Conservatives in an Age of Change

A. JAMES REICHLEY

Conservatives in an Age of Change
The Nixon and Ford Administrations

THE BROOKINGS INSTITUTION
Washington, D.C.

Library of Congress Cataloging in Publication data:
Reichley, A. James.
  Conservatives in an age of change.
  Includes bibliographical references and index.
    1. United States—Politics and government—1969–
1974.   2. United States—Politics and government—
1974–1977.   3. Nixon, Richard M. (Richard Milhous),
1913–   .   4. Ford, Gerald R., 1913–   .   I. Title.
E855.R44   973.9   81-1672
ISBN 0-8157-7380-3   AACR2
ISBN 0-8157-7379-X (pbk.)

9 8 7 6 5 4 3 2 1

THE BROOKINGS INSTITUTION is an independent organization devoted to nonpartisan research, education, and publication in economics, government, foreign policy, and the social sciences generally. Its principal purposes are to aid in the development of sound public policies and to promote public understanding of issues of national importance.

The Institution was founded on December 8, 1927, to merge the activities of the Institute for Government Research, founded in 1916, the Institute of Economics, founded in 1922, and the Robert Brookings Graduate School of Economics and Government, founded in 1924.

The Board of Trustees is responsible for the general administration of the Institution, while the immediate direction of the policies, program, and staff is vested in the President, assisted by an advisory committee of the officers and staff. The by-laws of the Institution state: "It is the function of the Trustees to make possible the conduct of scientific research, and publication, under the most favorable conditions, and to safeguard the independence of the research staff in the pursuit of their studies and in the publication of the results of such studies. It is not a part of their function to determine, control, or influence the conduct of particular investigations or the conclusions reached."

The President bears final responsibility for the decision to publish a manuscript as a Brookings book. In reaching his judgment on the competence, accuracy, and objectivity of each study, the President is advised by the director of the appropriate research program and weighs the views of a panel of expert outside readers who report to him in confidence on the quality of the work. Publication of a work signifies that it is deemed a competent treatment worthy of public consideration but does not imply endorsement of conclusions or recommendations.

The Institution maintains its position of neutrality on issues of public policy in order to safeguard the intellectual freedom of the staff. Hence interpretations or conclusions in Brookings publications should be understood to be solely those of the authors and should not be attributed to the Institution, to its trustees, officers, or other staff members, or to the organizations that support its research.

For Douglas, Richard, and Susan

Foreword

THE LATE Arthur Okun once wrote: "Nobody comes out of graduate school with a Ph.D. in priority setting or applied ideology. And yet these are major tasks in the executive's policymaking." The effects of ideology on policymaking in American government have been little studied—partly because many scholars have either dismissed the importance of ideology in American politics, or have held that almost universal agreement on a common "liberal" ideology has muted ideological dispute.

In this book A. James Reichley, a Brookings senior fellow, argues that there is a distinguishable tradition of conservative ideology in American political history, and he examines its effects on policy formulation in the administrations of Richard Nixon and Gerald Ford. Building on James L. Sundquist's critical analysis of policy formulation, *Politics and Policy: The Eisenhower, Kennedy, and Johnson Years* (Brookings 1968), Reichley's book studies the role of ideology in the deliberations and debates that led to positions taken by the Nixon and Ford administrations in foreign, economic, and social policy. Since the effect of ideology cannot be assessed in isolation, this book also deals with some of the personal rivalries and ambitions, partisan drives, economic interests, and national and international problems and challenges that influenced policymaking under Nixon and Ford.

The author is particularly grateful to his Brookings colleagues, Martha Derthick and James Sundquist, who provided advice and encouragement from the time the study began until it was finished and, for helpful comments and suggestions on the manuscript, to Joel

ix

D. Aberbach, Lawrence D. Brown, Paul R. Dommel, Stephen Hess, Herbert Kaufman, Paul Kennedy, Richard P. Nathan, Bradley H. Patterson, Paul Quirk, Helmut Sonnenfeldt, Gilbert Y. Steiner, and Joan Hoff Wilson. Valuable comments and corrections were offered by readers outside Brookings, including Karl H. Cerny, Richard Cook, Edwin L. Harper, Alan Henrikson, Everett Carll Ladd, Jr., Paul H. O'Neill, Roger B. Porter, Richard Rose, and William E. Timmons.

More than 150 participants in the two administrations, members of Congress, and practicing politicians gave time to be interviewed for this study. The author is especially grateful for help and advice given by Jana Hruska Fagan, Bryce Harlow, the late Rogers C. B. Morton, John Rogers, and Agnes Waldron. His debt to William W. Scranton for inspiration and guidance, which now extends over many years, was increased by Governor Scranton's helpful comments on the content of this book. None of these individuals, of course, are responsible for the facts or ideas presented here, and some will probably disagree with some of the author's interpretations.

The author is also grateful to Caroline Lalire, who edited the manuscript, to Patricia Foreman, who prepared the index, to the staff of the Brookings library, who tracked down obscure publications and file collections, to David Morse, Radmila Nikolic, Jo Ann Pinero, and Celia Rich, who typed—and retyped—the manuscript, and to Colleen Copley and Donna Verdier, who provided administrative assistance.

The views expressed in this book are the author's alone and should not be ascribed to the trustees, officers, or other staff members of the Brookings Institution.

BRUCE K. MACLAURY
President

March 1981
Washington, D.C.

Contents

Text Tables

Appendix Tables

1

The Conservative Tradition

THE CLOSING YEARS of the decade of the 1960s were a time of deep trouble for the United States. The war in Vietnam, already among the longest in American history, ground on, dividing the national public more bitterly than any military involvement since the Civil War. Inflation began taking off at a threatening rate for the first time since the Truman administration. Much of the American populace appeared to regard the nation's future with a mixture of apprehension and bewilderment.[1]*

On college and university campuses a "counterculture," associated with the recreational use of drugs and a bohemian life-style, persuaded many students that traditional American values and institutions were repressive, corrupt, and boring. Though immediately focused on opposition to the Vietnam War, the counterculture expressed broad hostility to such diverse social entities as industrialism, capitalism, governmental bureaucracy, scientific rationalism, and traditional morality, and, at a more fundamental level, to all forms of hierarchically structured authority.

The civil rights revolution, after securing substantial progress for black Americans through legislative victories in 1964 and 1965, turned violent during the second half of the decade, when spectacular riots took place in the black ghettos of Detroit, Newark, and other urban centers. Militance among blacks produced reactions of fear and resentment among many whites, some of whom in 1968 supported the

*Notes begin on p. 431.

1

presidential candidacy of George Wallace, the avowedly racist former governor of Alabama.

Social and economic reforms enacted during the middle years of the 1960s under the banners of John Kennedy's New Frontier and Lyndon Johnson's Great Society, after initially creating widespread hope and enthusiasm, were by the end of the decade generally believed to have fallen far short of their goals, and in some cases to have even made matters worse. Tom Wicker of the *New York Times*, hardly a conservative Cassandra, reported widely held impressions of "a 'war on poverty' that not only ended in defeat but virtually discredited the effort; a massive attack on urban ills that has left the cities in even greater disarray and tension; a welfare program that creates more dependency, rather than relieving it."[2]

The assassinations of Martin Luther King and Robert Kennedy in 1968 produced an almost dizzying sense that the entire social order was in danger of breaking down. Throughout 1968 the Gallup poll found the public ranking "crime and lawlessness" as a national problem second in seriousness only to the Vietnam War.[3] John Gardner, surveying the national spirit at the end of the Johnson administration, in which he had served as secretary of health, education, and welfare, observed "the anguish of the American people: the shattering of confidence, the anger, the bewilderment."[4]

As the party in national power during most of the 1960s, the Democrats were held accountable by many voters for the rising social turmoil. Between 1965 and 1969, the Democrats lost fifty-two seats in the House of Representatives and eleven in the Senate. In the 1968 presidential election, Hubert Humphrey, the Democratic candidate, received only 42.7 percent of the popular vote—a loss of more than 18 percentage points from the vote given to Lyndon Johnson four years before (almost exactly the same loss as that incurred by the Republicans between 1928 and 1932).

Loss of public confidence in the Democrats, however, did not seem to have been accompanied by any large swing toward their main opposition, the Republicans. Richard Nixon received only 43.4 percent of the popular vote in the 1968 election. (Most of the remaining 13.9 percent went to Wallace's third-party candidacy.) The Republicans were still far short of gaining a majority in either house of Congress.

Nevertheless, control of the executive branch gave the Republicans—or, more specifically, Nixon and his team of advisers and administrators—the opportunity to play a paramount role in shaping national policy. Did the Republicans draw on any store of values and ideas that might provide the basis for an alternative to the liberal social philosophy that had guided and inspired the Democrats since the 1930s? Or were they merely the out-party, offering different faces and perhaps an infusion of new vitality but no real change in direction?

Values of some sort the leaders of the new administration surely had. But were these values of a kind that had been, or could be, objectified into specific policy goals? And were these goals, if they existed, linked to ideas about such matters as how the economy operates, and how nations coexist, and how governments function? Would these ideas serve as a foundation for a structured approach to problems of administration, lawmaking, diplomacy, and leadership? Had the administration, in short, an *ideology*?

Definition of Ideology

In recent times the term *ideology* has acquired some pejorative connotations associated with closed-mindedness. Philip Converse has suggested that the term has been so "thoroughly muddled by diverse uses" that for purposes of practical study the neutral expression "belief system" should be put in its place.[5] Yet *belief system* and other possible alternatives like *social philosophy* or *political world view*, seem too vague, didactic, or cumbersome for regular use. The term *ideology* remains functional—so long as it is defined with some care, and kept free of semantic identification with dogmatism or fanaticism.

As used in this book, *ideology* will mean a *distinct and broadly coherent structure of values, beliefs, and attitudes with implications for social policy.* This definition is generally similar to Converse's definition of *belief system* as "a configuration of ideas and attitudes in which the elements are bound together by some form of constraint or functional interdependence"; and to Jerrold Schneider's more recent definition of *ideology* as "a theoretical construct . . . meant somehow to link beliefs, whether beliefs about facts or values, and attitudes . . . with behavior." It is somewhat broader than Martin Seliger's definition of *ideology* as "a group of beliefs and disbeliefs (rejections) expressed in value sentences, appeal sentences, and explanatory statements."[6] In my definition, *value* means an approved social goal or form of social conduct; *belief* means an opinion about the nature of political, social, economic, or geopolitical reality; and *attitude* represents a fusion of value and belief to create a predisposition toward particular behavior.

Every human being who participates in society operates on the basis of some kind of structure of values, beliefs, and attitudes, formed through a mixture of instinctual drives, social training, and individual experience and thought. Such individual psychological structures draw on ideology, or ideologies, but are not as a rule ideologies themselves—except in the hypothetical case of a person whose structure of social ideas corresponds exactly to a single ideology.

The number of conceivable ideologies is probably infinite. But in practice at any given time, the number of significant ideologies is limited to those that have an actual impact on the political process. Ideologies may rise out of or be associated with religions, economic systems (mercantilism, capitalism, collectivism), ways of defining the unit of ultimate social loyalty (tribalism, nationalism, humanism), systems of governance (monarchy, democracy, dictatorship), and comprehensive social value systems (conservatism, liberalism, socialism, fascism).

Ideologies may overlap. Modern conservatism, for instance, has important relationships with nationalism, capitalism, constitutional democracy, and religion, some of which are examined in this book. Ideologies are often given defining shape by an individual thinker (Locke, Burke, Marx), but in their operational forms usually represent the collective development of ideas through time (modern liberalism, conservatism, and socialism).

Much research has been done on the origins of ideologies, particularly on their sources in personal psychology or class attachments. Useful and illuminating though some of these studies have been, the approach has naturally tended to draw away attention from the social beliefs, values, and attitudes that constitute the ideologies themselves, which, I believe, may be judged as objectively true or false, constructive or destructive, whatever their psychological, biological, or economic sources.

Meanings of Conservatism

The Nixon and Ford administrations, while they were in office and since, have frequently been identified as "conservative" administrations—indicating that they in some ways drew on or represented a "conservative" ideology or point of view. What does *conservative* in this sense mean?

The term has been used as a political label for only a little more than a century and a half. Edmund Burke, Samuel Johnson, the two Pitts, Alexander Hamilton, and John Adams never thought of themselves as conservatives. In England during the 1820s, political defenders of established institutions began to describe their aims as "conservative" or "conservatory." In 1830 J. W. Croker, writing in the *Quarterly Review*, applied the adjective *conservative* to the Tory party (which, like its great rival, the Whigs, had first risen out of the controversy over the succession of James II to the English throne in the latter part of the seventeenth century). In 1832 Macaulay, a dedicated Whig, derided "the new cant word . . . Conservative"; and Daniel O'Connell, the champion of Irish liberty, spoke of "the fashionable, the new fangled phrase now used in polite society to designate the Tory ascendancy." The term was quickly taken up by Robert Peel and other Tory leaders, who were glad to find a title for their party less identified with the landed gentry, already a declining class in British politics. Benjamin Disraeli at first preferred *Tory* to *conservative*, but finally was persuaded to accept the new term, which made it possible for him to be identified in time as the founder of the modern British Conservative party.[7]

In the United States, opponents of the Jacksonian hegemony began using the term almost as soon as it became popular in England. In 1832 the platform of the National Republican party—the first party platform in American history—on which Henry Clay was to run for president, promised to maintain the Senate as "pre-eminently a conservative branch of the federal government."[8]

The development of a new political term during the 1820s and the 1830s to represent the bundle of attitudes that came to be known as "conservative" was not accidental, as will be discussed shortly. But some form of the general state of mind now identified with conservatism has probably existed in virtually all human societies.

Some writers, including Jefferson as well as Marx, have identified conservatism or its equivalent in earlier societies as simply the party of the rich and powerful.[9] Others, however, perhaps observing that modern conservative parties, though usually based on the middle class, draw support from all economic and social classes, have associated conservatism with more general social values or ideas. Robert

Michels, for instance, traced conservatism to belief in "norms, immutable in nature, determined by experience to be the best or least bad, and valid *sub specie aeternitatis*." Hugh Cecil found the origins of conservatism in "distrust of the unknown" and "a faculty in men to adapt themselves to their surroundings so that what is familiar merely because of its familiarity becomes more acceptable or more tolerable than what is unfamiliar." Karl Mannheim linked conservatism with the persistence of "pre-capitalist" social attitudes in modern societies. Daniel Bell has associated conservatism with an "authoritarian definition of leadership." Michael Oakeshott finds the roots of conservatism in "enjoyment of orderly and peaceable behavior." Samuel Huntington views conservatism as a "rationale of the institutional prerequisites of existence."[10]

An important key in sorting out these various suggested meanings is to recognize that, as Martin Seliger has pointed out, conservatism is both positional and ideational.[11] It applies, that is, both to an attitude toward social process and to a body of fundamental social beliefs and values. These two categories of meaning are in some ways related, but do not completely overlap. A political leader or party, therefore, may be conservative in one sense but not the other.

Positional Conservatism

Positional conservatism may be identified with Hugh Cecil's "distrust of the unknown," as well as with the determination among those who are doing well under a given social system to hang on to what they have. It is not, however, limited to simple support of the status quo. In times of social turmoil, or following disruption of established structures, positional conservatives may strongly condemn current social practices and conditions—as Burke condemned the French Revolution, or as Old Guard Republicans reacted against the New Deal in the 1930s. At such times positional conservatives tend either to idealize a prior state of social existence or to propose the establishment of a new order designed to maintain social stability. Burke may stand as an example of the first reaction, and Plato of the second.

Positional conservatives believe not simply in continuing what is going on at any given time, but in maintaining social forms that provide secure barriers against destructive change. The core value of positional conservatism is not so much continuity for its own sake as order. In the positional conservative view of things, order is the prerequisite for enjoyment of all other human values (security, community, affectional relationships, social justice, even freedom). But unfortunately, according to positional conservatives, order is also fragile, thinly stretched over the mouth of chaos, maintainable only through unremitting efforts at social discipline and self-restraint.

Human beings, according to positional conservatives from Aristophanes to Irving Kristol, are naturally inclined to indulge their selfish passions at the expense of the broader goals of society. But society is essential to the welfare of the individual, both for fellowship and physical support and for access to the inherited store of learnable knowledge and skills that is humankind's most precious treasure. Society, therefore, both to preserve itself and to serve the rationally conceived interests of the individual, must restrain the slothful and rebellious instincts of its individual members. For this purpose nations develop laws and customs, which should be strictly maintained and changed only slowly, if at all. It is in this sense that Huntington describes conservatism as a "rationale of the institutional prerequisites of existence," and Bell, less admiringly, as an "authoritarian definition of leadership."

People holding social power tend naturally over time to become positional conservatives, whatever their broader belief and value systems may be. In the Soviet Union at the present time, for example, members of the dominant Communist establishment are in this sense "conservatives"—leaders of the party of "law and order."

Ideational Conservatism

There is, however, another sense of conservatism, which Seliger calls ideational, that is far from the ends pursued by Communist regimes. Conservatism in this sense, as Robert Michels wrote, denotes adherence to "norms" that conservatives regard as "determined by experience to be the best or least bad, and valid *sub specie aeternitatis*."

The norms on which modern ideational conservatism is based are inherited from the distant past, most directly from the formative centuries of Western civilization, and beyond that from even earlier times. The history of the West has been so complex and varied that many scholars would question whether such a thing as a core or essential Western tradition may be said to exist. But from about the twelfth to the eighteenth century, at most times and in most places in the West, a few general ideas maintained dominance. Among these were: (1) the Judeo-Christian idea that God is working his will through history, thereby creating bonds of moral obligation tying all members of the community of believers to one another, and perhaps to all humanity; (2) the more distinctively Christian idea, derived also from parts of Greek culture and philosophy, that each human life possesses unique and transcendent value and significance; (3) the idea, older than the pyramids but developed most systematically by the Hebrews and Greeks, that societies and families constitute organic wholes, requiring loyalty and service from their individual members; (4) the related belief, also very ancient, that human institutions need to be structured around some form of hierarchically organized authority; and (5) a commitment to systems of laws and courts, usually based on Roman law or the common law, that establish individual and community rights and responsibilities.[12] In practice, most persons and groups commanding social power in those centuries fiercely resisted occasional attempts by members of the commonality to hasten the coming of the kingdom of God on earth; wars of conquest and subjugation, within and outside Christendom, were frequent; and the usual offenses of theft, debauchery, and violence were routine among all classes. Nevertheless, the convictions that history is moving toward some kind of definite conclusion, that each human life matters, and that every free man at least has standing before the law contributed to the development of societies and political structures markedly different from those of the East, where religious and legal traditions generally encouraged political and economic passivity.

From the Renaissance on, the importance assigned to the individual in Western social thought began to increase. Leon Battista Alberti, a fifteenth-century Florentine, wrote, "A man can do all things if he will." And Giovanni Pico della Mirandola agreed: "This is the culminating gift of God, this is the supreme and miraculous felicity of man . . . that he can be what he wills to be." But it was Thomas Hobbes, surveying the struggle between Royalists and Puritans in mid-seventeenth-century England, who decisively located the primary source of human values in the individual will rather than in transcendent purpose or in society conceived as an organic whole. For Hobbes, a positional conservative, the political conclusions drawn from this shift were authoritarian: if the individual wishes to save his skin, the philosopher argued, he had best submit to an absolute sovereign, to avoid waste and destruction in a "war of every man against every man."[13] Hobbes's belief in the primacy of the individual will as a determinant of value, it should be noted, grew out of an assumption already present in the Western tradition, but went outside the Western mainstream in basing value on the self-centered instinctual will to survive rather than on the role of the individual as a social and moral being.

John Locke, writing a short time later, rejected Hobbes's gloomy view of human nature, but essentially accepted his predecessor's innovative idea that the material welfare of the individual must be the standard for all political utility. On this basis Locke constructed a philosophy of political and economic individualism, asserting the right of every man to "life" and "liberty," and the enjoyment of whatever "property" he might acquire through "the labor of his body and the work of his hands" or through the accumulation of "gold and silver, which may continue long in a man's possession."[14] As George Sabine wrote: "The psychology which grew out of Locke's theory of mind was fundamentally egoistic in its explanation of human behavior. It ran in terms of pleasure and pain, and not like Hobbes's in terms of self-preservation . . . but the calculation of pleasure was exactly as self-centered as the calculation of security. Hobbes's better logic had its way in spite of Locke's better feeling. By a strange and undesigned cooperation the two men fastened on social theory the presumption that individual self-interest is clear and compelling, while a public or social interest is thin and unsubstantial."[15]

In the context of late-seventeenth- and eighteenth-century Britain, Locke's theory of human rights had effects that were, on the whole, politically conservative in the positional sense—providing a rationalization for the assimilation of the rising merchant class into the established social order. But when carried to France and to the British colonies in North America, where established authority resolutely opposed any dilution of its powers, the Lockean philosophy had revolutionary effects. Confronted by unyielding autocracy, writers like Helvétius, Voltaire, Jefferson, and Thomas Paine began to challenge the entire hierarchical structure of traditional society.

From this source and from some others—in particular, the allied development of scientific empiricism and the romantic exaltation of the primeval human will by writers like Rousseau—grew the three epochal revolutions that during the latter part of the eighteenth century launched the modern era: the industrial revolution, beginning in England, which arose partly as a result of government toleration of substantial economic freedom in accord with the free-market philosophy of Adam Smith; the democratic revolution, beginning in the United States and France, which proclaimed the political sovereignty of the general public, regardless of economic or class status; and the secular revolution, beginning mainly in France, which declared personal happiness to be the sole standard for judging human value. All three of these revolutions, though they ultimately led in somewhat different directions, contributed to the formation of the social and political philosophy that came to be known as "liberalism."

Modern conservatism, in the ideational sense, was created during the closing years of the eighteenth century and the early decades of the nineteenth century (the period when *conservatism* was coined as a political term) by writers and politicians who aimed to defend established values and institutions against what they regarded as the perils inherent in liberalism. At first, conservatives attempted to hold back all three of the liberal revolutions: against the advance of industrial capitalism, conservatives defended the interests of the landed gentry and the agricultural yeomanry; against democracy, conservatives tried to preserve government by what Fisher Ames in the United States called the class of "the wise, the good, and the rich"; and against secularism, conservatives upheld the locally dominant religious tradition (Anglicanism in England; Roman Catholicism in France, Italy, Spain, and southern Germany; Lutheranism in northern Germany and the Scandinavian countries; Orthodoxy in Russia; and various forms of Calvinism in Scotland, the Netherlands, and much of the United States).

From the start ideational conservatives could be divided into at least two categories: those, like Metternich and Joseph de Maistre, who dug in against almost any change, not only in values and fundamental beliefs but in the particular institutions and social forms associated with the European *ancien régime;* and those, like Burke, Kant, Hamilton, the Adamses, Tocqueville, and Peel, who sought, while preserving the essence of old tradition, to modify or reform established social structures to accommodate what they regarded as useful and good—or inevitable—in the new departures.[16] As Disraeli, speaking for the second approach, later put it, "You cannot form a party of resistance, pure and simple, because change is inevitable in a progressive country; the question is whether Reform shall be carried out in the spirit of the national customs and traditions, or whether you will follow abstract principles and general doctrine."[17] These separate strains of ideational conservatism have persisted to the present time (though the institutions and forms clung to by the bitter-enders have not always remained the same as those defended by Metternich and de Maistre).

During the course of the nineteenth century, liberalism split into at least three separate branches, all of which still exist today. One group, now generally known as libertarians, continued to promote expansion of both political and economic freedom. Another group, now generally called liberals in the United States and social democrats in Europe, remained committed to political freedom, but concluded that economic freedom would have to be substantially limited by government to prevent the strong from profiting at the expense of the weak. And a third group, following Marx, held that in a sense Hobbes had been right in the first place and that a system which bases all value on satisfying the drives of human nature is obliged, at least temporarily, to suppress political as well as economic freedom. (Marx parted crucially from Hobbes, however, in moving the locus of ultimate value from the individual will to humanity as *"species-being."*[18] This change had the effect of eliminating even the individual's last-ditch theoretical right to resist coercive authority to save his own life, on which Hobbes had insisted.) Many libertarians, viewing the new collectivists of the left as freedom's currently most dangerous enemies, in the latter part of the nineteenth century began moving toward practical alliances with conservatives.

Conservatism and Capitalism

While liberalism was dividing into mutually hostile elements, conservatism began evolving to meet new conditions and new opportunities—many of which came into being as a result of the successes of industrialization or democracy. The more farsighted conservative politicians, like Hamilton, the younger Pitt, William Huskisson, and Peel, were quick to recognize that conservatism and capitalism had profound common interests in protecting private ownership of property and maintaining social order, and that therefore over the long run they would be natural political allies.[19] The merchant and industrial capitalists, for their part, soon began to grow restless in tandem with political liberals. Not only did the successful capitalists develop tastes for the social honors and cultural pursuits associated with the older establishments, but some of them began to foresee the arrival of a time when liberalism would become a political force antagonistic to business. Moreover, most businessmen soon felt that the secular attack on religion, identified with liberalism, was going too far. In England many members of the business class were drawn from the dissenting sects; in Catholic countries they were disproportionately Protestant; and in the United States they usually subscribed to constitutional separation between church and state. Businessmen and their political associates, therefore, tended to deplore the link that existed in many countries between traditional conservatism and an established church. Most business liberals, however, strongly valued religion itself—both for its own sake and for the habits of honesty, sobriety, and hard work that it was held to foster.

In England business liberals, like Joseph Chamberlain, began gravitating toward the Conservative party during the latter part of the nineteenth century. In Germany many middle-class liberals after 1870 supported Bismarck, attracted in part by his nationalism. And in France most businessmen became staunch supporters of political conservatism under the Third Republic.

In the United States conservatism with an antibusiness orientation, though subscribed to by a few northern intellectuals like Henry Adams, was mainly limited to the South. Even there, most members of the planter class, beneath the froth of what Mark Twain called "Sir Walter's disease," held economic and social outlooks that were essentially capitalist. After the Civil War capitalism and conservatism were closely linked, normally dominating the Republican party, and exercising strong influence in the Democratic party as well.[20]

Yet capitalism and conservatism have remained somewhat uneasy partners. Some modern conservative political leaders, like Winston Churchill, Charles de Gaulle, Robert Taft, and Edward Heath, and conservative writers, like Walter Lippmann and Alexander Solzhenitsyn, have sought to maintain broader perspectives for conservatism than the values of the marketplace. On the other side, some contemporary writers who trace their intellectual origins to the libertarian strain of liberalism, like Milton Friedman and F. A. Hayek, have resisted identifying themselves as conservatives, preferring to be known as traditional liberals, or, in Hayek's case, as "old Whigs."

Friedman's view that the free man "recognizes no national purpose except as it is the consensus of the purposes for which the citizens severally strive" cannot be easily reconciled with the traditional conservative belief, classically stated by Burke, that society is an organic "partnership not only between those who are living, but between those who are dead, and those who are to be born."[21] Libertarians continue to identify with Jefferson and Gladstone, while disparaging Hamilton and Disraeli. To assign most social decisionmaking to the marketplace (which Adam Smith, incidentally, would not have dreamed of proposing) seems at odds with conservatism's traditional emphases on moral responsibility and community. Free-enterprise capitalism, as has often been pointed out, tends to promote just those demands for immediate gratification of instinctual appetites by consumers and those rejections of institutional ties that ideational conservatives warn threaten social harmony and discipline.

Louis Hartz has argued influentially that traditional conservatism never took root in the United States—that in America "Burke actually equalled Locke," because there the established order has always been based on liberal capitalism rather than on feudal hierarchy.[22] In America, according to this view, the individual is regarded as an atomistic unit, whether in the marketplace or at the ballot box, rather than as a participant in the kind of organic social whole that Burke had in mind. The political persuasion that goes by the name of conservatism, therefore, is in fact "business liberalism."

Yet the organic concept of social relationships has persisted, both in the United States and in other modern capitalist countries, as an influence in family life, as the organizing principle for many communities and institutions, and as the basis for national patriotism. Conservative politicians who support values based on the organic concept in these areas see no inconsistency in regarding market competition as generally the best means for allocating resources and stimulating economic growth. Capitalism, most modern ideational conservatives argue, is better suited than any other known economic system to maintain balance between economic progress and respect for noneconomic human relationships and values. The various statist means for organizing industrial economies, by contrast, crush personal dignity and suppress all interests and attachments that might compete with government for authority. Besides, conservatives contend, capitalism, though indubitably enriching the few, provides the highest achievable standard of living for the many and advances the economic development of society as a whole at an optimum rate of progress.

While conceding the dangers inherent in capitalism's glorification of material consumption, modern ideational conservatives hold that the resulting excesses of materialism or individualism may be offset by the moral authority of traditional institutions. Ideational conservatives therefore support capitalism as a generally useful means to complex and multifaceted ends, rather than, like Friedman and Hayek, as the invariably effective means to the almost solely valid end, individual opportunity and enrichment.[23]

Conservatism and Democracy

Democracy, the second element in liberalism's original triad, made irregular progress during the century following the American Revolution. In most countries expansion of the suffrage and extension of direct majority rule were usually resisted by conservatives, who tended to view mass politics as an insuperable barrier to responsible government. Conservatism won an early victory over unlimited democracy in the framing of the U.S. Constitution, which hemmed in majority rule with checks and balances, intended, according to James Madison, to make certain that "the rights of individuals, or of the minority, will be in little danger from interested combinations of the majority."[24]

As the size of the electorate grew, however, conservative party leaders in most Western countries came to recognize that they would either have to develop a mass base or accept political extinction. In England Disraeli in 1865 took leadership in further broadening the suffrage, and during his later ministry secured enactment of many measures designed to advance the interests of working-class voters. A Conservative party committee headed by Randolph Churchill recommended: "If the Tory party is to continue to exist as a power in the state, it must become a popular party."[25] Bismarck, too, by developing the West's first extensive welfare state and identifying conservatism with national patriotism, sought to offset the appeals of socialism and liberalism among German industrial workers.[26]

The most successful developer of mass support for essentially conservative policies was the early Republican party in the United States. From the start Republican leaders aimed to persuade voters of all classes that they had tangible stakes in the prevailing social and economic system. "I don't believe in a law to prevent a man from getting rich," Lincoln told striking shoe workers in New Haven in 1859. "It would probably do more harm than good. So while we do not propose war on capital, we do wish to allow the humblest man an equal chance to get rich with everybody else."[27] Four years later, as president, Lincoln informed a Republican workingmen's association in New York City: "The strongest bond of human sympathy outside the family relationship, should be one uniting all working people of all nations, and tongues, and kindreds. Nor should this lead to a war upon property, or the owners of property. Property is the fruit of labor; property is desirable; is a positive good in the world. That some should be rich shows that others may become rich, and hence is just encouragement to industry and enterprise."[28] From 1860 until 1932 the Republicans, through identification as the party of both social stability and economic progress, remained what Theodore Roosevelt called "the normal majority party" in American politics. During the New Deal period the Democrats achieved the majority status among registered voters and the dominance in Congress that they have since generally enjoyed. After the Second World War, however, the Republicans were again able to compete on at least equal terms for the presidency (winning a substantially higher average percentage of the popular vote than the Democrats in the nine presidential elections from 1948 to 1980),[29] as well as for statewide offices in most of the major industrial states.

In an age of near-universal adult suffrage in the industrial democracies, conservatives have usually sought, not limitations on the size of the electorate, which has turned out to be more conservative than most politicians and commentators expected, but maintenance of constitutional limits over the reach of governmental authority. Conservative arguments for constitutional as opposed to unlimited democracy are, first, that checks on government are needed to protect personal rights, and, second, that government intervention in many economic and social situations, because of the "inevitable ignorance" of governmental planners and the vulnerability of politicians to pressure from special interests, is likely to do more harm than good.[30]

Conservatism and Nationalism

In their pursuit of mass constituencies, as well as because of inherent ideological attraction, conservative parties have been led to identify themselves with the partly independent ideology of nationalism. In the eighteenth and early nineteenth centuries, nationalism, like capitalism, was more closely associated with liberalism than with conservatism. Liberals in the French Revolution, and in the related European revolutions that followed, generally allied their cause with support for the establishment of independent nation-states, based on common ethnic and cultural heritages.[31] Conservatives often defended extranational dynastic empires, like that of the Habsburgs, or sought to preserve particularist regional entities, like the Prussian and Bavarian kingdoms.[32]

As the modern political drama unfolded, however, conservatism and nationalism were found to possess natural affinities. The organic view of society was fundamental to both ideologies. Conservatives discovered that by claiming to speak for a common national interest, they could effectively counter the appeals to class interests being made by their liberal and socialist opponents. Patriotism and conservatism became intertwined, particularly in countries like England, where a conservative social establishment was one of the principal conveyers of the national identity, and in Germany and Italy, where national unification was brought about under conservative auspices (though many conservatives remained deeply suspicious of the new national governments). Even in France, where the idea of the nation continued to be closely associated with the tradition of the Revolution, nationalism during the nineteenth century became largely a conservative force in politics.

In the United States nationalism has always had a special quality, because Americans, even in the country's early years, and more so as new waves of immigration arrived, have not shared ethnic or cultural roots as have, say, Englishmen or Frenchmen. Scott Fitzgerald wrote: "France was a land, England was a people, but America [had] about it the quality of the idea."[33] American nationalism has therefore depended to an unusual degree on moral and intellectual principles, usually borrowed from other ideologies—most visibly from liberalism ("all men are created equal"), but also from elements of conservatism (such as the constitutional system of checks and balances, the work ethic, and the importance assigned to religion and community).

In national politics the Federalist and Whig parties in the early decades of the republic combined social conservatism with enthusiastic support for nationalism. Their successor as the more conservative of the two major parties, the Republicans, settled forever the question of the indissolubility of the national union in the Civil War. For the first half-century of its existence, the Republican party strongly espoused nationalism in both domestic and foreign policy. During the twentieth century many Republicans, for reasons to be discussed below, became advocates of decentralization of governmental authority in domestic policy. In foreign policy, however, both the interventionist wing of the Republican party, marshaled behind a series of leaders from Theodore Roosevelt to Dwight Eisenhower and Richard Nixon, and the isolationist wing, whose great champion was Robert Taft, continued to espouse nationalism, though proposing differing strategies for achieving nationalist goals.

Conservatism and Pluralism

Social pluralism has always found advocates among conservatives who feared and disliked heavy concentration of social power in a centralized national government. The Tory country squires of eighteenth-century England, Lewis Namier observed, "worshipped the throne and loathed the court, believed in authority and disliked government."[34] The German empire established in 1870 preserved major elements of internal decentralization, largely in response to the demands of conservative particularists in Prussia and the southern kingdoms and states.

During the first century of U.S. history, the cause of pluralism was promoted most ardently by Jeffersonian liberals, who valued diversity, both for its own sake and because they regarded a centralized national government as a threat to personal freedom. But the development of large national and international business corporations toward the end of the nineteenth century led many liberals to conclude that only a strong national government could deal effectively with the seats of private economic power. By the time of the New Deal, most liberals had become convinced of the beneficial effects of centralized government—at least when liberals held national power. Conservatives, meanwhile, had moved in the opposite direction. During the nineteenth century conservatives generally favored a strong central government as an aid to economic growth. But as federal government intervention in the private economy grew during the early twentieth century, conservatives went over to the side of decentralization. A "fact book" issued by the Republican National Committee in 1948 included "States Rights" as one of the four basic principles of Republican philosophy. (The others were "Constitutionalism, encouragement for American enterprise, and a minimum of government interference.")[35] At the time of Nixon's election in 1968, support for decentralization of government was an issue on which almost all shades of Republican opinion were agreed (though the extent and means of decentralization remained controversial).

Pluralism (not usually under that name) has been warmly supported by most white southerners, partly as a defense against federal intervention on racial matters and partly as a means for preserving local particularism. During the 1960s many urban "ethnics" (generally speaking, whites from other than northern European stocks) began to develop resentment against federal intervention in matters regarded as properly local or private concerns. In part, this antipathy, too, sprang from opposition to the federal promotion of racial integration, especially in school attendance and housing. But more than racial antagonism or fear was involved. The growing suspicion of governmental centralism expressed by urban ethnic groups also resulted from anger against federal court rulings that clashed with traditional moral and religious values, on issues like prayer in the public schools and (a bit later) abortion. In addition, the rise of social and moral "permissiveness" was blamed by many traditionalists on the national liberal elite, which was linked in the public mind with the federal bureaucracy.

So American pluralism, once primarily a liberal doctrine for the protection of dissent against dominant conservative institutions, had become by the end of the 1960s largely a way to defend traditional institutions and values against a perceived attack by the central government.[36] If the federal government could not be counted on to support inherited values, traditionalists had come to believe, it should at least be kept from undercutting their influence within local communities or in private relationships. "A government big enough to give you everything you want," Nixon, and later Ford, liked to remind their audiences, "is a government big enough to take from you everything you have."[37]

Conservatism and Religion

Religion during the course of history has maintained various relationships to government and secular politics. During the Middle Ages the Catholic Church was the chief competitor of the state for social power. Partly as a by-product of that rivalry, and partly as an expression of the concern for each individual human being that is inherent in the teaching of Jesus, the Church provided some support for what we now call human rights. The Protestant Reformation, beginning in the sixteenth century, was in some of its manifestations a protest against authoritarian structures within the Catholic Church, and in others a conservative reaction against the new humanism being spawned by the Renaissance. Within a short time Protestantism, in most of its branches, developed its own authoritarian tendencies.

After the French Revolution, organized religion, finding itself a major object of attack by secular liberals, generally lined up with political conservatism, sometimes of the reformist versions identified with Burke or Kant, but more often of the rigid conformist kind associated with de Maistre. In more recent times some of the more articulate churchmen, particularly in denominations closely associated with the middle class, have become outspoken critics of established social and economic systems in the Western democracies. Some of these religious liberals—religious persons, that is, with liberal or left-wing political views—have for all practical purposes gone over to the side of secularism, finding in political or social action the best available contemporary equivalent for religious experience.[38] Others have remained more or less traditional in their theologies, but have identified social and economic conservatism with just those evils of moral bigotry and social injustice that are repeatedly condemned by the sacred texts of both the Christian and Jewish faiths.[39]

Political conservatives have tended to react with bewilderment and indignation against attacks by liberal churchmen. In the view of most conservatives (except a few libertarians now lodged in the conservative camp), religious values and beliefs are among the most important elements of the heritage that conservatism exists to defend.

Most modern conservatives, at least in the United States, support constitutional separation between church and state, both because they want to protect religion against manipulation by politicians and because they recognize that religious diversity makes direct government support for religion legally inappropriate and politically impossible. Conservatives argue, however, that civic virtue over the long run is inextricably bound up with religious faith, and that many cherished Western values, including the sanctity of individual human rights, are ultimately rooted in religious belief. As a result, conservatives hold, democratic societies have deep interests in maintaining an atmosphere congenial to religion, though not in supporting any particular church or denomination.

Religious liberals tend to stress the role of religion as promoter of social justice, which they regard as impeded by existing social and economic systems. Conservatives, by contrast, are more likely to view the church as one of a cluster of traditional institutions, including the family and the community, that are expected to help the individual find his spiritual and moral bearings amid the challenges and mysteries of existence.

The "square virtues" that Nixon proposed to defend when he entered the White House, though not in most cases directly religious, sprang from the Puritan tradition that has always formed one part of the American identity.[40] The Puritan code, emphasizing moral restraint and the intrinsic value of work, influenced Republican leaders not only on issues with highly visible moral content, such as recreational use of drugs and abortion, but also, more subtly, on economic and welfare policies. "The work ethic is ingrained in the American character," Nixon said in a Labor Day speech in 1971. "As the name implies, the work ethic holds that labor is good in itself; that a man or woman at work not only makes a contribution to his fellow man, but becomes a better person by virtue of the act of working."[41] John

Calvin, Cotton Mather, and the authors of the Book of Proverbs would have thoroughly agreed.

Modern Conservatism

Lincoln once said that the Republican party by 1860 seemed to have stolen the clothes of its opposition. The same may almost be said of modern conservatism. Capitalism and nationalism were originally much more closely identified with liberalism than with conservatism. Social pluralism was always a conservative doctrine in Europe, but in America during the nineteenth century, and even through much of the twentieth, it was principally championed by liberals. All three doctrines, however, have developed into properties of contemporary American conservatism. Even democracy, though still a liberal cause in the sense that liberals usually still take the lead in broadening areas to be brought under the direct rule of popular majorities, has become in its constitutional form a pillar of conservative belief. Indeed, on some social issues, like school prayer and busing schoolchildren for integration, conservatives have argued from majoritarian principles, whereas liberals have dug in behind the nondemocratic authority of the courts.

Market capitalism, nationalism in foreign policy, social pluralism, constitutional democracy, and alignment with moral and cultural traditionalism were related within the structure of American ideational conservatism by the time of Nixon's election in 1968. Together with the emphasis on social order prescribed by positional conservatism, they provided the new administration with an ideological framework from which to derive the ideas, hunches, and social preferences that would go into the making of actual policy. Whether this framework could produce effective responses to the problems and opportunities of the final third of the twentieth century would be tested during the months and years that lay ahead.

2

The Republican Party in 1969

THE REPUBLICAN party has almost always been the more conservative, in both the positional and ideational senses, of the two major national parties in the United States. But like its Democratic rival, the Republican party has never been ideologically monolithic.

Somewhat arbitrarily and impressionistically, I have categorized the elements that made up the Republican party in the 1960s into four major and more or less enduring political groups: stalwarts, fundamentalists, moderates, and progressives. Ideology entered into the formation of each of these groups, although each also rose out of shared regional and economic interests, personal and what may be called tribal loyalties, and agreements on political strategy. The groups had no formal structures, overlapped around their edges, and fluctuated through time in size and influence. Some party leaders moved without much sign of strain from one group to another as political interests or personal associations dictated. Nevertheless, this scheme of classification will provide a useful preliminary guide to the frequently heated intraparty differences that affected policy development through the Nixon and Ford administrations.[1]

The Stalwarts

The stalwarts rose from the tradition of small-town, middle-class Protestant society that, through the Republican party, dominated American politics during the final third of the nineteenth century.

22

The last great hero of the stalwarts was Senator Robert Taft of Ohio, whom they loyally followed during his long and futile quest for the Republican nomination for president from 1940 to 1952.[2]

The stalwarts' political strongholds were in middle-sized cities like Peoria, Illinois; Canton, Ohio; Harrisburg, Pennsylvania; and Grand Rapids, Michigan. Most of these cities had by the 1960s acquired populations that were ethnically and socially diverse. They still, however, maintained at least the myth of identification with a relatively unified and homogeneous culture.

Like the nineteenth century New England "conservatives" described by Nathaniel Hawthorne in *The Blithedale Romance*, the stalwarts kept a tight hold "in this intangibility and mistiness of affairs . . . on one or two ideas which had not come into vogue since yesterday morning."[3] Among the ideas revered by the stalwarts were beliefs that the U.S. Constitution is an almost perfect charter for government and that the American free-enterprise system virtually guarantees long-run economic prosperity.

Loyalty to the Republican party as an institution was itself an important stalwart value. Brand Whitlock, looking back on his boyhood in a small town in nineteenth-century Ohio, wrote in 1915: "The Republican party was not a faction, not a group, not a wing, it was an institution like those Emerson speaks of in his essay on politics, rooted like oak trees in the center around which men group themselves as best they can. It was a fundamental and self-evident thing, like life, and liberty, and the pursuit of happiness, or like the flag or the federal judiciary. It was elemental like gravity, the sun, the stars, the ocean. It was merely a synonym for patriotism, another name for the nation. . . . It was inconceivable that any self-respecting man should be a Democrat. There were, perhaps, Democrats in Lighttown; but then there were rebels in Alabama, and in the Ku Klux Klan, about which we read in the evening, in the Cincinnati *Gazette*."[4] In many stalwart households, such sentiments, though somewhat diluted by twentieth-century sophistication, remained strong.

Like most of the founding generation of Republicans in the 1850s and 1860s (including such comparative radicals as Thaddeus Stevens), the stalwarts maintained a close relationship with American business. But also like the founders, they thought of themselves as speaking primarily for small business (Main Street) rather than for the giant corporations and the great New York banks (Wall Street). The stalwarts' approach to the economy was pragmatic, in the sense of being responsive to political interests, rather than doctrinaire. In general they favored reliance on the market, but they found room for "fair trade" laws for small retailers, selective tariff protection for American industry, and other items regarded with horror by laissez-faire purists.

In their social outlook the stalwarts were far from being libertarians. Though some of them did not appear to be burdened by moral inhibitions in their personal behavior, stalwart politicians publicly subscribed to the regulation of society according to the strict moral code preached by the so-called evangelical (largely Calvinist) Protestant denominations. Daniel Walker Howe, Ronald Formisano, and other researchers have recently shown that the struggle between moral puritanism, advocated by the evangelicals, and free-and-easy hedonism was an important source of the political division in the 1830s and 1840s between the Whigs and Democrats.[5] Except in the South, the Whigs passed on their side of the argument to the Republicans.[6] The stalwarts, and their allies among socially conservative southern Democrats, had by the 1960s long since conceded the impracticality of stamping out consumption of alcoholic beverages through national prohibition. But they continued to insist that government persevere in the fights against organized gambling, prostitution, pornography, and, above all, the newly flourishing trade in recreational narcotics.

In the area of civil rights, the stalwarts, though their voting alliance with blacks had long since been broken, and though they were often aligned on other issues with southern segregationists, remained generally loyal to the Republican party's progressive tradition. Memories of forebears who had been active in the abolitionist movement or who had fought in the Civil War helped produce votes among the stalwarts for the Civil Rights Act of 1964 and the Voting Rights Act of 1965. For example, Congressman Clarence Brown, Jr., a rising young stalwart in 1969, related his liberal record on civil rights to his proud recollection that "the main line of the old underground railroad [a network for smuggling escaping slaves to Canada] ran right through" his district in western Ohio.[7]

In foreign policy most of the stalwarts had shared Taft's isolationism—although a divergent strand led by Senator Arthur Vandenberg of Michigan (joined by the young Gerald Ford) had converted from isolationism to internationalism during the Second World War.

After Taft's final defeat at the Republican National Convention in 1952, and his death the following year, most of the stalwarts had abandoned overt isolationism, partly because of their concern over the growing power of the Soviet Union. But the old isolationist spirit still surfaced from time to time, chiefly in opposition to foreign aid and in attacks on the United Nations. By 1968 some stalwarts, such as Congressman Melvin Laird, who represented the once strongly isolationist seventh district of central Wisconsin, had grown critical of the prolonged American military involvement in Vietnam.

The stalwarts were conservatives, in the sense that they sought to preserve the social system in pretty much its existing form. But they did not oppose all change. They wished change to come slowly, and to develop through experience rather than in accord with abstract theories. Since the beginning of the New Deal in the 1930s, they had opposed each step in the growth of the welfare state, from social security to medicare. Once a particular welfare state measure was enacted, however, they tended simply to move their line of defense to a new position rather than seriously try to restore the former status quo.

The most visible stalwart leader at the time of Nixon's election was Senate Minority Leader Everett Dirksen of Illinois, who had nominated Taft at the climactic 1952 Republican convention in Chicago. Gerald Ford, the House minority leader, also adhered to the stalwart tradition except in his zealous internationalism. Other prominent stalwarts included Congressman Laird, House Minority Whip Leslie Arends of Illinois, Senators Robert Griffin of Michigan and Howard Baker (Dirksen's son-in-law) of Tennessee, and Republican National Chairman Ray Bliss of Ohio. The stalwarts were particularly identified with the old Republican heartland in the Middle West, but also drew support from upstate counties of Pennsylvania and New York, some parts of New England, the more sparsely populated regions of the Far West, and even some parts of the border states and the South.

After Eisenhower's election in 1952, the stalwarts had largely given up their long struggle to regain dominance within the Republican party—a resignation made easier by Eisenhower's surprising conservatism on many domestic issues. They retained, however, a powerful role within the party, partly because they had strength in Congress and partly because they held the balance of power between contending forces to their right and left. In 1964 Dirksen and other stalwart leaders had viewed with considerable misgiving the presidential candidacy of Senator Barry Goldwater of Arizona. But most of them had in the end supported Goldwater for the nomination. Understandably, some of the stalwarts regarded Goldwater's victory over the candidates of the eastern establishment as a kind of revenge for Taft's defeat in 1952.

In the competition leading up to the 1968 Republican National Convention at Miami Beach, most of the stalwarts actively and enthusiastically backed Richard Nixon. Though he had supported Eisenhower against Taft in 1952, Nixon had taken pains while serving as vice-president from 1953 to 1961 to build bridges to stalwart constituencies, and seemed responsive to stalwart values.

The Fundamentalists

To the right of the stalwarts on the ideological spectrum were the fundamentalists—a strain relatively new to the Republican party, nurtured much more than the stalwarts on political and economic theory, and attracting some support from groups like white southerners and Roman Catholics formerly not much drawn to the Republicans.

Fundamentalist conservatism had developed in the United States after the Second World War in response to a number of economic, social, moral, and even spiritual concerns. Some of the fundamentalists were primarily moved by determination to ensure the international military supremacy of the United States, for the protection of national security and economic interests (and also, among some fundamentalists at least, for the satisfaction of being "number one"). Others pursued the broader objective of carrying on a kind of worldwide crusade, spiritual as well as material, against the forces of international communism. Other fundamentalists were stirred mainly by domestic issues, such as racial tensions, spreading use of drugs, increases in crime, student disorders, and changing standards of sexual morality—concerns that were to be described collectively in 1970 by Richard Scammon and Ben J. Wattenberg as "the social issue."[8] Still others were chiefly aroused by the growth of the welfare state, which they viewed as threatening not only free-enterprise capitalism but also political and social freedoms.

Not all fundamentalists shared all these concerns. Some working-class Catholics angered by black militance or the unrestrained sale of pornography, for example, did not favor cutting back on major parts of the welfare state. Likewise some economic libertarians felt uncomfortable with proposals for more-restrictive regulation of personal morals. But at least for the time being, the fundamentalists were broadly united by their conviction that change had gone too far and too fast and that a return to an earlier condition of society, usually not very clearly defined, was now required. The fundamentalists, unlike the stalwarts, were no longer content with moderating the rate of change. They believed in the need for a "counter-reformation"— an evocative term used by Patrick Buchanan, Nixon's most conservative speechwriter.

On civil rights issues many fundamentalists were little affected by ties to the Republican past. Many southern fundamentalists, like Senator Strom Thurmond of South Carolina, the 1948 presidential candidate of the segregationist States' Rights Democratic party, had indeed switched from the Democrats to the Republicans in part as a strategic move to help carry on their fight against racial integration. Federal intervention to promote integration was opposed by most fundamentalists, even those like Senator Goldwater who were personally against segregation, on the ground that such action invaded areas of authority assigned by the Constitution to the states.

On foreign policy the fundamentalists favored aggressive American involvement wherever an issue could be defined as part of the struggle against international communism. The fundamentalists' foreign policy interests tended to be oriented more toward Asia than Europe— perhaps partly because Asia was free of the haze of conflicting emotions through which many Americans have regarded the continent of our main cultural origin, perhaps partly because of the spirit of "Westering" that seems always to have excited the American imagination.[9]

The fundamentalists had their greatest political strength in the rapidly developing states and regions that Kevin Phillips, a young political demographer on the staff of Nixon's campaign manager, John Mitchell, aptly titled the "sunbelt"—a vast area reaching from Florida across the Gulf states and Texas and the desert states of the Southwest to southern California.[10] In many parts of this area, Republicans had until recently been almost exotic creatures. Sunbelt fundamentalism in part arose from resistance to racial integration, but also in part was fed by the ethos of libertarian individualism inherited from John Locke by way of Thomas Jefferson. The fundamentalists also had substantial support in the rural parts of the Rocky Mountain and Great Plains states, another area in which the individualist self-image remained strong. In the metropolitan areas of the Northeast and Middle West, resentment against social change and aggressive anticommunism had produced some backing for conservative fundamentalism among traditionally Democratic working-class Catholics. In 1964, however, the outpouring of support that Goldwater's managers had hoped to attract from urban Catholics failed to materialize. Even in 1968 only about 33 percent of Catholic voters supported Nixon, while 59 percent supported Hubert Humphrey and 8 percent George Wallace.[11]

Under Goldwater's leadership the fundamentalists in 1964 had at least temporarily taken control of the national Republican party. Four years later the fundamentalists' cadres were divided at the Miami Beach convention. Most of what might be called the citizen activist wing of the movement supported the presidential candidacy of Ronald Reagan, a former Democrat who had campaigned vigorously for Goldwater in 1964 and had then been elected governor of California in 1966 on a platform stressing fiscal conservatism and social discipline. But key members of the fundamentalists' professional politician wing, including Senators Thurmond and John Tower of Texas, as well as Goldwater himself, supported Nixon—apparently having drawn the conclusion from the immensity of Goldwater's general election defeat in 1964 that the country was not yet ready to elect a fundamentalist true believer as president. Without the backing he received from the fundamentalists, Nixon probably could not have won the nomination. Of the 692 votes cast for Nixon on the first ballot—25 more than the necessary majority—252 (more than one-third) were from delegations from the South or Southwest, all of which were dominated by fundamentalists.[12]

The Moderates

During the years that most of the stalwarts were following Senator Taft in his struggle to give direction to the Republican party, the group I have called the moderates were gathered behind the leadership of Governor Thomas Dewey of New York. Dewey was twice nominated for president, in 1944 and 1948, but both times lost the general election. In 1952 moderate leaders, including Dewey, Senator Henry Cabot Lodge, Jr., of Massachusetts, and Congressman Hugh Scott of Pennsylvania, were instrumental in bringing about the nomination of General Eisenhower, who was known to be a strong internationalist in foreign policy but whose views on domestic issues were murky. Following Eisenhower's election, the moderates assumed relatively firm control of the national party for eight years.

The moderates were descended from the wing of the progressive movement of the first part of the twentieth century that had favored political reform, in the sense of making government more honest and efficient, but had remained conservative on most economic and social issues. These were men like the elder Henry Cabot Lodge and Elihu Root, who, after first being allied with Theodore Roosevelt, stood firm in 1912 with William Howard Taft, when Roosevelt sought a return to the presidency on a platform that contained elements of social radicalism.

During the 1930s, while the stalwarts fought delaying actions against the New Deal, the moderates concentrated on attacking the corruption and inefficiency that developed in some welfare-state programs. In the early years of the 1940s, when the political popularity of the New Deal began to ebb, moderates like Dewey in New York and Earl Warren in California led the Republicans back into control of several important industrial states. (Warren became more liberal on the Supreme Court after Eisenhower appointed him chief justice in 1953 than he had been as governor of California—and more liberal than Eisenhower had expected.)

The moderates were prepared to accommodate social change, which they, like Disraeli, regarded as inevitable in a developing industrial society, but they were cautious about initiating change themselves.[13] Their values tended to be managerial and—a term they particularly favored—"pragmatic." They claimed to have learned from the example of giant industrial corporations how to make large institutions operate more efficiently. Organization, and reorganization, were their favorite social tools.

In foreign policy the moderates from an early date were internationalists. Their quarrel with Senator Taft after the Second World War was much more over the issue of internationalism versus resurgent isolationism than over domestic issues. The moderates' internationalism was undisguisedly nationalist in motive, aimed at serving the national interests of the United States rather than based on Wilsonian altruism or democratic evangelism. Their commitment to an activist approach in world affairs grew partly out of their assessment of the nation's security needs and partly out of their eagerness to gather the benefits of foreign investment and trade. They favored maintaining close ties with Europe, especially Britain, but also were fascinated by prospects for economic and cultural interchanges with Asia and Latin America.

The moderates acted as spokesmen in national politics for corporate business, particularly for the business communities of New York, Boston, Philadelphia, and Baltimore and for outposts of the eastern business establishment in such cities as Pittsburgh, Cleveland, Detroit, Minneapolis, and San Francisco. Like many members of the postwar generation of corporate executives, they viewed a relatively close association between business and government as not only inevitable but in many respects beneficial.

Their emphasis on working out "pragmatic" compromise solutions to economic and social problems that were at least minimally acceptable to concerned interest groups gave the moderates tactical flexibility, but also tended to make them appear unprincipled. While steering the nation and the Republican party away from bitter ideological antagonisms, they seemed to sacrifice a capacity for arousing durable political enthusiasm or commitment. By the end of the Eisenhower administration, they were already losing ground within the Republican party to groups on both their right and left that had more clearly defined social objectives.

Before the 1964 Republican convention, the moderates joined the progressives in opposing Goldwater's candidacy, which they viewed as infected by the political vice of "extremism." But after Goldwater's nomination, most of them loyally supported the national ticket during the fall campaign—which many of the progressives did not. In 1968 the moderates, like the fundamentalists, were split. Some supported Nixon, whose own political origins were in the moderate camp. Others, regarding Nixon as now a political front-man for the fundamentalists or as a likely loser in the general election, backed candidates put forward by the progressives. After the Republican convention, the moderates gave full support to the Nixon-Agnew ticket.

Representative moderates at the time of Nixon's inauguration included Congressman Rogers Morton of Maryland, who replaced Bliss as Republican national chairman at Nixon's behest early in 1969; Hugh Scott, since 1959 a U.S. senator, who was elected Senate minority whip at the beginning of the 1969 session; and Governor James Rhodes of Ohio, a moderate in his governmental approach, though a flamboyant showman in political style.

The Progressives

The final group, which I call the progressives, traced its origins to the tradition of governmental activism embodied during the early years of the twentieth century by Theodore Roosevelt, and beyond that by the first generation of Republicans, led into control of the national government by Abraham Lincoln in 1860. If the stalwarts could claim continuity with many of the economic and moral attitudes of the Republican founders, the progressives more nearly approached their zest for social reform and their willingness to use government to promote economic growth and social progress. (During their first stay in complete control of the federal government, which ended with Lincoln's death in 1865, the Republicans, besides leading the Union to victory in the Civil War and bringing about the abolition of slavery, opened up public lands in the West for free settlement by homesteaders, provided for the establishment of state land-grant colleges, chartered the first transcontinental railroad, set up a national banking system, and raised a tariff wall to create an environment favorable to infant industries, among other items—a wave of governmentally initiated change probably unequaled in American history.)[14]

After Roosevelt's bolt to run for president on his own Bull Moose ticket in 1912, the progressives never fully regained their former strength within the Republican party. During the 1930s some of the old progressives, like Harold Ickes and George Norris, either participated in or actively supported the New Deal. By the beginning of the 1950s, the Republican progressive strain seemed almost to have disappeared.

With the election of Nelson Rockefeller as governor of New York in 1958, however, a new group of Republicans, consciously aiming to revive the tradition of progressive activism, began to emerge as a force within the party. During the 1960s the U.S. Senate came to include a small but influential (because they often held the balance of power) bloc of progressive Republicans, including Clifford Case of New Jersey, Jacob Javits of New York, Charles Percy of Illinois, Edward Brooke of Massachusetts, and Mark Hatfield of Oregon. Progressives also won the governorships of some of the heavily populated industrial states, including, besides Rockefeller, William Scranton and Raymond Shafer in Pennsylvania, George Romney in Michigan, Daniel Evans in Washington, and Richard Ogilvie in Illinois (elected in 1968 on the same ticket with Nixon).

Many of the new progressives seem to have been drawn to a more activist governmental approach, at least initially, because of pragmatic calculations that the stalwart or even moderate brands of Republicanism could no longer win elections, nationally or in the major industrial states, except when championed by a popular hero like Eisenhower. The fundamentalists largely agreed with this analysis, but argued that the way to solve the Republicans' political problem was to offer more sharply distinguished conservative alternatives to Democratic liberalism—"a choice, not an echo"—which they claimed would rally the conservative majority that public opinion polls suggested might exist among the electorate. The progressives' solution was quite different. The way for the Republicans to win and hold office, they maintained, was to demonstrate a capacity for meeting public needs, through government where necessary, but by means that would complement and encourage rather than stifle private enterprise and initiative.

In Congress, where they remained a minority within the minority, the progressives often felt that their interests, political and governmental, were best served by giving qualified support to programs initiated by the dominant Democrats. But in the state capitols progressive Republican governors during the 1960s proposed and won enactment of their own plans for revising state constitutions, expanding state services, broadening environmental protections, and carrying out other aspects of a general renaissance of state government.

Fundamentalist and stalwart Republicans often charged that the progressives were liberal Democrats in everything but name. The progressives did indeed share the Democrats' willingness to employ government to deal with social and economic problems that they believed could not adequately be met through private means. There were, however, some significant differences. First, on economic issues the progressive Republicans instinctively sought ways to work with business. The liberal Democrats, by contrast, though less antagonistic than they had once been, still approached business, especially big business, as the enemy. Second, the progressives gave somewhat greater weight than the liberals to the interests and moral attitudes of the rural areas in which the Republican party remained strong. Rural and small-town Republicans, for their part, particularly those in the East and Middle West, were more willing to support programs sponsored by the progressives than those initiated by Democrats. Third, the progressives, partly because they happened to control the governments of most of the major states in the 1960s but also to some extent for philosophic reasons, sought wherever feasible to put administrative control over government programs at the state or local level. Liberal Democrats on the whole remained enthusiastic federalizers. Finally, the progressives, true to the puritan heritage of the Republican party, tended to relate their proposals to moral absolutes (like Nelson Rockefeller's frequently invoked "brotherhood of man and fatherhood of God"—referred to by irreverent journalists as BOMFOG), whereas the liberal Democrats more often emphasized various kinds of personal and group "liberation."

While casting themselves as reformers, the progressives remained essentially conservative in that they viewed reform as a means for preserving the underlying soundness of the existing system. In Burkean terms, they aimed to repair "the deficient part of the constitution through the parts which were not impaired."[15] Like Theodore Roosevelt, looking back on his own career in 1916, they claimed that the progressive approach represented "not wild radicalism . . . [but] the highest and wisest form of conservatism."[16]

On many issues the progressives and the moderates took similar positions. The progressives, however, were more responsive to changing attitudes among the national news media and the national intelligentsia. On the issue of the Vietnam War, for example, the progressives moved earlier toward the dove position than most of the moderates (although Senator John Sherman Cooper of Kentucky, a moderate, became a leader in the effort within Congress to end the war).

The great political danger for the progressives was that by stretching to reach groups outside the normal Republican constituency, they would lose touch with and be rejected by the traditional Republican base—a fate that ultimately befell some progressive politicians, such as John Lindsay, the Republican who was elected mayor of New York City in 1965.[17] During the 1960s, however, progressive Republicans achieved substantial success at assembling winning coalitions in northeastern industrial states like New York, Pennsylvania, Massachusetts, and New Jersey; midwestern states like Michigan, Illinois, and Iowa; and far-western states like Washington and Oregon. Outside the South the progressives were weakest in a region where their counterparts in Theodore Roosevelt's time had been strong: the Great Plains and Rocky Mountain states, where most activists interested in reform had switched to the Democrats.

Most of the progressives had grown up within the Republican party, and many of them shared with the stalwarts a certain reverence for the party as an institution. Mark Hatfield, for example, liked to recall campaigning as a small boy for Herbert Hoover. Birthright Republicans among the progressives tended to regard fundamentalists like Goldwater and Reagan, not to mention Thurmond, as rather late arrivals, representing somewhat eccentric points of view.

In 1968 most of the progressives supported first Romney, then Rockefeller, for the Republican presidential nomination. They took pains, however, to avoid any repetition of the deep fission that had opened within the party following Goldwater's nomination in 1964. In the fall campaign most of the progressives campaigned dutifully, if without much private enthusiasm, for the national ticket. Nixon, in return, sought advice from the progressive leaders and indicated that, if elected, he would assign them important roles in the new administration.

Common Ground and Differences

On the spectrum of ideology, the four groups into which I have categorized the Republican party may be roughly arranged from right to left: fundamentalists the most conservative, followed by stalwarts, moderates, and progressives. In terms of positional conservatism, the progressives were prepared to promote change so long as it could be viewed as strengthening the existing system; the moderates accepted limited change and tried to make it work better; the stalwarts aimed to delay change as long as possible; and the fundamentalists believed that change had already gone too far. The relation of the groups to ideational conservatism was more complicated. The fundamentalists supported rigorous (their critics claimed simplistic) versions of various beliefs and attitudes that are a part of modern ideational conservatism: nationalism in foreign policy, market capitalism, and moral and cultural traditionalism, among others. By pressing each of these beliefs and attitudes to rather extreme positions, however, the fundamentalists tended to bring them into conflict with one another and with the organic view of society that lies at the heart of ideational conservatism. The fundamentalists, moreover, often advanced their views with a stridency that seemed likely to produce the opposite of social harmony. The complexity of conservatism, Nelson Rockefeller and others were able to argue, could better be served by the kind of innovations proposed by the progressives, or by the accommodations favored by moderates and many of the stalwarts, than by the bitterend resistance advocated by the fundamentalists.

In many areas of domestic policy, the four Republican groups maintained common goals and social assumptions, but supported differing means for implementing them. Even the most progressive Republicans placed greater trust in the beneficial effects of the market economy than most liberal Democrats did. Most Republicans from right to left viewed with alarm the promise of the Democrats' 1968 platform to make the federal government "the employer of last resort . . . for those who cannot obtain other employment."[18] For Republicans, the greater economic danger was not unemployment but inflation, which the 1968 Republican platform charged "has eroded confidence in the dollar at home and abroad . . . [and] severely cut into the incomes of all families, the retired, and those living on fixed incomes and pensions."[19] Fundamentalists and some stalwarts believed that to stop inflation it would be necessary to cut back drastically on federal spending for social programs enacted as parts of Lyndon Johnson's Great Society. But most progressives and moderates, who had supported passage of some of the Great Society programs, favored bringing down inflation gradually through more prudently managed fiscal and monetary policies.

Virtually all Republicans favored "decentralization of [governmental] power," which their 1968 platform claimed was "urgently needed to preserve personal liberty, improve efficiency, and provide a swifter response to human problems."[20] The Democrats, by contrast, far from backing away from the alleged centralizing tendencies of the Great Society, promised in their 1968 platform to create "a new federal banking structure to provide capital and investment guarantees" for reconstruction of inner city slums, and a federalized welfare system "in place of the present inequitable hodge podge state plans," among other new federal interventions.[21] Republican progressives, moderates, and many stalwarts were convinced that the best way to achieve decentralization was through the sharing of federal revenues with state and local governments. Fundamentalists, on the other hand, viewed revenue sharing as a cover for continued federal government expansion, and argued instead for a large cut in federal taxes, which, they claimed, would enable state and local governments to meet their legitimate needs out of their own resources.

Republicans almost unanimously applauded Nixon's promise to restore "law and order" throughout the nation, recently racked by riots and plagued by rising crime.[22] "Lawlessness," the 1968 Republican platform warned, "is crumbling the foundation of American society."[23] Fundamentalists and many stalwarts and moderates appeared willing to limit some civil liberties, particularly those most recently defined by the Supreme Court under the leadership of Chief Justice Warren, to strengthen "the forces of order." Progressives argued that a conciliatory approach by the new president toward minorities and the disaffected would go a long way toward restoring domestic tranquillity.

On foreign policy issues fundamentalists and stalwarts were usually hawkish, though some stalwarts still longed for withdrawal into a "Fortress America." Progressives and moderates were more prepared to take chances, and even to accept limited losses, for the sake of achieving peaceful solutions to international problems. All four groups were united in applying the test of "national interest" to foreign policy issues, but their interpretations of what constituted the national interest often differed.

Nixon, as will be described in chapter 4, carried out his promise to place representatives from all segments of the Republican party in high posts in the new administration. Those who took office generally tried, at least for a time, to put old differences behind them, and were often drawn into new patterns based on their current personal associations and governmental constituencies. Not far from the surface, however, the old divisions tended to survive—soon to reappear in the disputes over policy that broke out within the executive branch.

Nixon, as will be described in chapter 4, carried out his promise to place representatives from all segments of the Republican party in high posts in the new administration. Those who took office generally tried, at least for a time, to put old differences behind them, and were often drawn into new patterns based on their current personal associations and governmental constituencies. Not far from the surface, however, the old divisions tended to survive—soon to reappear in the disputes over policy that broke out within the executive branch.

The Nixon Administration

3

Richard Nixon

AT THE CORE of every modern presidency is the president himself. Henry Jones Ford's view that, "we deal with the oldest form of human governance: elected kingship" is perhaps extreme.[1] But few people would dispute Arthur Schlesinger's contention that Richard Nixon, when he entered the White House, was "on issues of war and peace the most absolute monarch (with the possible exception of Mao Tse-tung of China) among the great powers of the world."[2] On domestic matters Nixon's authority, even within the executive branch, was more limited, though still very broad.

To what ends did Nixon bend this enormous power? What were his values, aspirations, and social goals? What vision, if any, did he hold for the United States?

This chapter traces the development of Nixon's general social and political attitudes. In later chapters I will take up the evolution of his beliefs and attitudes in foreign policy and other particular policy areas.

Formative Influences

Richard Milhous Nixon, born in 1913, grew up in two small southern California towns, Yorba Linda and Whittier, both close to Los Angeles, but not in those days true suburbs. His early years were far from easy. His father, Frank Nixon, seems not to have had the knack to succeed at business, or perhaps was simply unlucky, and the family endured severe economic hardship. Frank Nixon is said to have had

41

a harsh temper, which he sometimes took out on his sons. When Nixon was a young teenager, his mother, Hannah, to whom he was deeply attached, went to live for almost three years in the Arizona desert to nurse his older brother, Harold, who was sick with tuberculosis. Harold died in his early twenties, and another brother, Arthur, died at age seven. (Hannah Nixon, who apparently had a romantic strain in her nature, named all but one of her five sons after early kings of Britain.) Nixon had very poor physical coordination, but he nevertheless strove to excel at athletics. (Pat Nixon has recalled that when she and her future husband began dating, they took up skating: "It was the gay thing to do. But it was awful for Dick. He almost broke his head two or three times, but he still kept going.")[3]

Whether as a consequence of these troubles, or some others, the young Nixon apparently developed unusual needs for self-justification and self-assertion.[4] Elliot Richardson, who served Nixon in three cabinet and one subcabinet posts before finally parting from the administration at the time of the so-called Saturday night massacre in October 1973, has speculated: "As a kid, Nixon seems to have been denied the satisfaction of being a winner. He was prevented from playing the roles that better-off types were able to play. He developed a compulsion to get even. He wanted to show the bastards."[5]

Such drives direct some men toward political radicalism. In Nixon they bred an iron determination to succeed within the existing system. The deciding factor may have been that Nixon, as a child and young man, did not view either his immediate social environment or the larger social system as hostile. "It was not an easy life," Nixon has recalled, "but it was a good one, centered around a loving family and a small, tight-knit, Quaker community. For those who were willing to work hard, California in the 1920s seemed a place and time of almost unlimited opportunity."[6]

As a boy, Nixon accepted pretty much intact the political culture of his family and community—a kind of distant extension of that small-town, Protestant Republicanism that Brand Whitlock described in his recollections of Ohio during the late nineteenth century. But the culture itself was changing, and becoming less secure. Southern California in the 1920s was approaching the worlds that Nathaniel West and Raymond Chandler later described; it was not Ohio in the 1880s. Economic and technological changes were undermining some of the values of the old Protestant culture, and new groups were challenging its social and political supremacy. Besides, Protestantism of the kind that developed in New England and the Middle West apparently had trouble adjusting to the alien environment of southern California, tending to wither or to produce exotic offshoots, like the evangelist Aimee Semple McPherson, whose revivals the Nixon family attended in Los Angeles.[7]

Frank Nixon had spent his childhood and early youth in Ohio, where he was, in his son's words, "a hard-line Republican." The elder Nixon continued to be a loyal Republican after he moved to California in 1907, when he was in his late twenties. But during the 1920s, possibly as a result of business reverses, he developed what Richard Nixon has called a "populist strain." Like many small-town Republicans, Frank Nixon disliked and feared the growing economic power of big business. He saw his small, independent retail grocery business in Whittier threatened by the competition of the rising chain stores. He believed, his son remembers, that "the Standard Oil trust was a blight on the American landscape." In 1924 the elder Nixon turned against the Republicans to vote for Robert La Follette, who was running for president on the Progressive ticket. Later, he became a strong supporter of the Townsend Plan, which proposed distributing $200 a month to everyone over sixty who would agree to spend the money and retire. He supported Hoover over Franklin Roosevelt in 1932 because he agreed with Hoover that prohibition should be continued. But in 1936, his son believes, he probably voted for Roosevelt instead of Alfred M. Landon, whom he described as a "stand-patter."[8]

Beyond somewhat irregular Republicanism, the Nixon family seems to have shared the growing scorn felt within the small-town Protestant culture toward all kinds of politics and politicians. In part this was a response to revelations of corruption in the national government. At the time of the Teapot Dome scandal in the mid-1920s, Nixon, then twelve years old, told his mother that he was going to be an "old-fashioned lawyer, a lawyer who can't be bought."[9] But this distrust of politicians also in part reflected the gradual displacement of small-town, evangelical Protestantism as the dominant force in American politics. Finding themselves outvoted by new coalitions, particularly in the urban and industrial states, evangelical Protestants for a long time disdained becoming one more interest group among many. Protestant values, for many Protestants, had been synonymous with Americanism. If these values were being rejected, there must be something wrong with the political system. This transition of attitudes had perhaps not gone very far in the 1920s—prohibition, the last great victory of evangelical Protestantism, had, after all, just been enacted—but there was an uneasy sense, especially in areas like southern California where other cultural forces were already strong, of coming change. Nixon's identification of political virtue as an "old-fashioned" value was probably not accidental.

The Nixon family were members of the Society of Friends, following the religious heritage of Nixon's mother; Frank Nixon had been a Methodist, but changed denominations when he married. The Friends—or Quakers, as they are commonly called—have always been somewhat special within the general family of American Protestantism. The West Coast branch of Quakerism to which the Nixons belonged was not so simple or austere as the eastern variety. The Whittier Quakers employed ministers and sang hymns, much like other Protestant denominations. The West Coast Friends, however, maintained the denomination's tradition of intense but rather good-natured moral piety. (Nixon's maternal great-grandmother was the model for the heroine of the Quaker novel, *The Friendly Persuasion*, written by Nixon's cousin Jessamyn West.) Before entering the navy during the Second World War, Nixon gave up the Quaker belief in pacifism, because, he had concluded, it "not only failed to stop violence—it actually played into the hands of a barbarous foe and weakened home-front morale."[10] But he continued to think of himself as a Quaker, even after he had abandoned many Quaker tenets.[11]

Early Career

While he was in high school, Nixon "dreamed of going to college in the East"—the beginning of a lifelong attraction, mixed with antagonism, to the values represented by the eastern academic and social establishments. He received the award for outstanding all-around student in his high school class given by the Harvard Club of California, and had a chance at a tuition scholarship to Yale. But the family's finances, undermined by the costs of his brothers' illnesses, and further flattened by the depression, required that Nixon live at home and attend Whittier College.[12]

On his graduation from Whittier in 1934, he won a scholarship to the new Duke Law School in Durham, North Carolina. His three years at Duke led to an enduring empathy with the South. Nixon has recalled: "We had some intense discussions on the race issue, and while I could not agree with many of my Southern classmates on this subject, I learned to understand and respect them for their patriotism, their pride, and their enormous interest in national issues."[13] The still somewhat backward condition of the South in the 1930s may have struck Nixon as analogous to his own situation: attuned to the finer things, but struggling for recognition in a rock-hard world. Harry Dent, who served as the White House's resident expert on southern politics from 1969 to 1972, has suggested: "Nixon's feeling about the South was more than political—he actually fell in love with the South. Nixon developed an insight into the southern mind during his years at Duke Law School. Nixon was actually a lot like the South. He grew up under poverty, and went on to better things."[14] Nixon's identification with the South may have contributed to his dislike for the "Battle Hymn of the Republic," almost a sacred anthem for generations of Republicans, which he once dismissed as "a Kennedy song."

During Christmas vacation of his senior year in law school, Nixon and two classmates made the rounds of prominent law firms in New York, looking for jobs. He was particularly impressed by Sullivan and Cromwell, where John Foster Dulles, Eisenhower's future secretary of state, was a senior partner. Nixon's friends found employment in New York, one with a major law firm, the other with a large oil corporation. But Nixon received no offers.[15]

Politically, Nixon in those years appears to have inclined toward a moderate liberal position. His first political hero was his father's old favorite, Robert La Follette. Nixon does not say in his memoirs whom he voted for in the 1936 presidential election, when he was twenty-three—although he guesses that his father voted for Roosevelt. In 1940, having returned to Whittier to practice law, Nixon made a few speeches in behalf of Wendell Willkie's presidential candidacy. "While I favored some of Roosevelt's domestic programs, particularly Social Security," he has recalled, "I opposed his attempt to break the two-term tradition."[16]

Nixon has usually dated his disenchantment with liberalism to his brief experience as a lawyer in the Office of Price Administration (OPA) in Washington in 1942. "While some career government workers were sincere, dedicated, and able people," he observed, "others became obsessed with their own power and seemed to delight in kicking people around, particularly those in the private sector."[17] Yet when he sought the Republican nomination for Congress from California's twelfth district (in Los Angeles County) in 1946, he still thought of himself as a kind of liberal. He wrote to the chairman of a local Republican candidate screening committee: "An aggressive, vigorous campaign on a platform of *practical* liberalism would be the antidote the people have been looking for to take the place of [Congressman Jerry] Voorhis's particular brand of New Deal idealism."[18]

In the opening speech of his campaign, Nixon contrasted the two routes he saw open for America: "One advocated by the New Deal is government control in regulating our lives. The other calls for individual freedom and all that initiative can produce." Under the tutelage of Murray Chotiner, a slick master of the burgeoning art of campaign consultancy, Nixon soon stopped arguing political philosophy and concentrated on the charge that Congressman Voorhis, the liberal Democratic incumbent, was supported by a left-wing political action committee that included "Communists and fellow travellers." In the general Republican sweep of 1946, Nixon was elected.[19]

During his first year in the House of Representatives, which was controlled by the Republicans for the first time since 1930, Nixon voted with the majority of his party on 84 percent of the roll calls on which there was a party division—not a particularly high level of party regularity in those days of tight Republican unity in the House. His voting pattern resembled that of a group of recently elected moderate Republicans, mainly from the East, including Kenneth Keating of New York (86 percent regularity) and Clifford Case of New Jersey (89 percent); but was considerably more regular than that of another first-term Republican representative, Jacob Javits of New York (67 percent).[20] In June 1947 Nixon voted for the Taft-Hartley labor relations bill, which was bitterly opposed by organized labor, as did Case and Keating, but not Javits.[21] Nixon consistently supported the Marshall Plan and other foreign aid measures proposed by the Truman administration (a divisive issue between the Dewey and Taft wings of the Republican party at the time), although a poll taken in Nixon's district in 1947 showed foreign aid opposed by about 75 percent of his constituents.[22]

In 1948, the year of Truman's upset victory over Dewey for the presidency, the Democrats regained control of the House, but Nixon, who received both the Republican and Democratic nominations then possible under California's cross-filing system, was reelected. In the new Congress Nixon achieved a party regularity score of 74 percent, the same as Keating, but much higher than Case (43 percent) or Javits (27 percent).[23] In 1950 Nixon was the only California representative to join a group of twenty-five Republican House members formed to develop more forward looking party policies, under the sponsorship of Javits and Keating.[24]

Nixon's most spectacular—and fateful—performance during his years in the House was his role, as a member of the House Un-American Activities Committee in 1948, in exposing Alger Hiss's involvement with the Communist party during the 1930s. Before Nixon ran for Congress, his attitude toward communism was one of "general disinterest." In the 1930s he sympathized with the Loyalists, who were fighting against Franco in the Spanish Civil War; and later he was "elated when both the United States and the Soviet Union supported the founding of the United Nations." By the time of his election to Congress in 1946, however, he had become convinced that international communism in general and the Soviet Union in particular threatened world peace and America's national interests. Even so, he accepted with reluctance when House Speaker Joseph Martin asked him in early 1947 to serve on the highly controversial Un-American Activities Committee.[25]

Nixon's successful pursuit of Hiss, carried out before newsreel cameras during the summer and fall of 1948, gained him a good deal of publicity and made him a minor hero with hard-line anti-Communists. It also earned him the lasting enmity of those members of the liberal community who either assumed that Hiss was innocent or were prepared to agree with Alistair Cooke's view that the Hiss case put "a generation on trial."[26]

Nixon strengthened his credentials with militant anti-Communists by achieving passage by the House in 1948 of the Mundt-Nixon bill, which would have required registration of all Communists and Communist-affiliated organizations. The bill died in the Senate. Nixon always took care, however, to avoid the impression that the pursuit of domestic Communists was his sole interest in public life. As a result, he missed both the instant celebrity and early political demise that befell Senator Joseph McCarthy of Wisconsin.

The circumstances of Nixon's election to the Senate in 1950 confirmed his identification as a scare figure for American liberals. His Democratic opponent, Congresswoman Helen Gahagan Douglas of

Los Angeles, had been one of the leaders of the opposition to the Mundt-Nixon bill in the House. She had also voted against military aid to Greece and Turkey, proposed by the Truman administration, and against investigation of the purchase of American patents by the Soviet Union, among other measures growing out of the developing world rivalry between the United States and Russia. These positions had frequently placed her on the same side as Congressman Vito Marcantonio of New York, the only avowedly pro-Communist member of Congress. Nixon, again following the advice of Chotiner, publicized this connection for California voters through a widely circulated "pink sheet" comparing the voting records of Douglas and Marcantonio. Congresswoman Douglas responded by charging that Nixon had voted with Marcantonio on foreign policy issues more often than she had, and by tagging her opponent with an enduring epithet: "Tricky Dicky." Governor Warren, running for reelection, and looking toward the Republican presidential nomination in 1952, declined to endorse Nixon in the Senate race. Nixon easily won election. But as a result of the campaign, he acquired national identification as a political polarizer—one likely to mobilize passions at either end of the ideological spectrum.[27]

In his two years in the Senate (1951 to 1953), Nixon's voting record closely resembled that of his California colleague, William Knowland, later identified as an extreme conservative, but then very much under the moderate influence of Governor Warren, who had appointed Knowland to the Senate in 1945. On foreign policy issues Nixon and Knowland often voted with the handful of Republican internationalists, such as Henry Cabot Lodge of Massachusetts and Irving Ives of New York, rather than with the neo-isolationist bloc led by Taft. On domestic issues the two wings of the party were relatively cohesive, both joining with the southern Democrats to oppose the liberal program of the Truman administration.[28]

Vice-Presidential Years: Association with Burns

Eisenhower wrote in his memoirs that he selected Nixon to run with him on the Republican ticket in 1952 for three reasons: he wanted a relatively young running mate (he was under the impression, however, that Nixon was forty-two rather than thirty-nine); he approved

Nixon's handling of the Hiss case; and he believed "through reports of qualified observers . . . that his political philosophy generally coincided with my own." The qualified observers who most influenced the choice were probably Dewey, Henry Cabot Lodge, and Herbert Brownell, who had been Dewey's campaign manager in 1948 and was Eisenhower's chief strategist at the 1952 Republican convention. Dewey had told Nixon at a Republican fund-raising dinner that Nixon addressed in New York three months before the convention that he planned to submit Nixon's name for the vice-presidency. Nixon subsequently helped convince the California delegation, officially locked up behind Warren, to support the seating of Eisenhower delegations from three southern states, which in effect determined the nomination. Before the convention Eisenhower had told only Brownell that he leaned toward Nixon for the second place on the ticket. When, on the night of his nomination, Eisenhower submitted to a small committee of party leaders a list of five possibilities for the vice-presidency, with Nixon's name at the top, the committee "enthusiastically approved" Nixon.[29]

If Nixon owed his promotion to the moderate eastern establishment headed by Dewey, he quickly found himself treated by the establishment as a cuttable loss. When the *New York Post* revealed in September that Nixon had been the political beneficiary of an $18,000 fund maintained by several California businessmen to assist his career, Dewey, speaking for "Eisenhower's top advisers," asked Nixon to resign from the ticket. The press, which had already begun to develop a dislike for Nixon, gave wide publicity to the story—much more than to the subsequent discovery that a similar fund had been maintained for Adlai Stevenson, the Democratic presidential nominee. Eisenhower waited almost a week before making clear—after the overwhelmingly favorable public reaction to Nixon's celebrated "Checkers" speech—that he wanted Nixon to continue as his running mate.[30]

In the campaign that followed, Eisenhower relied on Nixon to fire up the party troops while he himself pursued a more statesmanlike course. Nixon carried out the assignment with apparent gusto, producing such grubby rhetoric as the charge that Stevenson was a graduate of Dean Acheson's "Cowardly College of Communist Containment." Looking back long after, Nixon conceded: "Some of the rhetoric I used during that campaign was very rough. Perhaps I was unconsciously overreacting to the attacks made against me during and after the fund crisis; perhaps I was simply carried away by the partisan role Eisenhower had assigned me."[31]

During his eight years as vice-president, Nixon performed as a loyal subordinate to the president instead of allowing himself to become the focus of opposition to the administration within the incumbent party (the John Nance Garner model), or becoming the leader of an ideological faction (the Henry Wallace model). Within the administration he was usually on the side of a more activist role for the federal government in domestic affairs and of a hard line against the Communist powers in foreign policy. Once Eisenhower had made a decision on policy, however, Nixon loyally defended the position of the administration. In these crucial years of personal and intellectual development, therefore, his main role was to advocate views that he had had little real part in formulating.

Increasingly he became a target for abuse by liberals, particularly in the academic community and the press. Many liberals, some of whom had promoted Eisenhower for the Democratic presidential nomination in 1948, were reluctant to acknowledge Eisenhower's conservatism. Partly for this reason—and partly because of his own unremitting partisanship—Nixon was attacked with special fury by the opposition.

The person who most influenced the development of Nixon's views on domestic matters during this period appears to have been Arthur Burns, who in 1953 came from Columbia to become chairman of Eisenhower's Council of Economic Advisers. Burns, born in Austria in 1904, had made his professional reputation carrying on the study of the business cycle begun by his mentor at Columbia, Wesley C. Mitchell. Like Mitchell, who had been an economic adviser to Herbert Hoover, Burns favored a relatively limited role for government in management of the economy. He warned: "The imposing schemes for governmental action that are being bottomed on Keynes' equilib-rium theory must be viewed with skepticism." Burns, however, had accepted some elements of the Keynesian revolution. Government stimulation, he believed, was needed at times to overcome sluggish-ness in private spending and investment. During the depression he had supported the federal public works program instituted by the New Deal. "This policy," he wrote, "commends itself because it is a proposal for actual spending by the government, and because it directs additional spending to the industries in which there is the greatest proportion of unused resources." Burns's general conservatism was pragmatic and Burkean rather than dogmatic or doctrinaire. "Subtle understanding of economic change," he maintained, "comes from a knowledge of history and large affairs, not from statistics or their processing alone—to which our age has turned so eagerly in its quest for certainty."[32]

In their first encounter at a cabinet meeting, Nixon and Burns took opposite sides. Nixon spoke in favor of the administration's sponsoring a higher minimum wage, to demonstrate Republican concern for working-class voters. Burns objected, on the ground that the real effect of raising the minimum wage would be to deprive unskilled workers of jobs. Nixon was impressed by Burns's reasoning.

In later, more critical debates Nixon and Burns were often allied. In 1958, when unemployment rose above 7 percent, Nixon and Burns (who by then had returned to academic life, but retained substantial influence within the administration) tried unsuccessfully to get Eisenhower to propose a tax cut that would stimulate the economy—and improve Republican chances in that year's congressional elections. In 1960 Burns and Nixon again favored economic stimulation. Early in March Burns warned Nixon, who was then preparing to campaign for the presidency, that, contrary to many forecasts, the economy was headed for trouble. Burns recommended loosening credit and increasing defense spending. But once again Eisenhower, following the counsel of his more conservative fiscal advisers, stuck to restraint. "Unfortunately," Nixon wrote in his book *Six Crises,* "Arthur Burns turned out to be a good prophet. The bottom of the 1960 dip did come in October and the economy started to move up again in November—after it was too late to affect the election returns."[33]

During the Eisenhower years Nixon tried to act as a bridge between the moderates within the administration and the more conservative Republicans in Congress. The heart of the Republican party, he believed, lay with its right wing.[34] To win the Republican presidential nomination in 1960, therefore, he must make himself acceptable to the stalwarts and the fundamentalists. (He did not, of course, think of them by those names.) But once nominated, he would need to attract groups outside the normal Republican fold, as Nelson Rockefeller had done in New York in 1958.

Three days before the 1960 Republican convention was to begin, Nixon, with his nomination assured, made broad concessions to Rockefeller on the platform and tried to persuade the New York governor to be his running mate. Rockefeller declined.[35] Nixon then turned to another representative of the eastern establishment, Henry Cabot Lodge, Eisenhower's ambassador to the United Nations. (If Lodge had not insisted on seeking reelection to the Senate in 1952— a contest he lost to young John Kennedy—he might well have been Eisenhower's first choice for vice-president that year.)[36]

In the fall campaign Nixon claimed that he shared most of Kennedy's liberal goals, but that he offered more practical means for achieving them. In his fourth debate with Kennedy, Nixon even appeared relatively restrained in his attitude toward the Castro regime in Cuba—misleadingly, as it later turned out. Kennedy had been urging that the United States help launch an effort by anti-Communist Cubans to overthrow Castro, an operation that Nixon has charged— and Theodore Sorensen, Kennedy's aide and biographer, has denied—Kennedy knew, from briefings he had been given by the Central Intelligency Agency, the Eisenhower administration was already planning. In the televised debate Nixon took a strong stand *against* intervention in Cuba, which he had been arguing *for* within the administration—in order, he later claimed, to protect the security of the anti-Castro operation.[37]

The Road to the White House

His defeat in the 1960 general election by only 120,000 votes did not lead Nixon to conclude that his strategy on the issues had been wrong. Kennedy won, he believed, because of "unlimited money" and tactical mastery by "the most ruthless group of political operators ever mobilized for a presidential campaign." Never again, Nixon vowed, would he "enter an election at a disadvantage by being vulnerable to them—or anyone—on the level of political tactics."[38]

Seeking a political comeback, Nixon ran for governor of California in 1962. In the Republican primary he was opposed by Joseph Shell, the Republican leader in the state assembly, who received support from the awakening forces of conservative fundamentalism. "As I travelled through the state before the June primary," Nixon has recalled, "I met with a lot of heckling—but it was different from the heckling in 1950. Then I had been heckled by the far left; now I was being heckled by the far right."[39] He defeated Shell in the primary by about two to one—not a very good showing for the nominal head of the national party. In the fall Nixon lost to the Democratic incumbent, Pat Brown, by almost 300,000 votes, while Republican progressives were winning or holding the governorships of New York, Pennsylvania, and Michigan. After announcing his retirement from politics at a spectacular "last press conference," in which some reporters thought he seemed almost deranged, Nixon moved to New York City, setting out to fulfill his old ambition of becoming a successful Wall Street lawyer.

In 1964, edging back into political involvement, Nixon tried to act as a bridge between the Goldwaterite fundamentalists, who had taken over the Republican party leadership, and the more moderate party groups that had supported William Scranton for the presidential nomination. He found the exercise frustrating. Later he regretted the image of extremism that Goldwater had fastened to the party. "Republicans had always been tagged as reactionary," he lamented. "But after [Goldwater's] campaign we were portrayed as reckless and racist."[40]

After Goldwater's defeat Nixon was not above trying to rescue some political profit from the wreckage. Two days after the election he held a press conference at which he accused Rockefeller, who had not campaigned for Goldwater, of being "a spoilsport and a divider" who "could no longer be regarded as a party leader anywhere outside New York." His purpose, he later explained, was "to avert an irreconcilable split between conservatives and liberals within the party."[41]

Soon, however, Nixon began in earnest to try to take the sting out of ideological differences. In a series of speeches in 1965, he appealed for movement toward the center: "If being a liberal means federalizing everything, then I'm no liberal. If being a conservative means turning back the clock, denying problems that exist, then I'm no conservative."[42] He usually referred to himself as a "centrist" or a "pragmatist." In an interview in 1967, he said that he was "a pragmatist with positions grounded in pretty solid principles"—whatever that meant.[43]

As 1968 approached, Nixon found himself well situated to win the presidential nomination as a compromise candidate. He was at least minimally acceptable to both sides in the bitter struggle between fundamentalists and progressives that was dividing the party. Besides, he was the first choice of most of the stalwarts and of many of the moderates.

During the spring and early summer of 1968, after he had established himself as the front-runner for the nomination, Nixon gave a series of radio talks that were unusually philosophic for an American political campaign. Among "the central roots" of "the spread of violence and disorder," he argued in one talk, was "the steady erosion of the sense of person, of a place within the system, that we have allowed to accompany the development of our mass society." To rebuild "a sense of community," Nixon proposed that social power be decentralized. "After a third of a century of concentrating power," he said, "an old idea is winning a new acceptance: the idea that what we need is a dispersal of power."[44] In another talk, he seemed to place himself in the tradition of progressive activism—which, he appeared to suggest, should now lead the nation beyond the New Deal. "Franklin Roosevelt," he said, "promulgated the old, negative freedoms *from*. Our uncompleted task is to make real the new, positive freedoms *to*." (Emphasis in the original.)[45]

In a third talk, drafted by William Safire, one of his more liberal speechwriters (at that time), Nixon proposed a "new alignment," to include such unlikely partners as traditional Republicans, the "new South," some "black militants," the "silent center" (a tag lifted by Safire from a speech by former Senator Paul Douglas of Illinois, a New Deal Democrat), and "thoughtful critics like Daniel Moynihan and Richard Goodwin—both liberals."[46] Probably Nixon was no more than half-serious about some of the elements in his proposed alignment—particularly the black militants. But the talk showed the way his mind was working: he was groping toward new coalitions, examining unusual options.

The key to Nixon's success at the Miami Beach convention was that he was both the front-runner and the probable ultimate fallback candidate if the convention deadlocked. If he failed to win on the first ballot, he would probably lose strength on succeeding ballots to Rockefeller and Reagan. But since Rockefeller and Reagan each appeared to possess sufficient leverage to prevent the other from being nominated, the delegates would probably come back to Nixon in the end. Given this situation, Nixon's managers were able to pry loose enough wavering delegates to go over the top on the first ballot.

When it came time to select a candidate for vice-president, Nixon turned no more to the eastern establishment that had spurned him so often. At lunch with a group of journalists in New York two weeks before the Republican convention, when asked who would be his running mate, he replied that if he could select a vice-president without any consideration for party or political availability, his first choice would be Hubert Humphrey, and his second, John Connally.[47] His mention of Humphrey, the leading contender for the Democratic presidential nomination, was meant to get a laugh—though Nixon liked and respected Humphrey. But inclusion of Connally, then the Democratic governor of Texas, provided a deeper clue to the direction in which Nixon's political interest was turning: toward a new breed of nonestablishment, nontraditional conservatives; toward the "sunbelt," where John Mitchell's young political theorist, Kevin Phillips, was predicting the political future must lie.[48] Connally not being available—not yet—the choice went to Spiro T. Agnew, Republican governor of Maryland, marginally a southerner, marginally an ethnic (the son of a Greek immigrant, he had converted from the Greek Orthodox church to Episcopalianism); earlier an enthusiastic supporter of Rockefeller for the 1968 nomination, but a hard-liner during the urban riots that followed the assassination of Martin Luther King.[49]

In the fall campaign Nixon, apparently convinced that the disarray within the Democratic party following the riotous Democratic national convention in Chicago was sufficient to produce his election, played down the issues and made little further reference to "new alignments." He assigned Bryce Harlow, a former Eisenhower aide, and a few others "to meet with the interest groups, and find out what they wanted, and then promise them that the Nixon administration would give them what they wanted."[50] At the beginning of the general election campaign, he established a number of issue task forces, with Senator John Tower of Texas, a fundamentalist, as chairman, and Congressman Bradford Morse of Massachusetts, a progressive, as vice-chairman. On the hustings, however, Nixon confined himself largely to generalities.

The Pursuit of Balance

In the first months after his election, Nixon gave little clear indication of the administration's goals—probably because he was unclear in his own mind, except in the area of foreign policy, of the objectives he wished the administration to achieve or the direction in which he wished to lead the country.

On the one hand, he seemed intent on sweeping away many of the liberal programs enacted under Kennedy's New Frontier and Johnson's Great Society, as the fundamentalists and some of the stalwarts wanted. "In effect," he told his newly appointed cabinet, "we want to reverse the whole trend of government over the last eight years. We may only have four years in which to do it, so we can't waste a minute."[51] On the other hand, he wished to be associated with social progress. "Hell," he told Safire, "if all we do is manage things ten percent better, we'll never be remembered for anything. Republicans are supposed to manage things better, after Democrats break new ground—that's the old cliché. We have better things to do."[52]

Perhaps remembering his father's experience, Nixon retained strong sympathy for small business. "I know we can't go back to mom-and-pop grocery stores," he told a cabinet committee, "but does everything have to be sold in a super-market?"[53] But he believed that economic bigness represented the wave of the future. "I was convinced," he has written, "that American companies would be able to compete in the international market only if they were as big and strong as the government-sheltered monopolies in so many foreign countries."[54]

A key value for Nixon appeared to be individual freedom. "What we've got to say," he told Raymond Price, the speechwriter to whom he usually turned for philosophic messages, as they worked together on his inaugural address, "is, the emphasis in the past has been on material things and on governmental action. We've come to the ultimate limit in that respect. We've never had more programs, spent more money, or passed more laws than in the past third of a century. Yet we have these terrible problems today. . . . The missing thing is what's at the heart of the American experiment. While the United States is thought of as the wonder of the world, in terms of its material progress, its wealth, its productivity, what matters is the fact that the United States has provided a place for individual self-expression. We've got to provide that opportunity."[55]

Yet Nixon was concerned that in some areas individual self-expression had been carried too far. In one of his radio talks during the campaign, he observed: "All history has been a struggle between man's thrust toward violence and his yearning for peace. . . . The old violence parades today in a new uniform. . . . At home, it may masquerade as 'civil disobedience' or 'freedom,' and it sometimes marches under the banner of legitimate dissent."[56] He was eager, he has written, "to defend the 'square' virtues. In some cases—such as opposing the legalization of marijuana and the provision of federal funds for abortion, and in identifying myself with unabashed patriotism—I knew I would be standing against the prevailing social winds, and that would cause tension. But I thought that at least someone in high office would be standing up for what he believed."[57]

Early in 1969 Nixon circulated among members of his cabinet and his principal aides copies of the Godkin lectures recently delivered at Harvard by John Gardner, with a note saying they expressed "better than anything I have yet read what I hope will serve as the basic philosophy of this administration."[58] Gardner had paid tribute to the desirability of "a society (and institutions) capable of continuous change, continuous renewal, continuous responsiveness." But his emphasis was on the need for a restoration of traditional values and social order: "We have explored about as fully as a civilization can the joys of impulse, of indiscipline, of a world without forms, without order, and without limit. A balance must be struck."[59]

Nixon, of course, was not alone in simultaneously valuing individual self-expression and order based on traditional authority. Nor are these values necessarily incompatible. They have, however, maintained ideological tension in Western civilization at least since the beginnings of the industrial, democratic, and secular revolutions in the eighteenth century. The question was: how would the new president seek to reconcile freedom with order, and both with such other values as social justice and material abundance, in the context of his own time and place?

A Man for All Factions

Though his political roots were with the group I have labeled Republican moderates, and though he had served loyally as vice-president in the predominantly moderate Eisenhower administration, Nixon by 1968 was not closely identified with any of the major

Republican groups—one of his strengths in winning the nomination. His dedicated service to the party and his identification with traditional moral attitudes led most of the stalwarts to feel comfortable with him. His relative hawkishness on foreign policy had attracted support from many of the fundamentalists—though the economic libertarians among the fundamentalists viewed his economic eclecticism with considerable misgivings. The moderates maintained hopes that he would pursue a course generally similar to Eisenhower's. Among the progressives, most of the easterners and midwesterners regarded Nixon as at best an opportunist—all too likely to accommodate the fundamentalists on crucial economic and foreign policy issues. But some of the western progressives, remembering Nixon's restlessness in the relatively passive Eisenhower administration, predicted that he would turn out to be more of a governmental activist than most of either his supporters or his critics expected.

Among the leaders of the new administration, none seemed closer to Nixon than Robert Finch, the lieutenant governor of California who became Nixon's secretary of health, education, and welfare. Finch had become friendly with Nixon in the late 1940s while he was working in Washington for another California congressman. Twelve years younger than Nixon, Finch had served as a good sounding board, a companion on whom to try out ideas about government, about politics—about life. The two had remained friends. In 1960 Finch had managed Nixon's campaign for president. At the Republican convention in 1968, Nixon, before tapping Agnew, offered Finch the nomination for vice-president. On the eve of Nixon's inauguration, Finch fell into conversation with John Veneman, another Californian whom he had persuaded to join him at HEW as under secretary. "You watch that man," Finch told Veneman. "He's going to surprise people. He wants to be remembered in history, and, as a student of Theodore and Franklin Roosevelt, he knows that only presidents who come up with progressive social programs are likely to make a name."[60]

Surprises indeed there would be—not the least for Robert Finch.

4

The Nixon Team

ALTHOUGH the president is the single most important decisionmaker in almost every administration, the people he chooses for posts in his cabinet, particularly the so-called inner cabinet (State, the Treasury, Justice, and Defense), and for key jobs on the White House staff also exercise enormous authority. What sort of people did Nixon place in these important jobs? What ideological assumptions did they carry with them into the administration?

Like most of his predecessors, Nixon had made few firm decisions on executive branch personnel before his election. Aside from foreign policy, which he planned to manage from the White House, he aimed to delegate large amounts of control to the heads of the federal departments and agencies. "I've always thought," he liked to tell reporters, "this country could run itself domestically without a President. All you need is a competent Cabinet to run the country at home."[1] In May 1968 he told an interviewer: "I would disperse power, spread it among able people."[2] On election day the identities of most of the people who were to hold these enhanced cabinet posts, as well as other important jobs in the new administration, had yet to be determined.

The Inner Circle

The most natural place for Nixon to look first for personnel—as he began forming the new administration at his transition headquarters

59

in the Pierre Hotel overlooking Central Park in New York City—was the campaign organization that had just won him the presidency. The Nixon organization, as it had evolved by the fall of 1968, existed in layers. One layer reached back to Nixon's early days in California politics; another comprised associates from the Eisenhower administration; a third consisted of technicians who had worked in his 1960 campaign, some continuing with him through his disastrous race for governor of California in 1962; and a final layer was made up of more recent associates, acquired since he began practicing law in New York in 1963. Within each of these layers, and across layers, intricate webs of personal and political relationships had been formed.

In the early days of the campaign, when Nixon was still operating out of his law firm at 20 Broad Street, next to the New York Stock Exchange, the New York layer had seemed dominant. It included Nixon's personal staff, which besides Rose Mary Woods, his personal secretary since 1951, consisted mainly of two recently hired young press aides and speechwriters: Patrick Buchanan, a hard-line conservative fundamentalist on leave from the *St. Louis Globe-Democrat*; and Raymond Price, a Republican progressive and the former chief editorial writer for the old *New York Herald Tribune*. Other central figures in the New York group were members of Nixon's law firm, particularly John Mitchell, who liked to boast that he brought the firm "more business than Nixon"; and such junior members of the firm as John Sears and Leonard Garment, a trial lawyer whose own political heritage was Democratic liberal. On the outer fringes were a scattering of conservative intellectuals, mostly protégés of Arthur Burns, who had returned to the Columbia University faculty after leaving the Eisenhower administration: Martin Anderson, a young economist and critic of the federal urban renewal program, also at Columbia; Alan Greenspan, president of his own highly successful investment consulting firm; and Richard Whalen, former associate editor of *Fortune* magazine.[3]

As the primary campaign heated up—and the probability of Nixon's nomination grew—associates from earlier days returned, in some cases crowding out members of the New York layer. Late in April 1968 H. R. Haldeman, who had served as Nixon's chief advance man in 1960 and had managed his gubernatorial drive in 1962, joined the campaign. Haldeman's career as an advertising executive with the J. Walter Thompson agency in Los Angeles had recently been running down—but this was not known to others in the campaign, probably including Nixon. With Haldeman came John Ehrlichman, another former Nixon advance man, then practicing law in Seattle. Haldeman and Ehrlichman, both serious Christian Scientists, had worked together off and on since they were allies in campus politics at the University of California at Los Angeles in the 1940s. From the time of his arrival, Haldeman became Nixon's personal chief of staff, acting as a screen between Nixon and everyone outside his immediate family and a few personal friends. Ehrlichman's role was at first less visible, but, with Haldeman's approval, Ehrlichman soon began taking over administrative control of the candidate's professional staff.[4]

Only John Mitchell rivaled Haldeman for status within the Nixon campaign organization. The two warily developed a division of spheres: Mitchell would run the overall campaign; Haldeman would clear all decisions that required the candidate's approval or knowledge.[5]

Haldeman and Ehrlichman, with Mitchell's—and presumably Nixon's—concurrence, were principally responsible for keeping issue content low in the general election campaign. Some issue-oriented members of the earlier staff resigned. But most—attached, after all, to what appeared to be a winning drive for the presidency—hung on. Leonard Garment told Richard Whalen, who quit in August after a run-in with Ehrlichman: "If Nixon had put Haldeman and Ehrlichman in their slots six months earlier, he would never have gotten off the ground. Price and maybe Buchanan would have done what you did. But, coming in when they did, to take over and control the going machinery, they were very necessary."[6]

Neither Haldeman nor Mitchell seems to have had a highly developed political or ideological orientation before joining Nixon. Haldeman came from a well-established southern California family— he related in his memoirs, with amusement, that Nixon took pains to inform Oveta Culp Hobby, on a visit the two men made to Houston early in their association, that "Bob comes from one of the finest families in Los Angeles." His grandfather had been one of the founders of a militant anti-Communist organization in southern California. During his own youth, however, Haldeman recalled, he was "not only apolitical, but . . . a rah-rah college type." He was attracted to Nixon, he claimed, not for ideological reasons, but because he felt pride in Nixon as a fellow Californian and admired the vice-president as a "fighter." In the time of their association, before and during the White House years, Haldeman was, he maintained, essentially a "mechanic," executing Nixon's will. "I was a machine," he wrote. "A robot. . . . And I was a good machine. I was efficient"—surely among the saddest lines ever to appear in a political memoir.[7]

Some have argued there was more to Haldeman's role than that. Haldeman made himself the mysterious interlocutor of the administration. Soon after Nixon's inauguration he had a private dining room walled off for himself and a few members of the senior staff, apart from the general White House mess; before long, he ceased appearing even in the private dining room, taking lunch in his office. Quite a few people of considerable rank in the Nixon administration had virtually no contact with Haldeman during the more than four years he served as chief of staff. "It was a lot easier," Martin Anderson has recalled, "to see Richard Nixon in those days than it was to see Bob Haldeman."[8] He attended staff meetings on substantive issues infrequently. When he was present at meetings, he often said nothing. Yet, according to Alexander Butterfield, one of Haldeman's principal aides: "Sixty percent of the time the President spent with staff in 1972, he was with Haldeman—and ninety percent of that time, they were alone."[9] Leonard Garment, who worked closely with both Nixon and Haldeman, has observed: "It is true that Haldeman acted as a screen, but there is an old rule in physics that the ingredients of the screen affect the material that passes through the screen."[10] Perhaps Haldeman's main ideological effect on Nixon, as his own description of his role suggests, was not so much conservative as value-negating: as the good mechanic, who spent more time with the president than all other aides combined, he may have reinforced a tendency already present in Nixon's personality to view public issues as exercises in pragmatic logic, unaffected by standards of social justice or moral right.

Before coming into contact with Nixon, when Mitchell's small, prosperous law firm merged with the firm of Nixon, Mudge, Alexander and Guthrie early in 1967, John Mitchell seems to have been, if anything, a political moderate with loose ties to the New York Republican party. A partner from Mitchell's original firm has recalled his outspoken criticism of anti-Communist witch-hunting during the McCarthy period in the 1950s.[11] Mitchell had made his reputation and fortune by developing the ingenious device of "authority financing"—

a means for state and local governments to circumvent constitutional limitations on bonded indebtedness by guaranteeing bonds issued by special authorities for housing, school buildings, sewage plants, and other public purposes. Among his principal clients was the state of New York, then governed by Nelson Rockefeller. In the course of his municipal bond work for state and local governments all over the country, Mitchell acquired a keen sense of the way things work in the back rooms of American politics. It was this broad knowledge of state and local politics, as well as his apparent decisiveness and knack for organization, that made Mitchell appear invaluable to Nixon.[12]

During the campaign Mitchell was chief architect of the so-called southern strategy—really a border state strategy. When choice became necessary in distributing resources during the closing weeks of the campaign, Mitchell gave priority to winning the border states and the rim South over industrial states in the North. "I always believed," he told an interviewer in 1969, "that in the end the blue-collar workers in the North would go back to Humphrey."[13] (They did.)

After the election Mitchell was determined to return to his law practice—which was bound to grow more lucrative because of the firm's contacts in the White House. But he was persuaded by Nixon, who had come to rely on Mitchell's judgment, to accept the attorney generalship in the new administration. Mitchell proceeded to award top jobs at the Justice Department to lawyer-politicians from around the country whom he had earlier recruited for the campaign.[14]

Some other important participants in the campaign were appointed to cabinet posts or jobs on the White House staff. Robert Finch, given his choice of line departments or a place at the White House, picked the Department of Health, Education, and Welfare. "I was the fair-haired boy," Finch later recalled. "I could have had whatever I wanted. I was convinced, on the basis of recent developments, that the budget of HEW was going to get larger and larger. So that was what I took. I wanted to be where the action was."[15]

Raymond Price, Patrick Buchanan, and William Safire became White House speechwriters. Bryce Harlow, who had been functioning during the two Democratic administrations as chief Washington lobbyist for Procter and Gamble, agreed to take responsibility for congressional liaison, as he had during the closing years of the Eisenhower administration. Martin Anderson continued as an adviser on domestic issues, with duties at first not clearly defined.

Herbert Klein, Nixon's press secretary in 1960 and 1962, already in the process of being eased aside by Haldeman, became coordinator of public relations for the administration. Ronald Ziegler, a young protégé of Haldeman's at J. Walter Thompson, became Nixon's personal press spokesman. John Sears, one of the handful of aides who in 1966 had helped launch Nixon's campaign for the presidency, came on the White House staff to work on political liaison—but Sears, having aroused John Mitchell's dislike, was already under a cloud. "I was working for Nixon in the law firm for a year before the merger," Sears explained long after. "We had a good relationship. After Mitchell came onto the campaign, Nixon told him a couple of times to check things with me. That did not sit well with Mitchell."[16]

A few members of the campaign staff decided not to make the trip to Washington. Alan Greenspan, who had coordinated economic policy, agreed to work through the transition period, but announced that after that he would return to his firm in Manhattan. "I had the feeling there was an inner circle and an outer circle, and I was in the outer circle," Greenspan recalled in 1978. "I didn't like to work that way. I agreed with most of Nixon's policies, but I never quite hit it off with Nixon personally. I didn't feel comfortable with most of the people who were dominating policy in the Nixon administration. Except Bryce Harlow. If Bryce Harlow had been made chief of staff, I might have gone down and joined the administration. If Harlow and Arthur Burns had held the jobs that were held by Haldeman and Ehrlichman, it would have been a different administration. But then, of course, it was no accident that Nixon picked Haldeman and Ehrlichman rather than Harlow and Burns for those jobs."[17]

International Policy

For some important positions in the administration, Nixon's immediate campaign organization—or even his extended campaign organization—did not offer appropriate candidates. The most visible among these positions was secretary of state. Nixon planned to conduct his own foreign policy. "You need a President for foreign policy," he told an interviewer in November 1967. "No Secretary of State is really important; the President makes foreign policy."[18] Still, the secretary of state was the senior appointed official in the executive branch and would have to bring coherence to the operations of the State Department bureaucracy. Nixon's first choice for the post was William Scranton, recommended by a nominating panel the president-elect had set up for the purpose, which included William Rogers, Eisenhower's last attorney general; Herbert Brownell, still operating at the summit of Republican politics; and Walter Lippmann, the columnist, who had endorsed Nixon during the campaign. Scranton, who had developed a distrust for Nixon during the maneuverings that led up to the 1964 Republican convention, declined. The panel then recommended Douglas Dillon, senior partner in the prominent Wall Street investment firm Dillon Read, who had served as under secretary of state in the Eisenhower administration and had stayed on to be secretary of the treasury under Kennedy. Nixon, perhaps rankled by Scranton's rejection, turned down Dillon, who had nominated Clifford Case at the Republican convention in a vain effort to hold together the New Jersey delegation as part of the stop-Nixon coalition. Nixon's antipathy to Dillon was reinforced by the negative opinion of Melvin Laird, a rising power among Republicans in the House of Representatives, who had traveled on the Nixon plane during the final weeks of the campaign and was now busily participating in the selection and recruitment process at the Pierre.[19]

At this point, Brownell, with the concurrence of Dewey, now a Republican elder, suggested that the nominating panel itself included a fine choice for secretary of state: William Rogers. The relationship between Nixon and Rogers had once been so close that Nixon had kept Rogers almost constantly at his side in the days following Eisenhower's heart attack in 1956. But when Nixon moved in 1963 to New York, where Rogers headed a rival law firm, their old intimacy had not been resumed. Rogers told an interviewer in the fall of 1967 that he had not seen Nixon for many months and that he had no expectation of playing a role in any future Nixon administration. He took no part in the campaign. His foreign policy experience was meager. Still, Rogers had two important qualifications: the good opinion of the foreign policy establishment and a willingness to follow faithfully the direction of the president. Nixon asked Rogers to take the job, and Rogers accepted.[20]

The other major cabinet post dealing with the role of the United States in world affairs, secretary of defense, was first offered by Nixon, on Laird's recommendation, to Senator Henry Jackson, Democrat of Washington, a moderate liberal on domestic issues but an aggressive anti-Communist in foreign policy. Nixon and Laird believed that Jackson had tentatively agreed to accept. Jackson's recollection in 1980 was that he had never accepted the appointment, "even on a tentative basis." In any case, Jackson, vacationing in Hawaii during the first week in December, called the Pierre to tell Nixon that he had definitely decided to remain in the Senate. Nixon by then had announced that he would present his entire cabinet to the nation in a televised ceremony only twenty-four hours away. The president-elect asked Laird to step into the breach and fill the post left vacant because of Jackson's decision not to serve. Laird, who afterward insisted that he would have preferred to stay in the House, agreed to become secretary of defense.[21]

Laird's base in the House was among the Republican stalwarts, but he had maintained good relations with all factions. In 1958 he had introduced the first legislation in recent times to require the federal government to turn back a fixed portion of its revenue to the states. At the Republican convention in Chicago in 1960, he was called upon by Nixon to pull together the platform committee after the fundamentalists on the committee had staged a successful rebellion against the progressive committee chairman, Charles Percy, then a young Chicago businessman. Laird had supported Nelson Rockefeller for the 1964 presidential nomination until Rockefeller's remarriage, but ended up in 1964 as chairman of the platform committee, in which role he worked closely with the fundamentalists who controlled the convention. At the beginning of 1965, Laird was a leading participant in the insurgency through which Gerald Ford replaced Charles Halleck as Republican leader in the House; as part of the same revolt, Laird became chairman of the House Republican Conference.

In foreign policy Laird had acquired a reputation as a kind of cautious hawk. In a speech in September 1967 criticizing Lyndon Johnson for promising to withdraw from Vietnam six months after the end of hostilities, Laird made the Delphic observation: "If the choice is between turning South Vietnam over to the Communists in 1969 or right now in 1967, we might as well do it now and prevent further American casualties." This was regarded by some as a signal that Laird was preparing a fallback position among the doves.[22]

Since Nixon planned to run international policy directly from the White House, the job of director of the National Security Council was potentially more important than that of either secretary of state or secretary of defense. The NSC, established under Truman and used by Eisenhower to coordinate foreign and military policies, had, in Nixon's view, fallen into disuse under the Kennedy and Johnson administrations. "Since 1960," Nixon said in one of his radio talks during the campaign, "this Council has virtually disappeared as an operating function. . . . I attribute most of our serious reverses abroad since 1960 to the inability or disinclination of President Eisenhower's successors to make effective use of this important Council."[23] Nixon planned to use the NSC to gather instrumental control over all aspects of international policy into his own hands. For this purpose, he believed, he needed an NSC director not only substantively knowledgeable but also skilled in the Byzantine arts of bureaucratic management.

Nixon's foreign policy coordinator during the campaign had been Richard Allen, a young, militantly anti-Communist foreign policy intellectual. Allen had attached himself to Nixon at the low point of Nixon's career, after the defeat in California in 1962, because, Allen had concluded, "There would soon be a new Republican administration, and Nixon would either be the *éminence grise* behind foreign policy, would be secretary of state, or would be president himself."[24] Nixon felt comfortable with Allen, but evidently wanted someone with stronger credentials in the foreign policy community to direct the National Security Council. Besides, he may have regarded Allen as too inflexible to implement the new foreign policy initiatives then taking shape in his mind.[25]

Henry Kissinger had by 1968 established himself as the ranking Republican foreign policy expert within the academic community— but his loyalty seemed to run exclusively to Nelson Rockefeller, whom he had served in many campaigns. Kissinger had made some widely quoted disparaging remarks about Nixon, whom he had met only once before 1968. His expressed foreign policy views, however, were as hard-line anti-Communist as Nixon's, though more subtly articulated. Kissinger had maintained a continuing relationship with Melvin Laird, with whom he had negotiated, representing Rockefeller, at the convention that nominated Goldwater in 1964. At the 1968 convention he had helped put together with Richard Allen a vaporous plank on Vietnam ("Stop all bombing of North Vietnam when the action would not endanger the lives of our troops in the field; this action should take into account the response from Hanoi") that was acceptable to both Nixon and Rockefeller. Seemingly despondent after Nixon's nomination, Kissinger returned to his post on the Harvard faculty and declined an invitation to serve on the Republican candidate's foreign policy committee. After the election, Kissinger hoped to play some part in the new administration, but grumbled to friends that he would probably be offered no more than an assistant secretaryship at the State Department.

Toward the end of November, Nixon invited Kissinger to the Pierre. In a conversation that lasted several hours, the two men discovered that their views concerning most areas of foreign policy were the same. Nixon asked Kissinger what, in his opinion, should be the goal of the administration's diplomacy. Kissinger replied that "the overriding problem was to free our foreign policy from its violent historical fluctuations between euphoria and panic."[26] Two days later the president-elect offered Kissinger the directorship of the National Security Council. After a few days consideration, during which he consulted, among others, Rockefeller, Kissinger accepted. Moving with characteristic dispatch, Kissinger began assembling a staff of highly qualified, mostly young specialists in various areas of international relations and defense—many of them recruited from the liberal side of the foreign policy establishment and already committed to some kind of rapid withdrawal of American forces from Vietnam.[27]

Domestic Social Policy

On the domestic side of government, Nixon sought an alter ego who could be relied upon to devise and put into effect a program that would appear imaginative and daring, but would require little direct supervision by the president. Nixon had already discovered that the vice-president, whom he had originally hoped might fill this role, was not exactly suited for the responsibilities he had in mind. His choice therefore swung to his old friend and mentor Arthur Burns, then completing a distinguished academic career at Columbia. Nixon asked Burns to become, in effect, assistant president for domestic affairs, and, as an added inducement, he promised to make Burns chairman of the Board of Governors of the Federal Reserve System when that post became open at the beginning of 1970. But Burns declined. He was looking forward to moving to California, he explained, where he would pursue his work in economic research at Stanford. If Nixon wanted to talk again about the Federal Reserve when the time for appointing a new chairman approached, Burns would be glad to discuss it. But the prospect of returning to the White House did not appeal to him. Not easily put off, Nixon asked Burns to take charge of a small group that was preparing recommendations for the administration's domestic program, to be ready by the time of the inauguration. Burns agreed.[28]

While still hoping to bring Burns onto the White House staff, Nixon turned next to another academician, with a substantially different background and perspective: Daniel Patrick Moynihan, a Harvard political scientist who had served as assistant secretary of labor in the Kennedy and Johnson administrations. Moynihan had played an important part in developing the "war on poverty" division of Johnson's Great Society program. After returning to academic life in 1966, however, he had begun to express doubts about the efficacy of contemporary liberalism, and had become a moving force in the *Public Interest* group of "neoconservative" intellectuals. Soon he caught the attention of Republican politicians, particularly Melvin Laird, who were looking for more glittering alternatives to the Great Society than the traditional tenets of American laissez-faire conservatism. In an article included in a 1967 volume titled *Republican Papers*, edited by Laird, Moynihan, who still regarded himself as a liberal, wrote: "In our [the liberals'] desire to maintain public confidence in liberal programs, we have tended to avoid evidence of poor results, and in particular we have paid too little heed to the limited capacities of government to bring about social change."[29] In 1968 he was identified in one of Nixon's campaign talks as a "thoughtful critic."[30]

After the election Laird recommended that Nixon make Moynihan secretary of health, education, and welfare. Nixon's friend Finch, however, had staked a claim to that job; besides, Nixon seems at that time to have viewed academic intellectuals as normally better suited to staff than to line positions. Moynihan joined the trek to the Pierre. In his first meeting with Nixon, he was startled to find the president-elect offering him the directorship of a projected Urban Affairs Council—a kind of domestic counterpart to the National Security Council. Nixon told him that the president's chief assistant for foreign policy was to be Henry Kissinger; for economic policy, Paul McCracken of the University of Michigan; and for domestic policy—Moynihan. "I knew from the start that it could not work," Moynihan said in 1978, by then a Democratic senator from New York. "How could I, a lifelong Democrat, direct domestic policy in a Republican administration? I was not flesh of their flesh—not blood of their blood. But how could I refuse to try?"[31]

Conservative advisers to Nixon, like Burns and Martin Anderson, thought at the time and continued to think long after that Moynihan, as director of the new Council on Urban Affairs, set out, with astonishing success to preserve as much as possible of the liberal programs he had helped conceive under Kennedy and Johnson.[32] Moynihan's ideological motives, however, seem to have been more complicated than that. At times he implied to his new Republican colleagues that the Great Society programs had largely failed, but could not safely be dismantled for fear of bringing on a pitched battle with the liberal constituencies. He warned Nixon: "All the Great Society activist constituencies are lying out there in wait, poised to get you if you try to come after them: the professional welfarists, the urban planners, the day-carers, the social workers, the public housers. Frankly, I'm terrified at the thought of cutting back too fast."[33] At other times Moynihan presented a more positive vision: "In the past," he argued in a memorandum containing suggestions for Nixon's inaugural address, "the cry for decentralization was typically that of persons who wanted government, that is to say organized society, to attempt less, not more. This is not your purpose at all, nor is this why the surge toward decentralization arose. To the contrary, it has sprung from the desire that organized society should in fact achieve its goals, and that big centralized government simply cannot deliver on its promises." (Nixon wrote approvingly in the margin: "Decentralization is not an excuse for inaction, but a key to action.")[34]

Part of the motivation for Moynihan's shift in political direction, like that of some other members of the *Public Interest* group, seems to lie in the dynamics of the process of social science research. Some observers of scholarly behavior have argued that, paradoxically, despite the predominance of liberals in the social science community, research tends naturally to reinforce political conservatism. Henry Aaron has written: "The incentives of the academic world will encourage people, especially newcomers bent on promotion, to discover facts not consistent with previous theories and devise new theories to explain them. . . . The process by which research and experimentation are created corrodes the kind of simple faiths on which political movements are built." In an era when policymaking machinery is dominated by liberals, research will naturally expose conceptual contradictions and operational flaws in liberal solutions. "Over the long haul," Aaron suggests, "research and experimentation will be an intellectually conservative force in debates about public policy."[35] Perhaps this overstates the case. Research also exposes flaws in the status quo, which tends to promote change. It seems true, however, that by encouraging skepticism toward all kinds of political solutions, research, especially after a period of governmental activism and social change, guides both the public and some of the researchers themselves toward a kind of conservatism.

Moynihan's particular disenchantment with liberalism seems to have origins deeper even than this. Reared in the communal atmosphere fostered by the Irish-American variety of Catholic culture, Moynihan, even while grazing among the lotus-eaters of secular liberalism in Washington and at Harvard, appears to have felt deep twinges of remorse over the weakening of traditional social ties. *Beyond the Melting Pot*, the work that made both his academic and public reputations, written with Nathan Glazer in 1963, gave early encouragement to the revival of pride in ethnicity. His most visible—also his most controversial—contribution to the Johnson administration was a Labor Department study arguing the need to stabilize family ties among urban blacks.

Reflecting on his government experience, Moynihan came to conclude that the liberal state was harmfully overreaching itself. "The modern welfare state," he later wrote, "has not reached the point of picking every man a wife, but has come close enough to such imponderables to find itself held accountable for failure in areas where no person can reasonably promise success."[36] Early in 1969 he showed Nixon an article by Peter Drucker in *The Public Interest*, "The Sickness of Government." He emphasized Drucker's sentence: "The most despotic government of 1900 would not have dared probe into the private affairs of its citizens as income tax collectors now do routinely in the freest society."[37]

Yet Moynihan's way of dealing with the destructive effects of the welfare state was not a return to unrestricted laissez-faire. His quarrel with contemporary liberalism was not, like Milton Friedman's, that it interfered with the market, but that it threatened the underlying social fabric. He was not so much a neoconservative as a very old kind of conservative—the kind that had been fighting the disruptive effects of modernism since the beginning of the industrial, democratic, and secular revolutions in the eighteenth century. Organized society, Moynihan insisted, must not abandon its responsibility to help the weak and the poor. But this responsibility should not be made the excuse for establishing in power a new liberal elite—"the professional welfarists, the urban planners, the day-carers," and so forth. The solution, Moynihan concluded, was to give money directly to the poor, without intercession by liberal social workers—the "income strategy." In this way, he aimed, like Burke and Disraeli, to achieve broader distribution of the bounty of economic progress without tearing up the private roots of social order.[38]

Moynihan began recommending books to Nixon that presented models for his kind of conservatism: David Cecil's *Melbourne*, Robert Blake's *Disraeli*. Nixon, ever the eager learner, soaked them up. From the biography of Disraeli, the president gleaned the moral, as he told Moynihan: "Tory men and liberal policies are what have changed the world." Moynihan, as it happened, had not himself taken the trouble to read Blake's book—which runs to almost 800 pages—but he applauded the lesson.[39]

Economic Policy

In the crucial area of economic policy, Nixon set out, apparently somewhat casually, to assemble a team broadly conservative, in the sense of favoring a market-oriented economy, but free of domination by what he called "the New York–Boston banking establishment." When Safire remarked soon after the election that if Nelson Rockefeller became secretary of state or defense, it would not be possible to make David Rockefeller, chairman of the Chase Manhattan Bank, secretary of the treasury, because "you can't have two Rockefellers in the cabinet," Nixon dourly replied: "Is there a law that you have to have one?"[40]

Nixon's antagonism toward the eastern financial establishment seems to have been more personal than ideological—although Frank Nixon's dislike for the Rockefeller-dominated Standard Oil ("a blight on the American landscape") may have left its mark. In any case, suspicion of eastern bankers helped guide Nixon to choose most of the top members of his initial economic team from the Middle West: David Kennedy, chairman of the Continental Illinois Bank of Chicago, as secretary of the treasury; Robert Mayo, a vice-president at Continental Illinois, as director of the Bureau of the Budget; Paul McCracken, professor of economics at the University of Michigan, as chairman of the Council of Economic Advisers; and George Shultz, dean of the Graduate School of Business at the University of Chicago, as secretary of labor. (Kennedy and Mayo, though officers of the same Chicago bank, came to Nixon's attention through different routes. Kennedy's name was put forward by Charls Walker, then the well-plugged-in Washington lobbyist for the American Bankers Association, as an alternative to Maurice Stans, Nixon's chief fund-raiser in 1968, with whom Walker had had some run-ins when they both served in the Eisenhower administration.[41] Mayo was recommended to Nixon by Congressmen Wilbur Mills and George Mahon, the powerful Democratic chairmen of the two House committees dealing with fiscal matters, who had known Mayo as a competent civil servant during the nineteen years he had worked as a career employee at the Treasury before going to Chicago in 1961.[42] McCracken was recommended by Arthur Burns; and Shultz by Burns and Milton Friedman, his colleague and friend at the University of Chicago.) Of the initial first team, only Stans, who became secretary of commerce, and Peter Flanigan, who had worked in the campaign and became Nixon's personal aide dealing with economic matters, had direct links to the New York financial community.

The midwestern origins of so many of the principal economic policymakers led to speculation that the so-called Chicago school of conservative "monetarist" economists, which was closely aligned with the Republican fundamentalists, would play a dominant role in the new administration. Milton Friedman, who had generalized the libertarian social philosophy underlying some of the theories of the Chicago school, had advised Nixon during the campaign, as he had Barry Goldwater four years earlier.

Actually, however, most of Nixon's initial choices for top economic policymaking jobs were more in the moderate Republican tradition than in the fundamentalist line represented by Goldwater and Friedman. Kennedy, Mayo, Stans, and Flanigan were essentially pragmatic managerial types, with little interest or background in economic theory.

McCracken, a friend and protégé of Arthur Burns, had served on the Council of Economic Advisers (as one of two members in addition to the chairman) during the Eisenhower administration. In the context of that time, his approach was relatively market-oriented. At the end of a study of the balance-of-payments problem done after his return to the University of Michigan in 1963, McCracken wrote: "We need a society where the successful performance in the marketplace that gives rise to profits is not regarded as an antisocial act."[43] In philosophic moments he liked to place himself in a broad "British tradition" of conservative economic libertarians, like Burke, David Hume, and Adam Smith, as distinct from a competing "Continental tradition," fed by thinkers like Descartes, Voltaire, and Rousseau, which McCracken identified with aggressive intervention in economic matters by democratic governments.[44] But McCracken by no means favored an abrupt shift in the direction of economic policy in 1969. The federal budget, he believed, should be balanced—but only on the basis of "reasonably full employment." Like Friedman—and at the time like Burns—he strongly opposed any attempt by the federal government to control inflation through an "incomes policy." He believed in "appropriate" restraint in federal fiscal and monetary policies to bring down inflation—but such restraints, he maintained, should be applied only "gradually," so as not to upset the basic health of the economy.[45] McCracken did not regard himself as part of any "Chicago school." His degree, he pointed out, was from Harvard.

George Shultz shared his friend Friedman's confidence in the market as the most efficient means for regulating economic behavior. As a labor economist, however, he had become convinced of the need for a variety of government-sponsored insurance and welfare programs to cushion hardships caused by fluctuations in the job market.[46] At the Department of Labor, he at once began working to develop a spirit of détente between the administration and the leaders of the major trade unions, particularly George Meany.

Friedman himself remained at the University of Chicago. During the first two and a half years of the administration, he often sent recommendations to Nixon, but these had no great impact on administration policy—at least according to some who worked in the White

House. After the administration's dramatic reversal of economic policy on August 15, 1971, Friedman "spoke to Nixon only once again."[47]

The McCracken Task Forces and the Burns Report

Early in the fall campaign in 1968, Shultz had irritated Friedman by declining to take charge of a series of task forces that were being set up to prepare recommendations on domestic policy for the new administration, on the ground that he was committed to completing a book on wages in the urban labor market. Shultz did, however, accept the chairmanship of the task force on manpower and labor-management relations.

After being turned down by Shultz, Nixon asked McCracken, whom he had got to know in Washington during the 1950s while he was vice-president, to assume responsibility for the task forces. McCracken agreed. The task forces dealt with subjects like fiscal policy, employment, and public welfare. To chair them, McCracken recruited experts, with at least vaguely Republican credentials, from the business and academic communities. The chairmen picked their own task force members, sometimes without much attention to political or ideological inclinations.[48] Some of the task forces included liberal Democrats—a situation later deplored by Arthur Burns.[49]

During the transition period at the Pierre between November and January, the reports of the McCracken task forces became a principal resource for the small team headed by Burns, and including McCracken, Greenspan, Martin Anderson, and a few others, to whom Nixon assigned the job of preparing the administration's domestic program. Burns's group also drew on the Republican platform, on recommendations that were submitted by some Republican governors and Republican leaders in Congress, and on the sketchy pronouncements Nixon had made during the campaign.[50]

On January 6 Burns gave a draft memorandum, containing preliminary proposals, to Nixon; and on January 18, two days before the inauguration, he completed his final report, consisting of 110 separate items, some of which were divided into subrecommendations. Burns's report covered not only domestic policy but also international economic policy and even some areas of defense policy. Burns passed on many of the recommendations made by the McCracken task forces, but in some cases dissented from them. For instance, Burns reported to Nixon that the task force on public welfare, headed by Richard Nathan, a policy analyst formerly on the staff of Nelson Rockefeller, had "basically accepted the Johnson administration's approach to welfare problems and recommended liberalization of various benefits under existing law," making "another study . . . urgently needed."[51]

On revenue sharing, which had become a favorite issue with progressive and moderate Republicans, and which Nixon had endorsed during the campaign, Burns recommended: "Whatever the merits of any general revenue-sharing program may be, a decision should be deferred at this time because of budgetary constraints. You should also keep in mind the fact that a revenue-sharing plan is bound to defer or limit future reduction of the federal income tax." Burns recommended further study in some areas, such as the development of the supersonic transport (SST), and repeal of the Davis-Bacon Act (which was supposed to be inflating the cost of housing construction by requiring payment of the prevailing wage to construction workers). On many subjects, however, Burns made positive recommendations; for example, creation of a "single manageable program" for manpower training (as proposed by Shultz's task force); increase of the minimum standard deduction on the personal income tax from $200 to $300; special federal aid for inner-city schools; establishment of an all-volunteer army (one of Martin Anderson's particular interests, also strongly supported by Milton Friedman); enactment of a tax credit for employers to pay half the cost of starting or expanding on-the-job training programs; and a major initiative to reduce nontariff barriers to international trade.[52]

Nixon was delighted with Burns's report—so much so that he simply could not entertain the thought that Burns would not stay on to help implement its recommendations. On inauguration day Nixon took Burns into the cabinet room in the East Wing of the White House and showed him which was to be his chair at the cabinet table. Burns went to Haldeman and protested: "The president is suffering from a deep misunderstanding. He thinks I am going to come to work in the White House." Haldeman said he understood Burns's problem, but suggested that Burns come to the first cabinet meeting to present the recommendations included in his report.[53]

Actually, Burns, as he later admitted, was beginning to feel the lure of returning to White House service. Bryce Harlow, an old friend, later recalled: "Arthur was like a moth around the flame. He resisted, but at the same time he was attracted."[54] At the first meeting of the cabinet, the day after the inauguration, Burns presented his report. Nixon immediately began directing various cabinet officers to work with Burns to carry out their parts of the program. Burns at last capitulated. He told Nixon that he would work at the White House for four months—then he would proceed to Stanford.[55]

When the announcement of Burns's appointment to the newly created position of counsellor to the president came over the news ticker in the White House press office, Moynihan happened to be chatting with Ronald Ziegler, the new press spokesman. What does that mean? Ziegler asked. "It means," said Moynihan, who had been waiting for the conservative Republican shoe to fall, "that the president is bringing on his own people."[56]

A Shift to the Right

The administration team that Nixon had assembled by the end of January gave off mixed ideological signals. The president's principal speechwriters, for example, included a progressive (Price), a fundamentalist (Buchanan), and an eclectic moderate (Safire). The foreign policy machinery appeared to be dominated by progressives and moderates. The team for economic policy, though identified by the press with the Chicago school, was made up mainly of moderates. The major domestic service departments were headed by progressives or moderates: Finch, who had aligned himself in California politics with the Republican progressives rather than with Governor Reagan's fundamentalists, at HEW; Governor George Romney of Michigan, Nixon's progressive rival for the Republican nomination in the early primaries in 1968, at Housing and Urban Development; Governor John Volpe of Massachusetts at Transportation; Governor Walter Hickel of Alaska at Interior; Clifford Hardin, chancellor of the University of Nebraska, at Agriculture; Stans at Commerce; and Shultz at Labor. Nixon's assessment of the cabinet was that it was "a group less conservative than Eisenhower's cabinet, and in fact somewhat to the left of my own centrist position."[57]

Determined fundamentalists, however, were placed in important secondary posts, from which they could guide policy: Richard Kleindienst, Goldwater's campaign manager in 1964, as deputy attorney general; Harry Dent, Senator Thurmond's former administrative assistant, as special counsel to the president; and Robert Mardian, another veteran Goldwaterite, as counsel at HEW. The ultimate direction of domestic policy appeared to wait on the outcome of the almost certain clash between Burns and Moynihan.

Despite these ambiguities and uncertainties, the Nixon team as a whole was clearly more conservative, in both the positional and ideational senses, than either the Kennedy or Johnson teams that had preceded it. Like Nixon, most of the top members of the new administration felt that they had been called "to reverse the whole trend of government over the last eight years." Heeding their chief's advice not to "waste a minute," they prepared to do battle with their expected antagonists in the Democratic-controlled Congress.

5

Nixon and the Ninety-first Congress:
The Floating Coalition Strategy

"CONGRESS is not a milling mob of people," Bryce Harlow, Nixon's first director of congressional liaison, has said. "There are power levers, and one must know where the levers are, and how to pull them."[1] The strategy that the new administration would develop for moving these levers would reflect both its own goals and its evaluation of the balance of political and ideological forces in Congress.

The distribution of power in the Ninety-first Congress, which took office seventeen days before Nixon was sworn in, was still fundamentally affected by the political realignment of the 1930s that had made the Democrats the national majority party. Only twice since 1930—in 1946 and 1952—had the Republicans managed to win control of Congress. During the 1960s the growing advantages enjoyed by incumbents in most congressional elections, particularly for the House, provided added insulation for Democratic majorities.[2] As a result, Nixon entered the White House as the first president since Zachary Taylor in 1849 (the last Whig elected to the presidency) to face opposition majorities in both houses of Congress at the beginning of his first term.

Party alignments, however, did not fully measure either the president's potential influence in Congress or the number of congressmen who might share his general ideological outlook. The most important distinction in Congress was still party, which determined the selection of leadership, the control of committees, and the recruitment of the majority of staff. But within each of the parties there had grown up loosely formed factions, resembling in some ways separate parties within multiparty systems, such as those of France, the Netherlands, and Sweden. These factions were based not only on regional and economic interests but also to a considerable extent on ideology. If the factions divided on ideological rather than party lines, factions with broadly conservative tendencies held formidable power in both houses. Indeed, since the election of 1938, when the voters turned sharply against the New Deal, liberals had enjoyed secure majorities in both houses of Congress during only two terms: those following the Democratic landslide victories of 1958 and 1964.

Ideological Alignments in Congress

A rough guide to the ideological divisions in Congress is provided by the "conservative coalition index" developed by *Congressional Quarterly* magazine. The conservative coalition is supposed to have taken shape in Congress after the 1938 election, when conservative Republicans, mainly from the Middle West, and conservative Democrats, mainly from the South, appear to have concluded that their ideological affinities, at least on some issues, overrode their partisan differences.[3] *Congressional Quarterly* assumes that the conservative coalition is in operation on any roll call in which the majority of Republicans and the majority of southern Democrats, assumed to be conservative, oppose the majority of northern Democrats, assumed to be liberal. This coalition was evident on 27 percent of all roll calls in 1969, and on 22 percent in 1970—relatively high proportions considering that normally about two-thirds of the measures voted on by Congress are noncontroversial enough to be approved by majorities from both parties. (Bipartisan majorities appeared on 66 percent of the roll calls taken in 1969, and on 68 percent in 1970.)[4]

Congressional Quarterly calculates each member's "conservative coalition" score in each session as the percentage of roll calls on which he voted with the coalition when the coalition was in operation. Through a system of classification based on conservative coalition scores and party identification, I have distinguished eight ideological groups in Congress, four in each party. The four Republican groups correspond roughly to the intraparty divisions described in chapter 2, and I will use the same titles. I have called the Democratic groups liberals, regulars, centrists, and traditionalists. Democratic *liberals* may be defined as those belonging to the wing of the party that consistently promoted expansion of the federal welfare state, various kinds of personal liberation, and more equal distribution of status and wealth. In the final years of the Johnson administration, liberals were split by the issue of the Vietnam War, but after Nixon's election most of them swung quickly to opposition to the war. Democratic *regulars*, drawn particularly from big city political organizations and sections of the party closely aligned with the blue-collar labor unions, usually supported expansion of the welfare state, but were more cautious than the liberals on social issues like race and drug use. Regulars tended to be hawks on foreign policy. Democratic *centrists* supported the reforms carried out by the New Deal, but were leery of those enacted as parts of Johnson's Great Society. They resisted further government intrusion in what they regarded as private social matters and feared the economic effects of increased government spending. Democratic *traditionalists*, drawn almost entirely from the South, as a rule opposed expansion of the welfare state, especially on matters involving race. Traditionalists consistently supported measures to strengthen military defense.

The use of party as well as of conservative coalition scores to establish ideological categories may require some justification. It rests on the view that for most members alignment with a party continues to represent a meaningful commitment—though probably less so than at some other times in U.S. history. Perhaps the most important choice made by each member of Congress during each term is his decision (usually of course virtually automatic) on which party leadership to support for control of the house. As a member of a party caucus, he accepts some measure of party kinship, however loosely held. A study of the Eighty-eighth Congress by Randall Ripley showed that 94 percent of Democratic members and 96 percent of Republicans indicated that they "wanted to act in accord with their party's position."[5] David Vogler, writing in 1977, found party still the most important "cue source" in determining a member's vote.[6] As one conservative southern Democrat said, in explaining why he sometimes voted for liberal measures sponsored by northern Democratic colleagues, "Why be an S.O.B.?"[7]

Voting with the conservative coalition, composed of Republicans and only a minority of Democrats, has therefore a somewhat different significance for Democratic members than it has for Republican ones.

Southern Democrats who vote with the Republicans against their northern colleagues are giving a stronger indication of ideological commitment than Republicans who are simply voting with their party. Northern Democrats who vote with the conservative coalition are expressing a strong ideological preference indeed (or are guided by economic or regional interests sufficiently strong to dictate joining an ideological rather than a party alignment on a particular issue). Republicans, conversely, who vote against the conservative coalition give a different kind of signal from northern Democrats who are voting with the majority of their party colleagues. Distinction by party as well as by conservative coalition scores, therefore, seems appropriate.[8]

Within the parties, categories were based on conservative coalition support scores characteristic of members commonly identified by the press and by congressmen themselves as representative of broad ideological tendencies. Although the defining limits of the categories were established on impressionistic evidence, and are therefore to some extent arbitrary, they provide, at the least, a convenient means for classifying congressmen into groups with generally similar ideological voting patterns. (Another way to establish ideological categories would have been through use of "ratings" by avowedly ideological interest groups, such as the liberal Americans for Democratic Action or the conservative Americans for Constitutional Action, as has been done in some studies of Congress.[9] *Congressional Quarterly's* conservative coalition scores, however, have the advantage of being free from whatever biases may enter into the selection of "test" roll calls by outside groups with their own axes to grind. In any case, results appear generally similar.)

The eight categories based on party and conservative coalition support scores were as follows:

Republicans

Fundamentalists: 81 percent or more agreement with the conservative coalition, or less than 8 percent opposition (to pick up members who voted on relatively few roll calls)

Stalwarts: 61 to 80 percent agreement

Moderates: 41 to 60 percent agreement

Progressives: 40 percent or less agreement

Democrats

Traditionalists: 71 percent or more agreement, or less than 10 percent opposition

Centrist: 31 to 70 percent agreement

Regulars: 11 to 30 percent agreement

Liberals: 10 percent or less agreement

(Members who voted on less than 10 percent of roll calls, including the Speaker of the House, were not counted.)

These categories are used in table 5-1 to indicate the distribution of strength among ideological groups in the Congress that took office in 1969. An examination of the distribution shows that Republican fundamentalists and Democratic traditionalists, when they voted together, accounted for about three-tenths of the total memberships of both the Senate and the House. When joined by the Republican stalwarts, this alignment grew to about four-tenths of the memberships of both houses. Conservatives then needed to pick up only about half the Republican moderates and Democratic centrists to achieve majorities.

The strength of the conservative alignment was further enhanced by the dominance of southern Democratic traditionalists among the aging barons who chaired the key committees of Congress: Richard

Table 5-1. *Distribution of Strength among Ideological Groups in the Ninety-first Congress*

Group	Senate	House
Republicans		
Fundamentalists	17	72
Stalwarts	10	48
Moderates	7	44
Progressives	9	25
Total	43	189
Democrats		
Traditionalists	12	56
Centrists	9	49
Regulars	19	66
Liberals	17	72
Total	57	243

Sources: Based on *Congressional Quarterly Almanac*, vol. 25 (1969), pp. 1052–64; and vol. 26 (1970), pp. 1144–54.

Russell of Georgia at Senate Appropriations (also president pro tempore of the Senate); John Stennis of Mississippi at Senate Armed Services; John McClellan of Arkansas at Senate Judiciary; William Colmer of Mississippi at House Rules; George Mahon of Texas at House Appropriations; and Mendel Rivers of South Carolina at House Armed Services. In all, Democratic traditionalists in 1969 chaired six of the sixteen standing committees of the Senate and five of the sixteen standing committees of the House. Frequently they were joined by two powerful chairmen whose voting records put them among the Democratic centrists: Wilbur Mills of Arkansas at House Ways and Means, and Russell Long of Louisiana at Senate Finance.

At the other end of the spectrum, the Democratic liberals—the heart of a countervailing "liberal coalition"—included more than one-fourth of the Democratic majority in the Senate and close to one-third of the majority party in the House. In the Senate, however, the liberals, though half again as numerous as the traditionalists, held only one committee chairmanship: Joseph Tydings of Maryland at the District of Columbia Committee; and in the House, where they outnumbered traditionalists 72 to 56, held only two. (The reason the liberals held so few chairmanships was that they tended either to come from competitive districts or to move on in pursuit of other offices, which made them less likely to accumulate the seniority needed to rise to the top of committees.) The liberals in 1969 did command one post in the Democratic leadership: the office of majority whip in the Senate, held by Edward Kennedy of Massachusetts, who in 1968 had replaced Russell Long of Louisiana, a centrist. (But Kennedy's tenure in the whipship was not to be long: at the beginning of 1971, he was ousted by Robert Byrd of West Virginia, another centrist.)

The Democratic liberals were often joined by the Democratic regulars, including, in addition to Senate Majority Leader Mike Mansfield of Montana, such formidable figures as Senators Henry Jackson of Washington and John Pastore of Rhode Island and Congressman Daniel Rostenkowski of Illinois, leader of the powerful Chicago delegation. On many issues the liberals could also expect support from at least some of the Republican progressives, such as Senators Jacob Javits of New York, Clifford Case of New Jersey, and Charles Percy of Illinois and Congressmen Silvio Conte of Massachusetts and Paul McCloskey of California. These three groups together comprised almost half the total membership of the Senate, but only two-fifths of the House. In the Senate, therefore, the liberal coalition could triumph by winning over just a few of the Democratic centrists or Republican moderates. But in the House, even if all forty-nine of the Democratic centrists voted with the united forces of the three more liberal groups, the liberal coalition was still six votes short of a majority of the total body. The forty-four Republican moderates, among whom Rogers Morton of Maryland, John Anderson of Illinois, and Robert Taft, Jr., of Ohio were representative figures, were therefore crucial to the voting mathematics of the House. (Appendix A shows in greater detail the regional and social origins of the ideological groups in the Ninety-first Congress.)

The Floating Coalition Strategy

Such, roughly, was the distribution of ideological forces that confronted Bryce Harlow and the small staff that he deployed on Capitol Hill at the beginning of 1969. To achieve the administration's goals, Harlow recognized, he would have to reach beyond the 192 Republicans in the House (before the resignations of Laird and Congressman Edward Reinecke, who departed the House in January to take Finch's place as lieutenant governor of California) and 43 Republicans in the Senate. As William Timmons, who left the staff of Congressman William Brock of Tennessee to assist Harlow in managing relations with the House, has pointed out: "Lyndon Johnson had the luxury of enjoying large Democratic majorities in both houses during the time he was president. Therefore, he had no great need for Republican support. On occasion, he did cut some deals with Everett Dirksen, but as a rule he did not deal much with Republicans. He could pass legislation on the basis of party loyalty alone. We did not have that option."[10]

The most obvious place for Harlow to look for the additional votes needed to make up a majority was among the conservative Democrats. But on some issues the administration found itself pursuing goals that had little appeal to traditionalist Democrats or fundamentalist Republicans. Harlow therefore adopted what he called a "floating coalition" strategy, modeled to some extent on the approach taken in the House since 1965 by Gerald Ford. "We would begin by solid-ifying the Republicans," Timmons recalled in 1977. "Then we would reach out for whatever Democrats were needed. On many issues these would necessarily be conservative Democrats, but on some issues we would reach for the liberal Democrats—issues like the family assistance plan, foreign aid, and raising the debt ceiling. On issues like these, the liberals were the ones to whom we had to appeal."[11]

The floating coalition strategy had been devised by Ford after he replaced Charles Halleck as House minority leader at the beginning of 1965. Halleck, according to Richard Cook, a former House minority staff member who assisted Timmons, "had a policy of never voting against the southern Democrats unless it was absolutely necessary, so they would be available to support him the next time around."[12] Ford, who aimed to be Speaker of the House, not minority leader for the rest of his career, viewed this arrangement as impeding the growth of the Republican party in the South, and therefore the election of more Republican members from southern districts. Moreover, Ford believed, close alliance with the southern Democrats was hobbling the Republicans on civil rights issues, and giving the Democrats a free ride with blacks and other civil rights activists in the North. As minority leader, Ford, with the encouragement of Melvin Laird, there-fore switched to a more independent course, forming temporary alliances on particular issues but avoiding binding commitments to the southern Democrats.[13]

In the early months of the new administration, Harlow's team worked hard at firming up party loyalty among Republicans. Ac-cording to Timmons: "The Republicans had been out in the wilderness for a long time, and the new members in particular were happy to be on the inside, to participate in the development of legislation. Nixon has been criticized for failing to cooperate with Congress, but actually in those early days he spent a great deal of time having congressmen down to the White House and out to Camp David. Each Republican member of Congress was asked to submit in writing his ideas for legislation, and these ideas were taken into consideration in shaping the administration's program. In developing the defense budget, for instance, the Republican members of the armed services committees were brought into consultation. The congressmen some-times felt that their input was not considered, and this annoyed them, but they had no right to complain that they had not been consulted."[14]

Early Successes in the House

From the start, the administration's floating coalition strategy worked better in the House than in the Senate. In part, this was because Nixon himself had a surer feel for the House than for the Senate. According to Richard Cook: "Nixon was a man of the House, and he understood the House. The rules of the House create an entirely different kind of atmosphere from that of the Senate. The atmosphere of the House is Byzantine, and Nixon operated well in that kind of environment. He understood how congressmen are always putting things together in their whispering ways. He never acquired the same kind of feel for the Senate, although he presided over it for eight years as vice-president. He had closer friends in the House, from the time he had served there—people like Ford and [Minority Whip Leslie] Arends and John McCormack and [Majority Leader Carl] Albert and [Armed Services Chairman] Eddie Hébert and Mahon and Mills."[15]

In addition, Nixon had special claim on the loyalty of those House Republicans whom he had helped win election in the broad Republican advance of 1966. When talking with these members, according to Timmons, "he would remind them of the help he had given them by recalling the tremendous rally we had in Paducah—or wherever—when he spoke there in 1966." The congressional liaison staff, however, had no great respect for Nixon's talents as a lobbyist. As Timmons explained: "Nixon would never ask a member for his vote. He would discuss the issue and explain his position, but he would generally conclude by saying that he could understand that others might feel differently about the matter. On some issues, like the ABM and the SST [the antiballistic missile and the supersonic transport], when members were asked down to the White House to meet with the president, I really think it would have made a difference if the president had concluded with a frank appeal for a vote. But Nixon would not do it. I would put in the talking points, in capital letters at the bottom of the paper, ASK FOR HIS VOTE, and I would even underline it, but he would never do it. I think he felt it was somehow demeaning for the president to ask a member for his vote, and it was not in his personality to do it."[16]

Another factor that seems to have helped the administration in the House was the relative effectiveness of the House Republican leadership. "Jerry Ford felt he had a sort of dual role," Timmons has said. "He was loyal to his troops in the House, and at the same time he was loyal to the president. Ford very carefully worked over the voting lists to determine how members were likely to go on a given issue. He would call in his lieutenants and assign them different members to work on. He would say, certain fellows had best be contacted by the president. Then he would assign Les Arends to work on one list, and Bob Michel [the assistant whip] to work on another, and another list he would take for himself. When the roll was being called, Ford would prowl up and down the aisles, working on the members. On close votes he would get members who were reluctant to go along, but who were willing to be loyal if absolutely necessary, to line up in the back of the House. When the roll was finished, Ford would go down into the well of the House and examine the roll and determine how many we needed to win. Then he would turn and hold up his fingers and say, 'I need three,' or, 'I need four,' and that number would peel off from the line in the back and come down and change their votes and give us what we needed."[17]

Finally, the availability of manageable blocs on the Democratic side helped facilitate operation of the floating coalition strategy. "Nobody ever took the place of Judge Smith [Congressman Howard Smith of Virginia, who served in the House from 1931 to 1966] as leader of the southern Democrats," Bryce Harlow has said, "but Bill Colmer [of Mississippi] played somewhat the same role until he left Congress at the end of 1970. After Colmer left, there was a triumvirate, composed of Omar Burleson, Sonny Montgomery, and Joe Waggonner [of, respectively, Texas, Mississippi, and Louisiana]. Among those, Waggonner was the most visible."[18] According to Richard Cook, when Colmer, Burleson, Waggonner, and Congressman Alton Lennon (of North Carolina) agreed on an issue, they could deliver 50 to 60 votes to support the administration in the House.[19] Generally, Harlow, Timmons, and Cook negotiated directly with the southern Democrats, owing to Ford's aversion for open alliance with the bloc of Democratic conservatives. "Ford was reluctant to deal with the southern Democrats," Harlow has recalled. "He didn't like being placed in the position of having to return favors to the southerners. Les Arends, on the other hand, belonged to the other school, the Charley Halleck school, which had always believed in dealing with the southern Democrats."[20]

The southerners, according to the testimony of some of their leaders, were moved to cooperate with the Nixon administration because of common ideological objectives. Congressman Waggonner, who talked with Nixon for the first time when the president-elect called before the inauguration to thank him for defending an increase in the president's pay, has said: "I found over the years I had many mutual interests with President Nixon in such areas as defense and fiscal conservatism."[21] Or as Congressman Montgomery has put it: "President Nixon and I shared a common philosophy of saving the taxpayers' money and supporting the military. . . . Nixon did not go far enough with conservatism, but he was probably about as conservative as a president can be."[22]

Of course, the southern Democrats who supported the administration were not unmindful of the tangible rewards at the White House's disposal. According to Timmons: "We distributed such rewards as were at our command on the basis of detailed records of votes on key issues—not necessarily the same key issues you would find in publications like CQ, but votes to sustain the president's vetoes, on the budget, on defense matters, and things like that."[23]

When Nixon delivered his first veto on January 26, 1970—on the appropriations bill for the Departments of Labor and Health, Education, and Welfare, which exceeded the president's budget by more than 1 billion dollars—the majority of Democratic traditionalists in the House voted to sustain the president's action, in the face of a determined effort by the Democratic leadership and the education lobby to obtain the two-thirds majority needed to override. The distribution by ideological groups of the House vote on Nixon's veto, taken on January 28, was as follows (a yes vote being a vote to override the veto):[24]

Republicans	Yes	No	Democrats	Yes	No
Fundamentalists	3	64	Traditionalists	25	31
Stalwarts	4	43	Centrists	40	4
Moderates	7	38	Regulars	65	0
Progressives	13	11	Liberals	69	0
Total	27	156	Total	199	35

If all the traditionalists, plus the four Democratic centrists who voted to sustain, had voted to override, the forces opposing the veto would have needed to change the votes of only seventeen more members to achieve their goal. If the vote had been that close, some of the progressive or moderate Republicans who stuck with the administration might well have defected.

When the administration's objectives appeared to be more consistent with contemporary liberalism than with conservatism, as in the case of the family assistance plan (welfare reform), Harlow and his team sought support in the House from the Democratic Study Group, composed of about ninety Democratic liberals and regulars. "The Democratic Study Group was not deliverable as a group, in the same way that the southern Democrats were," Richard Cook has said. "But Phil Burton [Congressman Phillip Burton of California, chairman of the Democratic Study Group] was very effective in delivering votes for welfare reform."[25]

On April 16, 1970, the welfare reform plan proposed by the administration passed the House by a vote of 243 to 155. The distribution by ideological groups of those supporting and opposing the plan was as follows:[26]

Republicans			*Democrats*		
	Yes	*No*		*Yes*	*No*
Fundamentalists	13	57	Traditionalists	2	51
Stalwarts	30	12	Centrists	21	21
Moderates	37	3	Regulars	51	10
Progressives	22	0	Liberals	67	1
Total	102	72	Total	141	83

Without the support of a large share of the Democratic liberals and regulars who voted for the plan, the administration's proposal would have been defeated. The rate of defection among Republican fundamentalists on welfare reform, it may be noted, was much heavier than that among Republican progressives or moderates on Nixon's veto of the Labor-HEW appropriations bill.

On some issues the administration did not receive substantial support from either the Democratic traditionalists or the Democratic liberals, but was still able to prevail by obtaining support from key members of the Democratic leadership. Early in 1969 Nixon reluctantly asked for the extension of the 10 percent surcharge on the income tax, which had first been enacted in 1968 at the request of President

Johnson, when the combined costs of the Vietnam War and Johnson's Great Society programs began to push up inflation. The surtax had become unpopular both with liberals, who regarded it as a means for financing the war, and with conservatives, who opposed any tax rise on general principles. But Nixon's economic advisers convinced the president that its extension was needed to help check continued inflation. Ways and Means Chairman Wilbur Mills agreed, at a meeting in the White House with Nixon, to support renewal.[27]

When the extension of the surtax came to a vote in the House on June 30, 1969, it at first appeared to have been defeated. After a number of vote changes, however, it finally passed, 210 to 205. Republican members, under heavy pressure from Ford and Arends to maintain party regularity, voted for the surtax, 154 to 26. Most of the Republican defectors were fundamentalists, many of whom had made repeal of the surtax a prime issue in their campaigns the previous fall. On the Democratic side, 62 of the 65 liberals and 39 of the 55 traditionalists who voted on the issue were recorded against the surtax. The administration's winning margin came from 37 Democratic centrists and regulars, including Mills, Majority Leader Albert, Majority Whip Hale Boggs of Louisiana, and Democratic Caucus Chairman Rostenkowski, who voted for renewal.[28]

A Rougher Road in the Senate

In the Senate the floating coalition strategy proved much less successful. According to Harlow, this was partly because of the fragmented nature of the Senate by the end of the 1960s: "There were no strong leaders in the Senate, as there had been in Eisenhower's time. It was necessary to deal with the Democrats one-on-one. Senator Jackson could usually be relied on to help on national security problems. Stennis and Sparkman, who had been friends of mine for years, were helpful on a number of issues."[29]

A more important factor seems to have been that the Republican minority was less cohesive in the Senate than in the House. Many of the Republican progressives and moderates—a larger share of the total Republican representation in the Senate than in the House—felt they had little to gain politically by supporting the administration.

The administrative assistant to one Republican senator pointed out: "Senators like Dick Schweiker of Pennsylvania had run far ahead of Nixon in 1968, so it was not hard for them to figure out they were appealing to different constituencies than Nixon."[30]

In some cases, the progressives and moderates were committed by their previous records to programs that the administration aimed to dismantle. "For instance," Timmons has said, "Nixon felt that OEO [the Office of Economic Opportunity] should be spun off into other departments. Some of the liberal and moderate Republicans had voted for these [OEO] programs, and therefore opposed the change."[31]

According to Harlow: "Appealing to party loyalty among the liberal Republicans was not effective, whether on ABM, or on the Supreme Court, or on economic issues. On two occasions I arranged meetings between liberal Republicans in the Senate and officials of the administration. One of these was held in Senator Case's office. I brought in members of the White House staff in an effort to build a bridge between them and the liberal Republicans. What happened was that the senators, including Percy, Brooke, and some others, made speeches at the White House staff. When they had finished, one of them turned to me and said, 'Now Bryce, what do you have to say?' I concluded that the best way to deal with them was one-on-one."[32]

Harlow found that use of the "hard goods" at the administration's disposal—patronage and favors—on occasion brought some of the progressives around. In general, however, the tangible persuaders of politics were not very effective. In Harlow's view this was "partly because [the progressives] were acting on the basis of what they believed their constituencies wanted, and partly because they were acting on a personal ideology. These were men of strong conviction—people like Percy, Mathias, Case, Cooper, Packwood, Hatfield, and Pearson. They were men with strong notions of responsible government."[33]

The first important test encountered by the administration in the Senate was the challenge raised during the summer of 1969 to the antiballistic missile system, designed to provide a missile shield against incoming enemy attack. A similar effort in 1968 to eliminate authorization of the ABM system proposed by President Johnson had been defeated in the Senate, 46 to 27. Soon after inauguration, following a review of the arguments for and against ABM, Nixon ordered the reduction of Johnson's system, known as Sentinel, which had been planned to defend American cities, to a smaller system, known as Safeguard, which was intended to protect intercontinental missile emplacements.[34]

Despite this reduction in the scale of the program, Senator Russell, venerable chairman of the Senate Appropriations Committee and chief strategist for the Democratic traditionalists, predicted early in 1969 to Kenneth BeLieu, Harlow's chief assistant in the Senate, that the vote on Safeguard would be much closer than the vote on Sentinel had been the year before. According to his calculations, Russell said, if the full Senate voted, amendments to weaken Safeguard would either lose by a single vote or be tied.[35]

When Safeguard came to a vote in the Senate on August 6, 1969, after months of intensive lobbying by both the administration, which claimed that ABM was needed as a "bargaining chip" in negotiations on arms limitations with the Soviet Union, and opponents, who argued that the system might not work and in any case was exorbitantly expensive, Russell's prediction proved to be exactly correct. On an amendment to the military procurement bill to prohibit expenditures for the development of Safeguard, offered by Senator Margaret Chase Smith of Maine, the Senate divided 50 to 50. Vice-President Agnew added his vote—though the amendment had already fallen as a result of the tie—to the negative side. On a subsequent amendment, offered by Senators John Sherman Cooper of Kentucky and Philip Hart of Michigan, to prohibit deployment of Safeguard but permit continued research and development, Senator Smith switched sides—apparently on the theory that if the system were developed, it might as well be deployed—which gave the administration a 51 to 49 victory.

The distribution of the vote on the Smith amendment, cutting off all funds for Safeguard, was as follows (a yes vote being a vote against ABM):[36]

Republicans			*Democrats*		
	Yes	No		Yes	No
Fundamentalists	0	17	Traditionalists	1	11
Stalwarts	2	8	Centrists	3	6
Moderates	3	4	Regulars	15	4
Progressives	9	0	Liberals	17	0
Total	14	29	Total	36	21

As in the House, the administration attracted strong support from Democratic traditionalists for a position that appeared unambiguously conservative. Four Democratic regulars—Jackson of Washington, Pastore of Rhode Island, Thomas Dodd of Connecticut, and Gale McGee of Wyoming, all liberals on domestic issues but hard-liners on defense and foreign policy—also supported the administration.

All nine of the Republican progressives and three of the seven moderates, however, voted with the opposition. At the end of June, Nixon had personally presented the administration's case to five of the progressive and moderate Republican senators opposed to ABM (Schweiker, Percy, Marlow Cook, Charles Mathias, and James Pearson)—to no avail.[37] Haldeman and Ehrlichman at first thought they had obtained better results from a friendly chat with Senator Percy, with whom they believed they enjoyed special rapport as fellow Christian Scientists—and were subsequently outraged when Percy announced his continued opposition to ABM.[38] Threats to cancel government contracts in states represented by anti-ABM senators served only to widen the gulf opening between the White House and Republicans in the Senate, including many who supported the administration on Safeguard.

After the death of Everett Dirksen on September 7, 1969, the administration's problems with the Senate became even more difficult. Hugh Scott of Pennsylvania was elected minority leader over Howard Baker of Tennessee, Dirksen's son-in-law. Scott had almost unanimous support in the Republican caucus from the progressives and moderates, plus backing from some of the more senior stalwarts and fundamentalists, like Norris Cotton of New Hampshire, who evidently regarded Baker as something of an upstart.[39] Baker was supported by most of the stalwarts and fundamentalists.

"The White House," Eugene Cowen, who moved from Scott's staff to Harlow's staff in 1969, has recalled, "always felt that Hugh Scott, as minority leader, should be its leader in the Senate."[40] In Scott's view, his role was not that simple. "I owed responsibilities," Scott has explained, "first, to the voters of Pennsylvania who elected me; second, to the Republican members of the Senate; and, finally, to the President, as interpreter of his wishes."[41] The White House staff regarded Scott as unreliable and evasive. Scott, in return, while getting along well with Harlow, found Haldeman, Ehrlichman, and some of their assistants arrogant and heavy-handed. On one occasion Ehrlichman told Scott that it was his responsibility to hold the Republican senators in line to sustain one of Nixon's vetoes. Scott said some would refuse. "Well," Ehrlichman said, "you should make them." What weapons could he use, Scott asked, if they were adamant? "Well," Ehrlichman suggested, "you could hit them in the face."[42]

Shortly before Scott's election as minority leader, Nixon had nominated Clement Haynsworth of South Carolina, chief judge of the Fourth Circuit Court of Appeals, to the seat on the Supreme Court left vacant by the resignation of Justice Abe Fortas. After reviewing Haynsworth's record on the bench, organized labor, civil rights groups, and other important segments of the liberal community decided to oppose the nomination. Liberals in the Senate, led by Senator Birch Bayh of Indiana, charged that Haynsworth had not been sufficiently sensitive to the possibility that his personal financial interests were touched, however remotely, by a few of the cases that had been brought before him. But the main source of the opposition to Haynsworth's confirmation was clearly ideological. Liberal groups were against him primarily because he had delivered decisions reflecting relatively conservative assumptions in a number of cases involving school desegregation and labor-management relations.[43]

When the fight over Haynsworth's confirmation became intense, Scott and Senate Minority Whip Robert Griffin of Michigan, both representing states with large black and labor constituencies, recommended that Nixon consider withdrawing the nomination. Nixon refused. In a press conference on October 20, the president charged that Haynsworth had become the victim of "vicious character assassination," and said that he would not withdraw the nomination even if Haynsworth himself requested it.[44]

On November 21 Haynsworth's nomination was rejected by the Senate, 55 to 45. Voting against the nomination, along with 38 Democrats, were 17 Republicans, including Scott and Griffin. The distribution of the vote by ideological groups was as follows (a yes vote being a vote to confirm):[45]

Republicans			Democrats		
	Yes	No		Yes	No
Fundamentalists	16	1	Traditionalists	11	1
Stalwarts	5	5	Centrists	6	3
Moderates	5	2	Regulars	2	17
Progressives	0	9	Liberals	0	17
Total	26	17	Total	19	38

As in the vote on ABM, Republican fundamentalists and Democratic traditionalists voted almost unanimously with the administration, whereas Republican progressives and Democratic liberals were uniformly opposed. The difference between the ABM vote and the vote on Haynsworth's confirmation was due mainly to losses suffered by the administration among Republican stalwarts and Democratic regulars. (There were more senators switching to the opposition than the gross figures reveal, because some compensating gains offset some of the losses. In all, twelve senators voted *with* the administration on ABM, but *against* Haynsworth; and seven voted *against* ABM but *for* Haynsworth.) The Democratic regulars who had defected on ABM—Jackson, Pastore, Dodd, and McGee—returned to their party to vote against Haynsworth. Two moderate Republicans, George Aiken of Vermont and Pearson of Kansas, went the other way, having voted against ABM, but voting for Haynsworth. These, however, were more than offset by five Republican stalwarts, all from states with substantial labor union strength, who switched to the opposition.

The White House took Scott's defection particularly hard. "It really blew Haldeman and Ehrlichman up against the wall," Cowen has recalled.[46] The loss of all the progressives was regarded as further proof of the innate disloyalty of the progressive wing of the party. Senator Charles Mathias of Maryland, a Republican progressive who had been elected to the Senate in 1968 from a normally Democratic state, visited Nixon in the White House to explain the political and philosophic reasons for his vote against Haynsworth. The president expressed no resentment. But during the remainder of Nixon's time in the presidency, Mathias was never again invited to the Oval Office.[47]

Possible Alternative Strategies

The votes on ABM and Haynsworth, as well as later votes on the Vietnam War and Nixon's nomination of G. Harrold Carswell, another conservative southerner, to fill the Supreme Court vacancy, revealed a basic weakness in the floating coalition strategy, particularly in the Senate: Republican progressives and moderates, and even some of the stalwarts with large urban constituencies, could not be counted on to support the administration out of party loyalty when their personal ideologies or ideological pressures from their constituents pointed the other way. When the administration's welfare reform plan reached the Senate in 1970, Republican fundamentalists proved equally unwilling to sacrifice ideology to party loyalty. The administration, it became clear, was vulnerable to defeat by ideological groups at each end of the spectrum, combined with party-line Democrats—a sort of floating coalition in reverse.

The floating coalition strategy had worked well enough for the Republican minority in Congress when their chief objectives had been to harass and slow down the majority party allied with a Democratic White House. But for a Republican administration in the White House, with its own legislative program and other positive legislative objectives, reliance on the floating coalition was bound to be both hazardous and constricting.

There were essentially two ways in which the Nixon administration could seek relatively secure congressional majorities: by pursuing moderate reform of domestic institutions and prudent restructuring of foreign policy, which would attract support from Republican moderates and progressives and Democratic centrists without alienating most of the more conservative Republicans; or by trying to rally the supposed conservative majority among the national electorate to produce a Congress in which the more conservative groups would be clearly dominant.

During his first term, Nixon appeared to move back and forth between these two options. On August 8, 1969, he proposed to Congress a program for domestic reform, including revenue sharing and overhaul of the welfare system (described in chapters 7 and 8), that seemed designed to capture the broad middle ground of American politics. The following year, however, after the Senate's rejection of Carswell (by a vote of 51 to 45, on April 8, 1970)[48] and the rise of opposition to the administration's conduct of the Vietnam War, Nixon cut sharply to the right, appearing to cast his lot with the more extreme conservatives. Then, after the 1970 congressional elections failed to produce the conservative majority he had hoped for, he moved back toward the center, emphasizing domestic reform. But his domestic program was soon once again sidetracked as he concentrated on the Vietnam War and the dramatic new initiatives he was planning in foreign policy.

6

Foreign Policy: Passage to Détente

DURING most of his career before he was elected president, Richard Nixon had seemed almost the personification of militant resistance to the expansion of international communism. Yet within less than four years, by the summer of 1972, the Nixon administration had concluded a series of accords with the Soviet Union; exchanged vows of mutual forbearance with the Communist rulers of China; and announced triumphantly, in the president's State of the World message to Congress in 1972, the virtual interment of the cold war: "Our alliances are no longer addressed primarily to the containment of the Soviet Union and China behind an American shield. They are, instead, addressed to the creation with those powers of a stable world peace."[1]

In some secondary theaters, the more belligerent "old Nixon" from time to time seemed to take charge of policy, as in the administration's firm interdiction of the Syrian invasion of Jordan in 1970; the "tilt" toward Pakistan in the war between India and Pakistan in 1971; the campaign to bring down the Allende government in Chile; and, most of all, the administration's determined prosecution of the war in Southeast Asia. In the crucial areas of direct relations with the two Communist superpowers, however, Nixon's approach was more flexible and conciliatory than that of any president since Franklin Roosevelt.

Had Nixon risen above principle in the service of political expedience, as his fundamentalist conservative critics charged? Or were there consistent bonds of ideology between the cold war strategy of containment and Nixon's pursuit of détente? Or did ideology turn out to be, after, all, irrelevant to the conduct of foreign policy from the perspective of the Oval Office?

Kinds of Foreign Policy

To evaluate the influence of ideology on foreign policy, and specifically the foreign policies of the Nixon and Ford administrations, it is useful first to consider the kinds of foreign policies, relating to national goals and strategies, that may be affected by ideology. There are basically six kinds, not counting subtypes or hybrids.

1. *Autarky:* maintenance of national economic and military self-sufficiency, with minimum contact or relationship with the outside world. This policy has been popular at various times in countries protected by formidable natural barriers, such as Egypt, Japan, Russia, and the United States. It was essentially the approach attempted by the People's Republic of China from the time of the split with the Soviet Union in the early 1960s until Kissinger's arrival in Peking in 1971.

2. *Hegemony:* drive for world domination (or domination of the relevant world, as in Rome's mastery over the Mediterranean basin and western Europe in the first centuries of the Christian era). The idea of a world empire dominated by a single state or nation has lingered in the Western imagination, inspired in part by memories of "the grandeur that was Rome." If successful, this policy would achieve substantial military security and rich economic rewards for the dominant power. But it naturally arouses forceful and concerted resistance from all other nations, whose independent existences are threatened. Few nations have had the resources or military capacities to consider such a policy, and almost none have made it an avowed national aim. But it clearly has beckoned some, such as Napoleon's France and Hitler's Germany (perhaps also Wilhelmine Germany). The United States had at least the physical capacity to seek world hegemony at the end of the Second World War and was urged to do so by such savants as Bertrand Russell. By the end of the 1950s, this opportunity had passed, except at the cost of all-out nuclear war. In the opinions of some Western and Chinese military and political

theorists, the Soviet Union was by then developing the means—having always possessed the will—to attempt its own version of international hegemony.

3. *The power game:* the policy most frequently practiced by the great powers, and to a more limited degree the lesser powers, in the modern state system. Nations playing the power game seek through active diplomacy and trade to maximize their military security and economic advantage in relation to all other nations, but not at the cost of pushing their competitors to the point of responding with massive force. Alliances, treaties, colonization, establishment of spheres of influence, and even minor wars are regular tools of this policy. A favorite strategy is maintenance of a "balance of power," by which rival nations are poised against each other in a way that preserves reasonable security for all and allows each to achieve its reasonable economic goals. Britain was long the most skilled practitioner of the power game (though some nineteenth-century British statesmen and colonial administrators, like Cecil Rhodes, were attracted by the larger goal of hegemony).

4. *Clientship:* a variation on the power game practiced by nations that do not feel equipped to play an independent hand. Client states are often by no means completely under the thumb of the great power to which they are attached: the Soviet Union was unable to restrain Nasser during the weeks leading up to the Six Day War in 1967; and the United States had only limited control over a series of client governments in South Vietnam. Countries may move from clientship to participation in the power game as independent players. The Arab nations, for example, were usually regarded as client states of one or another of the great powers until their bold use of the oil weapon in 1973; then they became full-fledged players. Alexander Hamilton proposed that the young United States establish a kind of client-state relationship with Britain, preparatory to entering the power game. He was opposed by Thomas Jefferson, who believed that foreign relations should reflect larger moral considerations.

5. *International altruism:* pursuit of moral or ideological foreign policy goals, like making the world safe for democracy, or conversion to Christianity or Islam, or conquering world hunger, or fomenting the international revolution of the proletariat. This strategy may be combined with other goals, like hegemony (as when the seventh-century Muslims swept up out of the Arabian peninsula), or autarky (as when

the People's Republic of China tried during the 1960s to provide a model for the new proletarian society while developing military and economic self-sufficiency). Most international conquerors have sought fulfillment of some ideal, along with tangible enrichment. "We came here to serve God, and also to get rich," wrote Bernal Díaz del Castillo after the Spanish conquest of Mexico. In the nineteenth century, Christianity and liberalism, sometimes working in tandem, were dynamic international proselyting faiths. The prestige of both was severely damaged as a result of the First World War. Christian and liberal ideals, nevertheless, continued to influence the foreign policy of the United States and, to a lesser extent, those of other Western nations. After 1918 the incitement of international Marxist revolution became one of the avowed foreign policy goals of a major world power, the Soviet Union. The role Communist ideology has played in the actual formulation of Russian foreign policy has been debated by diplomats, scholars, and journalists ever since.

6. *Self-interested cooperation:* participation in world or regional compacts or federations to promote the common good, motivated not so much by moral altruism as by acceptance of the reality of international economic and security interdependence. Whereas approval of the League of Nations after the First World War was promoted as a moral duty, formation of the United Nations was presented to the American public after the Second World War as a worthwhile investment in security and economic progress that would directly benefit the United States. The difficulty with justifying mutual assistance through appeals to self-interest is that support for it is bound to wither if important national interests are regularly thwarted—as many Americans had begun to feel was happening to the United States in the United Nations by the end of the 1960s.

Ideology normally influences, but hardly ever determines, which of these kinds of foreign policy, or crossbreed among them, a given nation practices at a given time. (Other factors that may influence a nation's choice of foreign policy may include: political, military, and economic capabilities; geographic realities and perceptions; internal politics; ethnic or religious ties to other nations; institutional traditions and structures; personalities of leaders.) A purely nationalist ideology, for example, discourages altruism or prolonged clientship, but it may be carried out, in different ways, through pursuit of autarky, hegemony, or the power game. By contrast, moralistic ideologies, emphasizing values like human rights or equality, establish a natural tug against foreign policies aimed solely at hegemony or at ruthless practice of the power game. (This does not mean, of course, that moral goals may not be joined to the pursuit of power—as has been done with spectacular results at various times by, among others, imperial Spain, Britain, the United States, and the Soviet Union. But almost always those concerned primarily with moral objectives are eventually drawn into internal opposition against leaders and groups concerned primarily with increasing national power.)

Conservative ideology, to the extent that it is associated with nationalism, weighs against a foreign policy founded mainly on altruism. On the other hand, the cautious, pragmatic side of positional conservatism militates against bold drives for hegemony, or even against particularly daring participation in the power game. Autarky appears to be the instinctive foreign policy of positional conservatism. But the commercial interests that form important constituencies in most modern conservative parties in the West work against extreme isolationism or protectionism because of the heavy economic costs that would result from any substantial reduction in foreign trade, even for relatively self-supplying systems like the United States. Also, conservative leaders and publicists with international perspectives, often attached to the reform wings of conservative parties, warn against the political and military hazards of withdrawal into a "Fortress America" or "little England" or unaligned European community. Finally, the association of ideational conservatism in the West with the moral values of the Judeo-Christian religious tradition creates a compelling mandate within conservatism for acceptance of some kind of transnational responsibility for the welfare of the human race.

In practice, modern conservative parties have usually been broadly nationalistic; more concerned with national defense than liberal or socialist rivals; moderately supportive of steps to promote freer world trade, but responsive to the particular needs of threatened domestic industries; and prepared to practice, generally on an ad hoc basis, international cooperation for humanitarian purposes. In the particular context of the conduct of relations with the Communist powers, conservative parties have usually taken the lead, along with some social democrats, in promoting resistance to Communist advance. In office, however, conservative leaders have sometimes proved to be flexible negotiators with the Communist rulers.

American Experience

In the early years of the United States, division over foreign policy based partly on ideological differences was a primary cause of the development of the first party system. The Federalists, following Hamilton, favored an aggressively pro-British policy in the war that broke out between Britain and France after the French Revolution, on the theory that alliance with the former mother country would be helpful to the economic development of the new nation, and that in any case the British were defending civilized interests and values against the equalitarian and atheistic frenzy rising out of France— which, the Federalists insisted, had nothing in common with the principles for which the struggle for American independence had been fought. The Republicans, following Jefferson, favored France in the belief that the French Revolution was a critical further step in the international movement toward human freedom and enlightenment, of which the American Revolution had also been part. Profiting from public indignation over slights and insults inflicted on American diplomats by French leaders, the Federalists at first seemed to be carrying the country with them, but ultimately they were frustrated when President Adams, himself a Federalist, decided to undertake a conciliatory policy aimed at avoiding war with either side.[2]

The division over foreign policy during the Washington and Adams administrations was between aggressive conservatism and aggressive liberalism. Aggressive conservatism for a time held the advantage, only to give way when a more cautious brand of conservatism achieved a calming of international tensions. Ultimately, liberalism triumphed on the basis of domestic issues in the climactic presidential election of 1800.

In the nineteenth century the republic turned its attention inward, devoting its energies to buying or conquering, and developing, a vast continental empire, while settling internal social differences and launching American versions of industrialization and urbanization. During this period of absorption in internal problems, many Americans continued to think of themselves as carrying out a moral responsibility to humankind, performed by building a "city upon a hill" to serve as an international beacon and model for all who aspired to republican virtues.

When the nation vigorously entered the global power game after the Spanish-American War, this sense of moral mission found expression in attempts at democratic evangelism, particularly during the administration of Woodrow Wilson. The carnage of the First World War, followed by wrangling among the victors over the peace settlement, dissipated moral commitment and contributed to a partial return to isolationism in the 1920s.

In the years leading up to American participation in the Second World War, the struggle between isolationists and internationalists was fought more along regional and ethnic than ideological lines. People from inland states or of Germanic or Irish descent, very broadly speaking, sought to avoid involvement in the expanding conflict, whereas those from coastal states or of English or Jewish stock were more inclined toward intervention. Both sides made heavy use of moral as well as practical arguments.

After the Second World War, most Americans were determined not to repeat the mistakes of passivity that were believed to have encouraged the aggressions of the Axis powers. Soviet obduracy in Eastern Europe, followed by Communist victory in the Chinese civil war in 1949, were met by American resolve to offer forceful resistance against further Communist territorial expansion. The policy of containment, embodied in specific moves proposed by the Truman administration and approved by bipartisan majorities in Congress, was based on the lesson of Munich (aggression cannot be deterred by appeasement), now joined by the new lesson of Poland, Czechoslovakia, and finally China (the appetite of the worldwide Communist movement for expansion is insatiable). Among those supporting containment, a few were prepared to go the whole way to benevolent hegemony; but for most of its adherents, containment required only aggressive pursuit of the power game, accompanied by limited self-interested cooperation with the rest of the "free world."

The conceptual argument for containment included important ideological elements, drawn partly from American nationalism and partly from broader faiths in political democracy, constitutional rights, and economic freedom. This ideological structure, combining resistance against fundamental change in the established order in the capitalist democracies with concern for human rights and welfare, helped attract support from a very wide range of American political opinion. Opposition developed only among left-wing zealots (grouped behind

Henry Wallace), who argued the practicality of renewed collaboration with the Communist powers; and among conservative stalwarts (led by Senator Taft), who, while no less anti-Communist than those proposing containment, maintained that neither the national interest nor the moral responsibilities of the United States required resistance against communism all over the globe.[3]

Left-wing opponents of containment were routed within the Democratic party by forces loyal to President Truman, and they failed to attract significant support for Wallace's third party presidential candidacy in 1948. The more broadly based conservative opposition was finally overwhelmed at the Republican National Convention in 1952, when Taft's last bid for the presidency was turned back by Republican internationalists supporting Eisenhower, who promised continuation and indeed more positive application of the containment policy.

The Cold Warrior

From the time he entered public life in 1946, Richard Nixon identified with the internationalist wing of the Republican party. He recalled in his memoirs that Winston Churchill's "Iron Curtain" speech at Fulton, Missouri, in March 1946, warning of the effects of Communist domination of Eastern Europe, helped "jolt" him into awareness that "the defeat of Hitler and Japan had not produced a lasting peace, and freedom was now threatened by a new and even more dangerous enemy."[4] In the struggle between Republican internationalists and isolationists in 1952, Nixon, at considerable political risk to himself (though not of course without awareness of the possible rewards), actively helped round up support for the internationalist candidate, Eisenhower. During his eight years as Eisenhower's vice-president, Nixon almost always sided with those in the administration who favored the strongest possible response to any sign of further Communist advance.[5]

When he returned to private life in 1961, Nixon continued to espouse hard-line anticommunism. While visiting President Kennedy in the White House shortly after the Bay of Pigs attack on Cuba, Nixon recommended intervention in both Cuba and Laos, "including if necessary a commitment of American air power." When Kennedy appeared loath to take further action in either area, Nixon was, he has written, "surprised and disappointed" that the new president did not grasp "that the Communist threat was indivisible, and unless it was resisted everywhere there was really no point in resisting it anywhere."[6] As the war in Vietnam expanded, Nixon placed himself among the most belligerent of the hawks. "Neutralism in Vietnam," he warned in 1964, "would be surrender and defeat in our time." In August 1966 he told the national convention of the American Legion: "In the event that Vietnam is either lost at the conference table or on the battlefield, it will mean that the Pacific will become a Red Sea, that Communist China will become the dominant power in that area of the world, and that World War Three will be inevitable."[7]

By 1967, however, Nixon had begun to rethink some of his foreign policy assumptions. His hostility to communism was undiminished, but he was moving toward the view that changed circumstances had created conditions under which the old goals might better be served through new policies. The split between the Russian and Chinese Communists during the 1960s had created the intriguing possibility that the two in the future might be used to check each other. Meanwhile, practical hopes for displacing Communist regimes in China and Eastern Europe had faded. Perhaps most important, the American public was clearly tiring of the sacrifices and exertions needed to maintain the role of international policeman.

On a visit to Taiwan in 1967, Nixon listened sympathetically, but skeptically, to the aging Chiang Kai-shek's confident talk of returning to the mainland. "I wondered whether he might be right," Nixon later commented, "but my pragmatic analysis told me that he was wrong. His burning desire to return to the mainland was understandable and admirable. But it was totally unrealistic in view of the massive power the Communists had developed."[8] Nixon's celebrated article on "Asia after Vietnam," published in the October 1967 issue of *Foreign Affairs*, though less prophetic of his future China policy than has since been claimed, contained a significant concession: "Taking the long view, we simply cannot afford to leave China forever outside the family of nations, there to nurture its fantasies, cherish its hates, and threaten its neighbors."[9]

Vietnam, meanwhile, had begun to seem a cuttable loss—if an exit could be arranged that did not damage the credibility of continued American resistance against Communist expansion. Nixon agreed with Eisenhower in a conversation in 1967 that Lyndon Johnson had erred in Vietnam by failing to use sufficient force at the outset.[10] He doubted, however, that public opinion would now support the steps needed to achieve a decisive military victory. Meeting with a group of journalists in New York a few weeks before the Republican convention in 1968, Nixon said that he would end the war by bringing pressure on the North Vietnamese through the Russians. And if that failed? His answer was terse: "A phased withdrawal."[11]

Divisions within the New Administration

After his election Nixon immediately set in motion foreign policy initiatives designed both to relieve some of the international burdens that had been assumed by the United States and to preserve containment through a new approach that would draw the two major Communist powers into blocking each other. "After a period of confrontation," he announced in his inaugural address, "we are entering a period of negotiation."[12]

To carry out his new policies, Nixon determined to make extensive use of the National Security Council, as he had promised during the campaign. The NSC, he believed, had functioned most effectively during the Eisenhower administration, as a means for bringing all aspects of foreign and military policy under central direction and coordination. Nixon was not, however, entirely happy with the Eisenhower model. He aimed to avoid the excessive homogenization of policy alternatives that the NSC had tended to produce during his earlier experience in the executive branch.[13]

Meetings of the NSC—composed of the president, the vice-president, the secretary of state, the secretary of defense, the director of the Office of Emergency Preparedness, and, at Nixon's designation, the attorney general—were not, by all accounts, usually occasions for lively policy debate. Discussion was led by the president, who, according to a staff member who attended meetings for about a year, took care "not to tip his hand, trying to elicit the views of others." Despite Nixon's best efforts, the cabinet members "would try to guess which way the president was going, and then come down on that side." Secretary of State Rogers and Secretary of Defense Laird sometimes tried to influence policy by pointing out that they would have to defend the administration's conduct before congressional committees: "Remember, Mr. President, I will have to testify on this next week." Both were careful, however, not to take strong stands that might run counter to Nixon's ultimate position. Attorney General Mitchell said little unless he had been previously primed by Nixon to be "loquacious" on a specific issue. Vice-President Agnew, his colleagues joked, "got the countries mixed up."[14]

The real importance of the National Security Council, it soon became apparent, was that it gave Nixon a base on which to build a White House foreign policy secretariat, directed by his assistant for national security, Henry Kissinger. At meetings of the full council, Kissinger's role was mainly limited to summarizing views contained in memoranda submitted by the departments on subjects listed for discussion. But during the first hundred days of the new administration, Kissinger set his own sizable staff to work on fifty-five separate studies of major and minor foreign policy and defense issues. Soon he was able to give Nixon the means for making key decisions over the heads of the State and Defense bureaucracies. The focus for major foreign policy and military decisionmaking became the daily meetings between Nixon and Kissinger in the Oval Office or in the president's working office in the Executive Office Building.[15]

Kissinger's rise was abetted by H. R. Haldeman. Although Haldeman and Kissinger do not seem to have liked each other much, Haldeman, as one of Kissinger's assistants has put it, "was loyal to the president, and he had the shrewdness to see that Kissinger served the president's interests." At the beginning of the administration, phone calls made by Secretary Rogers to Nixon were at first routed through Haldeman, who soon began turning them over to Kissinger. The assistant for national security would then ask if he could take a message for the president. When it became clear that Rogers was willing to communicate with Nixon in this way, the secretary's authority over policy inevitably dwindled.

Rogers's decline, however, was more gradual than is now generally remembered. In the first foreign policy crisis faced by the administration, Rogers, supported by Laird, prevailed. On April 15, 1969, the Communist North Koreans shot down an unarmed American reconnaissance plane. At first, Nixon's inclination—somewhat ambiguously supported by Kissinger—was to respond by bombing a North Korean airfield. But Rogers and Laird urged restraint. Wishing to avoid an all-out conflict in Korea while the United States was heavily involved in Vietnam, Nixon finally decided to settle for sending armed escorts with future reconnaissance missions.[16]

As the administration unfolded, Rogers, like Laird, became identified with taking the "soft" option on most issues—no more a compliment in the Nixon White House than it has been in the White Houses of Kennedy or Johnson. Kissinger, by contrast, usually favored the "tough" option, which appealed to Nixon's hard-line preconceptions if not always to his pragmatic judgment. Given a difficult case, Rogers presented it poorly. "The secretary of state," according to one account, "refused to go into detail and would arrive at White House meetings with a short memo on the subject in hand. Kissinger would come with a huge briefing book and, sometimes, aides to check facts and lend dignity."[17] Nixon told Safire: "Henry thinks Bill isn't very deep and Bill thinks Henry is power crazy. In a sense they are both right."[18]

Rogers's loss of standing became precipitous when, in the spring of 1970, Nixon became convinced that the secretary had allowed word to reach the press that he had opposed the president's decision to order an American ground attack against North Vietnamese staging areas in Cambodia. Rogers lost the president's confidence—and did not regain it until April 1973, when Nixon, beginning to suffer the agonies of Watergate, once more sought the counsel and company of his old friend.[19]

The eclipse of Rogers by Kissinger resulted in large measure from the latter's superior competence and craftiness. But it also reflected, at least symbolically, their underlying ideological differences. Rogers's operational lethargy and confusion expressed the doctrinal ambiguity of what remained of the old American foreign policy establishment: a vague commitment to long-run international cooperation and human progress, and to gentlemanly conduct of foreign affairs, but an immediate concern with keeping the United States economically and militarily "number one." Kissinger stood for a more ruthless view, based on the experience of European conservatives since the French Revolution: that the defenders of civilized values cannot afford indulgence in moral posturing or imprecise thought. In the Nixon White House, as on the larger stage of international politics, the old establishment's conceptual confusion tended to undermine focused effort.

Melvin Laird was another story. The secretary of defense's inclination toward a more conciliatory approach in world affairs was based not on vague moralistic scruples but on an experienced politician's judgment of what the American people were prepared to take. Laird's old congressional district in central Wisconsin had been a stronghold of isolationist sentiment before the Second World War. Though himself an internationalist, in the cold war sense, Laird had concluded that the United States could not, or would not, indefinitely maintain primary responsibility for checking the expansion of communism all over the world. As early as 1964 he had issued a personal "white paper" questioning the wisdom of carrying on a land war in Asia.[20]

When he arrived at the Pentagon at the beginning of 1969, Laird quickly assembled an experienced policy planning staff, composed of both holdovers from the Johnson administration and new appointees. In the first months of the new administration, while Kissinger's NSC staff was still finding its bearings, Laird's policy planners did much of the preliminary work on some of Nixon's early foreign policy initiatives, including the Nixon doctrine (calling on America's allies to assume more responsibility for their own defense), and Vietnamization (establishing a program for turning over the land war in Vietnam to South Vietnamese forces, while withdrawing American troops).[21]

Laird has said that he got the idea for Vietnamization from a plan developed by Paul Warnke, assistant secretary of defense in the Johnson administration, later a foreign policy adviser to George McGovern, and still later disarmament coordinator for President Carter. When Laird told reporters during the 1968 campaign that the Johnson administration had a plan to withdraw 50,000 American troops from Vietnam, his statement was hotly denied by Johnson and Clark Clifford, Johnson's secretary of defense. But after Laird took Clifford's job, he called on Warnke, who stayed on at the Pentagon for a few months under the new administration, and together they worked out the plan for the gradual withdrawal of American forces. Laird himself coined the term *Vietnamization*.[22]

Along with political cunning and broad understanding of international affairs, however, Laird had one damaging liability: an almost aesthetic delight in political intrigue. "Mel Laird," Eisenhower had told Nixon in 1967, "is the smartest of the lot [among Republican leaders in Congress], but he is too devious."[23] Nixon had asked Laird to take charge of the Defense Department only when he had been left in the lurch by Senator Jackson. As the administration came under increasing attack for continuing the war in Vietnam, Nixon began to suspect that Laird was planting stories critical of administration policy with selected columnists and reporters. Hawks among the military in the Pentagon found their way around Laird to Kissinger—or directly to Nixon.[24]

Throughout most of Nixon's first term, Laird—partly because he maintained influence in Congress and within the structure of the Republican party, and partly because Nixon, while questioning his loyalty, continued to respect his intellect—retained substantial influence within the administration's policymaking structure. But as time went on, and particularly after the invasion of Cambodia, which Laird like Rogers opposed, the secretary of defense gradually slipped away from the inner circle of power.[25]

As Nixon lost confidence in Rogers and Laird, he naturally relied more and more on Kissinger. The star of the assistant for national security was in any case probably destined to rise. In addition to skill at negotiation and broad knowledge of international relations, Kissinger brought to Nixon a capacity for conceptualizing policy that the president, who liked to have a sense of how the pieces fitted together, greatly valued. Also, Kissinger was unswervingly loyal to the administration. Unlike Rogers and Laird, he was prepared to risk losing the respect of his natural constituency—in Kissinger's case, the community of academic intellectuals. After going a certain distance with Nixon, Kissinger seems to have concluded that his best chance was to continue, in the hope that the administration's policies would, in the end, be regarded as having been reasonably successful. Besides, Kissinger's world view, formed under very different circumstances, was essentially similar to Nixon's.

Kissinger: Conservative Intellectual

Despite his show of militance in White House policy debates—probably adopted in part to impress Nixon—Kissinger was by no means a bitter-end opponent of international change. The former Harvard professor traced his intellectual descent from the traditions of Kant and Burke, both of whom in different ways had aimed to come to terms with and give direction to progressive forces in the modern world, rather than from the tradition of Metternich and de

Maistre, who had tried to build walls of resistance against all forms of change.

Kissinger's early years, as is well known, were disrupted by calamities far more horrendous than those experienced by the young Nixon. As a boy of fifteen, after five years of exposure to growing Nazi terror, Kissinger fled with his family from their German homeland to the United States. He later commented: "Twice, once in 1933 when the Nazis came to power, then in 1938 when I came to the United States, all the things that had seemed secure and stable collapsed and many of the people that one had considered the steady examples suddenly were thrown into enormous turmoil themselves and into fantastic insecurities."[26] In another sense, however, Kissinger's childhood seems to have been more secure than that of Nixon or many of his contemporaries in the United States. The future secretary of state grew up in a relatively fixed and supportive immediate social environment, whose ultimate disruption was the result of catastrophe that could in no way be interpreted as self-inflicted. "I was not consciously unhappy," Kissinger has said. "I was not so acutely aware of what was going on. For children those things are not that serious."[27] Before the Nazis came to power, Kissinger's father was a successful secondary school teacher—a position of higher status in Germany than in the United States. The family adhered strictly to the rituals and traditions of Orthodox Judaism. In the United States the Kissingers soon became an integral part of the Jewish community in the Fort Washington section of Brooklyn.[28]

Both early security and traumatic disruption seem to have contributed to the development of a profoundly conservative character. "You have never seen the dissolution of a society," Kissinger warned young members of his staff inclined to protest against Nixon's policies in 1970—referring, apparently, not only to the social turmoil he had experienced before his family's flight from Germany in 1938, but also to the ravaged German society he had witnessed as a sergeant in the American army of occupation after the Second World War.[29] Experience of social tragedy, it seems, caused Kissinger to value all the more highly the sense of order and respect for traditional authority with which he was imbued during his youth.[30]

After his experience in the army, Kissinger enrolled at Harvard, where he soon demonstrated a talent for attaching himself to influ-

ential academicians. Abandoning earlier plans to become an accoun-
tant, he set out to pursue a career in international studies.

Kissinger's undergraduate hero is said to have been Immanuel
Kant, the eighteenth-century German philosopher (partly of Scottish
descent) who strove, perhaps more successfully than anyone else has
ever done, to reconcile liberal principles with conservative values. In
his undergraduate thesis, which ran to 377 typed pages (causing the
Government Department at Harvard to set new rules for the permissible length of such works), Kissinger was already dealing with big
ideas. The paper, a commentary on the philosophies of history of
Kant, Spengler, and Toynbee, argued that history teaches the limits
to what man can achieve and yet also teaches man's responsibility to
advance toward unlimited goals.[31]

For his doctoral dissertation, completed in 1954, Kissinger under-
took a study of the efforts of post-Napoleonic statesmen, particularly
Metternich and Castlereagh, to restore the traditional order in Europe
after the Congress of Vienna. Kissinger's admiration for Metternich,
the conservative Austrian foreign minister, has been considerably
exaggerated, as Stephen Graubard and others have pointed out. While
praising Metternich's diplomatic skill in his dissertation, Kissinger
nevertheless observed: "The 'Metternich system' answered the question of the cause of revolution, but it gave no indication of how to
cope with it once it had occurred."[32] Kissinger distinguished two
strains of European conservatism: the conservatism of Burke, which
aimed to "protect the social sphere by timely political concession";
and the conservatism of Metternich, for whom "political concession
was the equivalent of social surrender."[33] Kissinger seemed to identify
his own position with that of Burke, as represented by the British
foreign secretary Castlereagh.

While clearly on the conservative side in his political sympathies,
Kissinger did not choose to play the role of apologist for the conservative Eisenhower administration in office during the 1950s. Conservatism, he argued, must be at least as imaginative and intellectually
resourceful as its opposition, rather than bound to outmoded concepts
or irrational convictions, like the French generals at the beginning of
the Second World War. In a 1956 article in *Foreign Affairs*, Kissinger
wrote: "There can be little doubt that the foreign policy of the United
States has reached an impasse. For several years we have been groping

for a concept to deal with the transformation of the cold war from an effort to build defensive barriers into a contest for the allegiance of humanity. But the new Soviet tactics, coupled with equally unassimilated increase in the destructive potentialities of the new weapons technology, have led to a crisis in our system of alliances and to substantial Soviet gains among the uncommitted peoples of the world."[34] During 1956 he attached himself to young Nelson Rockefeller (elected governor of New York in 1958), who agreed with him in scorning what they regarded as Eisenhower's passivity in foreign and military affairs.

In 1961 Kissinger joined the rush of Harvard academicians to help staff the new Kennedy administration in Washington. He signed on as part-time consultant to his former Harvard colleague McGeorge Bundy, President Kennedy's special assistant for national security. It did not turn out to be a happy experience for Kissinger. He seems to have cut a poor figure at Camelot. There were "ball games" in the White House, he complained, that he did not understand. His advice was too belligerent for even the relentlessly tough-minded Kennedys—when the Russians built the Berlin wall in August 1961, he recommended the use of force to tear it down. Finding himself excluded from the inner circle, Kissinger tried to go around Bundy to the president. In February 1962 Bundy politely suggested that he resign.[35]

During the 1960s, particularly after his failure in Washington and his divorce from his first wife in 1964, Kissinger seemed to turn back to the humanistic values expressed in his senior thesis at Harvard. He wrote often, sometimes pompously, of the need for "tragic vision." American idealism, he maintained, "would gain in depth if leavened by the European sense of tragedy."[36]

As the 1968 presidential campaign approached, Kissinger predicted, in his contribution to *Agenda for the Nation*, published by the Brookings Institution: "The age of the superpowers is now drawing to an end. Military bipolarity has not only failed to prevent, it has actually encouraged multipolarity." Under such changed circumstances, Kissinger argued, some reduction in American responsibility was not only possible but inevitable: "Regional groupings supported by the United States will have to take over major responsibility for their immediate areas, with the United States being concerned more with the overall framework of order than with the management of every individual enterprise." Henceforth, he believed, "the most profound challenge to American policy will be philosophical: to develop some concept of order in a world which is bipolar militarily but multipolar politically."[37]

On the specific issue of the war in Vietnam, Kissinger set down his views in an article written before his selection by Nixon, but appearing in *Foreign Affairs* almost simultaneously with his arrival in the White House. "However we got into Vietnam," Kissinger wrote, "ending the war honorably is essential for the peace of the world. Any other solution may unloose forces that would complicate prospects of international order." The American commitment to Vietnam, he reasoned, was limited by two propositions: "First, the United States cannot accept a military defeat, or a change in the political structure of South Vietnam brought about by external military force; second, once Vietnamese military forces and pressures are removed, the United States has no obligation to maintain a government in Saigon by force." Within these limits, Kissinger suggested, a settlement might be achieved through a bilevel system of negotiations, in which the United States and the North Vietnamese would bargain on mutual troop withdrawals, while the Saigon government and the indigenous Communists in South Vietnam (the NLF) sought agreement on an internal governmental structure.[38] This proposal, as Kissinger himself soon discovered, reflected almost total misunderstanding of the Communists' minimum objectives in Vietnam.[39]

Installed as Nixon's assistant for national security at the beginning of 1969, Kissinger was able to apply some of the ideas he had developed over the previous two decades. The impact of Kissinger's formulations can be seen not only in conceptual rationalizations of administration policy, particularly the annual State of the World messages presented by Nixon from 1970 through 1973, but also in the design of the strategies themselves, particularly détente.

Yet the role of Kissinger under Nixon should not be exaggerated. The controlling intelligence behind foreign policy in the Nixon administration was not Henry Kissinger's but Richard Nixon's—at least until the fall of 1973, when the president's preoccupation with the threat of Watergate became overwhelming. The first steps in the process that led to the new China policy were taken by Nixon in December 1968, before Kissinger had joined his staff. Kissinger, though he had written a position paper for Nelson Rockefeller during the 1968 campaign proposing that China be encouraged to develop "constructive relationships with the outside world,"[40] is said to have at first taken a skeptical view of the new policy.[41] Nixon's important proposal for a new international order based on "five great power centers"—the United States, Western Europe, the Soviet Union, China, and Japan— was made while his assistant for national security was flying toward China in July 1971, and had not even been read by Kissinger, according to one of his closest associates, until it was shown to him by a delighted Chou En-lai in Peking.

The Problem of Vietnam

Both Nixon and Kissinger looked upon détente, at least initially, as a way to achieve the goals of containment by substituting negotiation for confrontation—ideological warfare carried on by other means. Their aim was to develop a classic balance of power between the Soviet Union and China, with the United States maintaining the balance, much as Britain had done in Europe during the nineteenth century. For this design to succeed, it was necessary that American power remain credible, so that neither of the Communist superpowers could act against the other, or against one of the lesser powers, without fear of retaliation by the United States. To gain this end, as well as to maintain authority within its own spheres of influence, the United States must not allow itself to be pushed around "like a pitiful, helpless giant" in Southeast Asia, the Middle East, Latin America, or other areas where American interests were substantial or where American prestige had been committed.[42]

Carrying out the logic of this policy, Nixon promoted the overthrow of the Allende government in Chile, restrained Egyptian and Syrian aggression in the Middle East, maintained a tough stance toward the Castro government in Cuba, and propped up Pakistan against India. But the most serious threat to the credibility of American will, Nixon believed, lay in the still unsettled war in Vietnam.

In terms of Nixon's grand design, the principal American goal in Vietnam had become more strategic than ideological: the Vietnamese Communists must be denied victory, not primarily because they were Communists, but because they had challenged American resolve (although Nixon believed—as it turned out, correctly—that Communist victory would result in the brutal repression of the Vietnamese people). At another level, the aggressive tendencies of world Communism, even though no longer monolithic, remained the ultimate enemy. The United States could not accept defeat, or the appearance of defeat, in Vietnam, Nixon had concluded, because such a setback might upset the developing balance of power and uncage the renewed threat of aggression by one or both of the Communist superpowers.[43]

While still at the Pierre Hotel, between the election and the inauguration, Nixon reviewed the possible means by which the Vietnam War might be brought to an end. Military victory—a "blow that would both end the war and win it"—he reckoned, could be achieved either by using tactical nuclear weapons or by bombing irrigation dikes in North Vietnam to cause devastating floods. But he concluded that "the domestic and international uproar that would have accompanied the use of either of these knockout blows would have got my administration off to the worst possible start." As for escalating conventional warfare to the extent needed to produce victory, which he thought would take at least six months, he decided: "There was no way I could hold the country together for that period of time in view of the number of casualties we would be sustaining."[44] Nixon determined to seek a negotiated peace—but a peace concluded on terms that would meet the standard of Kissinger's first proposition: prevention of "a change in the political structure of South Vietnam brought about by force."

Despite the extraordinary complexity of the negotiations between the United States and the Saigon government on the one side and the Vietnamese Communists on the other, the basic issues and stakes were relatively simple. The United States aimed to withdraw its ground forces while leaving the Saigon government with a decent chance for survival. The Thieu regime in Saigon sought to win the civil war with the Communists in South Vietnam. The Communists were determined to continue hostilities until they were virtually assured of control over all Vietnam. To achieve the American objectives, Nixon at first set out to force the North Vietnamese government to pull its forces out of South Vietnam as a condition for American withdrawal. During the first year and a half of his administration, Nixon believed that this condition could be won through a combination of diplomatic pressure on the Russians and application of sufficient force in Southeast Asia.

To maintain public support for his strategy, Nixon accepted Laird's plan for Vietnamization: the gradual replacement of American ground units with South Vietnamese troops. In private, however, the administration continued to explore the possibility of ending the war through a knockout victory over the North Vietnamese. In September 1969 Kissinger established a special task force drawn from the NSC staff to examine new military options, including, according to Tad Szulc, possible one-time use of a nuclear device. "I refuse to believe," Kissinger reportedly told members of the task force, "that a little fourth-rate power like North Vietnam doesn't have a breaking point." The task force concluded, however, that there could be no certainty that a "savage blow," as Kissinger had termed it, would knock North Vietnam out of the war. Meanwhile Melvin Laird had learned of the project and argued strongly against it on both political and military grounds. Nixon decided not to go ahead.[45] Kissinger later wrote: "In truth I never examined [the military option] more than halfheartedly, largely because I and all members of the Administration not only wanted to end the war but yearned to do so in the least convulsive way."[46]

According to someone who participated in policy formulation at the highest level, the "savage blow" option of 1969, and other military solutions considered from time to time, were thought of as "means for shooting our way out of the saloon." However, this source conceded: "If we had taken one of these actions, and it had succeeded, it might have whetted our appetite for more. Public opinion might have changed in a very dramatic way."

Nixon does not seem to have finally abandoned the possibility for military victory—and with it his original condition for American withdrawal—until he faced the results of his decision to send American troops into Cambodia to clean out North Vietnamese staging areas on April 30, 1970. The president was not wholly unprepared for the wave of national protest that followed his televised speech announcing the incursion into Cambodia, and he had the satisfaction of knowing that, at least in the short run, he had a strong plurality of the public behind him—a Gallup poll taken in May found 50 percent approving the military attack and only 35 percent opposed.[47] The depth and extent of the protest, nevertheless, seem to have shaken his confidence that he could maintain the domestic base needed to end the war on what he had regarded as acceptable terms. Nixon's wounds were emotional as well as political—he seems to have been particularly seared by the deaths of four young men and women at Kent State University in Ohio, shot during a riotous confrontation between National Guardsmen and student demonstrators.[48] But his chief shock came from the rapidity with which opposition was mounted in Congress. On June 30 the Senate voted 58 to 37 in favor of an amendment submitted by Senators Cooper of Kentucky (a Republican moderate) and Church of Idaho (a Democratic regular) to prohibit use of funds for American military operations in Cambodia after July 1. The distribution of the vote by ideological groups was as follows:[49]

Republicans			Democrats		
	Yes	No		Yes	No
Fundamentalists	1	15	Traditionalists	1	10
Stalwarts	2	8	Centrists	8	0
Moderates	4	3	Regulars	17	1
Progressives	9	0	Liberals	16	0
Total	16	26	Total	42	11

The administration lost not only all the Democratic liberals and centrists, and all but one regular, but also all the Republican progressives and a majority of the Republican moderates. Although the House nine days later rejected the Cooper-Church amendment by a vote of 237 to 153—after the last American troops had left Cambodia—Nixon's room for maneuver had been greatly reduced.

Nixon wrote in his memoirs: "Because of the success of the Cambodia operation, I felt that now, for the first time, we could consider agreeing to a cease-fire in place in South Vietnam without first requiring that the North Vietnamese agree to withdraw their forces."[50] Circumstantial evidence indicates that, in reality, the political and social repercussions from Cambodia convinced Nixon that he could not hold out for the withdrawal of North Vietnamese troops—the only condition that would give the Saigon government a fair chance at prolonged survival. On October 7, five months after the attack on the North Vietnamese staging areas in Cambodia began, Nixon proposed in a televised address that "all armed forces throughout Indochina cease firing their weapons and remain in the positions they now hold," to be followed by complete withdrawal of American troops, according to a negotiated timetable. Nixon seemed to hedge by making complete American withdrawal contingent not only on "the proposals I am making tonight" but also on "the principles I spelled out previously"—which some commentators interpreted as including his former demand for mutual withdrawal. In essence, however, Nixon had conceded the most important issue of the war: North Vietnamese forces would remain in South Vietnam while American forces withdrew.[51]

For almost two more years negotiations with the North Vietnamese remained deadlocked by the Communists' demand that the Americans depose the Thieu regime in Saigon as a condition for ending hostilities. This Nixon would not do. (The United States also insisted on the return by the North Vietnamese of American prisoners of war as an irreducible condition for American withdrawal. But for the North Vietnamese the prisoners of war were simply a bargaining chip.) Finally, in June 1972, after Nixon's successful meeting on nuclear arms limitation with Leonid Brezhnev in Moscow, the Russians at last busied themselves to persuade the North Vietnamese to settle for a cease-fire under which each side would maintain control over areas currently occupied by its forces. Negotiations then began in earnest. Although they were delayed by Thieu's understandable reluctance to accept an agreement that he recognized would provide nothing but a short respite before the renewal of Communist attack (as though George Washington had been pressured by the French into approving a cease-fire under which British troops continued to occupy large parts of New England, Pennsylvania, and Virginia), and were set back from time to time when one side or the other tried to gain better terms, they moved inexorably toward the truce that finally was signed in Paris on January 27, 1973.

Did the United States achieve its goals in Vietnam? Not entirely, of course, in that Nixon finally accepted terms that left the Saigon regime with only a small chance for long-term survival. On the night the cease-fire went into effect, Nixon felt "a surprising sense of sadness, apprehension, and impatience"[52]—partly because of emotional letdown at the end of the ordeal, no doubt, but also because of his recognition that the settlement was only temporary for the Vietnamese. Within little more than two years, the Communists had established control over all Vietnam.

Yet the prolonged American presence, at however horrendous a cost, had not been entirely in vain. Fairly stable and prospering societies, resistant to further Communist advance, had developed in the nations of Southeast Asia outside the former Indochina. The new policies toward the Soviet Union and China had been launched without signaling any relaxation of American will. China had been given time to recover somewhat from the effects of its own cultural revolution during the 1960s, and was able, by the time the United States left Vietnam, to provide a formidable counterweight to the Soviet Union in eastern Asia. By Nixon's standards, the United States had withdrawn from Vietnam without suffering unacceptable strategic damage.

Whether this result could have been achieved sooner and with less bloodshed—American and Vietnamese—and devastation is another question. But after October 1970, at least, the Vietnamese Communists appear to have been more responsible than Nixon for prolonging the war.

Détente

Meanwhile, during 1972, Nixon had dazzled the world with his spectacular journeys to China and Russia, apparently dispelling some of the acrimony that had characterized relations between the United States and the two Communist superpowers for more than twenty-five years. In the short run, at least, these moves toward détente more than fulfilled Nixon and Kissinger's hopes that they would draw the Soviet Union and Communist China into checking each other, and would contribute to an overall reduction of international tensions. After the opening to China, the Russians became much more receptive to American initiatives for limiting the nuclear arms race. Even after Nixon had taken the supposedly reckless step of mining Haiphong harbor in North Vietnam in April 1972, the Russians the following month eagerly welcomed the American president to Moscow to conclude a preliminary nuclear arms limitation agreement. After the nuclear arms treaty was signed, the Russians helped persuade the North Vietnamese to accept a compromise settlement with the United States. In 1973 the Soviet Union pulled back from a potentially dangerous confrontation with the United States in the Middle East at the time of the Yom Kippur War.

A funny thing happened to Nixon, however, on the way to détente. Not only did the reduction of overt hostility between the West and the Communist powers naturally loosen some of the bonds of anxiety that had helped hold together the Western alliance, and further undermine readiness among the American public to accept continued risks and sacrifices in the cause of containment. But also Nixon himself seems to have developed doubts whether containment, under changed international conditions, could provide an adequate framework for the conduct of American policy.

While negotiating in Moscow and Peking with the Communist leaders, Nixon somewhat uneasily recognized that his lifelong adversaries shared some values that he treasured and that he feared might be running dry in the West: discipline, order, industry, patriotism. After his return from China, the president told his cabinet, as recorded by Safire: "Whatever the failures of their system, there is in their leader class a spirit that makes them formidable either as adversaries or—not friends—as people with whom we have some understanding. . . . The leader class in the United States sometimes lacks the backbone, the strength that they have."[53] Later he wrote in his diary: "We emphasize the material to the exclusion of the spiritual and the Spartan life [in aiding countries abroad]. . . . On the other hand, the enemy emphasizes the Spartan life, not the material, emphasizes sacrifice."[54]

Nixon did not believe that the Communists had given up the goal of world revolution. "I believe that it is essential," he observed in the talking points that he prepared for his negotiations with the Chinese leaders in Peking, "not to let the assumption exist at all on their part that their system will eventually prevail because of its superiority."[55] Until détente became a reed for his own political survival, he tried not to raise exaggerated hopes over the new relationships. In his 1973 State of the World message, he warned of the Soviet Union: "Areas of tension and potential conflict remain, and certain patterns of Soviet behavior continue to cause concern." And of China, he cautioned: "Although we have come a remarkable distance, two decades of blanket hostility cannot be erased completely in two years. In any event, our ideologies and views of history will continue to differ profoundly."[56]

Still, if the United States remained strong, and the Soviets and the Chinese continued to check each other, a prolonged period of international stability might be achieved. In that case, containment would have achieved its direct goal. What then would be the guiding concept for American foreign policy?

Nixon's answer seems to have been a form of the power game, supplemented by cautious international cooperation. Nixon talked grandly of keeping the United States "number one," but he appears to have had no real hegemonic ambitions. Though he liked to think of himself as a Wilsonian, he had little trust in altruism as a motivating force in foreign policy. He vehemently rejected return to isolationism as a viable course for the United States. The "pentagonal strategy"— set forth in a speech to midwestern news media executives in Kansas City on July 6, 1971, when the president knew, though his audience did not, that Kissinger was on his way to Peking—seems to have come closest to representing Nixon's view of what a post-détente American international policy might be like.

"What we see," the president told the news executives, "as we look ahead 5 years, 10 years, perhaps it is 15, but in any event within our time, we see five great economic super powers: the United States, Western Europe, the Soviet Union, Mainland China, and, of course, Japan. . . . When we see the world in which we are about to move, the United States no longer is in the position of complete preeminence or predominance. That is not a bad thing. As a matter of fact, it can be a constructive thing. The United States, let us understand, is still the strongest nation in the world; it is still the richest nation in the world. But now we face a situation where four other potential economic powers have the capacity, have the kind of people—if not the kind of government, but at least the kind of people—who can challenge us on every front."[57]

A system dominated by five great power concentrations, each pursuing its interests through competition, Nixon suggested, would promote general economic progress and produce a kind of watchful peace. It sounded rather like Adam Smith's model of a laissez-faire market economy in which each player "by pursuing his own interest . . . frequently promotes that of the society more effectually than when he really intends to promote it."

One flaw in such a system if only mechanically conceived, Nixon and Kissinger recognized, was that it would lack the authority of common moral purpose. Without some base in shared moral assumptions and ideals, the system would be subject to breakdown through miscalculation or inordinate ambition among the individual players (as happened in Europe in 1914) or through challenge by new political religions (as happened during the 1930s). "We must identify interests and positive values beyond security," Kissinger told the editors of the Associated Press in 1973, "in order to engage once again the commitment of peoples and parliaments. We need a shared view of the world we wish to build."[58]

Another potential flaw—less clearly recognized by Nixon and Kissinger before the oil crisis in the fall of 1973—was that the system seemed to assume passive acceptance of subordination by the nations and peoples of southern Asia, the Middle East, Africa, and Latin America—the third world. Most of the third world countries had not yet advanced very far into the industrial revolution. But their populations and their resources made them forces that would not submit indefinitely to domination by the five concentrations of power arrayed across the northern temperate zone.

Above all, the question remained open whether the Soviet Union, devoting a huge share of its economic resources to building up its military capabilities, would be content to participate in the power game as a player with limited goals, or whether it was bent on world hegemony. If the latter, the system would crumble, as it had in 1939.

As matters worked out, Nixon was not able to go very far in developing the pentagonal strategy, let alone in dealing with its potential flaws. By the end of 1973, the president's authority had been gravely weakened by public and congressional reactions to Watergate. During the first seven months of 1974, Kissinger, now secretary of state, was de facto director of most aspects of American foreign policy—a situation in which the launching of any further major initiatives was impossible.

Nixon's foreign policy legacy was a greatly transformed international geopolitical landscape. Relations had been opened with the mainland Chinese. Negotiations were under way with the Russians for further limitations on nuclear arms and for mitigation of outstanding differences. Soviet influence in the Middle East had been greatly reduced. World affairs appeared ripe for further constructive change. Whether these possibilities for change would be realized—and whether they were real or rested on illusions—remained to be tested.

Ideology and Foreign Policy

To what extent did ideology affect the Nixon administration's conduct of foreign policy? Nixon's foreign policy ideology, both before he became president and during the time he was in office, remained essentially conservative and nationalistic. Though he professed attachment to the internationalist idealism of Woodrow Wilson, a political hero of his youth, and though he was no doubt sincerely devoted to the establishment of world peace, the standard by which he measured policy seems almost always to have been the national interest of the United States, conceived as a capitalist industrial power. Experience before and during the Second World War, and association with the wing of the Republican party concerned with international trade and finance, had convinced him that America's national interest was best served through military alliances and commercial interchange with other nations. He favored, that is, an internationalist strategy as the best means for pursuing nationalist goals.

In the period after the Second World War, Nixon accepted the view, widely held among both conservatives and liberals, that American interest, as well as world peace, was critically threatened by the expansive tendencies of world communism. He favored the rigid application of the doctrine of containment to any sign of Communist territorial advance. But he never based his opposition to communism outside the United States on its inherent authoritarianism. The existence of authoritarian governments in foreign countries, Nixon said, should not directly concern the United States so long as they did not threaten American interests or security. Authoritarian regimes like that of Franco in Spain or Somoza in Nicaragua were not very nice, but were acceptable, even as allies. Some authoritarian regimes, like that of the shah of Iran, might even be appropriate for the current state of their nations' social and political development. But authoritarian regimes motivated by Communist ideologies must be resisted and opposed because the very nature of their ideology impelled them to attack American interests and to upset international stability, on which American security to a great extent depended.[59]

This part of Nixon's ideology may be said to have been based on an anti-ideology: opposition to communism because of its tendency to foment trouble for the United States. But anticommunism was not itself a basic value for Nixon, as it was for much of the anti-Communist movement (both liberal and conservative). If a Communist regime could be shown to have relaxed its antagonism toward the United States and American interests, as, for instance, the Tito regime in Yugoslavia had done, there was no necessary reason why it should not rise to the level of respectability enjoyed by Franco and Somoza.

As president, Nixon modified some of these beliefs, and at times acted contrary to some that he continued to hold. But not as much as is now generally supposed. Nixon went to China not because he believed the inner nature of the Chinese Communist regime had changed, or because he had decided that the United States should cooperate with the Communist superpowers to advance the general good of mankind, but because he had concluded that the Chinese Communist government was not going to be dislodged and was too important a power, whatever its nature or goals, to be ignored, and because he hoped that the interests of the Chinese might lead them to help block the aggressive tendencies of the Soviet Union. He accepted a compromise truce in Vietnam not because he expected the Communists to keep the peace but because he was convinced that continuation of direct American military involvement in Vietnam, with its divisive effects at home, no longer served America's national interest. He signed the nuclear arms limitation agreement with the Russians partly because he believed it would to some degree reduce the possibility of a nuclear holocaust (which would serve everybody's national interest, as well as the common interest of the human race), but also because he was persuaded that it would help maintain an acceptable balance of forces between the United States and the Soviet Union. He dealt harshly with Allende, Castro, the Syrians, and the neutralist Palme government in Sweden because he believed that these represented adversary forces with which it was not necessary for the United States to come to terms.

But would not any American administration elected in 1968, regardless of ideological preconceptions, have behaved pretty much the same? Were not Nixon and his advisers in fact the captives of external events, or their hunger for electoral approval, or the bureaucratic structures on which they depended, or some combination of all of these?

To deal with the bureaucratic structures first: presidents must of course to a great extent act through and rely for information and advice on the federal government's career civil service. Often this bureaucracy appears to have a will (or wills) of its own, and may sometimes frustrate a president's intentions, particularly on minor matters. (Presidents and their staffs, however, are not very good witnesses on the extent or effectiveness of bureaucratic obstructionism. From the perspective of the White House, even minor delays or objections in the departments are commonly viewed as monstrous insubordination.) Policymakers frequently go along with the collective judgments of their bureaucracies, either because they believe the bureaucracies know best or simply because they want to keep peace within their agencies. (D.P. Moynihan, for instance, reports that he originally recommended that the United States should not veto the admission of the Vietnams into the United Nations in 1975, largely because that was the unanimous opinion of the permanent staff of the U.S. mission at the United Nations. Moynihan was overruled by Kissinger and President Ford.)[60] But on major policy issues, only a very weak president would permit the bureaucracy to override his settled objectives. *How* the administration's objectives are to be achieved may be deeply influenced, if not determined, by an imaginative or stubborn bureaucracy, as when Laird's policy planning staff provided the plan for Vietnamization in 1969. But the overall direction of policy, and the major strategic decisions, rest with the president and his closest advisers. There was nothing in the institutional network that compelled Nixon to send Kissinger to Peking, or to settle for a truce in Vietnam, or to sign the nuclear arms treaty with the Russians. These decisions, each of which most people would agree significantly affected the course of history, were all made at the presidential level.

The view that policy decisions simply reflect the president's opinion of what will attract the most votes rests on the observation, valid in itself, that presidents are eager to win reelection or, in their second terms, to aid the election of a chosen successor. These aspirations undoubtedly influence their choice of policies. Nixon, for example, decided against a "savage blow" to produce victory in Vietnam partly because he believed to do so would produce an "uproar" among the American public and Congress. After policies are selected, presidents of course seek to present and implement them in ways that will gain maximum approval from the voters—as when Nixon arranged his return from China in 1972 so that he could go directly from the airport to appear before Congress during prime time television. But this does not turn presidents into mere vote-maximizing machines, at least not on issues that truly matter to them, as foreign policy surely mattered to Nixon. A president seeking nothing but electoral success would probably, as Nixon regularly told the American people over television, have taken the "easy road" and got out of Vietnam as quickly as possible, regardless of the strategic consequences. The China opening might not have seemed worth the risks if only votes were at stake—though Nixon's reputation as a veteran cold warrior made it politically more feasible for him to seek rapprochement with the People's Republic than it would have been for Hubert Humphrey or George McGovern. Certainly, a pure vote-maximizer would not have mined Haiphong harbor in 1972, jeopardizing the United States' whole relationship with Russia only six months before the presidential election. Nixon's foreign policy maneuvers proved popular with the voters and contributed to his landslide reelection in 1972. Even in 1974, on the eve of his departure from office, when only 26 percent of the voters still approved his overall conduct of the presidency, his foreign policy was still admired by 54 percent.[61] This resulted, however, more from the astuteness of his analyses of international conditions, and the values he shared with the voters, than from relentless calculation of which policies would prove the most popular. A president preoccupied with discovering which approaches were most likely to win maximum voter approval would probably have been less successful at developing policies that met the actual needs of the time.

Finally, external events obviously play a major part in forming the policies of an administration. Events provide the stimuli to which an administration must respond. But events do not contain their own interpretations or create the values that shape the response. If the Russians and Chinese had not split, Nixon probably would not have attempted the China opening. If the Vietnamese Communists had proved less resilient, or Congress more tractable, he would probably not have accepted a compromise truce in Vietnam. If Allende had followed a course more friendly to the United States and American business interests, the administration probably would not have worked for his overthrow. But such events do not so much determine policy as establish conditions that cause policy to be made. Humphrey might have gone to China whether or not the Russians and the Chinese had split. Goldwater or Reagan would probably have pressed on for victory in Vietnam—and would have been much more cautious negotiating with the Russians—regardless of foreign or domestic opposition. McGovern would surely not have tried to overthrow Allende.

Any politically conceivable administration taking office in 1969 would probably have sought some reduction of American commitments abroad, and would have explored the possibility of exploiting the division between the Russian and Chinese Communist regimes. But an administration of the Goldwater-Reagan right would have followed such courses more slowly and cautiously than Nixon did, and would not have approved the cuts in military spending that Nixon permitted. In general, Goldwater or Reagan would have based foreign policy on a conceptual framework that accepted the power game as self-evident and assumed the hegemonic ambitions of the Soviet Union. An administration of the Kennedy-McGovern left would have moved more quickly to get out of Vietnam; would have cut back faster and deeper on foreign defense commitments and military spending; would have sought friendly relations with Allende, Castro, Palme, and perhaps even Hanoi; and would in general have taken greater risks to move foreign policy toward a conceptual framework based on international altruism and self-interested cooperation.

The international policies pursued by the Nixon administration represented the center-right point of view that Nixon had held when he took office and that he maintained with little change throughout his presidency. Nixon's opening to China and his move toward détente with the Soviet Union expressed a shift in operational strategy. But his basic world view and his strategic goals did not greatly alter. His failure to give American foreign policy much positive content perhaps resulted from limitations inherent in his ideology, and pointed to problems that would have to be dealt with by his successors.

7

Domestic Social Policy I: Welfare Reform

DURING his tenure in the presidency, Richard Nixon devoted far more time and attention to foreign policy than to domestic social and economic policies combined. At times he spoke to his staff and even to members of the press as though he regarded his domestic responsibilities as onerous burdens, as distractions from the really important work of bargaining with the Russians or holding together the Western alliance.[1]

Yet when Nixon thought more grandly, he liked to envision a series of major domestic reforms that would fit harmoniously with his foreign policy triumphs as parts of the Augustan legacy he aimed to leave to the nation. "Nixon had a sense of architecture, in both domestic and foreign policy," Elliot Richardson has said. "Some parts of the programs were more important than others, but they all belonged to the design."[2]

The most controversial, indeed astonishing, element in Nixon's domestic program was his proposal for reform of the nation's system for providing aid to low-income families, which he presented in a televised address on August 8, 1969. The family assistance plan, as it was called, seemed to propose further expansion and centralized administration of government services—exactly the opposite of what Nixon had appeared to be promising during the campaign. Had Nixon become a liberal? Or had the administration's welfare reform program been put together by liberals in the executive branch while the president was preoccupied with foreign policy? Or was the plan somehow consistent with conservative values, as Nixon and others in the administration kept arguing?

The Rivals

Initially, Nixon had hoped to subcontract responsibility for the administration's domestic policies to Arthur Burns. When Burns resisted joining the White House staff after the 1968 election, Nixon transferred this assignment, though with more limited authority, to Daniel P. Moynihan—much to the horror of his conservative domestic advisers like Burns and Martin Anderson. "Haldeman and Ehrlichman regarded Moynihan's appointment as a master stroke," Anderson has recalled, "a way of bringing in a Democrat and giving the impression that this would indeed be an open administration, with a very broad base. They thought they could use him as a figurehead, with no real authority. But Moynihan was practically the only person in the White House, with the exception of Bryce Harlow [before the appointment of Burns], with previous experience in Washington. Not surprisingly, he turned out to be extraordinarily effective."[3]

On the day after the inauguration, Burns at last agreed to come on the staff for a limited period. Nixon then had two domestic suzerains, one an avowed conservative and the other an avowed liberal—though, in Moynihan's case, a liberal who had recently been making distinctly conservative sounds. Some former members of the White House staff have suggested that Nixon deliberately set up the competition between Burns and Moynihan as an administrative technique—like Franklin Roosevelt's practice of playing off one adviser against another. But as Stephen Hess, a political scientist and biographer of Nixon who became Moynihan's principal assistant, pointed out: "[This] had never been Nixon's style, nor was he employing internal adversaries in other parts of government. More likely Nixon slipped into this mode by inadvertence. . . . That Burns and Moynihan were given vague and overlapping jurisdictions may have most reflected the President's limited attention to domestic policy."[4]

Burns, with Anderson as his chief lieutenant, set out to implement the domestic program that he had prepared at the Pierre and that Nixon had approved, almost *in toto*, during the first cabinet meeting.

"We were very naive," Anderson has said. "We thought that, once the president had approved a policy, all we had to do was to communicate that decision to a department, or to a cabinet secretary, and the department would carry it out. That is not the way the government really operates, as we soon found out."[5]

Moynihan was not so innocent. Using the Urban Affairs Council, established by Nixon's first executive order, as his base, he set up a well-staffed secretariat, much as Kissinger was doing with the National Security Council in another corner of the White House basement. "Moynihan was expert at dealing with the president," Hess recalled. "This was, after all, the third president he had worked for. He kept a steady stream of memos flowing into Nixon, and these began to have an effect. . . . There was a competition that developed between the Burns group and the Moynihan group. In this competition Moynihan moved quickly, and Burns found that he was spending most of his time reacting to proposals developed by Moynihan's staff. Burns did a very good job at this. He was a very intelligent critic. But he did not have the time or the staff, once the administration was under way, to develop many initiatives of his own."[6]

The Nathan Plan

The test issue between the two groups became—somewhat surprisingly for a Republican administration—welfare reform. Except for rhetorical promises to get the poor "off the welfare rolls and onto the payrolls," Nixon had not given much attention to welfare during the campaign. In a statement issued about a month before the election, he had said: "One of the reasons that I do not accept—and at the present time I do not see a reasonable prospect that I will recommend—a guaranteed annual income or a negative income tax is because of my conviction that doing so first, would not end poverty, and second, while it might be a substitute for welfare, it would have a very detrimental effect on the productive capacity of the American people."[7]

Once in office, however, Nixon quickly came under pressure from the Republican governors of New York, Pennsylvania, Illinois, and Michigan, among others, to take some action to relieve the states of the rapidly growing costs of welfare, particularly the aid for families with dependent children program (AFDC), which paid benefits for children in poor families lacking an employed adult (limited in about half the states to families with fathers absent because of death, disabilities, or desertion). AFDC was specially troublesome to the governors of the urban industrial states, because benefits varied widely from state to state, depending on the level of state contributions (from a low in 1968 of average per person monthly benefits of $8.50 in Mississippi to a high of $71.75 in New York).[8] As a result, the higher welfare benefits available in the industrial states were thought to be acting like a magnet to attract poor families, including many blacks, from the low-benefits states, mainly rural and southern.[9]

Welfare was not originally among the subjects assigned to Paul McCracken's task forces set up to develop an administration program in the period just before the election. John Mitchell, however, had been bothered by this omission, and directed that a welfare task force be established. Mitchell asked John Gardner to recommend someone with professional qualifications and respectable Republican credentials to head such a task force. Gardner suggested Richard Nathan, a Brookings Institution social policy analyst who had served as chief domestic affairs adviser to Nelson Rockefeller during Rockefeller's campaign for the 1968 Republican presidential nomination. Mitchell passed along Nathan's name to McCracken, and Nathan, who already was serving as chairman of the task force on intergovernmental fiscal relations, took the additional job.[10]

Nathan's welfare task force, most of whose members were political liberals, recommended that the aid for families with dependent children problem be dealt with by establishing a minimum national standard that would require the states to pay benefits enabling recipients to maintain an average monthly budget of at least $40 per person. The federal government would pay the additional cost for the first $30 in benefits. The task force proposed further that the federal government pay 50 percent of welfare benefits per person from $30 to $70—which would provide substantial aid to the higher benefit states. The total additional federal cost, the task force estimated, would be about $900 million. The administration's ultimate goal, the task force recommended, should be "complete federal financing" of AFDC and aid to the aged, blind, and disabled.[11]

As was noted in chapter 4, Burns reacted negatively to the proposals of the Nathan task force, and advised Nixon that "another study—

whether by a special task force or some other way—is urgently needed."[12] The report, however, received a more friendly reception from Moynihan and from the new secretary of health, education, and welfare, Robert Finch. Moynihan had for years ardently championed the enactment of a federal program to pay allowances for all dependent children, regardless of family income ($12 monthly for the first child and $8 for each additional child, at a cost to the government of about $8 billion). Similar programs in Europe, Moynihan claimed, had roots in conservative as well as social democratic ideologies: "The *theory* of Family Allowance developed in Europe as an accommodation of the social theory (in this case Catholic) that holds it to be the responsibility of society to provide families with an adequate income to the modern industrial practice that gears wages to the productivity of the worker without regard to differing levels of need. . . . The *practice* began in Europe under fairly conservative regimes, usually a pronatalist policy. Soon enough, however, it became a standard feature of social-democratic welfare policies."[13] Judging the conservatism of the Nixon administration to be based on a somewhat different mixture from that which he had observed in Europe, Moynihan believed the chances that the administration would sponsor family allowances were practically nil; he therefore supported the Nathan proposal as the best available alternative. Finch, who was anxious to develop an activist and progressive image for the administration, was so taken by Nathan's recommendation of a national standard for AFDC that he endorsed the idea during an impromptu press conference held outside the White House after he visited President Johnson two weeks before Nixon's inauguration.[14]

As a means for getting welfare reform on the administration's agenda, Finch scheduled a meeting of the Urban Affairs Council welfare subcommittee (of which he was chairman) for the first week in February, to consider the proposal for a national standard. Nathan, who had joined the administration as assistant budget director, presented his task force's recommendations to the subcommittee, composed of Attorney General Mitchell, Secretary of Labor Shultz, Secretary of Agriculture Hardin, and Secretary of Commerce Stans, as well as Finch. The members of the subcommittee, all of whom were by then occupied with departmental concerns of their own, talked over the national standard idea and asked some probing questions, but adjourned without taking any action. Finch and Nathan decided independently that the proposal would have to be put into more concrete form to persuade the subcommittee to recommend it to Nixon.

The Negative Income Tax Idea

Meanwhile some holdover appointees from the Johnson administration at HEW were mulling the possibility of replacing Nathan's plan with a much bolder concept—the guaranteed annual income. As long ago as 1943, Milton Friedman, then a young economist working in the Treasury Department, had developed the idea of supplanting welfare with what he called a "negative income tax": direct payment of cash to people whose incomes were too small to make them liable for the federal income tax. The negative income tax appealed to Friedman as a means for relieving suffering among the poor without maintaining a massive welfare bureaucracy. For the plan to function as he intended, however, Friedman insisted that it must include two important conditions: first, all other forms of welfare, such as subsidized housing and school lunches, must be terminated; and second, the marginal tax rate on welfare (the rate at which welfare payments were reduced as income from other sources rose) must be kept low so that loss of welfare would not discourage welfare recipients from seeking regular jobs. To meet the second condition without continuing some welfare payments up to a relatively high level of earned income, it would be necessary to keep maximum per person benefits low—no problem for Friedman, who believed that welfare payments should not in any case provide for more than minimal subsistence.[15]

The idea for some form of guaranteed income thus entered serious political discourse in the United States under conservative auspices. It developed some vogue among conservative intellectuals, particularly after Friedman gained national visibility as Senator Goldwater's chief economic adviser in 1964. But for rank-and-file conservative and moderate voters, who tended to look upon the negative income tax as just one more way for government to give away something for nothing, it never seems to have generated much appeal. A question by the Gallup poll on a guaranteed income in January 1969 produced a response of 62 percent opposed and only 32 percent in favor.[16]

Most liberal politicians shied away from the idea, both because many of them regarded it as inherently unsound and because they believed the labor unions would oppose it out of fear that it would undermine wages. But some liberal intellectuals and government officials, including Alice Rivlin, assistant secretary of health, education, and welfare in the Johnson administration, and her deputy, Worth Bateman, were attracted by the negative income tax as a means for giving help to a group largely excluded from benefits under existing welfare programs: the "working poor"—families that included an employed adult, but nevertheless earned very low incomes. In the final year of the Johnson administration, Rivlin and Bateman urged Wilbur Cohen, who became secretary of HEW early in 1968, to endorse the negative income tax as a way to provide the working poor with incomes at least comparable to those received by persons living off welfare. Cohen, doubting the social value and political feasibility of a federal relief program for all low-income families, refused.[17]

After Nixon took office, Rivlin and Bateman, who stayed on for a few weeks before giving way to Republican successors, found the new administration's top management at HEW, including Finch and his under secretary, John Veneman, surprisingly eager to undertake major welfare reform. In this atmosphere they felt encouraged to try again, during the brief time they remained on the federal payroll, with some of the ideas that had been turned down by the Democrats. Rivlin and Bateman favored the negative income tax over Nathan's proposal for national standards because of a conscious decision that it would be better to expand coverage to the working poor than simply to increase payments to families currently living off welfare—a choice that many later participants in the welfare reform controversy either did not understand or refused to make. In a memorandum forwarded in mid-February to Finch, Bateman criticized Nathan's plan on the grounds that it would "intensify present inequities in the treatment of male and female headed families and provide increased financial incentives to break up intact households, particularly those low income families headed by a man who works." In place of national standards, Bateman proposed a "program which is income tested but provides supplementary income to all families with children." Such a program, Bateman acknowledged, "is a Negative Income Tax plan for families with children, but it could be called by a different name."[18]

At this time Finch, increasingly harried by conservative attacks on the relatively liberal policies being pursued by his department on school desegregation and other issues, turned over responsibility for welfare reform to John Veneman, who had acquired some expertise in welfare matters during the previous six years as a member of the California legislature. A self-described "passionate moderate" Republican, Veneman in 1967 had led the opposition in the legislature against Governor Reagan's attempt to reduce medicaid benefits. Reviewing Nathan's plan for national standards and Bateman's alternative proposal for a federal floor under income for all families with children, Veneman concluded that Bateman's approach would be much more far-reaching and ultimately more beneficial to most of the poor. The fact that the negative income tax would be more likely to stir up the fundamentalist conservatives was not necessarily a mark against it in Veneman's appraisal. Bateman's plan would guarantee an annual income of $1,500 for a family of four, with benefits to be reduced fifty cents for each dollar earned. The cost of the Bateman plan would be $600 million above what Nathan had estimated as the cost of national standards, but the HEW economists claimed that national standards would cost at least $300 million more than Nathan had forecast. Veneman had little difficulty in selling the shift from national standards to the negative income tax to Finch, who seems to have been anxious to propose some kind of dramatic change in welfare, without worrying too much about the substance.[19]

Moynihan, informed that Finch was coming up with a plan to guarantee incomes for families with children (one much closer to his own plan for family allowances than the Nathan plan had been), happily swung his support to the new alternative. Recognizing the unfavorable connotations that had become attached to the title "negative income tax," Finch, Veneman, and Moynihan agreed to change the name to family security system (FSS).

When the welfare subcommittee of the Urban Affairs Council reconvened on March 24, 1969, Moynihan took the lead in promoting the new plan. Martin Anderson, who attended the meeting representing Burns, recalled: "Moynihan laid out this plan that was contrary to the whole thrust of the campaign and the administration, as I understood it. To my astonishment, all of the people sitting around the table—John Mitchell and John Ehrlichman and Maurice Stans—began nodding agreement. They simply did not grasp that what he was talking about was a negative income tax."[20] Anderson attacked the plan as contrary to Nixon's announced intention during the campaign not to recommend "a guaranteed annual income or a negative income tax." The important thing, Moynihan responded, was not what Nixon had said during the campaign but what he wanted as president. Again, the subcommittee wandered off in discussion, and adjourned without reaching a decision.[21]

By this time Nixon had begun to worry over the fact that his administration, already more than two months old, had not presented any major domestic legislation. In a meeting with Burns, Finch, and Moynihan at his home at Key Biscayne, Florida, over Easter weekend early in April, Nixon pressed his advisers for some substantive legislative initiatives. Finch and Moynihan responded with the family security system. Burns was caught without an alternative.

Birth of the Family Assistance Plan

Returning to Washington, Burns worked out a complicated proposal that combined some aspects of Nathan's plan for national standards for welfare with a modest revenue-sharing program—both ideas that he had viewed critically in his original memorandum to Nixon written before the inauguration. Burns recommended that national standards for AFDC recipients be set at $40 average monthly benefits, the same figure suggested by Nathan. These standards would not be mandatory on the states, but states that did not meet the standards would not be eligible for revenue sharing. Burns also proposed an expanded job-training program and a requirement that ablebodied adult welfare recipients accept either work or job training— the so-called work requirement that Nixon insisted be included in all subsequent versions of welfare reform.[22]

Nixon readily accepted the revenue-sharing part of Burns's recommendation—too readily, in Burns's judgment. "The president sometimes would accept my arguments without hearing them out," Burns years later recalled. "This bothered me. I was able to persuade the president to go ahead with revenue sharing in two minutes. This was an achievement of which I was not very proud. It was wrong for the president to make decisions without being fully acquainted with the problem."[23]

On the issue of welfare reform, however, Nixon was faced with two competing proposals: some form of national standards or FSS. Since the president appeared undecided, the Burns group and the Moynihan group in the White House began to maneuver to win the decision. In this rivalry Burns had the advantages of long familiarity with Nixon and, presumably, greater ideological compatibility. But Burns could not match Moynihan as a bureaucratic tactician. Besides, as Bryce Harlow has recalled, "The truth is that Nixon was getting bored with Burns. He became tired of having Burns lecture him. Burns did not realize it, but he was beginning to get on the president's nerves." In addition to which, according to Harlow, "Behind the scenes, Haldeman and Ehrlichman were cutting him down." Burns, for his part, was developing serious reservations about the direction the administration was taking. One day in early spring, Burns came into Harlow's office clearly upset. He had just been talking with John Ehrlichman, Burns related, and had told Ehrlichman that the guaranteed income being pushed by Moynihan and Finch was not in agreement with the president's philosophy. Ehrlichman had laughed, Burns said, and asked, "Don't you realize the president doesn't have a philosophy?" Burns concluded: "Bryce, if that is true, our country is in serious trouble."[24]

The conflict between the two groups over welfare reform began to affect other areas of domestic policy. Kenneth Cole, who served as staff secretary at the White House in 1969 and then became deputy director of the Domestic Council under Ehrlichman, has recalled: "Confusion began to spread through the departments. Nobody was sure whether the Burns group or the Moynihan group really spoke for the administration."[25]

In this situation Nixon turned increasingly to Ehrlichman as a kind of impartial mediator. Martin Anderson has said: "Haldeman and Ehrlichman came on board [in 1968] to try to bring some order into the chaos that was engulfing the campaign. But they were regarded as political technicians. Ehrlichman made some suggestions on domestic policy during the transition period between the election and the inauguration, but they were not treated seriously by the people working on policy. When Ehrlichman became the president's counsel, this was taken as further evidence that he would have no role in domestic policy."[26] By the spring of 1969, however, Ehrlichman, under

Haldeman's sponsorship, was rapidly becoming Nixon's principal adviser on domestic affairs.

Moynihan put up no serious resistance to Ehrlichman's rise— partly because he regarded himself as primarily a producer of ideas and was glad enough to have somebody else take responsibility for implementation, partly because he usually found Ehrlichman to be an ally on policy matters.[27] Burns, on the other hand, was outraged. In conversation with a journalist friend, Burns complained that Haldeman and Ehrlichman did not understand the problems of the country, did not understand the issues they were trying to deal with. "The only thing they are interested in," Burns said, "is getting votes for the Republican party. And they don't even know how to do that."[28]

During this time George Shultz, too, was acquiring influence over matters of domestic policy that went well beyond the normal purview of the Department of Labor. "Shultz made it on brains," Stephen Hess has said. "He was barely known to the president at the time he was appointed, but he soon began to make a strong impression at meetings. His style was to hang back until others had presented their views, and then to cut through to the heart of the subject, summarizing what others had said, and giving his own opinion."[29] Early in May Nixon asked Shultz to analyze the family security system. Shultz's evaluation of FSS was generally favorable, but the plan had, he concluded, one serious flaw: the fifty-cent reduction in benefits for every dollar of earned income, when coupled with work-related expenses, would dissuade welfare recipients from seeking regular employment. Shultz's solution to this problem was to disregard the first $20 earned each week when figuring the reduction of welfare benefits for an employed person. In other words, if a worker receiving family security payments found a job paying $60 a week, he would lose only $20 in benefits, rather than $30 as called for in Bateman's draft of the plan. The added cost of the disregard to the federal government, Shultz estimated, would be $1 billion. But the increased expenditure, he argued in a memorandum to the President, "is not a welfare cost, i.e., not a payment for non-workers. Instead, it is a fundamental girder in building a solid bridge from welfare to work."[30]

Late in June Nixon directed Ehrlichman to prepare a proposal that combined the basic features of FSS with Burns's work requirement and Shultz's job incentive disregard. The president suddenly announced in the course of a Saturday afternoon meeting with his chief aides: "I've decided we should try to advance a welfare reform proposal along the lines we've been studying. It will be expensive, but in the long run the present system will be more expensive if we don't change."[31]

While Ehrlichman, assisted by Nathan and others, labored to produce a program that carried out the president's instructions, Burns sought allies for a final stand against FSS, and Moynihan and Finch worked to cement their victory. "Both Burns and Moynihan began recruiting allies, but particularly Burns," Hess recalled. "Burns tried to gather support for his point of view within the cabinet. Moynihan did not pursue that strategy. It was Moynihan's view that only the president would make the decision in the end, and that to some extent Burns was spinning his wheels in his efforts to line up support in the cabinet."[32]

On August 1, 1969, Ehrlichman, bearing a completed draft of the revised FSS, flew to Bucharest. There he met Nixon, who was visiting Rumania on the last leg of a round-the-world tour that had included the president's welcome, in the middle of the Pacific Ocean, of the astronauts returning from the first human visit to the moon. Ehrlichman carried with him a message from Burns, cosigned by Secretary of the Treasury Kennedy, Budget Director Mayo, and CEA Chairman McCracken, urging rejection of FSS. In a formal garden in Bucharest, Nixon and Ehrlichman reviewed the draft. Nixon was apparently less troubled by the objections of his economic advisers than by a last minute plea from HEW that the floor be raised to provide more adequate support. Could the floor be increased to $1,600 within the same overall cost through a moderate reduction in Shultz's disregard? Nixon asked.[33]

Two days later, back in Washington, Ehrlichman and his collaborators worked out the change the president wanted. The floor was set at $1,600, and the exempted income was reduced to $720 a year.[34]

Finally, on the morning of August 6—the same day the Senate was voting on ABM—Nixon presented the family security system to the full cabinet, meeting at Camp David. Among the eleven cabinet members present, Nixon later estimated, only Finch, Shultz, and Laird favored the plan. Vice-President Agnew was strongly opposed. Conservatives, he argued, would charge that the plan provided a guaranteed income, while liberals would claim that the benefits were shabby. Budget Director Mayo protested the cost. HUD Secretary

Romney argued that adding people to the welfare rolls would increase dependency. Burns gave his final summation of disapproval. For the most part, however, the cabinet members who opposed the plan said little, evidently regarding its sponsorship by the administration as a *fait accompli.* Melvin Laird—an experienced hand at the technique of concentrating debate on insignificant issues—complained that the title family security system sounded New Dealish. Nixon agreed. Cabinet members devoted the rest of the meeting to jotting down proposed new names for the plan. Agnew left during lunch—to go to the Senate, where he was expected to cast a tie-breaking vote on ABM. (A tie would defeat the attempt to amend ABM, but Nixon wanted the psychological lift of a majority victory for the administration.) "Mr. President," the vice-president said as he departed, "if there's a tie I may call you to see if you've changed your mind about FSS!" Everybody laughed.[35]

Two days later, on August 8, Nixon presented the administration's welfare reform proposal, as part of the domestic social program that he titled the "New Federalism," in a televised address to the nation. The welfare plan had acquired a new name: the family assistance plan (FAP). It was not, Nixon insisted, a "guaranteed income," because it included a work requirement. At the end of his talk, Nixon asked for approval of the administration's reform program "in the spirit of APOLLO"[36] (the name of the spacecraft in which the astronauts had flown to the moon)—an invocation presumably gratifying to the shade of Julian the Apostate.

Reasons for Nixon's Decision

Why did Nixon reject the advice of his conservative economic advisers and decide to sponsor a welfare reform proposal drafted by holdover liberal Democrats in HEW and promoted by a donnish Harvard intellectual who had formerly held high office under liberal Democratic presidents? Several answers have been suggested:

—Moynihan charmed him (the favorite explanation of conservatives like Burns and Anderson).

—Nixon wanted to give a victory to Finch, "the son he never had," according to some who have known both men. Finch was then already beleagured on several fronts at HEW and was beginning to acquire the look of a loser.

—The intellectual arguments for FAP, and against continued efforts to patch up the existing welfare system, were so overwhelming that Nixon was won over by the sheer logic of the case presented by Moynihan and HEW. This explanation gains plausibility from the fact that Caspar Weinberger, a conservative so dedicated to austerity that he was called "Cap the Knife" by resentful bureaucrats when he served as Nixon's budget director in 1972, was converted to support an even broader form of income guarantee after he became secretary of HEW in 1973.

—Nixon wanted to make a splash, and he recognized that FAP would get more attention than any proposal for incremental reform.

—FAP was part of Nixon's political balancing act. While the conservatives got a change in school desegregation guidelines, the liberals got FAP. Or FAP was a bone thrown to the liberals to distract them from harassing Nixon on Vietnam.

—Milton Friedman's identification with the negative income tax persuaded Nixon that it must have some conservative attributes. (Friedman, however, disowned the plan in the form that it was introduced by the Nixon administration in 1969, arguing that the marginal tax rate was too high and that too many other forms of welfare were allowed to continue.)

—The fact that FAP was supposed to do away with the welfare bureaucracy made it attractive to Nixon as a conservative measure.

—Nixon liked the idea of giving help to the working poor, a class that he had always respected and that he may have identified with because of experiences in his own childhood and youth. "Nixon had a very thin life as a child," Moynihan has said, "and his instinct was always to identify and sympathize with poor people. He did not feel that he had to apologize for his own success, as some people do who were born to wealth. But he did not think that society was operating under a perfectly equitable arrangement, and he was prepared to use government where appropriate to make this arrangement more equitable."[37]

Probably several of these factors, perhaps all, influenced Nixon's decision. In any case, FAP, for a time at least, put an end to charges that the administration had no positive domestic program.

Congressional Response

Nixon expressed satisfaction with the widely favorable response
given to the program set forth in his August 8 speech—and almost
immediately began disassembling the system that had delivered it.
Whatever the value of the product, he seems to have felt, the mess-
iness of the process should not be repeated. On November 4 Ehrlichman was formally installed as chief of the White House domestic
staff. Moynihan and Bryce Harlow were elevated to the roles of
counsellors to the president—positions in which they were held to
require no significant professional staff assistance. In January Burns
became chairman of the Federal Reserve. The Burns and Moynihan
staffs were dispersed: some were given jobs under Ehrlichman, some
were assigned to other duties, and some left government service
entirely. "After I became counsellor to the president," Moynihan
recalled, "I stopped going to staff meetings, took no further role in
administration. I stayed on at Nixon's request to help with implementation of the family assistance plan and with desegregation in the
South."[38]

Although ultimately the least successful of the proposals offered
in Nixon's New Federalism message, FAP at first attracted most
interest and activity. Hearings were held before the House Ways and
Means Committee in October 1969. Influential groups lined up behind
the plan: the Committee for Economic Development (composed of
representatives of the corporate elite); the National Association of
Manufacturers; representatives of Protestant, Catholic, and Jewish
welfare agencies (although usually with the demand that benefits be
increased). Organized labor, George Meany announced, supported
"the principles embodied in the family assistance bill proposed by
the administration," but demanded some changes—principally a
guarantee that persons in the work training programs be paid the
federal minimum wage or the prevailing wage, whichever was
higher.[39]

Conservative opposition to FAP at first centered on the national
Chamber of Commerce, which charged that the administration's plan
would create "the beginning of a national guaranteed income arrangement." On the left, the National Welfare Rights Organization,

a small but militant organization of welfare recipients, led by George A. Wiley, a flamboyant activist who had once been a chemistry professor at Syracuse University, denounced the plan as "anti-poor and anti-black . . . a flagrant example of institutional racism." In place of FAP, the welfare rights organization demanded a guaranteed annual income of $5,500, to approach the goal of "an adequate income for everyone." This plan, according to a government estimate, would cost $71 billion a year, and would bring more than half the population under welfare.[40]

In December Wilbur Mills, chairman of Ways and Means, commented: "The public isn't ready for [FAP]—and won't be for years." Two months later, however, under prodding from Congressman Hale Boggs of Louisiana, the House Democratic whip and second-ranking Democrat on Ways and Means, and Congressman John Byrnes of Wisconsin, the ranking Republican, Mills announced that he would support FAP, and predicted that his committee would send it to the floor.[41] Opposition to FAP on Ways and Means was led by Congressman Al Ullman of Oregon (later chairman of the committee), a Democratic centrist, who expressed himself "shocked . . . almost to the point of being speechless" by the administration proposal. "It looks to me," Ullman told Finch during the October hearings, "like you are opening up the Treasury of the United States in a way it has never been opened up."[42] On March 5, 1970, Ways and Means approved FAP by a bipartisan majority of 21 to 3. Ullman was joined only by Congressmen Burleson of Texas and Landrum of Georgia, both Democratic traditionalists, in voting no.[43]

Appearing before the House Rules Committee in April to obtain floor clearance for the bill, Mills, by now a firm advocate, described FAP as the "only ray of hope" for ending the "welfare mess."[44] On April 16 the House passed FAP by a vote of 243 to 155. Republican fundamentalists and Democratic traditionalists, as was shown in chapter 5, voted heavily against the bill. But Republican stalwarts, held in line by Minority Leader Ford, were overwhelmingly in favor, as were Republican moderates and progressives and Democratic regulars and liberals. Democratic centrists divided evenly, 21 to 21.[45]

On April 29—the day before Nixon sent American troops into Cambodia—the Senate Finance Committee, chaired by Senator Russell Long of Louisiana, opened hearings on FAP. Finch, Veneman, and Moynihan entered the hearing room in a euphoric mood—a humor that, as Moynihan has recorded, they quickly lost. In his opening remarks, before introducing Finch, Long complained: "Work disincentives are a feature of the present law which we should certainly try to remove. Unfortunately, [FAP] does little more than perpetuate and enlarge upon these work disincentives."[46]

After delivering the prepared testimony, Finch found himself under aggressive interrogation by conservative members of the committee, particularly Senator John Williams of Delaware, a Republican stalwart then completing his fourth and final term in the Senate. Under FAP, Williams pointed out, many welfare recipients would actually have less "spendable income" if they found jobs, because as their earned income increased they would be disqualified from receiving various kinds of welfare benefits. In New York City, for instance, under FAP a family of four with annual earned income of $720 could receive $3,888 in direct welfare payments, $522 in food stamps, $1,153 in average medical benefits, and $2,052 in public housing benefits, for total income and benefits of $8,298—$272 more than a worker with the same size family who had a regular job paying $9,599 would have left after taxes![47]

Finch and Veneman, who also testified, tried to argue that Williams's examples were extreme, and that, in any case, the worker would be no more unfairly penalized than under existing law. But Williams persisted: "Aren't you trying to correct the inequities in the law, or are you just trying to proceed and write in all the economic weights and expand them?"[48] What Williams had got on to, as Moynihan later admitted, was that FAP was not in fact welfare reform at all in the sense of cleaning up welfare abuses permitted by the existing law—the sort of thing that Nixon had seemed to be talking about during the campaign—but rather reform in the sense of trying to correct inequities in the way the social system dealt with poverty. As Moynihan wrote: "The planners of FAP had no idea how absurd the welfare system had become. It *did* invite abuse, and needed changes directed to the elimination of abuse. Once the Senate Finance committee began to press the point, the case for FAP as welfare reform was bound to collapse."[49]

At the end of the third day of hearings, Long announced that Finch had agreed to take FAP back to the executive branch and "devise an overall plan for welfare reform which will take account of the benefits such as public housing, food stamps, etc., which are made available to low income families." Williams added: "We had no objections, in fact we have a responsibility, to take care of those who through no fault of their own, are unable to work. But the time comes when we should end a program which rewards idleness and discourages personal initiative of those who can provide for themselves. I think that with all of us working together, this can be done."[50]

The administration, to say the least, had not been adequately prepared for the onslaught. "We were taken by surprise," Veneman later conceded. "While the bill was in the House, I went to see a few of the senators, but John Williams told me not to bother with people in the Senate until the bill had passed the House. Looking back afterward, I felt sure that Williams had set out to block the bill from the start."[51]

On May 18 Finch, while preparing to go before a conclave of HEW employees gathered to protest Nixon's invasion of Cambodia, suffered a physical collapse. "I had burned myself out," he later explained. "I let myself become too much involved on too many fronts. Besides all the problems that I was dealing with at HEW, I was constantly being called to the White House to advise the president on problems that had nothing to do with HEW."[52] In the view of one of his subordinates at HEW, "Finch spent so much time playing the White House game that he didn't begin to learn the HEW game until it was too late." On June 6 Nixon moved Finch to his own staff as another of the growing group of counsellors to the President, and appointed Elliot Richardson secretary of HEW.

Richardson, the product of an established Massachusetts family, many of whose members had been medical doctors, had played an active role in various fields of social policy since serving as assistant secretary of HEW in the Eisenhower administration. The Republican party, he had concluded, should observe what he called, borrowing from the law, a "principle of rest"—acceptance that some issues had been settled once and for all and should not be reopened. Most of the New Deal reforms, he believed, were now in this category. The issues that currently needed to be debated were chiefly questions of process: how social needs, like welfare assistance for the poor and more accessible health care, which almost everybody acknowledged, could be satisfied without infringing unduly on other values, such as personal freedom or economic productivity. The family assistance plan, he was persuaded, offered just the kind of procedural reform that it should be the special mission of a Republican administration to undertake.[53]

On July 21, 1970, Richardson went before the Senate Finance committee with a revised version of FAP. Under the new plan, prepared by the HEW technicians, there would be less chance that a worker would actually lose real income by earning more money at his job. To make this improvement, however, it had been necessary to lower some welfare benefits. Long and Williams were little impressed. Under the new version, Long claimed, "thousands of welfare recipients would be cut off the rolls, and many thousands more would find their welfare payments reduced substantially."[54]

The changes made in the bill, not unnaturally, caused George Wiley and his National Welfare Rights Organization to step up their attacks. In November Wiley persuaded Senator Eugene McCarthy of Minnesota, who had decided not to seek reelection in 1970 after losing his bid for the Democratic presidential nomination in 1968, to hold hearings that would give some actual welfare recipients an opportunity to testify. The members of the organization who appeared at McCarthy's hearings concentrated their criticisms on FAP's work requirement. For instance, Mrs. Ethel Camp, a mother of five, separated from her husband and living on about $5,400 in welfare benefits and food stamps, testified, to the accompaniment of cheers and applause from others in the hearing room: "We only want the kind of jobs that will pay $10,000 or $20,000. . . . We aren't going to do anybody's laundry or babysitting except for ourselves."[55]

On November 20 the Finance Committee rejected a one-year trial of FAP by a vote of 10 to 6. Long, after a personal appeal from Nixon, ultimately voted to send the bill to the floor, as did two Democratic regulars (Ribicoff and Fulbright), two Republican fundamentalists (Bennett and Jordan), and a Republican stalwart (Miller). Voting in the negative were Williams, three Republican fundamentalists (Curtis, Fannin, and Hansen), two Democratic traditionalists (Talmadge and Byrd), two Democratic liberals (McCarthy and Harris), a Democratic regular (Gore), and a Democratic centrist (Anderson—reportedly influenced by Harris).[56] The bill's chances evidently suffered from the lack of Republican progressives or moderates on the Finance committee, and even more from the defection of the Democratic liberals, for which Wiley and his welfare rights organization claimed chief credit. "It's a big win," Wiley told a reporter for the *Washington Star* after the vote.[57]

The Second Round

The next year, facing a Congress slightly more conservative as a result of the midterm election, the administration tried again with family assistance. In his 1971 State of the Union message—in which the New Federalism was briefly, and grandiosely, retitled "the New American Revolution"—Nixon announced: "I will call upon Congress to take action on more than 35 pieces of proposed legislation. . . . The most important is welfare reform."[58] To make the bill more acceptable to liberals, the administration, on Wilbur Mills's advice, agreed to raise the income guarantee for a family of four from $1,600 to $2,400, while making welfare recipients ineligible for food stamps. The change increased the cost of FAP by $6 billion.

Mills again guided the bill through the House. Opposition in the House, however, was much greater than it had been in 1970. On June 22, 1971, a motion by Congressman Ullman to delete family assistance from H.R.1, a comprehensive welfare–social security bill cosponsored by Mills and Byrnes, was rejected by only 187 to 234—a decline of 41 votes in the margin by which FAP had passed the House in 1970. Slippage was particularly heavy among Democratic liberals, who had voted 67 to 1 for FAP in 1970 (Congressman Shirley Chisholm of New York being the only liberal in opposition). In 1970, 20 of the 60 liberals voting supported Ullman's motion. Eleven of the 12 black liberal Democrats in the House, possibly influenced by Wiley's charge that FAP was "racist," supported deletion of family assistance from H.R.1.[59]

As in 1970, FAP once more came up against an apparently insurmountable barrier of opposition in the Senate Finance Committee. Senator Abraham Ribicoff of Connecticut, who had voted for FAP in the Finance Committee in 1970, proposed to get around this roadblock by offering his own version of family assistance as an amendment to another bill on the Senate floor. Ribicoff's amendment, however, raised the guarantee for a family of four to $3,000 a year—almost double Nixon's initial proposal—and contained other liberalizing features, which together, according to his own estimate, would increase the annual cost of welfare by $13 billion.[60]

Lengthy negotiations followed between Richardson and Ehrlichman, representing the administration, and Ribicoff, representing a group of liberal and regular Democratic senators who appeared to hold the balance of power on FAP. On June 16, 1972, Richardson recommended to Nixon that the administration compromise with Ribicoff on a guarantee of $2,600 for a family of four, plus cost-of-living increases in the future. By then, however, the 1972 presidential campaign was under way, and George McGovern had proposed his famous "demogrant"—a plan to pay every man, woman, and child in the United States $1,000 a year, taxable at the same rates as ordinary income. (The demogrant was, in effect, a form of guaranteed income with a very high break-even point, so that it would extend some welfare benefits to about half the population.) In the California primary, held on June 6, Hubert Humphrey had come from far behind to a relatively close finish with McGovern, chiefly by publicizing what he held to be the likely destabilizing social and economic effects of the demogrant. Nixon, who sensed that attacking McGovern's plan promised more political profit than securing passage of a more costly version of FAP, declined to compromise with Ribicoff. This killed any chance for welfare reform in 1972.

In the winter of 1978, looking back on the failed effort at compromise six years before, Richardson said: "It never occurred to me to resign on the welfare issue. I disagreed with the president's judgment on the matter, but I recognized that there was a lot to be said on the president's side. He would have had a tremendously difficult time delivering on the compromise, even if he had wanted to. McGovern's gaffe had created an embarrassment among the liberals. It had put them on the defensive on the issue. . . . The president had already gone far beyond his original proposal. To accept the Ribicoff compromise would have been to accept a bill more liberal than that passed by the House, which itself had been a compromise."[61]

On October 3, 1972, a month before the presidential election, Ribicoff's amendment, unsupported by the administration, came before the Senate. A motion by Russell Long to table and thus kill the amendment carried by a vote of 52 to 34. The distribution of the vote by ideological groups was as follows (a yes vote being a vote to kill FAP in the form proposed by Ribicoff):[62]

Republicans			Democrats		
	Yes	No		Yes	No
Fundamentalists	15	1	Traditionalists	9	0
Stalwarts	7	4	Centrists	12	1
Moderates	2	3	Regulars	6	4
Progressives	0	7	Liberals	1	14
Total	24	15	Total	28	19

The distribution of the vote tends to bear out Richardson's contention that even with Nixon's support the Ribicoff amendment would still have faced an uphill fight. Even if the administration had been able to switch all the Republican stalwarts and moderates who voted in favor of the tabling motion—an unlikely achievement—the amendment would still have been one vote short of passage.

On October 17, 1972, Congress gave final approval to H.R.1, stripped of any form of family assistance, but containing a program for supplementary security income, which in effect provided a guaranteed annual income for the elderly, blind, and disabled. With little public notice, Congress thereby accepted the principle of the guaranteed income for a portion of the population—though not for poor families with children, the proposed beneficiaries of Nixon's original bill.

The Weinberger Plan

At the beginning of Nixon's second term, Caspar Weinberger, who replaced Richardson as secretary of HEW in 1973, ordered a thorough review of the entire welfare issue. After examining the results of this study, Weinberger concluded, essentially, that the administration had been on the right road all along: the best way to deliver welfare benefits at minimum cost to the truly needy was through a system of cash allowances, backed up by a strict work requirement. On November 13, 1974, Weinberger presented a new plan called the income supplemental plan to President Ford, who had replaced Nixon three months before. Under this plan, cash benefits, amounting to $3,600 a year for a nonworking family of four, paid through the Internal Revenue Service, would completely replace not only AFDC but also food stamps and supplementary security income.[63] Milton

Friedman praised Weinberger's plan as coming closer than any of the previous efforts to his original negative income tax idea.[64]

At Ford's direction Kenneth Cole, then heading the Domestic Council, asked Martin Anderson, long since moved on to the Hoover Institution at Stanford, to head an ad hoc group to evaluate the income supplemental plan. Anderson had the satisfaction of winning the current round in the argument that he and Burns had lost in 1969. His group concluded that the HEW analysts had "grossly underestimated the costs and grossly overestimated the benefits" of the new proposal.[65] Partly because Anderson's verdict was negative, and partly because economic conditions were not favorable to the introduction of a major new domestic program, Ford decided not to go ahead with Weinberger's proposal—and that was that for welfare reform in the period of the Nixon and Ford administrations.

The Flaw in FAP

Whatever its substantive merits, the proposal for a guaranteed income for families with children had at least the pragmatic flaw that it lacked the political qualities needed to achieve passage. To produce practical results, therefore, Nixon evidently would have been wiser in 1969 to have sponsored some form of the proposal for national standards for welfare, first recommended by Nathan and finally favored by Burns. The effects of the Nathan plan, while less far-reaching than those projected for the family assistance plan, would have been important: poor families in some of the southern states would have more than tripled their incomes; the industrial states would have received significant help with their fiscal problems; and the disparity in benefits paid by welfare systems in different parts of the country would have been greatly reduced. The plan for national standards would undoubtedly have encountered strong opposition, from some of the same sources that opposed FAP, but it probably was simple enough and broad enough to have passed.

FAP, by contrast, created concern all across the political spectrum about just the kind of incalculable side effects that conservatives regularly warn against. Its originality and complexity made it an easy target for those who, out of varying motives, decided to oppose it. The briefing of the cabinet at Camp David in August 1969, Moynihan wrote, "had scarcely begun before a fact of first importance became unmistakably clear. *The proposal was hard to understand.* Burns, from the beginning, had sensed that this would make it easy to misrepresent, and in this as in much else he proved altogether correct."[66] (Emphasis in the original.)

In its origins, FAP rose from bold and imaginative analyses in some ways similar to those that produced Nixon's major foreign policy initiatives. Unlike the move toward détente with the Russians or the opening to China, however, FAP failed in the end to provide a usable channel through which to guide the flow of events. Chronic poverty among a minority (or minorities) cut loose by the industrial system remained a national problem for which American society had not yet found a solution. Proposed remedies seemed either to discourage low wage earners from working to increase their incomes, or to place politically unacceptable burdens on the middle class, or both. FAP represented a daring attempt to break through this dilemma, but it turned out to be, at best, as Nixon later conceded, "an idea ahead of its time."[67]

8

Domestic Social Policy II:
The New Federalism

NIXON'S New Federalism, first presented to the public in his television address on August 8, 1969, was a legislative program before it was rationalized into a governmental theory. Perhaps for this reason, the theory of the New Federalism, when it was worked out by William Safire and Richard Nathan during the winter of 1969–70, never seemed to fit snugly around all elements of the program, especially the family assistance plan. This does not mean, however, that the New Federalism did not express fairly consistent social values and attitudes. Revenue sharing, which with FAP was one of the two principal elements in the original program, in particular was based on goals and assumptions that form essential parts of modern ideational conservatism.[1]

Origins of Revenue Sharing

Revenue sharing—the distribution of federal aid to state and local governments through broad money grants, to be spent for purposes determined by the recipient units, rather than through payments for narrowly defined and closely regulated "categorical" programs—had a diverse political history. The idea was first proposed in the 1820s by Henry Clay as part of his "American System," which became the basis for the Whig party's domestic program. The first revenue-sharing bill in modern times was introduced in the House in 1958 by Melvin Laird, who remained a strong proponent thereafter. In the Johnson administration, Walter Heller, chairman of the Council of Economic Advisers, recommended that projected federal surpluses be distributed to the states to spend for purposes of their own choosing. Johnson set up a task force, headed by Joseph Pechman, director of economic studies at the Brookings Institution, to evaluate Heller's proposal. Though initially opposed to revenue sharing, Pechman came to support the idea, chiefly because he concluded that turning federal surpluses over to the states for expenditure on services would be socially more beneficial than making further cuts in federal taxes. In the fall of 1964, the Pechman task force recommended to Johnson a plan under which a fixed percentage of the federal income tax would be set aside for distribution to the states, which were to have almost unlimited discretion in how they used the money. Johnson, however, rejected what became known as the Heller-Pechman plan—reportedly in part because he was annoyed that it had received premature publicity in the press.[2]

Advocacy of revenue sharing then shifted mainly to the Republicans, and particularly to Republican governors of the major industrial states, like Romney of Michigan and Rockefeller of New York, who viewed the plan as a potential source of relief from their growing fiscal problems. Although revenue sharing was most closely identified with the progressive wing of the Republican party, it held attraction for most ideological shades of Republicans, largely because it could be presented as a means for implementing the party's almost united support for strengthening the roles of state and local governments. Some fundamentalists, however, opposed it on the grounds that it was just one more way of promoting the continued growth of government, state and local as well as federal; and that government funds should be raised at the level at which they are spent.

Proponents of revenue sharing were divided, as Paul Dommel has pointed out, over whether funds distributed under the program were to be a *replacement* for federal money transferred to state and local governments under existing categorical programs (that is, programs for narrowly defined purposes in areas like education, health care, and municipal services), or an *addition* to the categorical programs. The replacement approach, which was favored by Laird and most of the conservative supporters of revenue sharing, was designed purely to give the states and localities more freedom in the way they spent federal subsidies. The "add-on" approach, which was contained in a bill introduced in 1965 by Congressman Ogden Reid of New York, a progressive Republican (later a Democrat), was intended to provide the state and local governments with more federal money, as well as to give them increased administrative freedom.[3]

During the 1968 campaign Nixon announced: "Generally, I favor a no-strings approach to the sharing of federal tax revenues with local and state governments."[4] Whether he supported the replacement or the add-on concept of revenue sharing, Nixon left unclear.

Before accepting the chairmanship of Nixon's preelection welfare task force, Richard Nathan was already serving as chairman of another task force dealing with intergovernmental fiscal relations. The report of the intergovernmental fiscal relations task force, submitted to Nixon at the end of November 1968, recommended a revenue-sharing program through which one-half of 1 percent of federal revenues from the personal income tax (about $1.8 billion in 1969) would be distributed to state and local governments. These funds, the task force recommended, should be "a supplement to existing federal aids." The Nathan task force also recommended consolidating many categorical aid programs into broad "block grants" in "functional areas," such as education, which would give states and localities more administrative leeway.[5]

Nixon's Proposal

Following the advice of Arthur Burns, Nixon at first moved slowly on revenue sharing. As part of his strategy against FAP, however, Burns early in the spring of 1969 shifted to a position of advocacy for revenue sharing, and the plan began to advance inside the administration. In April Nixon appointed an interagency committee on revenue sharing, which included Burns, Nathan, and Assistant Secretary of the Treasury Murray Weidenbaum. Nathan and Weidenbaum thereafter became the principal drafters of the administration's revenue-sharing program.

In a meeting with representatives of the National Governors' Conference, the Conference of Mayors, and other organizations of state and local government officials at the White House on July 8, 1969, administration officials were able to head off a potential dispute between the state and local governments over how the federal funds were to be distributed. Participants in the meeting tentatively agreed that distribution to the states would be through a formula based on population and the state's own tax effort; and that there would be a mandatory pass-through requirement directing each state to forward to its localities a share of the federal funds proportionate to the percentage of state-local revenues raised by local government in that state.[6] In other words, since California took a higher percentage of its citizens' incomes in taxes than New Hampshire, California would receive a proportionately greater share per person of revenue-sharing funds; and within California, the state would forward to the localities about 50 percent of the total grant, since that was the portion (approximately) of state-local revenues raised in the state by local governments.

After including revenue sharing among the programs called for in his speech on August 8, 1969, Nixon set forth details of the plan in a message to Congress on August 13. The president's message recommended that the federal government set aside one-third of 1 percent of the revenues from the personal income tax (about $500 million) in the first year the plan was in operation for distribution to the states and localities; the percentage of income tax revenues set aside was then to rise until it reached 1 percent in fiscal 1976 (producing, with expected economic growth, about $5 billion).[7]

As prospects for enactment of welfare reform declined during 1970, John Ehrlichman gradually concluded that the administration should make revenue sharing the top priority item in its domestic program. Nixon proved hard to convince. Revenue sharing, he complained, lacked political "sex appeal."[8] But another factor had entered the picture. Nixon had been persuaded by his economic advisers, Paul McCracken and George Shultz, that the budget should be "balanced at full employment"; that is, designed to produce a deficit corresponding to the difference between actual revenues and the revenues that federal taxes would bring if the economy were operating at full employment. The resulting fiscal stimulus, they argued, would lift the economy toward actual full employment. To reach this target deficit, it would be necessary to increase federal expenditures. The added funds, Nixon decided, could be spent more advantageously on revenue sharing than on increased support for categorical programs.

Toward the end of July 1970, Nixon, in the course of a budget review conference at his home in San Clemente, California, directed that the revenue-sharing program be expanded and pushed during 1971.[9] During the fall Edwin Harper, one of Ehrlichman's assistants, directed a portion of the Domestic Council staff to comb the list of categorical programs in search of items that could be replaced by revenue sharing. Harper applied to each program a fourfold test devised by Raymond Waldman, another member of the Domestic Council staff. Was there a need for national consistency in administration of the program? Was the federal government "absolutely" more efficient in providing the service? Was there need for a "federal cutting edge"? Was there an "overriding necessity" for federal participation? (The last category evidently included political as well as fiscal considerations.) If a program did not pass any of these tests, it was marked for elimination.[10]

The amount to be allotted for revenue sharing was not finally determined until all the rest of the budget had been put together. According to Harper: "We simply subtracted the cost of everything else in the budget from the figure that would balance the budget at full employment and what was left over went for revenue sharing. The final number was teletyped from Washington to San Clemente just before New Year's Day [1971]."[11]

The revised plan was proposed to Congress by Nixon in his State of the Union message on January 22, 1971. It provided $5 billion for general revenue sharing—up from $1 billion in 1969—to be divided about evenly between the states and the localities. Also, the president proposed taking $10 billion from existing categorical programs and adding an extra $1 billion in new money to provide $11 billion for "special revenue sharing"—block grant programs in six broad functional areas: education, urban development, transportation, job training, rural development, and law enforcement.[12] Nixon's plan thus looked both ways in the division between those who viewed revenue sharing as a means for replacing categorical programs and those who thought of it as an addition to existing programs. General revenue sharing was to be a substantial add-on, while special revenue sharing was to be accompanied by elimination of many of the categorical programs.

Most members of Nixon's cabinet knew nothing of the plan for special revenue sharing, which would profoundly affect the operations of their departments, until informed of it in briefings by Ehrlichman, Shultz, and Nathan during the week before Nixon spoke to

Congress. HUD Secretary Romney expressed outrage over having been kept so long in the dark. When Nathan described the plan at a meeting of the full cabinet, however, there was little controversy. "That's what we're all for," Attorney General Mitchell said after Nathan had finished his presentation. Nobody disagreed.[13]

Action by the House

A Gallup poll released on January 24 showed 77 percent in favor of revenue sharing and only 14 percent opposed.[14] But reaction in Congress was cool at first. Part of the reason that Wilbur Mills had reversed his position and decided to support the family assistance plan was that he thought it would help block revenue sharing, which he viewed as a fiscal monstrosity. John Byrnes of Wisconsin, the ranking Republican on Ways and Means, who had helped win Mills over to FAP, was opposed to revenue sharing on both fiscal and philosophical grounds. "If Uncle Sam raises the money," Byrnes recalled arguing to the president, "Uncle Sam should pretty much determine how it is spent."[15] On January 25, 1971, Mills announced that Ways and Means would hold hearings on revenue sharing, "not for the purpose of promoting the idea—for the purpose of killing it."[16]

Mills's attitude was probably shared by a large majority in the House at that time. Members of Congress were naturally reluctant to allow federal funds to be used to finance programs for which state and local officials would receive political credit. As Congressman John Brademas of Indiana put it: "They [the state and local officials] don't even invite us to the ribbon-cutting ceremonies."[17] William Timmons, who had succeeded Harlow as director of congressional liaison for the administration, has said: "It went against a very basic instinct of Congress to turn over tax money voted by Congress to other units of government to spend with no strings attached."[18] Many members of congressional committees dealing with categorical programs were particularly hostile to revenue sharing, not only because they viewed it as a political threat but also because they were concerned that their favorite programs might not be continued by state and local governments given unrestricted use of federal funds.

Revenue sharing, however, had a powerful constituency: the elected officials of state and local governments, many of whom were by now facing fiscal crises of staggering proportions. Some of the governors and mayors regarded special revenue sharing with considerable skepticism, since the special-interest lobbies that promoted the categorical programs in Washington were helpful in shaking loose federal dollars, and the officials hesitated to upset mutually profitable alliances. But general revenue sharing was an unconditioned boon. Senators and representatives found themselves under heavy pressure from government officials in their home bailiwicks, some of whom controlled parts of the political machinery on which they depended for election. One member of the Ways and Means Committee, Sam Gibbons of Florida, was warned by the president of the Florida state senate that he would be redistricted out of his seat if he did not vote for revenue sharing.[19] Another congressman, Louis Stokes of Ohio, who viewed revenue sharing with considerable misgivings, was forcefully lobbied by his brother and political ally, Carl Stokes, the mayor of Cleveland.[20]

By the middle of 1971, even Wilbur Mills had begun to waver. Mills had developed a farfetched ambition to run for president in 1972. Continued opposition to revenue sharing, he seems to have concluded, would make him anathema to the local political leaders whose support he hoped to obtain at the Democratic National Convention. Mills, therefore, produced a revenue-sharing plan of his own. Under his plan all funds would go to local governments, where, Mills argued, the most serious fiscal problems were to be found.[21] Mills's exclusion of the states was perhaps not unrelated to the fact that most of the major states were then governed by Republicans.

After many months of negotiations, Mills and the administration agreed on a compromise, under which a general revenue-sharing program, paying benefits to both state and local governments, would be authorized for five years. In the first year $5.3 billion would be distributed, with two-thirds going to local governments and one-third to the states. In subsequent years the states' share would increase, until by the fifth year the states would receive $3 billion and the local governments $3.5 billion.[22]

Before taking a bill to the floor, Mills always aimed to build not merely a majority but a broad consensus of support on Ways and Means. To develop such a consensus behind revenue sharing, the chairman acceded to the inclusion of numerous special factors in the distribution formula. Of the twenty-five members of Ways and Means in 1972, no less than fifteen came from the urban-industrial states of the Northeast, the Great Lakes region, and the Pacific coast. To win the backing of these members, Mills accepted a provision in the formula giving special bonuses for heavily urbanized areas. Bonuses were provided for areas with large concentrations of low-income families—a factor appealing to members of the committee from relatively low income southern and border states as well as from core cities in the Northeast. Also, benefits were linked to the amount each state collected through its own income tax—a provision particularly helpful to two states with high income taxes, New York and California, both of which had two members on the committee. To satisfy members representing small towns and rural townships, a provision in the bill limiting benefits to localities with populations over 2,500 was dropped. Congressman James Corman of California later admitted: "We finally quit, not because we hit on a rational formula, but because we were exhausted. And finally we got one that almost none of us could understand at the moment."[23]

On April 17, 1972, Ways and Means voted by a majority of 18 to 7 to send revenue sharing to the floor. Voting in the negative were John Byrnes and two other Republicans, and Sam Gibbons and three other Democrats.[24]

Five weeks later, on May 23, Mills went before the House Rules Committee, seeking a closed rule for the bill that would prohibit amendments on the floor—the customary procedure for bills reported by Ways and Means. Congressman George Mahon of Texas, chairman of the Appropriations Committee, appeared before the Rules Committee to oppose the request for a closed rule by his frequent ally Mills, on the ground that revenue sharing should be subjected to the regular annual appropriations process—a change that revenue-sharing proponents feared would undermine the program as a reliable support for state and local budgets. The Rules Committee approved the closed rule by a vote of 7 to 6.[25] The one-vote margin was provided by Congressman Spark Matsunaga of Hawaii, who after initial skepticism shifted over to support of the bill at the request of his state's governor, John Burns.[26]

Both sides prepared for what seemed likely to be a close division on the floor. The bill was supported by both the Democratic and Republican House leaderships, as well as by the administration; it was opposed by an unusual combination of liberals who distrusted the priorities of state and local governments, conservatives who viewed revenue sharing as another spending program, and self-interested congressmen who disliked funding expenditures for which they would be unable to take political credit. Richard Cook, Timmons's assistant in the House, has recalled a conference of the bill's supporters as the floor vote approached: "We met in [Speaker] Carl Albert's office. There were governors and mayors there, and the floor leaders of both parties. Everyone was assigned a list of members to go out and line up. Governor Rockefeller [of New York] enthusiastically left the office with a list of fifteen members that he said he would be good for. Mayor Moon Landrieu of New Orleans left with another list. It was one hell of a coalition!"[27] Majority Leader Hale Boggs later said it was the only time in his experience in the House when floor leaders of the two parties exchanged vote counts.[28]

In the floor debate John Byrnes taunted Mills by quoting criticisms of revenue sharing that the Ways and Means chairman had made in times past.[29] On June 21 opponents of the bill planned to challenge the closed rule, so that an amendment could be offered to make revenue-sharing funds dependent on regular appropriations, as Mahon had demanded. Congressman T. P. O'Neill of Massachusetts (later House majority leader and Speaker), a supporter of the bill, moved to end debate on adoption of the closed rule. O'Neill's motion carried, 223 to 185. The bill thereby passed what had been expected to be its most difficult test, and approval of revenue sharing appeared assured. The distribution of the vote on O'Neill's motion by ideological groups was as follows (a yes vote being a vote in favor of retaining the closed rule):[30]

Republicans			Democrats		
	Yes	No		Yes	No
Fundamentalists	45	38	Traditionalists	6	40
Stalwarts	33	16	Centrists	27	41
Moderates	21	3	Regulars	43	24
Progressives	14	0	Liberals	34	23
Total	113	57	Total	110	128

As this distribution shows, ideology was by no means irrelevant to the division of the House on revenue sharing.[31] Democratic traditionalists—conservatives relatively uninfluenced by the White House—voted overwhelmingly with the opposition. Republican moderates and progressives were even more overwhelmingly in favor, which suggests that moderates and progressives found revenue sharing a particularly apt expression of their kind of Republicanism.

Other factors besides ideology, however, were clearly at work. Two of the most ideologically consistent groups in the House, Republican fundamentalists and Democratic liberals, were deeply split on the issue. (Without the affirmative votes of 13 Democratic liberals from New York, the liberals divided on the issue almost evenly: 21 to 23.) The bill, apparently, gave off mixed ideological signals. As a result, more parochial interests held sway with many members. In some state delegations a single strong political leader seems to have exerted determining influence. Of the 38 New York congressmen voting on the O'Neill motion, all but 2 took the side of revenue sharing—which suggests that Governor Rockefeller may have been good for most of the 15 members on his list. In the Texas delegation, 22 of the 23 members voting joined George Mahon in opposing the motion. The special interests of dominant members of the committees handling categorical programs also seem to have been influential: of the 11 chairmen of such committees voting on the O'Neill motion, 10 voted in the negative. The Appropriations Committee also contributed a large block of negative votes—of the 26 members of Appropriations recorded, 19 voted no.

The next day, June 22, revenue sharing carried on final passage by a vote of 275 to 122—a margin 115 votes larger than had been achieved on the motion to retain the closed rule.[32]

Final Enactment

The Senate Finance Committee, fresh from scuttling welfare reform for the second time, now turned its attention to revenue sharing. Russell Long and his colleagues on the Finance Committee, it soon became apparent, were prepared to vote out a bill—but only after making major changes in the distribution formula approved by the House. Senate Finance in 1972 comprised five members from the southern and border states, six from the Rocky Mountain and Great Plains states, four from the Great Lakes states, and only one (Ribicoff of Connecticut) from the Northeast or Pacific region. The only senator on the committee representing one of the ten most populous states was Robert Griffin of Michigan, the most junior member on the Republican side. Not surprisingly, the committee proceeded to remove the factors in the House distribution formula that related benefits to urbanization and state income tax collections. The formula approved by the Finance Committee based benefits on only three factors: population, relative income, and state tax effort—criteria that generally favored the poorer, less densely populated states of the South and West.

On the Senate floor, amendments offered by Ribicoff and other senators from urban states to restore some of the factors in the House bill favoring urban areas were consistently defeated by large margins. On September 12, 1972, the bill was approved on final passage by a vote of 64 to 20, with five Republicans and fifteen Democrats voting in the negative. Both supporters and opponents were drawn from the full range of the ideological spectrum.[33]

In the conference committee appointed to reconcile differences between the House and Senate versions of revenue sharing, argument centered on the distribution formula. At the suggestion of James Cannon, a special assistant to Governor Rockefeller assigned to work full time on the bill (later director of the Domestic Council under President Ford), the conference agreed to accept *both* formulas, determining each state's share on the basis of the formula that gave it the larger benefits. All benefits were then to be trimmed proportionately to keep the total cost of the bill for the first year at $5.3 billion. As a result of Cannon's stratagem, New York obtained $88 million more than it would have received under the Senate bill (though $54 million less than under the House version). Louisiana (Long's state) received $38 million more than under the House formula. But some states, such as Pennsylvania, Wisconsin, Indiana, and Virginia, received less than they would have obtained under *either* the House or Senate version.[34]

On October 20, 1972—eighteen days before the presidential election—President Nixon, surrounded by hundreds of state and local government officials, signed the revenue-sharing bill into law in front of Independence Hall in Philadelphia. "Today," Nixon said, "we are giving the distinguished people here—the mayors, the governors, the county officials, and your colleagues all across the country—we are giving you the tools, now you do the job."[35]

The administration's effort to consolidate categorical programs into broad block grants achieved partial success through the enactment of manpower revenue sharing in 1973 and the community development block grant program in 1974—somewhat to the surprise, apparently, of the White House, which by then was preoccupied with the fight against impeachment. President Ford took up the battle for block grants, but no further movement had been achieved at the end of 1976. Following Ford's recommendation, Congress renewed general revenue sharing in 1976.

The New Federalist Papers

On October 2, 1969, H. R. Haldeman sent a memorandum to William Safire that said in part: "Few seem aware of the Nixon political philosophy, of his vision of America—outside of his hope for domestic tranquility. . . . The President feels that this general subject area of what the President's philosophy is would be worth some work and effort by our PR group. Would you please follow up?"[36]

Setting out on his assignment, Safire at once encountered a serious difficulty: the family assistance plan and revenue sharing, the two major proposals in Nixon's domestic program up to that time, seemed to point in opposite ideological directions. The family assistance plan called for shifting more authority to the federal government, whereas revenue sharing was intended to strengthen the roles of the states and localities. What was needed was a common rationale that would cover both of these apparently conflicting tendencies. "Strange," Safire later wrote, "fitting a philosophy to the set of deeds, but sometimes that is what must be done."[37]

In January 1970 Safire circulated among members of the White House staff the product of his labors—an essay on government theory, which he titled "New Federalist Paper No. 1" and signed "Publius" (the pseudonym adopted in 1787–88 by the authors of the original Federalist papers). The Publius essay, Safire later revealed, incorporated changes suggested by Moynihan, Ehrlichman, and the president himself.

The New Federalism, according to Publius, was based on the Nixon administration's recognition that contemporary American society requires satisfaction of paradoxical sets of needs: "a need for *both* national unit and local diversity; a need to protect *both* individual equality at the national level and individual uniqueness at the local level; and a need *both* to establish national goals and to decentralize government services."[38] (Emphasis in the original, in this and succeeding quotations.) To mediate between these apparently competing needs, Publius explained, the administration employed a standard based on "the cause of Fairness." In a "proudly diverse, pluralistic society," fairness was determined "not by government policy, church decree, or social leadership" but by a strictly relative scale of values: "What is moral is what most people who think about morality at all think is moral at a given time." Currently, this national moral consensus held that "fairness *in principle* still lies in Federal standards and minimums, but that fairness *in administration* usually lies closest to home." Applying these judgments, the administration had conceived a domestic program Publius called "national localism" (a phrase fortunately soon forgotten). Under national localism, the role of the states was to be strengthened—but only on the understanding that " 'States' rights' have now become rights of first refusal." Similarly, local communities were to be given wide administrative leeway—but only so long as they lived up to nationally established standards. Publius warned: "National localism says to communities, 'Do it your way,' adding coolly, 'but do it.' " The family assistance plan was a mechanism to establish a "national minimum" for welfare that the states would have to meet. (Actually, the rejected Nathan plan for national standards would have fitted Safire's argument better than FAP.) Revenue sharing would give the states and localities more authority over administration. Block grants would give "local authority more room to maneuver" in broad areas designated by the federal government.[39]

New Federalist Paper 1 stirred up considerable reaction among the squad of intellectuals, both progressives and fundamentalists, who had found their ways onto the White House staff. One of the fundamentalists, Tom Charles Huston, a former president of Young Americans for Freedom, was sufficiently moved to compose a lengthy reply. (Nominally a member of the speechwriting staff, Huston was in fact devoting much of his time to pondering weaknesses in the way the federal government gathered intelligence on potential subversives. The result of this study was later to gain him brief fame as author of the notorious Huston plan, a proposal for presidentially authorized burglaries and other illegal operations that helped pave the way to Watergate.)

Huston's essay, signed "Cato" (a pseudonym used by Thomas Gordon and John Trenchard, eighteenth-century English libertarian Whigs), argued that the New Federalism, as formulated by Publius, was really no more than a camouflaged revision of New Deal liberalism. "In the New Federalist Society," Huston wrote, "there is no real room for individuality, for behind every apparent private choice lurks the iron fist of Government. . . . [Publius] envisages a New Federalism in which national authority says to local authority, 'Do it your way, but do it.' Such a political scheme is necessarily authoritarian in implication, if not in practice; it denies discretion and thus denies freedom, for no man is free who lacks the power to say No."[40]

At a more basic level, Huston attacked Publius's reliance on moral relativism as sufficient ground for ethical standards. "Not all questions are open questions," Cato wrote, "for the spirit of community is rooted in a shared view of man's meaning and destiny, in agreement about right and wrong, good and evil. There is room for debate and disagreement, but consensus, not dissent, is the rock upon which ordered liberty rests." Moral relativism, Huston warned, could encourage "temporary political leadership" to pick and choose among moral options to obtain those that best suited its pragmatic interests.[41] (But it was Huston, the moral absolutist, rather than Safire, the relativist, who later proved indifferent to limitations on executive authority established by law.)

If Publius's views represented the administration's social philosophy, Huston's position on the White House staff was uncomfortable, perhaps untenable. (He evidently did not know that Nixon had played some part in the composition of New Federalism Paper 1.) Rather than advance a rival philosophy of his own, Huston chose to argue that the items in the administration's domestic program were "mere solutions to contemporary social problems." They had been drafted, he insisted, "as specific answers to specific problems: measures whose redeeming social value is to be found in the likelihood that they may work."[42]

Richard Nathan, who had actually participated in the evolution of the substantive programs that the New Federalism was supposed to explain, entered the debate with a functional definition of the administration's domestic strategy. Using the pseudonym "Althusius" (the seventeenth-century Dutch political philosopher who composed the first modern defense of federalism), Nathan wrote that the policies of the New Federalism were aimed at two procedural objectives: "to improve the performance of the federal government" in areas of exclusive or predominant federal responsibility; and to provide more opportunity "for recipient jurisdictions to make their own choices" in areas of "primarily state-local responsibility." The trick, of course, was to determine which responsibilities were properly federal and which were primarily state and local. Nathan used the criterion of administrative efficiency. The federal government, he claimed, did a better job at running large-scale cash transfer programs (like welfare) and at dealing with problems that overlapped state and local jurisdictions (like air and water pollution). State and local governments, in contrast, were more effective at managing most service functions (like education, manpower training, and public health). The administration, therefore, had proposed national solutions for welfare and pollution control, while seeking, through revenue sharing and block grants, to restore state and local authority over many other government services.[43]

Beyond Equity and Efficiency

Those who, like Huston, argued that the administration's domestic program consisted of essentially unrelated "specific answers to specific problems," rather than various expressions of a consistent social philosophy, were able to point to the fact that the main items in the program, FAP and revenue sharing, were developed in response to concrete and particular political and economic problems. When the theory of the New Federalism was formalized, whether in Safire's or Nathan's version, FAP did not seem to fit very well.

Yet the proposals brought together under the New Federalism shared at least one quality: all attempted to deal at the federal level with national social problems (national at least in the sense of being found to some degree almost everywhere) like poverty, support for education, and health care costs, while avoiding the large amounts of federal control and regulation that had come to be associated with Johnson's Great Society. Nixon and his advisers were concerned about the administrative unwieldiness and the rising costs of many Great Society programs. But a major generative impulse behind the New Federalism came from a concern deeper than desire for administrative efficiency or budgetary restraint.

In one of the radio talks he gave during the 1968 campaign, Nixon spoke of the need to "re-establish the sense of community, and thus the framework within which *all* the elements of our society at last can function." Increasing centralization of social authority in large and impersonal institutions, particularly big government, he argued, was a major cause of current individual alienation and social disorder. "The machinery of government seems increasingly remote, increasingly incapable of meeting [the individual's] needs when action is needed. The community itself begins to appear less relevant, and its standards and restraints become less effective."[44] Kennedy's New Frontier and Johnson's Great Society, Nixon wrote in his memoirs, "aimed at using the power of the presidency and the federal government to right past wrongs by trying to legislate social programs." He claimed that he approved their objectives: "The problems were real and the intention worthy." But the centralizing approach taken by the New Frontier and the Great Society, he argued, had by the end of the 1960s "undermined fundamental relationships within our federal system, created confusion about our national values, and corroded American belief in ourselves as a people and as a nation."[45] The fundamental goal of Nixon's domestic social program—the unifying theme of the New Federalism—was to continue moving toward social progress, but by means that would enhance rather than undermine natural community structures.

From the end of World War II to the middle of the 1960s, political debate on domestic issues dealt mainly with finding ways to achieve optimum balance between the right of the individual to social justice (equity) and the interests of both the individual and society as a whole in maintaining economic production (efficiency). Liberals tended to be more concerned with achieving increased fairness in the distribution of social and economic benefits, whereas conservatives gave somewhat greater weight to preserving incentives for economic growth. But these differences were chiefly over emphasis: most liberals and most conservatives gave high priorities to both equity and efficiency (expressed in preferred slogans and catch phrases). By 1960 there was broad, though not universal, agreement among public officials and social scientists that economic efficiency was best served by a relatively free system of economic exchange, supported by appropriate federal fiscal and monetary policies, but that social equity required some government intervention—with plenty of room for argument over where trade-offs should occur. The reforms of the first half of the 1960s, enacted under the banners of the New Frontier and the Great Society, were designed to produce greater equity in the distribution of benefits without unduly burdening economic efficiency—a welfare state harnessed to a market economy.

Development of broad consensus on governmental goals among political and intellectual elites and enactment of liberal reforms did not, however, lead to overall social harmony. Quite the contrary: the latter years of the 1960s were marked by social turmoil perhaps unprecedented in the United States since the Civil War. Protest against the Vietnam War and the drive for racial equality were the immediate causes of the most violent upheavals. But there was a widespread sense that something more fundamental had gone wrong, or was going wrong, in American society, something that the Great Society reforms were unlikely to cure, and might even be making worse.[46]

Political leaders seeking to increase social fairness without slowing economic growth had tended to take for granted or ignore a third category of values that have at least as direct a bearing on the actual experience of most people as either equity or efficiency: bonds of affection and obligation to such institutions or associations as the family, the church, the local community, and various kinds of voluntary groups. In the two decades after World War II, while economic growth in the West proceeded at astonishing rates, and equity gradually improved in most Western societies, many of the ties sustaining these relationships were clearly eroding. At least partly as a result, most of the Western democracies suffered from epidemics of the modern social disease known as alienation, along with rises of such attendant disorders as crime, alcoholism, drug addiction, social terrorism, and plain bad manners. Weakening of social ties was variously blamed on the effects of industrialization, urbanization, increasing social mobility, and secularism. But the cause most often attacked, perhaps because it appeared the most tangible and susceptible to reform, was the dehumanizing impersonality of dominant social institutions, particularly the modern bureaucratic state (formed to promote a favorable balance between social equity and economic efficiency, as well as to carry on modern warfare).

During the middle years of the 1960s, concern about alienation, though not usually under that label, and its related symptoms rather suddenly became an important issue in American politics. Candidates running for national office promised to reduce street crime, break up the traffic in drugs, and defend traditional moral standards. At a deeper level various forms of antistatist or nonstatist social idealism developed and gathered strength all across the political spectrum. These included the romantic anarchism of the New Left, the crusade against "big government" undertaken by libertarian conservatives, and assorted expressions of "populism" and "voluntarism" in between, as well as the doctrines of numerous exotic religious cults.

Some of the architects of the Great Society, especially Moynihan and Richard Goodwin, understood and even participated in the revolt against institutional depersonalization and tried to find a place for it within the liberal agenda. Moynihan favored substituting cash payments to individuals or families for social services, in the hope that stabilizing relationships might take root naturally in untended social spaces. The prevailing view among Great Society planners, however, was that humanizing effects could be built right into the federal programs themselves and packaged out to the localities from Washington. The result of this conclusion was the opposite of that wished for by Moynihan—more federal control rather than less. Great Society programs in areas like housing, income maintenance, and job training were designed, Moynihan wrote, "to affect such outcomes as who *thinks* what, who *acts* when, who *lives* where, who *feels* how."[47]

The Great Society's attempt to impose ready-made personal and community values from Washington must be judged a failure, at least in terms of public acceptance. Large majorities of the national public continued to support most of the equity goals toward which the Great Society programs were directed. In 1969, for example, the Harris poll found that 83 percent of a national sample favored the use of federal funds to "wipe out slums in the cities."[48] But as early as the summer of 1966, the Gallup poll found that a large majority of those with an opinion had turned against the Great Society as a governmental mechanism—partly no doubt because of its identification with the still controversial goal of racial integration, but also because of resentment against what was perceived as too much federal intrusion into complex and essentially private or local social relationships.[49] In August 1968 Gallup reported that 46 percent of the public believed that "big government" posed "the biggest threat to the country in the future," against 26 percent who feared "big labor" most, and 12 percent who saw the main danger coming from "big business."[50]

The election of Nixon opened the way for a new approach. Contrary to liberal complaints, the New Federalism was *not*, at least during Nixon's first term, a device for cutting back the federal budget for domestic social programs. Nixon, however unwillingly, proceeded on the assumption that to change the structure of programs, it would be necessary to introduce "grandfather clauses" and "fail-safe" provisions that would maintain existing levels of payment for most current beneficiaries and inevitably increase total costs.[51] In Nixon's budget for fiscal 1974—the budget in which he at last declared war on the rise in federal spending—the administration's request for social programs totaled 58 percent more than in Johnson's last budget, figured in constant dollars, whereas its requests for defense were 17 percent less (made possible in part of course by withdrawal of ground forces from Vietnam).[52]

Nixon took only intermittent interest in domestic social policy. Despite the hyperbole with which he customarily described the administration's domestic program ("the New American Revolution"), he was often privately skeptical about its possible effects. "Let's not kid ourselves into thinking [revenue sharing's] a bold domestic program," he told some of his advisers at the end of 1970. "Or that it will pass. It's not dramatic."[53]

But other members of the administration, and at times Nixon, too, were convinced that they were advancing a coherent program aimed at producing a major change in underlying social conditions. Burns, Nathan, Moynihan, Anderson, Finch, Veneman, Ehrlichman, Shultz, Richardson, Weinberger—all, in their different ways, seem to have regarded themselves as advance agents for a new social era. "What does the New Federalism have to say about this?" John Ehrlichman would ask, during the period of his ascendancy, when a new problem was set before him.[54]

Even before Watergate, the Nixon administration, for reasons to be examined in chapters 11 and 12, had turned away from some of the more optimistic and generous aspirations represented by the New

Federalism. As the threat of impeachment grew, the administration's domestic program, like everything else, became geared to Nixon's battle for political survival. Later, in both the Ford and Carter administrations, some of the themes expressed through the New Federalism were to reappear. But the felt loss of community that gave birth to the New Federalism remains, at the beginning of the 1980s, largely uncured—a continuing source for potential conflict or constructive growth in American life.

9

Civil Rights Policy:
The Busing Controversy

NO ITEM in the administration's domestic program left so bitter a taste as the president's attempt to end the busing of schoolchildren for racial integration. Civil rights activists and many blacks became convinced that Nixon was deliberately exploiting the busing issue to gain political profit. They were partly right. Nixon seemed at times almost obsessed by fear that George Wallace, who was expected to run again for president in 1972, would draw away enough conservative voters in both North and South to make Nixon vulnerable against a Democrat without strong liberal identification, such as Edmund Muskie or Henry Jackson. Opposition to busing, Nixon believed, would earn him the gratitude not only of whites fighting a holding action against desegregation in the South, but also of millions of voters in the urban areas of the North who regarded busing as an invasion of their personal liberties and as a threat to the welfare and safety of their children.[1]

Yet the air of righteous anger with which Nixon addressed the busing issue does not seem to have been feigned. He appears to have felt that the administration's position was morally unassailable, irrespective of politics. Busing, he said, was "a new evil . . . disrupting communities and imposing hardship on children—both black and white."[2]

Nixon and the South

As vice-president during the 1950s, Nixon had consistently supported liberal positions on civil rights issues. In his role as presiding

174

officer of the Senate, he delivered rulings favorable to those who were trying to impose limitations on the filibusters through which southern senators customarily blocked enactment of civil rights legislation.

If the Democrats had nominated Lyndon Johnson or even Adlai Stevenson for president in 1960, Nixon would probably have written off most of the traditionally Democratic South and gone all-out to win the support of black voters. Eisenhower had received about 40 percent of the black vote in 1956. If Nixon did almost as well, he would be sure to carry most of the densely populated industrial states of the North. But the nomination of John Kennedy, whose Catholicism was expected to cause him problems among southern Protestants, produced a competing political enticement: what if white voters in the deep South would shift at last to the Republican side?

Since his days at Duke Law School in North Carolina, Nixon had felt a special empathy for the South. He disapproved of segregation, but he believed he understood the psychology of southern whites—perhaps, as Harry Dent has suggested, Nixon saw a parallel between his own career and the South's long struggle to regain its rightful place in the national firmament. Throughout the 1960 campaign Nixon made no overt appeal to racial antagonism, but also took care not to identify himself with black aspirations in a way that would turn off potential support among southern whites. Then, two weeks before the election, Martin Luther King was arrested for refusing to leave an Atlanta department store restaurant reserved for white customers. Nixon did nothing. Kennedy intervened to help secure King's release on bail. King's father, the leading Negro Baptist minister in Atlanta, who several weeks before had endorsed Nixon, announced: "I've got a suitcase of votes, and I'm going to take them to Mr. Kennedy and dump them in his lap."[3] Even so, Nixon won 32 percent of the black vote—a good showing for a Republican, but not quite good enough to bring him victory in Illinois, Pennsylvania, or Michigan. On the other side of the political balance, Nixon, despite his caution on the race issue, lost eight of the eleven southern states.

During the years of the Kennedy and Johnson administrations in the 1960s, Nixon did his best to steer the Republicans away from becoming the party of last-ditch opposition to desegregation in the South. He endorsed the Civil Rights Act of 1964, and took no part in the effort by some of Senator Goldwater's managers to attract the support of southern segregationists. In 1966 he warned in Jackson,

Mississippi, that there was "no future in the race issue" for the Republican party. He strongly opposed the introduction of segregationist planks into Republican state platforms in the South.[4]

Nevertheless—and perhaps paradoxically—Nixon's own support within the Republican party was increasingly built on a southern base. After the 1964 election debacle, many southern Republicans, like Senators Thurmond of South Carolina and Tower of Texas, came to see Nixon as their best defense against the resumption of party control by the more moderate groups that had dominated the national party from 1940 through 1960. Perhaps, as Harry Dent has said, the southerners viewed Nixon with suspicion, thinking of him as "Tricky Dick"[5]—but better Nixon by far, they seem to have felt, than Romney, Percy, or, worst of all, Nelson Rockefeller. At the 1968 convention at Miami Beach, Nixon received 228 of the 310 votes cast by southern delegates—60 of the remainder going to Ronald Reagan, probably the first choice of most southern Republican leaders if the need to nominate a candidate likely to win in November had not seemed so imperative.[6] Without the support he received from southern delegations, Nixon would have fallen 203 votes short of a majority on the first ballot, and probably would have lost the nomination.

From Brown to Green

Desegregation of the public schools had been hanging like a sword of judgment over many southern whites since the Supreme Court's decision in the case *Brown* v. *Board of Education* in 1954 that "in the field of public education the doctrine of 'separate but equal' has no place."[7] In 1955 the Court, in its second ruling on *Brown,* seemed to countenance delay by requiring only that desegregation proceed "with all deliberate speed"—though insisting that school districts formerly legally segregated "make a prompt and reasonable start" toward compliance with the 1954 decree.[8] During the years between 1955 and 1968, most southern districts with substantial black populations yielded ground slowly to federal pressure for desegregation. Under "freedom of choice" plans, established during the 1960s, many districts, while ending legal segregation, gave all students the option of attending formerly all-white or all-black schools. In practice, these plans usually led, as their authors had intended, to white students almost without exception continuing to attend schools formerly reserved for whites, and most black students still going to the former black schools. By 1968—fourteen years after the first decision on *Brown*—68 percent of black children in the South were still going to all-black schools, and 82 percent were going to schools at least 95 percent black.[9]

In May 1968 the Supreme Court ruled in the case *Green* v. *Board of Education* that freedom-of-choice plans failing to produce "a unitary system in which racial discrimination would be eliminated root and branch" would no longer be tolerated.[10] Since the 1964 Civil Rights Act empowered the federal Department of Health, Education, and Welfare to cut off all federal aid to school districts that failed to desegregate, and authorized the Justice Department to bring civil rights cases against such districts, the bell appeared to have tolled at last for segregation in rural districts throughout the South, where whites and blacks had always lived in close proximity and been assigned to separate schools on the basis of race alone.

But what about heavily urbanized metropolitan areas, in the North as well as the South, where blacks were largely confined to inner city ghettos, so that the traditional American pattern of dividing school districts into compact attendance areas, based on neighborhoods, would in many cases produce all-black or all-white schools? The language of *Brown*, forbidding "segregation of children in public schools *solely* on the basis of race" (emphasis added), seemed to suggest that though *de jure* segregation, resulting from previous state or local laws, was illegal, *de facto* segregation, caused by residential patterns, was perhaps socially deplorable but nevertheless not unconstitutional.[11] This view was expressed by the finding of a federal district court in the case *Briggs* v. *Elliot* in 1955: "The Constitution . . . does not require integration. It merely forbids discrimination."[12] Decisions based on this assumption in several similar cases were allowed to stand by the Supreme Court.

In 1961, however, another district court ruled in the case *Taylor* v. *Board of Education* that the school authorities of New Rochelle, New York, a suburb of New York City, were required to transport some students to schools outside their own areas in order to achieve racially mixed student bodies, even though New Rochelle schools had never been segregated by law. Judge Irving Kaufman held in the *Taylor* case that *Brown* had established the constitutional right of all Negro children to "educational and social contacts and interaction" with white children in the same district.[13] The Supreme Court also allowed this decision to stand. If the apparent difference between the interpretation offered by *Briggs* and that offered by *Taylor* were resolved in favor of *Taylor*, virtually every heavily urbanized school district in the United States would be required to transport large numbers of children of both races to schools outside their normal attendance areas. Out of the fear and resentment created by this possibility, the busing controversy was born.[14]

Both sides at times interpreted the label "busing" to suggest that their opponents in the controversy were primarily arguing over the bus ride itself. Nixon denounced "busing simply for the sake of busing,"[15] as though somewhere there were maniac judges or social planners who took sadistic pleasure in forcing small children to take long bus rides to and from school each day. Proponents of busing argued that busing had long been an established adjunct of American education, and in fact had been used extensively to maintain segregation in the South in areas where housing was not segregated, so that parents and children had no reasonable right to oppose busing for integration. In some cases, the length of the bus ride, when it stretched to inordinate extremes, did become an issue. But the opponents' main complaint, as most of them forthrightly indicated, was that some children were to be carried out of their own areas, even if by a means not in itself particularly burdensome, to schools perceived as educationally inferior, in uncongenial and potentially dangerous neighborhoods.

The impact of the growing fear of busing in urban areas of both the North and South was first felt in Congress during the debate that preceded passage of the Civil Rights Act of 1964. Under pressure from Senator Robert Byrd of West Virginia (later Senate majority leader), Senator Hubert Humphrey, manager of the bill, stated that the provision authorizing cut-off of federal funds from school districts that failed to desegregate could not be applied in cases of de facto segregation.[16] The act as passed specified that "'desegregation' shall not mean the assignment of students to public schools in order to overcome racial imbalance."[17]

"Freedom of Choice"

Nixon's own disposition had been to hold that freedom-of-choice plans, which did little more than halt segregation enforced by law, met the requirements of *Brown*. "The Court was right on *Brown* and wrong on *Green*," he told Safire in June 1968.[18] In an interview over a television station in Charlotte, North Carolina, on September 11, 1968, Nixon seemed to extend hope to the rural South that the *Green* decision would not be enforced after all: "With regard to freedom of choice, I would have to look at each one of the states involved to see whether actually it was a true freedom of choice. If it were, I would tend to favor that. I tend to look with, I would say, great concern, whenever I see Federal agencies or whenever I see the courts attempting to become in effect, local school boards. I think the decision in the local areas should be made primarily by people who are more familiar with those problems."[19]

When his statement produced protests from northern Republican progressives, including Senators Brooke of Massachusetts and Javits of New York, Nixon backed off to the extent of saying that he would favor withholding federal funds from school districts that clearly were using "freedom of choice" to maintain segregation, but he continued to insist that he would not cut off federal funds to produce integration "in a positive way through busing and the like."[20] In a statement issued in October, Nixon called attention to the language in the Civil Rights Act of 1964 prohibiting "busing to achieve racial balance in the schools."[21]

Ardent campaigning for Nixon by Senator Thurmond, who in 1948 had been the presidential candidate of the avowedly segregationist States' Rights party, seems to have been sign enough for many die-hard opponents of desegregation, particularly in the Carolinas, that a Republican administration would bring a change in enforcement policies. On November 5 Nixon carried five southern states (Virginia, Florida, Tennessee, and both Carolinas), while losing five deep South states to Wallace, and Texas to Humphrey. He received 12 percent of the black vote nationally—20 percent less than in 1960.[22]

In his first inaugural Nixon indicated, in accordance with views he had expressed during the campaign, that he would ask for no further civil rights legislation: "The laws have caught up with our consciences." What was needed now, he said, was "to give life to what is in the law."[23]

Under the Civil Rights Act of 1964, responsibility for enforcement of desegregation lay with both the Department of Justice and HEW. Many in the press and the political community expected the new attorney general, John Mitchell, architect of Nixon's "southern strategy," to trim the law to suit the allies he had recruited for Nixon in the South. By contrast, Robert Finch, the new secretary of HEW, was widely viewed as a progressive activist, likely to press on moral grounds for strict enforcement of civil rights laws. Neither man quite fitted the stereotype assigned to him. Mitchell was indeed sensitive to the interests of the South. But he also based his recommendations for moderation in civil rights policy on an argument for social fairness. The South, he maintained, had been singled out long enough, and desegregation policies applied in the South should henceforth be enforced equally throughout the nation.[24] Finch, rather than draw on any competing ethical or moral view, seems usually to have relied on the pragmatic argument that the administration should balance concern for its southern white supporters with awareness of the growing role being played by minority groups in national politics.

Perhaps Finch emphasized the political aspect of his case because he believed this was the only argument for racial equality that had a chance of winning acceptance at the White House. Long after he had left the administration, however, he remained anxious to stress his interest in the political side of the problem: "I want to make it clear that the course I was following at HEW was not motivated entirely by concern for good works or support for social programs. I was trying to deal with the cutting issues that were affecting the Republican party. I thought that it was very important, for instance, that Republicans gain a foothold in the Chicano community. I thought that it was important that we not write off the black vote. Simply from a partisan standpoint, it was important that a Republican administration deal effectively with some of the problems that came under my authority at HEW."[25]

Whether for political or policy reasons, or some of both, Finch assembled at HEW a battery of lieutenants markedly more liberal in social outlook than were most officials found elsewhere in the Nixon administration. Foremost among these was John Veneman, who did employ, when the occasion arose, the moral arguments that Finch eschewed. Veneman, however, early decided not to make civil rights one of his particular areas of concern. "Integration," he later explained, "was a real hot potato. Much of the top leadership at the department, including Finch, were being preoccupied with it. I decided to bail out. They were well qualified to deal with the issue, and I had other things to devote my time to. . . . I decided at an early time not to play the silly White House game. I would keep rolling on the programs that I believed in until somebody told me I was wrong. . . . I always believed that the telephone works both ways."[26]

With Veneman devoting himself to other things, like welfare reform, Finch turned for assistance in the formulation of civil rights policy to his young director of the HEW Office of Civil Rights, Leon Panetta. Like Finch and Veneman, Panetta was a Californian. He had served on the staff of Senator Thomas Kuchel, a California Republican progressive, who had been defeated in the 1968 primary by Max Rafferty, an outspoken fundamentalist (who in turn lost in the general election to a Democrat, John Tunney). In the book he later wrote about his experiences at HEW, Panetta (who in 1976 was elected to the U.S. House of Representatives as a Democrat) described the differences that he sensed at the beginning of the administration between Nixon and himself: "We were both from California, both from families which stressed achievement and solid old virtues. . . . Both believed strongly in the Republican party as one-half of an eminently successful two-party political system. But there was, in fact, a gulf. Oversimplified, it was the difference between 1960's-style liberalism and a brand of orthodox conservatism which had been around for some generations. . . . I had thought of myself as a practical type who believed that it was the federal government's role at the end of the decade to bring into the American homestead those millions who had been left out of it, to provide them a stake in society, and to help society make room. I doubted that the President, as a conservative man, shared this view. But I had hopes that he would see the need when he stopped campaigning and became President."[27] Panetta, though a registered Republican, had voted in 1968 for Hubert Humphrey. He did not mention this to Finch or anyone else in the administration when he was approached about the job at HEW, but, he later explained, he "always thought they knew it."[28]

Panetta agreed to become director of the Office of Civil Rights, he later said, because he believed that "Finch was committed to enforcement of the law, and enforcement of the law under the Supreme Court decisions required that an end to segregation of the schools in the South be carried out rapidly." His realistic hope, he said, was that "the Nixon administration would continue slow momentum forward on civil rights, or at least that there would be no retreat." But looking back in 1977 on the record of the Nixon administration, Panetta concluded that there had been "a massive retreat on civil rights."[29]

Along with the band of progressives he installed in high posts at HEW, Finch also appointed a few strict conservatives. One of these was L. Patrick Gray, who became executive assistant to the secretary (later director of the FBI, fired when he admitted to the Senate Judiciary Committee that he had destroyed evidence relating to Watergate). Another was Robert Mardian, who became general counsel (later found guilty of participation in the Watergate cover-up). Mardian, who had been western chairman of the Goldwater campaign in 1964 and had formed a close friendship with John Mitchell in 1968, told Panetta that it was his understanding that the administration planned to move slowly on desegregation.[30] Finch, however, publicly stated early in February: "I consider it neither legally nor morally defensible to 'turn back the clock' and to accept as public policy so-called 'freedom of choice' plans which do not bring about effective school desegregation."[31]

Outside HEW, the strongest resistance to the strict enforcement policy favored by Panetta came at first, not from the Justice Department, but from the White House. During the transition period, Harry Dent, former administrative assistant to Senator Thurmond, had been appointed special counsel to the president. It was understood that Dent, among other duties, was to serve as White House representative for the interests of Republican leaders in the South. "Nothing should happen in the South without checking with Harry Dent," Nixon repeatedly told his cabinet, Dent later recalled.[32] As soon as the administration took office, Dent busied himself seeking revocation of orders issued by the departing Johnson administration to cut off federal funds to five southern school districts that had failed to comply with desegregation guidelines. Dent's effort was supported by Bryce Harlow, conveying protests from Senator Thurmond and other southern members of Congress. Despite resistance by Panetta and Veneman, Finch agreed to delay the cutoff for sixty days. Roy Wilkins,

executive director of the National Association for the Advancement
of Colored People, denounced the delay as "a terrible decision and
a miserable way to start four years of working for the health, education, and welfare of American citizens."[33] Senator Thurmond told
the press that Finch's action "assures the American people that the
policies of this administration on school desegregation guidelines will
be consistent with President Nixon's statements during the campaign."[34]

Mitchell and his assistant attorney general for civil rights, Jerris
Leonard (coordinator of the Nixon campaign in the Wisconsin primary
in 1968 before he ran unsuccessfully for the U.S. Senate in the general
election), began to argue that enforcement against noncomplying
districts should be carried out mainly through lawsuits brought by
the Justice Department, rather than through cutoffs of federal funds
to the districts by HEW. This course could be expected to shift the
blame for desegregation in the eyes of southern whites from the
administration to the courts. There is no reason to believe, however,
that Mitchell was not sincere in arguing that recalcitrant districts could
more readily be brought into compliance through court orders than
by fund cutoffs[35] (a view that had also been held by John Doar, the
assistant attorney general for civil rights in the Kennedy and Johnson
administrations).[36] "We found," Jerris Leonard later claimed, "that
many school districts in the South had desegregation plans in their
bottom desk drawers, but they had built up such a feeling of antagonism toward the HEW people that they were unwilling to use them
unless required to do so by court orders. Often they would tell us,
'You must make us do it if you want us to do it.' "[37]

Panetta, at least nominally supported by Finch, argued in response
that thousands of southern districts had already agreed to desegregate
by the beginning of the school year in September 1969, under the
impression that if they failed to do so, their federal funds would be
cut off. Any change now, Panetta insisted, would "not only encourage
the recalcitrant districts but undermine the efforts of those that have
complied." In the debate that followed within the administration,
Panetta came to develop a certain respect for John Mitchell: "He did
not give us a runaround. He was perfectly clear and straightforward
about his position. Although it was not a position that I agreed with,
I admired him for being candid about his objectives." Finch, on the
other hand, Panetta came to believe, "did not have strong philosophic

convictions on the issue, one way or another. He was under heavy pressure from the White House, and he wished chiefly to do what the White House wanted him to do."[38]

Nixon assigned Leonard Garment, who joined the White House staff during the spring of 1969, to mediate the dispute. Though sharing Panetta's liberal orientation on civil rights in general, and desegregation in particular, Garment, formerly a member of Nixon and Mitchell's law firm in New York, approached his assignment pragmatically. He soon found himself, he later recalled, "among those who were critical of the fund cutoff approach." Fund cutoffs, Garment concluded, "led to confrontations, which tended to make difficult situations intractable." He found that "HEW by that time had developed such distrust among southern school districts that some change in approach by the federal government was needed." He came, he said, "to favor the court route—allowing each of the communities to have their day in court. It seemed to me that this would bring about more compliance in the long run."[39]

On July 3, 1969, the administration issued a statement, largely composed by Garment, announcing a shift in emphasis to enforcement through the courts, and indicating that deadlines requiring desegregation by the beginning of the school year in September might be extended. At a hectic press briefing at the Justice Department conducted jointly by Leonard, Veneman, and Panetta, the representatives of Justice and HEW each tried to put their own interpretations on the new policy.[40] The press generally reported that the administration had announced a more lenient approach to enforcement. Informed of the change during the NAACP national convention in Jackson, Mississippi, Roy Wilkins accused the administration of "breaking the law." Wilkins declared: "It's almost enough to make you vomit. This is not a matter of too little too late; rather, this is nothing at all."[41]

Panetta, back in Washington, denied that desegregation guidelines had been significantly weakened. Within a few hours Panetta received a phone call from John Ehrlichman, who was spending the holiday weekend with the president at Key Biscayne, Florida. Ehrlichman told Panetta, as Panetta later recalled, to "cool it," and not to get into any arguments with the NAACP over interpretation of the new policy. Panetta came away from the conversation convinced that Ehrlichman and, presumably, the president were not unhappy with the angry reaction from the NAACP.[42]

"The Supreme Court Has Spoken"

In August Finch, under heavy pressure from the White House, requested delay in court-ordered desegregation of twenty-three Mississippi school districts scheduled to begin in September. Veneman told Panetta that the White House was responding to demands by Senator John Stennis of Mississippi, chairman of the Armed Services Committee, who at that time was leading the fight on the floor of the Senate to save the administration's antiballistic missile program.[43] For the first time since the fight against segregation began in the 1950s, lawyers representing the federal Justice Department argued on behalf of those resisting desegregation and against lawyers representing civil rights organizations. Jerris Leonard could find only two HEW education experts willing to testify in favor of the delay. Some of the experts who refused to testify were threatened, according to Panetta, with loss of their jobs.[44]

In October the Supreme Court, headed by Warren Burger, the new chief justice appointed by Nixon, ruled unanimously that no further delay in desegregation was permissible and that the twenty-three Mississippi districts should "begin immediately to operate as unitary systems within which no person is to be effectively excluded from any school because of race or color."[45] In a hurried meeting at HEW after the announcement of the court's ruling, Mardian suggested that further delay might be possible, depending on how the lower courts implemented the decision. But Patrick Gray, who had previously argued stoutly for the administration's position, insisted: "No, this is over. The Supreme Court has spoken. Now we must obey the law."[46] Finch issued a statement promising that the department would not "tolerate any further delays in abolishing the vestiges of the dual system." Nixon followed with a statement that "the administration will carry out the mandate of the Court and will enforce the law."

White House pressure to slow desegregation enforcement was in part generated by objections from southern politicians, conveyed through Dent and Harlow. These were usually seconded by H. R. Haldeman and John Ehrlichman, who, although they did not get along very well with Dent personally (because, Dent believed, he was "not from southern California and not an advance man"), shared his opinion that the national public was cooling on desegregation. To support their case, they cited a Gallup poll of July 1969 showing that

44 percent of the public felt integration was moving too fast, 22 percent felt that it was not going fast enough, and 25 percent felt that it was proceeding about right.[47] Ehrlichman once told Panetta: "Blacks are not where our votes are, so why antagonize the people who can be helpful to us politically?" Moreover, the administration's political interests, as perceived by the White House, do not seem to have conflicted with the president's essential beliefs. Dent has recalled: "Basically, Nixon was very conservative. . . . He would keep a Len Garment around to speak for liberals and blacks and other minorities. He would let Garment and Finch make their liberal arguments. But after they were finished, almost always, he would come down on the conservative side—he would say what Harry Dent wanted him to say."[48]

During the fall Finch asked Panetta if he could tell the White House that Panetta, as a sign of loyalty, was willing to resign if it would be for the good of the administration. Panetta agreed that Finch could deliver such a message.[49]

On the morning of February 17, 1970, the front page of the *Washington Daily News* announced that Panetta was about to be fired. Similar stories had appeared before, but Panetta feared the worst. He brought the matter up with Finch while they were going over testimony that the secretary was to deliver before a congressional committee. We'll deny it, Finch said, the way we did all the others. But, Panetta pointed out, Ziegler will be asked about it at his press briefing at the White House this morning. Yes, Finch said, that bothers me, too. Panetta realized then, he later recalled, that it was all over.[50] A short time later, Ziegler announced that Panetta's resignation, "submitted some time ago," had been accepted. In Leonard Garment's view, "Panetta had become the symbol of everything that was arguably wrong with civil rights enforcement."[51]

Resistance in Congress

On February 19—two days after Panetta was fired—the House refused, by teller vote (members not recorded by name) of 122 to 145, to delete the so-called Whitten amendment, prohibiting use of federal funds to "force busing of students," which the Appropriations Committee had attached to the Labor-HEW appropriations bill. The Whitten amendment, at that time primarily aimed at forestalling desegregation in the rural South, had first been submitted by Congressman

Basil Whitener of North Carolina in 1966, but was always identified by the name of Congressman Jamie Whitten of Mississippi, who resubmitted it annually thereafter. In 1969 the House had passed the Whitten amendment, but it had been defanged when the Senate, on motion of Senator Hugh Scott, added the modifying language, "except when required by the Constitution"—a fate that was again to befall it in 1970.[52]

Those aiming to stop busing for desegregation could not yet command a majority in the Senate. On the day the Whitten amendment was approved by the House, the Senate voted 36 to 49 against an amendment offered by Senator Sam Ervin of North Carolina (later the folksy scourge of Watergate) to forbid courts or federal agencies from requiring busing in order to change the racial composition of any school. The vote in the Senate on the Ervin amendment by ideological groups, which gives a fair picture of the distribution of forces before resistance to busing intensified in the North, was as follows (a yes vote being a vote to prohibit busing):[53]

Republicans			*Democrats*		
	Yes	No		Yes	No
Fundamentalists	13	2	Traditionalists	12	0
Stalwarts	2	8	Centrists	7	2
Moderates	1	5	Regulars	1	12
Progressives	0	7	Liberals	0	13
Total	16	22	Total	20	27

Support for flat prohibition of busing for desegregation was pretty much confined to Democratic traditionalists and centrists, mainly from the South and the border states, and Republican fundamentalists, largely representing western states with very small black populations and therefore presumably voting primarily to maintain ideological solidarity with Democratic traditionalists. Even border state Republican senators, like Baker of Tennessee, Cooper of Kentucky, and Bellmon of Oklahoma, voted against the Ervin amendment. The administration, however, took no position.

Desegregation of the Rural South

After the Supreme Court's decision on the Mississippi case, Nixon appears to have decided that desegregation in the rural South could no longer be delayed, and to have set out to bring it about as harmoniously as possible. "Nixon's attitude on integration," Bryce Harlow has said, "was that it was a hell of a problem that the country had to get past."[54] On February 16, 1970—the day before Panetta was fired—Nixon announced the formation of a cabinet-level "working group," chaired by Vice-President Agnew, with Secretary of Labor Shultz as vice-chairman, to explore means by which the administration might assist school districts going through desegregation. "The Courts have spoken," Nixon acknowledged. "Many schools throughout the country need help."[55]

Agnew turned out to be an inactive chairman. "The vice president," Harry Dent wrote, "was not appreciative of the assignment as the 'Number One Integrator of the South.'"[56] George Shultz, who through the Department of Labor had established the controversial "Philadelphia plan," requiring construction unions to accept quotas of black apprentices for work on federal contracts, became effective chairman of the group. "I developed a plan," Shultz has recalled, "based on the assumptions that the dual school system was going to have to come to an end, and that political support would be needed in the South to end it peacefully." Shultz established advisory committees of prominent citizens to aid with desegregation in the seven states where he judged resistance to be most serious (Mississippi, Louisiana, Arkansas, Georgia, Alabama, and the Carolinas). "I aimed at getting significant figures from both races on the committees," Shultz later explained. "Of necessity, these included many Democrats, because practically all of the blacks in the South at that time were Democrats. . . . John Mitchell was very helpful in making contact with the existing political establishments. The existing political leaders in many cases would not get into the same room with people interested in integration, but Mitchell was able to approach them as one who understood their problems and wanted to help. . . . I was also able to identify a small amount of federal money that could be given to school districts going through the process of desegregation. This was to enable the districts to stay on top of the process operationally."[57]

As the advisory committees (except the committee for Louisiana) were formed, they were brought to the White House, where Shultz, as he said, "moulded them into groups out of bunches of individuals." After meeting with the cabinet-level working group, the members of the advisory committees were taken in to see the president, who told them their states could have "good schools, inferior schools, or no schools"—it was up to them. Under the spell of the Oval Office, racial antagonisms appeared to fade.[58] Shultz's biracial advisory committees worked effectively to smooth the way for desegregation throughout the deep South—an example of the invaluable contribution that a social establishment motivated by strong political leadership can bring to reform.

When the Louisiana advisory committee was set up, Nixon went to New Orleans on August 14, 1970, and told its members and the chairmen and vice-chairmen of the committees from the other six critical states: "The highest court of the land has spoken. The unitary school system must replace the dual school system throughout the United States. . . . In the event that the law is not complied with, in the event that there are difficulties, as has been predicted in many quarters, those who will suffer will not simply be this generation, it will be primarily the next generation, the students, the children in the school districts involved. They will pay the price for the failure, a failure of leadership. . . . As I approach this problem, I emphasize this is one country, this is one people, and we are going to carry out the law in that way, not in a punitive way, treating the South as basically a second class part of the nation, but treating this part of the country with the respect that it deserves, asking its leaders to cooperate with us and we with them."[59]

The administration's effort to achieve peaceful desegregation of the South, however reluctantly undertaken, proved remarkably successful. In the fall of 1970, school districts throughout the South desegregated in compliance with the Supreme Court's *Green* decision, without serious upheaval or resistance. Within four years the percentage of black children attending totally black schools in the South, still 68 percent in 1968, had fallen to 8 percent.[60]

A Middle Ground

The problem of school segregation resulting from racially distinct residential neighborhoods, mainly in the metropolitan areas of the North, still lay ahead. Although the share of black children attending schools 95 percent or more black had declined to 20 percent in the

South by 1974, the share of blacks attending such predominantly black schools in northern and western states had risen to 50 percent.[61]

Some within the White House viewed efforts by civil rights groups, in some cases supported by the courts, to attack de facto segregation as a golden opportunity for political gain. On February 12, 1970, Patrick Buchanan, who had recently been acquiring a reputation as a writer of vitriolic prose for Spiro Agnew, addressed a memorandum to the president: "The national mood among blacks and whites *alike* is toward black separatism and white separatism. Where the Court in 1954 ruled at the crest of a national tide, their current rulings go against the grain of rising and angry public opinion. . . . Let me say candidly that for the foreseeable future, it is all over for compulsory social integration in the USA. . . . The second era of Re-Construction is over; the ship of Integration is going down; it is not our ship; it belongs to national liberalism—and we cannot salvage it; and we ought not to be aboard. For the first time since 1954, the national civil rights community is going to sustain an up-and-down defeat. It may come now; it may come hard; it may be disguised and dragged out— but it can no longer be avoided."[62]

Partly in reaction to Buchanan's memorandum, Nixon assigned Raymond Price and Leonard Garment, two of the more liberal members of his staff, to prepare a presidential statement setting forth the administration's general view on desegregation. As with his effort in 1969 to resolve the differences between Justice and HEW on civil rights enforcement, Garment approached the project with what he regarded as a realistic attitude toward the dynamics of social change. "Change," he said later, "requires a certain amount of zigging and zagging. The great trick is to keep operations directed at change within the law, while at the same time preventing those antagonistic to change from becoming too enthusiastic in their antagonism. What is needed is to maintain enough balance to keep going."[63]

In their research Garment and Price consulted, among others, James Coleman, who was the author of the 1965 Coleman report recommending integration as a means for improving black students' educational performances, but who had begun to question whether under some circumstances integration was worth the social costs; and Alexander Bickel, Yale Law School professor, who had written a widely quoted article in the *New Republic* arguing for a moderate approach to integration.[64] The draft submitted to Nixon early in March, written largely by Price on the basis of an analysis prepared by Garment, called for action to achieve "conditions in which neither the laws nor the institutions supported by law any longer draw an invidious distinction based on race; and going one step further, . . . to repair the human damage wrought by past segregation"; but warned that "in a free society, there are limits to the amount of coercion that can reasonably be used; . . . [and] we cannot afford to sacrifice the education of an entire generation on the altar of an abstract ideal, no matter how desirable."[65]

Nixon turned this draft over to Bryce Harlow, a native of Oklahoma inclined by role and by temperament to a conservative point of view. Harlow produced his own draft, which, he believed, "did not so much change the substance, as take out the sentimental language."[66] Garment and Price felt that Harlow's draft was, Harlow has recalled, "insensitive." Nixon then turned out a version of his own that was based on Price's original draft but that included many changes suggested by Harlow.

In the final statement, issued by the White House on March 24, 1970, Nixon placed the administration on a middle ground, between those who "feel that the only way to bring about social justice is to integrate all schools now, everywhere, no matter what the cost is in the disruption of education," and those "who believe that racial separation is right, and wish the clock of progress would stop or be turned back to 1953." The president's statement drew "a fundamental distinction between so-called *de jure* and *de facto* segregation." De jure segregation, whether resulting from legally established dual school systems or from attendance zones deliberately gerrymandered to produce racially distinct schools, would have to be eliminated "root and branch." But "in the case of genuine *de facto* segregation (i.e., where housing patterns produce substantially all-Negro or all-white schools, and where this racial separation has not been caused by deliberate social action) school authorities are not constitutionally required to take any positive steps to correct the imbalance." De facto segregation, though "undesirable," should not "by itself be cause for federal enforcement actions." School districts were required to assure that schools within "individual districts do not discriminate with respect to the quality of facilities or the quality of education delivered to the children within the district." But "transportation of pupils beyond normal geographic school zones for the purpose of achieving racial balance will not be required." Racial isolation should be combatted through "innovative approaches," such as making integrated supplemental education opportunities available outside of regular schools (an idea suggested by Coleman), but not through "such concepts as compulsory 'busing'—taking children out of the schools they would normally attend, and forcing them instead to attend others more distant, often in strange and even hostile neighborhoods."[67]

The Swann Decision

Nixon hoped that his statement would guide the courts to preserve the distinction between de jure and de facto segregation, and to rule out extensive use of busing for integration. On April 20, 1971, however, the Supreme Court held unanimously, in the case of *Swann* v. *Charlotte-Mecklenburg Board of Education*, dealing with the school district of Charlotte, North Carolina, and its surrounding county, that busing under some circumstances was an appropriate means for rooting out the effects of prior segregation. Desegregation plans, the Court ruled, in an opinion written by Chief Justice Burger, could "not be limited to the walk-in school." Remedies "administratively awkward, inconvenient, and even bizarre" would sometimes be needed.[68]

At the same time, however, the chief justice established a number of limits to the criteria and remedies that could properly be employed by the courts. The Constitution, Burger wrote, does not require "that every school in every community must always reflect the racial composition of the school system as a whole"; abstract "racial balance," achieved through racial quotas, therefore, could not be required by the courts. In some cases, even in districts like Charlotte where segregation had long been established de jure, some schools could "remain all or largely of one race until new schools can be provided or neighborhood patterns change,"—though such cases "will require close scrutiny." School districts, once they had achieved desegregation, could not be required "to make year-by-year adjustments of the racial composition of student bodies" to keep schools integrated. Objections to busing might have validity "when the time or distance of travel is so great as to either risk the health of the children or significantly impinge on the educational process."[69]

Despite its generally moderate tone, the *Swann* decision sent new tremors through the nation's major metropolitan areas, many of whose residents had been hoping for a flat prohibition against extensive busing. Cases involving busing were moving in Detroit, Boston, Atlanta, Richmond, and Denver, among other cities, many of which had never maintained legally segregated school systems. In the Richmond case, federal district judge Robert Merhige ruled in January 1972 that students in suburban counties surrounding Richmond would have to be bused into the city to achieve genuine desegregation. Merhige argued that school districts maintaining schools identifiable as "black" or "white" could not be in compliance with the Supreme Court's holding in *Green* that there should be not "a 'white' school and a 'Negro' school, but just schools."[70]

In the Detroit case, federal district judge Stephen Roth delivered a series of rulings, beginning in July 1971, requiring that children from suburban districts as well as those in Detroit be bused to achieve integration of schools in the entire metropolitan area. Residential segregation in the Detroit area, Roth held, was in part the result of federal and state housing policies; school segregation resulting from such residential patterns must therefore be overcome, just as much as if separation of the races in the schools had been directly established by law.[71]

In the bitter controversy that followed *Swann*, within Congress and between the administration and Congress, at least six identifiable positions emerged in debate—although two of these six enjoyed only a kind of fictive existence, seriously defended by almost nobody at the national level and maintained chiefly for political or rhetorical purposes. Ranged along the spectrum roughly from left to right, these positions were the following:

1. Use of busing to achieve "racial balance" in the public schools—that is, systems in which approximately the same proportions of blacks and whites would attend all schools in a given district or metropolitan area. All knowledgeable participants in the debate understood that this had been prohibited by the Supreme Court in *Swann*, but since much of the public believed that "racial balance" was supposed to be the objective of busing, legislators who wanted to go on record against busing without placing real restrictions on the courts regularly proposed and enacted prohibitions against "busing for racial balance."

2. Elimination of racially identifiable schools—the real objective of the more extreme busing proponents following *Swann*. So long as schools could be identified as "black" or "white," those holding this position argued, education could not possibly be "equal." Everyone recognized that, for the foreseeable future, integration to this extent could not be achieved in most large cities without busing that mixed students from city and suburban districts.

3. Elimination of schools identifiable as "black" or "white" within city limits. In many large cities, including Philadelphia, Detroit, Chicago, and Washington, the most that could be achieved along these lines was elimination of schools identifiable as "white," since comprehensive mixing would produce large black majorities in all schools. This, it was eventually agreed by almost everybody, would increase "white flight" from the cities and lead to further residential segregation and decline in city tax bases.

4. "Open transfer" for minority children from core city schools whose parents wanted them to attend schools elsewhere in the metropolitan area, with federal funds paying the cost of busing. This alternative, which was supported by many moderates, was proposed in 1972 by Congressman Richardson Preyer of North Carolina, a Democratic centrist, on the basis of a plan drafted largely by Alexander Bickel. It was opposed by liberals as likely to produce only token integration, and by fundamentalist conservatives who would not countenance busing for desegregation in any form.

5. Elimination of discrimination of any kind on the basis of race, so that children would not be bused outside their normal attendance areas for the purpose either of segregation or of integration. This was the actual position held by most opponents of any form of busing for integration.

6. Return to segregation on the basis of race—not seriously proposed by any politician of national stature, except possibly George Wallace, after the desegregation of most southern schools in 1970, but kept alive for rhetorical purposes as an alternative in debate by some proponents of busing.

A large majority of the national public was clearly lined up behind position five, though position four, the Preyer-Bickel plan, never received much national discussion. The Gallup poll in November 1971 found 18 percent favoring and 76 percent opposing "busing of Negro and white school children from one school district to another." Even among blacks, 45 percent favored and 47 percent opposed "busing," when formulated in these terms.[72]

The Griffin Amendment

On November 4, 1971, in a late night session, the House of Representatives, reacting to the rising national furor against busing, approved by a vote of 234 to 124 an amendment to the higher education bill offered by Congressman John Ashbrook of Ohio, a Republican fundamentalist (who was to run the following year in the Republican presidential primaries as a right-wing opponent to Nixon), barring the use of federal funds for busing students to "carry out a plan of racial desegregation of any school or school system."[73] The Ashbrook amendment was itself amended before passage to include an amendment offered by Congresswoman Edith Green of Oregon, a Democratic centrist, forbidding federal employees to "urge, persuade, induce or require" local officials to use state or local funds for busing for integration.[74] The House also approved a third antibusing amendment, proposed by Congressman William Broomfield of Michigan, a Republican stalwart whose district included part of Detroit's suburbs, to prevent any court order requiring busing to achieve "racial balance" from taking effect until all appeals had been exhausted.[75]

The distribution of the vote on the Ashbrook amendment, the most drastic of the three, by ideological groups was as follows:[76]

Republicans			Democrats		
	Yes	No		Yes	No
Fundamentalists	72	0	Traditionalists	42	0
Stalwarts	36	4	Centrists	40	14
Moderates	13	7	Regulars	25	39
Progressives	4	9	Liberals	2	51
Total	125	20	Total	109	104

Only Democratic liberals held their lines firmly against the amendment. Republican progressives suffered some erosion, and a majority of Republican moderates supported Ashbrook. A majority of Democratic regulars voted against the amendment, but there were many defections—including four regulars from the Detroit metropolitan area, two from Chicago, and two from Boston. All other groups voted overwhelmingly in favor of the amendment.

When the higher education bill reached the Senate floor early in 1972, as part of an omnibus education bill, Senators Scott and Mansfield, the minority and majority leaders, offered a compromise, accepting the Ashbrook and Green amendments with little change, but adding the qualifying language "unless constitutionally required."[77] Scott and Mansfield accepted the Broomfield amendment without the qualifier, apparently on the theory that the courts, under *Swann*, could not in any case require "racial balance."

On February 25, 1972, Senator Robert Griffin of Michigan, who in 1967 had helped lead the fight against antibusing legislation proposed by Everett Dirksen, proposed, in place of the Scott-Mansfield compromise, a flat prohibition against federal courts ordering that children be bused "on the basis of their race, color, religion, or natural origin."[78] After angry debate, the Senate approved the Griffin amendment by a vote of 43 to 40—the "up-and-down defeat" for the civil rights community that Patrick Buchanan had predicted two years before. The distribution of the vote on the Griffin amendment by ideological groups was as follows:[79]

Republicans			*Democrats*		
	Yes	No		Yes	No
Fundamentalists	20	0	Traditionalists	8	0
Stalwarts	4	5	Centrists	9	3
Moderates	0	4	Regulars	2	9
Progressives	0	7	Liberals	0	12
Total	24	16	Total	19	24

The difference between the votes on the Ervin amendment in 1970 and the Griffin amendment in 1972 in part reflected the fact that an unusually large number of Democratic liberals and regulars were absent from the Senate chamber when the latter vote was taken. But also the antibusing forces had made significant gains among Democratic centrists and Republican fundamentalists and stalwarts—one of the last being Griffin himself.

On February 29 the Senate recanted, first voting down a broader amendment, which contained both the Griffin amendment and the Scott-Mansfield compromise, by the narrow margin of 49 to 48, and then reenacting the Scott-Mansfield compromise. The reversal was achieved when eight senators who had been absent and without pairs when the Griffin amendment passed on Feburary 25 (including Senators Muskie and McGovern, who were campaigning for the Democratic presidential nomination in New Hampshire) voted against Griffin the second time around, and Senator Fulbright of Arkansas changed his vote from yes to no. On the other hand, Senators Mathias of Maryland and Bellmon of Oklahoma, border state Republicans, switched from no to yes.[80]

Nixon's Legislative Proposals

In the winter of 1972, Nixon, observing Congress's apparent inability to take effective action against busing—and looking toward the coming presidential election—decided to enter the conflict with some antibusing proposals of his own. "Forced busing is wrong," he told Safire, "and I don't care if it sounds like demagoguery—I want to say so loud and clear. The courts don't understand the folks."[81] The preparation of a presidential position on the issue was entrusted chiefly to John Ehrlichman. Garment, though still on the White House staff, was given little role.

Nixon considered supporting a constitutional amendment that stated flatly: "No public school student shall, because of his race, creed or color, be assigned or required to attend a particular school." He was dissuaded from this course by Attorney General Mitchell and HEW Secretary Richardson (who had succeeded Finch in 1970), both of whom expressed lawyerly scruples against cluttering the Constitution with what amounted to legislation on a presumably passing issue. Vice-President Agnew, no shrinking violet on the busing issue, also opposed going the amendment route on the ground that it would "trivialize" the Constitution.[82]

On March 14 George Wallace, campaigning on a promise to stop busing, won a plurality of 42 percent in the Florida Democratic presidential primary—24 percent ahead of his closest rival (Hubert Humphrey). Two days later, in a nationally televised address, Nixon proposed two strong statutory measures against busing: a "moratorium" on court-ordered busing until July 1, 1973, or until Congress passed new guidelines for busing, whichever was sooner; and an "equal educational opportunity" bill, which would strictly limit busing, while providing increased federal financial support for schools primarily serving poor children. The president sought once more to

identify his position as a middle course, one disliked both by "extrem-
ists on the one side who oppose busing for the wrong reasons" and
by "extreme social planners on the other side who insist on more
busing, even at the cost of better education," but favored by "the
majority of Americans of all races [who] want more busing stopped
and better education started."[83]

He had rejected proposing a constitutional amendment to stop
busing, Nixon said, because the amendment approach "has a fatal
flaw: It takes too long." His recommended moratorium "would call
an immediate halt to all new busing orders by federal courts."[84] The
"equal educational opportunity" act, which was to follow, would
prohibit busing for integration altogether for students in the first six
grades, and permit busing for students above the sixth grade only
under the most extreme circumstances. To improve education for
children in poor neighborhoods, the president called for allocation of
$2.5 billion in federal funds for "compensatory education" programs
in schools "in which substantial numbers of students are from poor
families." By this means, he maintained, "schools in the central cities"
would be "upgraded so that the children who go there will have just
as good a chance to get quality education as do children who go to
school in the suburbs."[85] This recommendation represented a notable
change of view by the president, who as recently as 1970 had rejected
increased federal support for compensatory education, because, as
he put it, "we must recognize that our present knowledge about how
to overcome poor background is so limited that major expansion of
such programs could not be based on such results."[86] Nixon's proposal
also included a very limited form of the "open transfer" plan, providing a federal bonus to schools that accepted students transferring
from "poor" to "non-poor" schools, but only within a single district.[87]

The constitutionality of Nixon's recommended moratorium on
court-ordered busing was quickly challenged by many authorities on
constitutional law. Alexander Bickel, who had been critical of some
of the court's busing decisions, protested that the enactment of such
a moratorium would represent an attempt at "a more far-reaching
limitation on judicial power, a greater qualification of the power of
judicial review established by *Marbury* v. *Madison* than ever before"
in American history.[88] Robert Bork, also of the Yale Law School (later
solicitor general under Nixon), almost alone among recognized legal
experts argued that the moratorium could be justified under article

1, section 8, of the Constitution, which empowers Congress "to make all laws which shall be necessary and proper for carrying into execution" all authority vested in the federal government. "The constitutionality of the proposed moratorium act," Bork argued, "is likely to turn upon the factual showing by Congress that the freeze is 'necessary and proper' to the exercise of the power to regulate remedies. . . . This means, essentially, a showing of the likelihood of the entry of further large-scale busing orders with their concomitant heavy expenditure of funds, administrative disruptions, and student inconvenience all tending to disrupt and make less effective the educational process."[89] Perhaps shrinking from such a direct confrontation with the courts, Congress allowed the moratorium bill to die in committee.

On June 10, 1972, the House reluctantly approved a conference report accepting a higher education bill with antibusing provisions largely modeled on the Scott-Mansfield compromise. Opponents of busing then turned their attention to Nixon's proposed equal educational opportunity bill. When the administration bill reached the House floor on August 17, 1972, large majorities voted for an amendment offered by Congressman Ashbrook to require that students be assigned to schools closest to their neighborhoods, and one by Congresswoman Green to permit the reopening of desegregation cases already settled by the courts.[90]

When the bill was taken up by the Senate in October 1972, with only a few weeks to go before election, liberals decided that the only way to head off its passage was by resorting to a device they had frequently denounced when it was employed by conservatives: the filibuster. Three attempts at invoking cloture failed, and on October 12 the administration and its allies in the Senate finally conceded defeat.

The Courts and the Public

Although action against court-ordered busing had been temporarily forestalled in Congress—through exactly the kind of obstructionist techniques that liberals had often claimed were undermining the credibility of the governmental system when they were used by conservatives—few informed people believed that the issue was simply going to vanish. By the beginning of 1973, a majority of the national public seemed ready to support almost any legal action to stop busing for integration, even if it meant challenging the autonomy of the courts and the authoritative role of the Supreme Court in the federal system. The Supreme Court, as Justice Felix Frankfurter once pointed out, has always been an "undemocratic aspect of our scheme of government."[91] As such, it has usually been accepted and even revered by most of the public as a means for maintaining the authority of constitutional principles against the whims of transitory popular majorities. Yet in a system in which all authority is derived ultimately from the will of the people—or, in another formulation, from objective rules of moral obligation as perceived by a majority of the people— constitutional principles themselves must finally rest on some kind of popular approval.

This does not mean that the Court is answerable to the public in the sense that the president and the Congress are viewed as answerable. Because of presumed objectivity and legal wisdom, gained through training and experience, the Court is vested with authority to interpret the Constitution by no other standards than the rules of reason and the traditions of American jurisprudence. "We are under a Constitution, but the Constitution is what the judges say it is," Charles Evans Hughes remarked, before he rose to the Supreme Court.[92] This state of affairs is acceptable to the national public only so long as the public retains confidence that the judges are deciding pretty much as the ordinary citizen would decide *if* the ordinary citizen possessed extensive legal experience and training, and *if* he were able to detach himself from his personal interests. Since these conditions are by their nature unattainable, and therefore untestable, the citizen's confidence must rest to a great extent on faith—a faith that the citizen has usually been prepared to grant in order to preserve the advantages of a constitutional, as distinct from a purely democratic, system.

During the 1960s the Supreme Court, through such decisions as those prohibiting prayer in the public schools and placing new restrictions on the investigative procedures of the police, began to impose heavy burdens on that faith. Still, a majority of the public seemed willing to concede that the Court, in its legal wisdom, probably knew best, or at least they were not willing to take the risks involved in changing the Constitution to overthrow the unpopular decisions. With the decisions requiring extensive school busing for integration, however, the courts seemed to a majority of the public to have pushed to the breaking point the unarticulated assumption that judges decide as the ordinary citizen would decide, given legal training and objectivity. Defenders of the busing decisions argued that the courts were merely enforcing the Constitution. The public did not believe it. The public knew that from 1896 until 1954, the courts had held, under the *Plessy* decision approving "separate but equal" facilities for black citizens, that the Constitution permitted legal segregation of schools by race. Now, some courts held that the Constitution required busing of children out of their own communities and away from their neighborhood friends to achieve racial integration in areas that had never practiced legal segregation. Had the Constitution changed so much?

The courts had acted, in the *Brown* decision and subsequent decisions putting an end to the dual school system, not only out of humanitarian principles or new insights into the Constitution but also out of recognition that the nation was approaching a constitutional crisis.[93] Blacks and civil rights activists had given sign that they would not indefinitely tolerate curtailment of rights supposedly guaranteed to all Americans by the Constitution. The Supreme Court had led in securing constitutional rights for black citizens, but the executive and legislative branches and a majority of the national public had eventually given support to what were accepted as needed reforms.

Now, however, the courts, or some courts, seemed to be driving the nation toward an even graver constitutional crisis, in which not the minority but the majority felt threatened in their fundamental interests and rights: the cohesion of their communities, the welfare of their children.

In 1973 the Supreme Court began to indicate that it was prepared to limit the reach of busing. On January 15—five days before Nixon's second inaugural—the Court agreed to hear arguments on the Richmond case, on which the Fourth Circuit Court of Appeals had ruled that Judge Merhige had exceeded his authority in requiring that children from suburban counties be bused into Richmond to integrate the metropolitan area. Later that year the Court announced that it had split 4 to 4 (Justice Lewis Powell, appointed by Nixon, having disqualified himself because he had formerly been a member of the Richmond school board), and the circuit court's judgment was therefore permitted to stand.[94]

On November 19, 1973, the Court accepted jurisdiction over *Milliken* v. *Bradley*, the Detroit case, in which the Sixth Circuit Court of Appeals, by a vote of 6 to 3, had approved Judge Roth's ruling that busing must be carried out between Detroit and fifty-three suburban school districts to integrate the entire metropolitan area.[95] On February 27, 1974, the Supreme Court, by a vote of 5 to 4, reversed both Judge Roth and the circuit court, and ruled that suburban districts could not be required to bus students into Detroit, even though an integration plan limited to Detroit "would result in an all black system, with an overwhelming white majority in the total metropolitan area."[96] Voting with the majority were the four justices appointed by President Nixon, and Justice Potter Stewart, appointed by President Eisenhower. Chief Justice Burger, writing for the majority, held: "Boundary lines may be bridged where there has been a constitutional violation calling for interdistrict relief, but the notion that school district lines may be casually ignored or treated as a mere administrative convenience is contrary to the history of public education in our country. No single tradition in public education is more deeply rooted than local control over the operation of schools; local autonomy has long been thought essential both to the maintenance of community concern and support for public schools and to quality of the educational process. . . . Disparate treatment of white and Negro students occurred within the Detroit school system, and not elsewhere, and on this record the remedy must be limited to that system."[97] Justice Thurgood Marshall (who twenty years before had argued for the plaintiffs in *Brown* v. *Board of Education*) wrote in dissent: "Today's holding, I fear, is more a reflection of a perceived public mood that we have gone far enough in enforcing the Constitution's guarantee of equal justice than it is the product of neutral principles of law."[98]

The Supreme Court's decision in *Milliken* did not end either busing or the busing controversy. It certainly did not end the problem at which busing was directed—the existence of racially identifiable schools in many American cities. But it did appear to limit sharply the portion of the population vulnerable to busing (although some liberals, forgetful for the moment of their insistence when decisions of the Court promoted desegregation that the Court's judgments must be accepted as final, continued to hold out hope that a differently constituted Court would approve busing across school district boundaries). Most suburban residents, except when city and suburbs were included in one school district, as in Charlotte, North Carolina, and Louisville, Kentucky, seemed to have been exempted from busing for integration. In many cities with large black majorities in their public schools, like Detroit and Philadelphia, busing appeared increasingly futile. The chief areas still vulnerable to busing were the combined city-suburban districts and the cities, like Boston, with sufficiently small minority populations to make mixed schools achievable through busing within city limits. (In the process, as Gary Orfield has pointed out, the burden for integration would be placed on "working class white families, those most threatened by racial change and least able to handle it successfully.")[99]

Judges did indeed push ahead with busing orders in some districts in these two categories, which lead to renewed outcries for curbs against busing in Congress and among the public. In 1976 President Ford asked Congress for legislation to limit busing to districts with proved histories of practices leading to segregation.[100] On the whole, however, by the end of the 1970s the busing controversy had at least temporarily subsided—leaving the authority of the courts pretty much intact, the rights and interests of middle-class suburban families relatively secure, and the core city schools increasingly segregated.

Liberal versus Conservative

The political struggle over busing for integration produced an almost classic confrontation between liberal and conservative points of view. Liberals were prepared to risk social disruption and personal hardship among many white families, which they of course minimized, to gain access to "equal" education for poor blacks and to promote the eradication of racial distinctions in society. Conservatives gave lower priority to combating black deprivation, which they preferred not to acknowledge, than to preserving traditional systems and protecting what were regarded as constitutionally established rights.

President Nixon and many officials of the Nixon administration claimed that they favored a middle course. "I could deliver the Sermon on the Mount and the NAACP would criticize the rhetoric," Nixon told members of his staff in 1969. "And the diehard segregationists would criticize it on the grounds that I was being motivated solely by public pressure rather than by conscience."[101] Nixon viewed himself as a moderate reformer in that he proposed means, like increased federal support for schools attended largely by children from poor families, that would help reduce inequality. But in their more candid moments Nixon and his associates conceded that the remedies they offered would not put an end to racial separation in American life. In a memorandum to John Ehrlichman in January 1972, Nixon wrote: "This country is not ready at this time for either forcibly integrated housing or forcibly integrated education. . . . We simply have to face the hard fact that the law cannot go beyond what the people are willing to support."[102]

To what extent was Nixon motivated by conviction in his handling of the busing issue, and to what extent by political expediency? He appears to have sincerely shared the indignation of white families threatened by court-ordered busing. "There is no doubt whatever," he told Ehrlichman in 1972, "that education requiring excessive transportation for students is definitely inferior. I come down hard and unequivocally against busing for the purpose of racial balance."[103] Instead, however, of offering leadership toward some means, like the Preyer-Bickel plan for open transfers, that would at least provide a way out of segregation for highly motivated families and students, Nixon dug in hard against any remedy that would cause even mild concern among the southern, suburban, and white working-class constituencies that he aimed to win by large majorities in 1972. It would be hard not to conclude that his judgment was heavily influenced by his immediate political interests.

As matters turned out, Nixon obtained the majorities he sought, carrying practically all the voters who had gone for George Wallace in 1968 and even some of the white working-class voters who had supported Hubert Humphrey. In the process, however, he passed up whatever opportunity he may have had to lead the public toward some at least partial remedy to the potentially catastrophic problem of racial separation in the nation's major metropolitan areas.

10

Economic Policy:
The Great Reversal

OPPOSITION to any form of "incomes policy"—government intervention to affect wage and price adjustments in the market—had long
been a cherished doctrine among economic conservatives. Even voluntary controls, Arthur Burns warned in 1964, would "throttle the
forces of competition" and lead to costly inefficiencies.[1] Milton Friedman went even further. Attempts to suppress inflation through government intervention, the Chicago economist said, would "produce
waste and misallocation of resources, encourage bribery, corruption,
and disrespect for the law. They are a far greater hindrance to economic development than open inflation."[2]

Richard Nixon quite agreed. During the campaign Nixon had dis-
paraged the Johnson administration's policy of announcing wage and
price "guideposts" as a means for combating inflation. Guideposts,
he said, would not work, and might lead to mandatory wage and
price controls. Mandatory controls, he insisted, citing his own experience with the Office of Price Administration at the beginning of
the Second World War, "can never be administered equitably and
are not compatible with a free economy," and result in "rationing,
black markets, regimentation."[3]

Inflation, as measured by the rise in the consumer price index, was
4.7 percent in 1968, more than twice the average annual rate of
inflation from 1956 through 1967. Unemployment, on the other hand,
at the end of the year had fallen to 3.3 percent, its lowest level since
1953.[4] The new administration's primary economic problem was to

bring down the first without greatly increasing the second. Nixon was prepared to pursue this goal through gradual tightening of the federal budget, accompanied by a moderately restrictive monetary policy, as recommended by his conservative economic advisers.

Yet the president, as his advisers recognized, was not prepared to take extreme political risks for the sake of economic dogmas. Paul McCracken, chairman of the Council of Economic Advisers during the first three years of the administration, later said: "Nixon was predisposed toward using the market to make most economic decisions, and toward maintaining a free-market economy. Mixed with this philosophy, he had a pragmatic turn of mind which tended to keep him free of being confined by any ideology." On budgetary matters, according to Arthur Burns, "Nixon was very much of an improviser—sometimes hard as nails, but at other times allowing expenditures to swell." Or as Milton Friedman put it: "My principles were Nixon's prejudices."[5]

Nixon's tendency to waver in the application of conservative economic policies may have in part reflected the fact that the subject, unlike foreign policy, did not excite his intellectual interest. To McCracken, his attitude toward economics was "somewhat like that of a little boy doing required lessons." Sometimes, particularly in the early days of the administration, Nixon got his economic signals mixed up. Herbert Stein, who served as a member of the CEA throughout the first term and succeeded McCracken as chairman at the end of 1971, recalled that when Nixon spoke at a press conference in 1969 of "fine-tuning" the economy, his advisers took him aside later and told him: "That's not what we do; that's what the other people believe in doing."[6]

The deeper reason for Nixon's economic flexibility, however, seems to have been his fear that strict adherence to the conservative approach would lead to political disaster. It would interfere with his ability to operate an "activist" presidency, and might throw the economy into recession before curbing the rate of inflation. "You can't explain economics to the American people," he told Charls Walker, whom he had made under secretary of the treasury, in 1969.[7] Nixon believed that he had lost the presidency to John Kennedy in 1960 in large part because Eisenhower had refused to stimulate the economy during the spring of the election year. He was determined not to be willingly twice victim of the same mistake.

Troika and Quadriad

During the first year of the administration, economic policy was largely managed by the so-called troika, composed of McCracken, Secretary of the Treasury David Kennedy, and Budget Director Robert Mayo. These three midwesterners, who had known each other professionally for many years, met over breakfast at least once a week, usually at the Cosmos Club, a social club for writers and scholars located in an elegant former town house along Massachusetts Avenue. About once a month this group was joined by William McChesney Martin, Jr., chairman of the Board of Governors of the Federal Reserve, to form the "quadriad"—an informal association of top economic policymakers modeled on a group first formed during the Eisenhower administration. Arthur Burns, though a member of the administration and a close friend and sponsor of McCracken, seems most of the time to have deliberately kept his distance from economic policy during the year he spent in the White House.

Although the members of the troika appear to have dealt with one another on a basis of amiable equality, McCracken soon became the most visible of the economic policymakers. Within the business community and the government's various economic policy establishments, this was viewed as a reduction in status for the Treasury, normally the fulcrum of economic decisionmaking in most administrations. David Kennedy's career in banking turned out not to have prepared him very well for the more public role of secretary of the treasury. According to Charls Walker, who had originally recruited him for the job, Kennedy was too anxious to avoid "shootouts" with other members of the administration. In the view of another who served at the Treasury, Kennedy had been "used to relying on strong staff support at Continental Illinois. That did not work out so well at the Treasury, because the secretary, rather than the staff or deputy secretaries, must testify before congressional committees."

Besides the troika and the quadriad, Nixon established a Cabinet Committee on Economic Policy—largely as "a sop to [Secretary of Commerce] Maurice Stans," according to one of its members. The larger group consisted of the members of the troika, Stans, Secretary of Labor George Shultz, Secretary of Agriculture Clifford Hardin, John Ehrlichman, D. P. Moynihan, and one or two other members of the White House staff. In McCracken's view: "The Committee on Economic Policy was too large and unwieldy to serve as an effective policymaking board. It did not comprise a natural group. Unlike the troika, many of its members spoke for identifiable constituencies, which tended to hinder its effectiveness."[8] The Committee on Economic Policy did, however, provide a sounding board for Shultz, who aimed to play a larger role in formulating economic policy.

The Nixon Game Plan

McCracken set forth the administration's basic economic strategy—called the "game plan" (perhaps through association with Nixon's highly publicized interest in professional football)—in his first appearance before Congress's Joint Economic Committee on February 17, 1969. "The American economic system," McCracken told the committee, "did not spring full blown from the brow of some Scottish philosopher or Virginia gentlemen 200 years ago. It evolved over the decades." The central truth about the economy in 1969 was "not that it has problems but that it is highly successful." Still, the problem of inflation, rising at an annual rate of 5 percent in the final quarter of 1968, must be dealt with. Inflation had been caused, McCracken maintained, by the attempt of the Johnson administration and Congress to finance the Vietnam War without cutting spending for domestic programs or increasing taxes, until enactment of the 10 percent surcharge on the personal income tax in the spring of 1968. To curb inflation while keeping unemployment relatively low, it would be necessary "to slow down the growth of total demand gradually." The administration had rejected the idea of an "incomes policy," McCracken said, because such a policy "can apply only to a limited segment of the economy—. . . the centralized national unions and large corporations," which "become resentful and resistant, for understandable reasons." The administration intended to employ two principal weapons against inflation: maintenance of "a budget whose expenditures are at least matched by the revenues from the tax system—assuming reasonably full employment"; and "an appropriate degree of monetary restraint."[9]

In March Nixon asked Congress to extend the surcharge, and simultaneously announced cuts in the budget for fiscal 1970 and the

postponement of scheduled reductions in the automobile and telephone excise taxes. Meeting at the White House with congressional
leaders to discuss cuts in the budget, Nixon asked if they felt any
further steps were needed. Russell Long (according to Charls Walker,
who was present) replied: "We should get rid of that goddam [7
percent] investment tax credit"—first enacted in 1962 as part of President Kennedy's program to encourage industrial expansion. As the
meeting was breaking up, Nixon took Walker and John Byrnes aside
and asked what they thought of Long's proposal. Walker replied that
the administration might as well come out for the repeal, since the
Democrats in Congress were going to do it anyhow and the administration should get some of the credit. Nixon told Walker to sound
out Republican members of the Ways and Means Committee on the
question. In a few days Walker reported back that the Republicans
on Ways and Means all believed that repeal of the investment credit
was inevitable and should be supported by the administration, even
though the change would be unpopular with business. Nixon was
particularly impressed that Congressman James Utt of California, the
most conservative Republican on Ways and Means, joined in this
recommendation.[10]

Responding to demands from Senate Democrats, particularly Edward Kennedy, that extension of the surcharge should be accompanied by "tax reform," Nixon on April 14 sent Congress a comprehensive reform proposal calling for repeal of the investment tax
credit, limitations on tax shelters, and removal of 2 million people
with incomes below the poverty level from the income tax rolls. The
net effect on revenues of the tax reform bill was calculated by the
Treasury to be a long-term annual gain of $720 million—which at least
would not make inflation worse.

During the spring and summer the administration's game plan
began to slow the growth of the economy, but had no immediate
effect on inflation. Unemployment at the end of September had edged
up to 4 percent, and the consumer price index during the third quarter
rose at an annual rate of 5.8 percent.

In August Arthur Burns warned that high wage settlements in the
construction industry were becoming targets for unions and workers
throughout the industrial labor force. Burns recommended suspension of the Davis-Bacon Act, which, by requiring that workers on
federal construction projects be paid at "the prevailing wage in the

locality," established an artificial wage base for all construction workers. Suspension of Davis-Bacon was opposed, however, by Secretary of Labor Shultz, who was assiduously cultivating good relations for the administration with George Meany and other members of the AFL-CIO hierarchy.[11]

Burns also recommended that the president announce a 75 percent reduction in federally financed construction projects. Despite heated protests from many of the nation's governors, predominantly Republican for the first time in many years, Nixon ordered this cut on September 4.

By the end of summer, many economists, within and outside the administration, had begun to worry that the tight money policy being pursued by the Federal Reserve was going too far. In August Milton Friedman wrote in his column in *Newsweek* that the Federal Reserve's policy was approaching "overkill," and would throw the economy into recession if continued much longer. By November McCracken had joined the critics of extreme monetary restriction, and suggested to McChesney Martin at a meeting of the quadriad that the time had come to ease up on the brakes. Martin was unconvinced. In December George Shultz, with Nixon's private approval, criticized the Federal Reserve's tight money policy in a Department of Labor bulletin.[12]

Actions taken by Congress toward the end of 1969 on Nixon's tax reform proposal put further pressure on inflationary expectations. The version of the tax bill approved by the House in August included a cut in personal income tax rates, drafted by Wilbur Mills, that would result in a net annual revenue loss of about $2.4 billion. This loss was hugely increased in December when the Senate approved, by a vote of 58 to 37, an amendment offered by Senator Albert Gore of Tennessee, an oldtime southern populist waging a losing fight for reelection, to increase the personal exemption on the income tax from $600 to $800. Among Senate Democrats, only Russell Long and four southern traditionalists voted against the Gore amendment. The Senate also attached an amendment to the bill increasing social security benefits 15 percent—5 percentage points more than had been recommended by Nixon.

Though the increase in the personal exemption was cut back to $750 in conference, the bill that went to the president would still result in a heavy revenue loss. On December 19 Kennedy, McCracken, and Mayo sent a memorandum to the president concluding: "The country needs strong medicine to bring it to its fiscal senses. A cogent veto message would be a dramatic vehicle for reaffirming your commitment to the Nation's priorities and the Government's responsibilities."[13] Nixon, nevertheless, signed the bill on December 30, with the grumbling comment that its "effect on the budget and on the cost of living is bad."[14] The net result of the new law was a long-term annual revenue loss of about $5 billion.[15]

The 1971 Budget

Meanwhile, work had gone forward on the budget for fiscal 1971, to be presented by the president at the beginning of 1970—the first budget for which the new administration would be fully responsible. Budget Director Mayo, exercising real authority for the first time in his career, had set out to confound predictions by some of his former associates that he would prove too passive for the job. "During the Eisenhower administration," Mayo has said, "[Budget Directors] Brundage and Stans approached the budget essentially as accountants, but under the Democrats [in the 1960s] Kermit Gordon and Charles Schultze took a broader, more philosophic approach to the budget. I decided to continue the approach taken by Gordon and Schultze. . . . I persuaded Nixon that through the budget he could get control over the whole direction of government."[16]

During the administration's first year, Nixon devoted about forty-five hours to working on the budget. In keeping with the budgetary frugality called for in the game plan, he directed Mayo to make deep cuts in budget requests submitted by the departments. On many politically sensitive items, however, Nixon reversed cuts recommended by the budget director. "For a few days in 1969, I had Nixon talked into getting rid of Saturday mail deliveries," Mayo said later. "But then he caved in to the politicians, and Saturday deliveries were restored." Nixon also yielded to pressure from Senator George McGovern, of all people, to turn down Mayo's recommendation that the then infant food stamp program be terminated. Over Mayo's strong objection, the president decided to go ahead with the supersonic transport program (SST). Nixon told him, Mayo recalled: "Bob, I must keep in mind some other things." John Ehrlichman, who as the year went on increasingly sat in on budget sessions, later explained to Mayo that Nixon had meant that the SST was needed to maintain American prestige.[17] (Despite the administration's best effort, the SST was voted down by the Senate in December 1970.)

When the budgetary process was completed (including a series of appeal sessions in which Nixon allowed each cabinet member seven minutes—except Melvin Laird, who was given an hour—to argue against cuts made in his requests), the expenditure total was just over $200 billion (about twice the size of Eisenhower's last budget nine years before). After the budget document had gone to press, Arthur Burns, whose appointment as chairman of the Federal Reserve had already been announced, protested to Nixon that breaching the $200 billion mark would have extremely damaging psychological effects. Burns's position was supported by HUD Secretary Romney, who feared that a budget viewed as exorbitant would drive up interest rates, undermining the market for housing. To Burns's delight—and Mayo's mortification—Nixon ordered that the printed budgets be destroyed and further cuts made to bring spending below $200 billion. The additional cuts that were made, Mayo felt, were "cosmetic"—the kind of thing the Republicans had criticized Lyndon Johnson for doing. In any case, the new cuts had no durable effect. "Within a few weeks," Burns later complained, "the same expenditures had found their way back into the budget."[18]

Nixon wanted no more of detailed budget making. Early in 1970 Ehrlichman came to Mayo and told him: "The president is very concerned that he spent too much time last year on the budget. Next year, decisions on the budget are going to be made by two people: Ehrlichman and Mayo." Mayo protested that major budget decisions should be made by the president himself. Ehrlichman insisted: "That's the way the president wants it." In March 1970 Mayo, getting a minute alone with Nixon, warned him that Ehrlichman was "getting too much power." The president was noncommittal. In June Haldeman called Mayo into his office and told him that George Shultz would become director of the newly created Office of Management and Budget (OMB). Mayo was to join Moynihan, Harlow, and Finch among the counsellors to the president. In July Mayo resigned to become president of the Federal Reserve Bank of Chicago.[19]

Breaches in the Line

As inflation continued to grow during 1970, some second- and third-rung officials within the administration, particularly at the Treasury, began privately to express doubts whether fiscal and monetary restraint alone would bring the rise in prices under control. In March Assistant Secretary of the Treasury Murray Weidenbaum (a principal architect of revenue sharing) sent the first in a series of internal memoranda to Paul Volcker, the under secretary for monetary affairs, arguing that excess demand had already been drained out of the economy, and that current pressure on prices came mainly from "cost-push" adjustments by companies and unions. These, Weidenbaum claimed, were largely immune to fiscal or monetary discipline. Some positive action by government was therefore needed to cool inflationary expectations. In Weidenbaum's view at that time, mandatory wage-price controls were "too coercive and perhaps self-defeating," and guidelines had been "discredited in part because of the demand-pull inflation which we have since successfully fought." The best available remedies, he concluded, were a temporary voluntary freeze and establishment of wage-price objectives by a board of citizens.[20]

On May 18 Arthur Burns, now installed as chairman of the Federal Reserve, moved away from his long-standing opposition to any form of incomes policy. The "worldwide inflationary trend," Burns told a conference of the Amercian Bankers Association at Hot Springs, Virginia, could be ascribed in part to "humanitarian impulses" that had caused rapid increases in government spending for such purposes as health, education, income security, housing, manpower training, and community development. Burns saw little prospect that the public would tolerate reduced government effort for these purposes. Indeed, "substantial further expenditures" would be needed "to help halt the decay of our central cities, to bring air and water pollution under control . . . to provide better housing for the less privileged, better medical services to the indigent and aged," among other purposes. These needed expenditures would put a heavy strain on national economies, but through careful management could be "offset by monetary and tax policies, supplemented by more selectivity in public expenditures."

In general, Burns said, the fiscal and monetary policies undertaken by the administration had been fruitful: "The excess demand that bedeviled our economy during the past four or five years has been eliminated." But to rely on fiscal and monetary restraints alone to overcome the "cost-push" pressures that were now the principal cause of inflation "would be most unwise." Too much restraint would "increase greatly the risks of a very serious business recession." If a recession should occur, "the outcries of an enraged citizenry would probably soon force the government to move rapidly and aggressively toward fiscal and monetary ease." In that case, "our hopes for getting the inflationary problem under control would . . . be shattered." Under these circumstances, Burns suggested, "we should not close our minds to the possibility that an incomes policy, provided it stopped well short of direct price and wage controls and was used merely as a supplement to overall fiscal and monetary measures, might speed us through this transitional period of cost-push inflation."[21]

Testifying before the Joint Economic Committee on June 2, Murray Weidenbaum became the first official under presidential authority to breach publicly the administration line against any kind of incomes policy. Under close questioning from Senator William Proxmire of Wisconsin, the committee's chairman, Weidenbaum acknowledged: "I think the time has come to give some serious consideration to some form of incomes policy." Weidenbaum declined to go much further on the ground that it would not be "appropriate to pass on the confidential counsel" he was giving to the secretary of the treasury. He did say, however, that he thought the most effective action would lie somewhere between mandatory controls and mere exhortation by the president.[22]

George Shultz, taking over his new duties as director of OMB, strongly advised Nixon that all talk of an incomes policy must be squelched. Suggestions like those of Burns and Weidenbaum, Shultz argued, were themselves inflationary, because they motivated businessmen to raise prices quickly, before an incomes policy was instituted.[23]

On June 17, while the effects of the Cambodia incursion still traumatized the nation, Nixon made his first concession to the growing public demand for some forceful government action against inflation. In a speech over national radio and television, the president announced that he had ordered the Council of Economic Advisers to issue "periodic Inflation Alerts," which would "spotlight the significant areas of wage and price increases," and "call attention to outstanding cases of price or wage increases." Moving quickly back toward the position held by Shultz and McCracken, however, the president maintained that these "alerts" should not be regarded as "guidelines" or "controls in disguise." He realized, Nixon said, "that there are some people who get satisfaction out of seeing an individual businessman or labor leader called on the carpet and browbeaten by Government officials." But this kind of "grandstanding" would "distract attention from the real cause of inflation" and could be "a dangerous misuse of the power of Government." As for mandatory controls, the president flatly insisted: "I will not take this nation down the road of wage and price controls, however politically expedient that may seem."[24]

In a statement issued on July 18, Nixon warned that the rising tide of spending bills flowing out of Congress was demolishing the balanced budget he had submitted in January. Since he did not wish to lock himself into commitment to a budget balanced regardless of economic (or political) circumstances, which would have inhibited his ability to stimulate the economy when stimulation seemed opportune, Nixon offered a device that seemed to combine flexibility with fiscal discipline: the concept of balancing the budget at full employment, developed by Herbert Stein, among other economists, during the 1940s.[25] "In raising the issue of budget deficits," the president said, "I am not suggesting that the Federal Government should necessarily adhere to a strict pattern of a balanced budget every year. At times the economic situation permits—even calls for—a budget deficit. There is one basic guideline for the budget, however, which we should never violate: Except in emergency conditions, expenditures must never be allowed to outrun the revenues that the tax system would produce at reasonably full employment."[26]

Apparently hoping to shift blame for continued inflation back to the White House, Congress in August attached an amendment to a bill extending the Defense Production Act of 1950 that granted the president the authority to freeze wages, salaries, prices, and rents. While signing the bill on August 17, Nixon said that he would have vetoed the authority to impose controls if it had come to him separately. "I have previously indicated that I did not intend to exercise such authority if it were given to me," he said. "Price and wage controls simply do not fit the economic conditions which exist to-day."[27]

Burns in Opposition

During the fall the economy slipped into a mild recession, caused in part by a three-month strike against General Motors. In the fourth quarter of 1970, unemployment averaged 5.8 percent—the highest level it had reached since 1961. Yet inflation for the year was 5.5 percent—only slightly less than in 1969. As the CEA report issued in February 1971 drily commented: "Sophisticated econometric analysis of the relation between the behavior of prices and a large number of variables that might help to explain it . . . did not generally predict the rate of inflation experienced in 1970, given the actual conditions of 1970."[28]

Doing poorly against the unions at collective bargaining tables, corporate leaders began to take up the cry for some sort of government-imposed restraint on wages. In October 1970 the Business Council, composed of the top executives of some of the nation's largest corporations, harshly criticized the administration for failing to check excessive wage increases and price inflation. The following month the Committee for Economic Development, another corporate sounding board, recommended appointing a three-man prices and income board to promulgate "broad norms of appropriate noninflationary wage and price behavior."[29]

While corporate chief executives deplored inflation, the major oil companies, pursuing their own immediate interests, during November announced sharp increases in prices of crude oil and gasoline. Government investigation showed that conservation boards maintained by some oil-producing states had cut allowable crude oil production to sustain the new prices, in the face of unusually high petroleum inventories.[30]

Speaking to the National Association of Manufacturers (NAM) at the Waldorf-Astoria Hotel in New York on December 4, Nixon signaled that he did not intend to be a pushover either for his friends in the business community or for the trade unions that were again winning huge settlements in the construction industry. Reacting to the increase in oil prices, the president announced that he was suspending the authority of the states to restrict oil and gas production from federal offshore leases and was increasing the amount of oil that could be imported from Canada. Taken together, Nixon said, these actions would "increase the supply of oil and can be expected to help restrain the increase of oil and gasoline prices." Turning to the construction industry, where first-year wage and benefit increases averaged 19.6 percent during 1970, Nixon warned: "Unless the industry wants government to intervene in wage negotiations on Federal projects to protect the public interest, the moment is here for labor and management to make their own reforms in that industry." But these actions, the president maintained, were "not moves toward controls; on the contrary, these are moves away from the kind of government controls that cause artificial market shortages."[31]

While he was working on the NAM speech, Nixon had again been privately urged by Arthur Burns to suspend the Davis-Bacon Act. Reportedly, an announcement suspending Davis-Bacon was at one point included in the speech. At the last minute, however, George Shultz persuaded Nixon that such a move would needlessly antagonize "hard-hat" unions, then giving strong support to the administration's policies in Southeast Asia.[32]

On December 7 Burns rose at Pepperdine College in Los Angeles to deliver what was widely regarded as a reply to the president's address before the NAM. While commending Nixon's "stern warning to business and labor to exercise restraint in pricing and wage demands," Burns went on to argue, with less equivocation than in his speech to the bankers at Hot Springs in May, that "it would be desirable to supplement our monetary and fiscal policies with an incomes policy." The nation must recognize, Burns said, "that we are dealing, practically speaking, with a new problem—namely, persistent inflation in the face of substantial unemployment—and that the classical remedies may not work well enough or fast enough in this case."[33]

Appointment of Connally

One week later, on December 14, Nixon announced, not an incomes policy, but a daring move that he clearly hoped would shake up the administration's approach to the economy (while, not incidentally, changing the nation's political map): the appointment of John Connally as secretary of the treasury. Connally—former administrative assistant to Lyndon Johnson, business and political agent for Texas oil millionaires, secretary of the navy under John Kennedy, and three-term Democratic governor of Texas (1963 to 1969)—possessed political and personal clout of a dimension up till then absent from Nixon's cabinet. In 1968 Connally, paying final homage to Lyndon Johnson, had in the last week before the election thrown the full weight of his political organization and personal authority behind the Democratic drive in Texas, which enabled Hubert Humphrey to carry the state. But now Connally was moving toward alignment with more like-minded political conservatives in the Republican party.

Connally's conservatism was goal-oriented rather than procedure-oriented. "Connally was not the most conceptual person in the world," according to Peter Peterson, who worked with him managing international economic policy in 1971, "but he did have certain values by which he steered."[34] Latter-day liberals, the new secretary complained, were undermining national solidarity by "running over the country denouncing the Government" and taking potshots at big business. "The days are past," he later said, "when we could enjoy the luxury of an antagonistic relationship between business and government." Current conditions, he argued, require a kind of partnership between big government, big business, and big labor—a concept he never defined very precisely.[35] Connally may be thought of as bringing together salient characteristics of Franklin Roosevelt and Barry Goldwater: governmental activism to promote conservative values.

Connally's drive and confidence had long fascinated Nixon, who even before the 1968 election seems to have regarded Connally as a possible successor. Only two people in America besides himself, Nixon once said, understood power: Nelson Rockefeller and John Connally. For reasons of political circumstance and personal antipathy, Rockefeller could never be Nixon's protégé. But Connally, Nixon felt, could carry on the work of national reconstruction and revitalization he saw himself beginning—Pompidou, perhaps, to Nixon's de Gaulle. More immediately, Nixon looked to Connally to give leadership in finding a way out of the economic quagmire in which the nation seemed to be descending, while the president planned epochal foreign policy moves.

At the Treasury, Connally's arrival produced mixed feelings of apprehension and excitement. "We viewed him as a political animal," according to one high Treasury official, "but also as an advocate who would stand very close to the president." To another former Treasury executive, Connally "in some ways went against the grain. He reminded us of Lyndon Johnson, who was then not long off the scene. But there also was a feeling that a strong, new force was coming to the Treasury."

Connally arrived in Washington an agnostic on the issue of wage and price controls—which already set him off sharply from the adamant opposition to controls still preached by Shultz and McCracken. "I did not come to Washington thinking that controls were needed," Connally has said, "but I could see that economic troubles were ahead."[36] Within a short time Volcker and Weidenbaum, who had by now concluded that a wage-price freeze would be the best way to jolt inflationary expectations out of the economy, had convinced the new secretary that the authority to impose controls should at least be preserved as an available option.

"I Am Now a Keynesian"

Because of the 1970 recession and the refusal of Congress to hold down the level of spending, the budget for fiscal 1971 was headed toward the second highest deficit since the end of the Second World War. (Ultimately, the deficit for the fiscal year ending in June 1971 was $23 billion, far more than in any postwar year except 1968, when the deficit, reflecting the costs of the Vietnam War and the Great Society programs, had reached $25 billion.) Fearing that sharp abatement in the rise in government expenditures would prolong and deepen the recession, Nixon used the concept of the "full employment budget" to justify a projected deficit of $11.6 billion in the budget for fiscal 1972, submitted in January 1971.[37] When Nixon briefed the Republican congressional leadership on the budget, House Minority Whip Leslie Arends complained: "I'm going to have to burn up a lot of old speeches denouncing deficit spending." Nixon admitted: "I'm in the same boat."[38]

In a television interview on January 4, 1971, Nixon soothingly explained that the budget was not "inflationary . . . because it will

not exceed the full employment revenues." After the interview had
gone off the air, Nixon told Howard K. Smith of the American
Broadcasting Company, one of the participating correspondents: "I
am now a Keynesian in economics"—rather like, Smith later commented, "a Christian crusader saying, 'All things considered, I think
Mohammed was right.'"[39] Keynesian or not, Nixon was not winning
high marks from the public for economic performance. A Harris poll
taken in January found 68 percent disapproving and only 28 percent
approving of the administration's handling of economic problems.[40]

During the winter and early spring, Nixon intervened to restrain
price increases in selected industries. On January 12 the president
publicly denounced a 12.5 percent increase in the price of steel plates
and structural shapes posted by Bethlehem Steel. When United States
Steel a few days later announced increases only about half as large,
Bethlehem rolled back its prices to meet those of its competitor. On
February 23 the president, observing that management and labor in
the construction industry had not complied with his request to hold
down settlements, at last suspended the Davis-Bacon Act. On March
29 Davis-Bacon was reinstated, after an agreement within the industry
to form a tripartite committee, representing management, labor, and
the public, charged with responsibility for moderating wage increases.
"There are times," Nixon told the annual meeting of the U.S. Chamber
of Commerce on April 26, "when economic freedom must be protected
from its own excesses." Still, the president insisted, "the road to full
employment with price stability . . . will be the road of free markets,
free competition, free bargaining, and free men."[41]

Inflation appeared to be responding, though slowly, to the decline
in economic growth. The annual rate of rise in the consumer price
index for the first six months of 1971 was 5 percent, against 5.5 percent
in 1970 and 6.1 percent in 1969. At the Treasury, however, Volcker
called Connally's attention to another statistic: as summer got under
way the wholesale price index for industrial commodities, which he
argued provided the best clue to future inflationary pressures, was
going up twice as fast as the consumer index. Testifying before the
Joint Economic Committee in July, Burns observed: "The rules of
economics are not working in quite the way they used to. Despite
extensive unemployment in our country, wage rate increases have
not moderated."[42] Wage settlements in the can, aluminum, and telephone industries called for increases of 12 percent or more in the first

year. I. W. Abel, president of the United Steelworkers, let it be known that he aimed to win a settlement in forthcoming wage negotiations for the steel industry at least equal to those gained by brother unions.[43]

When the economic stabilization act came up for renewal, Connally announced that the administration would not object if Congress continued the president's authority to impose wage and price controls. "Why," he asked Nixon, "do you want to be against something that Congress wants to give you?"[44]

Burns's Jeremiah-like warnings that the administration's economic policy was not working became such an irritant to Nixon that he finally unleashed the resourceful Charles Colson to bring the Federal Reserve chairman back into line. Colson called Alan Greenspan in New York and asked him to talk to Burns. Greenspan declined to become involved. Colson then planted a story with United Press International that Burns, while proposing restraint on wage increases for others, was seeking a raise in his own salary—a palpable falsehood, since Burns, though he had recommended that the chairman's salary be increased, had insisted that the raise take effect only after he had left the post and after economic stability was achieved. Burns's rage at the attempted smear was so great that Nixon had to back down. The president admitted at a press conference that Burns had "taken a very unfair shot," without telling where the shot had come from.[45]

Decision to Go for Controls

Unemployment, meanwhile, pushed up to 6 percent in April and 6.1 percent in May. At a meeting of the president and his top economic policymakers at Camp David on June 26, McCracken admitted discouragement with the pace of recovery from the recession and recommended increased stimulation to prevent unemployment from hovering around 6 percent to the end of the year. Connally, fearing the political as well as economic effects of continued high unemployment, supported McCracken. Shultz, however, foreseeing that increased stimulation would rekindle inflation and lead almost inevitably to controls, argued for continuation of what he called a steady-as-you-go policy. Nixon, who may have been preoccupied with plans for Henry Kissinger's coming secret trip to Peking, decided, at least for the time being, to follow Shultz's advice.[46]

Perhaps wishing to give something to the other side while resolving public confusion over conflicting reports from the Treasury and the CEA, Nixon at the same meeting designated Connally as the administration's chief economic spokesman. Returning from Camp David, the secretary of the treasury announced with his customary ebullience the continuation of the policy he had argued against within the inner circle. The administration, he told the press, would not budge from the "four noes": no tax cut, no increased federal spending, no wage and price review board, and no controls.

On July 15 Nixon stunned the world with his announcement of Kissinger's meeting with the Chinese Communist leaders and of his own intention to visit China in 1972. By this time most of the top economic policymakers had moved toward accepting the inevitability of controls. "I cannot put my finger on exactly when I came to believe that controls were going to be needed," Connally has said. "It was part of an evolving package of economic measures that were taking shape in my mind."[47] Early in August the Steelworkers, as Abel had predicted, won a three-year wage increase of about 30 percent. At some point in late July or early August, Connally persuaded Nixon that controls were the only solution. "If we don't propose a responsible program," Connally told the president, "Congress will have an irresponsible one on your desk within a month."[48] According to George Shultz: "In the end, the only people opposed to controls were Richard Nixon, Milton Friedman, and myself."[49] Finally, even Shultz gave in.

In two long Monday night sessions, on August 2 and 9, Nixon, Connally, and Shultz discussed how and when controls should be applied. Connally presented a plan for mandatory controls. "I am not sure this program will work," he said. "But I *am* sure that anything less will not work."[50] Shultz advised beginning with a total freeze. "There was danger," he recalled, "that a Band-Aid approach would be used, which would bring the bad effects of controls without getting any of the good that could come from a major change in economic policy."[51]

Though the decision had been made to go to controls, the date remained uncertain. According to McCracken, Nixon was anxious that controls not be imposed too early "for fear the warts would begin to show by the time of the election in November 1972." Initially, Nixon planned to announce the change in economic policy early in 1972.[52] In the meantime it was essential that no word of the president's intention leak out. Only McCracken was let in on the secret. "Studying how to make a major change in policy," Shultz has pointed out, "always presents serious problems of how to deal with expectations and anticipations. If it becomes known that you are considering change, this may tip off your intention, leading to reactions exactly the opposite to those you want." Already, some companies were raising prices on the hunch that some kind of incomes policy was in the offing. Still, it was necessary to carry out some technical studies on the effects of different kinds of controls. "Luckily," Shultz has said, "the Senate Republicans at that time were beating the drums for an incomes policy, and were demanding that we express our views. Hearings were to begin right after Labor Day." Shultz used the scheduled hearings as a pretext for directing a few members of his staff to study the likely effects of various incomes policies.[53]

The date for imposition of controls was moved up in response to calamitous developments in the international money markets. At the beginning of the administration, Milton Friedman had urged Nixon to "close the gold window"; that is, to stop convertibility of the dollar into gold for foreign holders of U.S. currency. Friedman later said that he gave this advice because he foresaw that the dollar would have to be cut loose from gold sometime during Nixon's term, and that if it were not done immediately, the president would feel obliged to accompany this change with some kind of politically popular action—like imposing wage and price controls.[54] Arthur Burns, however, argued against ending convertibility on the ground that this would be interpreted as a sign of economic weakness, and Nixon had followed Burns's advice. Later, Volcker and his associates at the Treasury had opposed ending convertibility, because, as Volcker put it, "the United States was committed to play the game straight until it was absolutely clear that the jig was up."[55]

During the first two and a half years of the Nixon administration, the dollar had steadily grown more vulnerable in the international exchanges. In the second quarter of 1971, trade statistics indicating a sharp deficit in American exports compared with imports had caused a heavy shift away from dollars, chiefly into deutsche marks. In the latter part of July, McCracken advised the president that the time had come to cut the dollar loose from gold. On August 6 the Joint Economic Committee issued a report calling for an incomes policy and recommending devaluation of the dollar. In the next few days the flight from the dollar in the money markets grew to rout proportions. Finally, the Bank of England requested that the United States guarantee convertibility of Britain's dollar holdings into gold. Even Volcker concluded: "The jig was definitely up."[56]

August 15, 1971

On the afternoon of Friday, August 13, Volcker reached Connally at his ranch in Texas, where the secretary was spending the weekend, with word that "a major crisis was developing in the world's monetary exchange system." The under secretary reported the British move. Connally "saw at once that we would have to find means for dealing with the situation by Monday morning." Now, he concluded, was the time to move the entire package of economic measures that he had been contemplating. Returning immediately to Washington, Connally quickly persuaded Nixon of the need for action. "The president agreed," Connally has recalled, "that this was a very sensitive situation. He decided that we had best get somewhere where we would have complete control over communications, coming in and out."[57]

On Friday evening the administration's top economic policymakers—McCracken, Shultz, Volcker, Peterson, and Stein, in addition to the president and Connally—plus a few members of the White House staff assembled without fanfare at Camp David. Arthur Burns, swallowing his resentment over the Colson incident, joined the group. "By the time the meeting assembled," McCracken has said, "the decision to go to wage and price controls had already been made. Nevertheless, the president, as was his custom, went around the room and asked each man if he agreed with the policy that was about to be announced."

On a fall afternoon in 1978, McCracken, back at his post at the University of Michigan, recalled the discussion seven years before: "I have sometimes wondered if perhaps I should have taken an opposition role that night. But I did not. I thought in balance it was an acceptable package. I liked the idea of the tax cut [which was to be included in the new policy]. I liked closing the gold window. Since wage and price controls came as part of that package, I thought I could accept it. In retrospect, I sometimes think I should have disembarked at that time. But I did have some hope that controls would break the inflationary momentum. At least, I was able to rationalize it that way in my own mind."[58]

Shultz, too, made no further argument against controls. "I would have continued to oppose controls if the plan had been to impose them in isolation," he later said. "But as part of an overall change in economic policy, I was able to accept them. It was absolutely necessary to close the gold window. The old exchange rate policy was basically bankrupt."[59]

Burns welcomed the move to an incomes policy, but continued to oppose ending the convertibility of the dollar into gold. If the dollar were devalued, Burns warned, "*Pravda* would write that this was a sign of the collapse of capitalism."[60] Once the president announced his decision, however, Burns promised to support the new policy.

On Sunday evening, August 15, Nixon, in an announcement exceeded in shock effect only by his revelation of Kissinger's mission to China exactly one month before, presented his "New Economic Policy" to the public over television and radio. The president briefly described each of the steps he was ordering or proposing to Congress: a ninety-day freeze on wages and prices; suspension of convertibility of the dollar into gold; a 10 percent surcharge on all imports; a $4.7 billion cut in federal spending (requiring postponement of the administration's requests for welfare reform and revenue sharing); a 10 percent tax credit to business for investment in new equipment; repeal of the 7 percent excise tax on automobiles; and acceleration of the increase in the personal income tax exemption from January 1973 to January 1972.[61]

Immediate public reaction to the president's announcement was immensely favorable. The wage-price freeze, as Herbert Stein later said, "was the most popular economic move made by a president since Roosevelt closed the banks." A Gallup poll taken the week after the new program was announced found 73 percent approving Nixon's action. Even Milton Friedman, while deploring the move to controls, admitted in an interview with *Playboy* magazine that Nixon, having failed to convince the public that inflation could be vanquished without controls, acted "the only way a responsible leader of a democracy could."[62]

Preparing for Election

For a time inflation abated. During the final quarter of 1971, under
the freeze and the Phase II guidelines that followed, the consumer
price index rose at an annual rate of less than 3 percent. Unemployment, however, despite the stimulative elements in the August package, continued to hover around 6 percent.

During the fall of 1971, while much of the domestic bureaucracy
was busily implementing the new economic policy, a few technicians
at OMB were assigned to develop statistical models plotting the effect
of economic conditions on the outcomes of presidential elections. This
study, the results of which were reported to George Shultz and John
Ehrlichman, not surprisingly showed that rapid economic growth
strongly benefited an incumbent president seeking reelection.[63]

Nixon hardly needed statistical models to know that falling unemployment in 1972 would increase his chances for reelection. Perhaps nerved by the apparent success of controls, he decided to plunge
ahead with increased federal spending to produce boom conditions
during the months leading up to the election.

For a short time the president's conservative economic advisers,
even Shultz and Stein, joined the euphoric rush toward stimulation.
The 1973 budget, presented at the beginning of 1972, projected outlays
of $246 billion and a deficit of $25.5 billion (almost balanced at full
employment).[64] During calendar 1972 federal spending rose 10.7 percent. Orders spread through the departments to accelerate purchase
plans. Melvin Laird recalled: "Every effort was made to create an
economic boom for the 1972 election. The Defense Department, for
example, bought a two-year supply of toilet paper. We ordered
enough trucks to meet our expected needs for the next several years—
and they turned out to be good buys, because of the way prices rose
later on."[65] At the Federal Reserve Burns accommodated Nixon's
expansionary fiscal policy with a parallel increase in the supply of
money. During 1972 the supply of money (M-1) grew 9 percent—as
opposed to an average annual increase of 5.2 percent from 1965 to
1970.[66] Shultz has defended the stimulation carried out by the administration in early 1972 by pointing out that most of the liberal Democrats, who later accused Nixon of setting out to buy the election with
federal dollars, were at that time advocating *more* stimulation, not

less.[67] A fair response may be that whereas the liberals' economic philosophy called for intense stimulation under such circumstances, Shultz's did not.

By May 1972 the administration's economic policymakers returned to a more conservative stance. On May 16 Connally resigned as secretary of the treasury and Shultz took his place. Stein had succeeded McCracken as chairman of the Council of Economic Advisers in November 1971. Shultz, Stein, and Caspar Weinberger, who succeeded Shultz at OMB, reckoned that an inflationary bubble was growing in the economy that controls could not restrain indefinitely. In an effort to head off a price explosion, they began trying to put the brakes on government spending. "Our fight with Congress," Shultz recalled, "was to hold spending below the $250 billion level."[68] In October 1972 the House actually voted to allow the president to cut appropriations already passed to fit under the $250 billion limit. The Senate, however, refused, by a vote of 27 to 39, to grant Nixon such extraordinary power. Outlays for fiscal 1973, nevertheless, were held to $247 billion—about a billion more than Nixon had asked for in his budget proposal at the beginning of 1972.

The 1974 Budget

In the months immediately before and after Nixon's reelection, Shultz, Weinberger, and Stein set out in earnest to curb the growth in federal spending. Having countenanced heavy spending in 1972, in part to assure Nixon's victory in November, they now intended to use that victory to achieve what they regarded as desirable government goals. The budget for fiscal 1974, submitted in January 1973, projected a reduction of the deficit to $12.7 billion and more severe economies for the following years. Several Great Society programs, which Nixon had left untouched during his first terms, were marked for extinction.[69]

"I argued to Nixon at the time," Shultz later said, "that the political cycle provides a window every eight years when a president can make some significant impact on economic policies. At the beginning of his second term, a president understands his job much better than he did when he took office, and he no longer has to worry about reelection. Even the Congress has a three- or four-month period in which it is not worrying too much about the next election. . . . The programs that we cleaned out hardly anybody could defend, except on political grounds."[70] If Congress voted appropriations for programs recommended for termination, the president vowed, he would impound the funds. Nixon told a press conference on January 31, 1973: "The Constitutional right for the President of the United States to impound funds— . . . that is not to spend money, when the spending of money would mean either increasing prices or increasing taxes for all the people—that right is absolutely clear."[71]

The administration's budgetary offensive of 1973 succeeded for a time in curbing the growth of federal spending. The deficit for fiscal 1974 fell to $4.7 billion. Inflation, however, burst through controls in 1973. The consumer price index for the year rose 8.8 percent—partly because of the stimulative policies of 1972, though also because of huge increases in international food and petroleum prices. In 1974, when most controls were finally abandoned, the consumer price index rose 12.2 percent. This rise contributed directly to the deep recession of 1975, which in turn produced the horrendous federal budget deficits of $45 billion in fiscal 1975 and $66 billion in fiscal 1976. This spiraling chain of economic disasters was in part traceable to Nixon's decision to impose wage and price controls in August 1971, which provided the deceptive security on which the excessive stimulation of 1972 was based.

Paying the Piper

The Nixon administration's break with the free-market ideology in the summer of 1971 was preceded, as has been shown, by a number of preparatory steps. The failure of the administration's fiscal and monetary game plan to bring down inflation as quickly as had been expected weakened the confidence of the president, and to some extent that of his professional advisers, in the practical validity of the principles on which it was based. Nixon's avowal of the concept of balancing the budget at full employment, which permitted an actual deficit, may have had ample theoretic justification. But it represented a giving in to the other side, which probably helped make further giving in appear more acceptable. The defection of some of the market ideology's high priests, particularly Burns, sapped the will of those who tried to remain faithful. The desertion of much of the business community, the ideology's natural constituency, further weakened resistance. The development of a school of thought favorable to controls at the Treasury provided an intellectual resource for Connally when he decided that dramatic action—almost any action—was needed. Finally, Connally's personal dynamism proved far more compelling and reassuring than the abstract arguments of the professional economists. Under the circumstances, it seems surprising that Nixon held out as long as he did.

Once the central doctrine of the ideology had been violated, at first with apparent impunity, all associated maxims, like the caution against extreme deficit spending, for a time seemed to lose relevance. As Herbert Stein has said: "The administration that was against expanding the budget expanded it greatly; the administration that was determined to fight inflation ended by having a large amount of inflation." Stein has attributed these deviations to "circumstances."[72] But in the winter of 1972, even such true believers as Shultz and Stein seemed to join the revelers who were pumping up federal spending.

The free-market ideology, however, like a Freudian superego, maintained latent force, even while its commandments were being violated. When inflation began to rise again in the latter part of 1972, the administration's economic policymakers—Nixon, Shultz, Stein, Weinberger—returned to conservative orthodoxy with the passion of remorseful penitents. The result was the budgetary offensive of 1973— an important contributor to the atmosphere of confrontation between president and Congress, which helped lead to Nixon's final downfall in August 1974.

By 1978 almost none of the policymakers who had participated in the decision to impose controls in 1971 were prepared to defend the rightness of the move. In McCracken's opinion: "Politically, controls made sense, but economically they turned out to be disastrous." To Shultz: "The imposition of controls was wonderful politics, but the economy would have been better off without them." Stein recalled: "I didn't think controls were a good idea at the time, and Nixon didn't think they were a good idea, but the uproar was such that something had to be done." Volcker, who in 1975 became president of the Federal Reserve Bank of New York (and in 1979 rose to the chairmanship of the Federal Reserve), continued to believe that "controls served a purpose for a time," but acknowledged that "unfortunately, they lingered on."[73] Connally, in an appearance at the American Enterprise Institute in September 1978, confessed: "If I had the wisdom of hindsight, I probably would have recommended against wage and price controls. . . . The wage and price controls imposed in 1971 were a mistake."[74] Nixon himself wrote in his memoirs: "The August 15, 1971, decision to impose [controls] was politically necessary and immediately popular in the short run. But in the long run I believe that it was wrong. The piper must always be paid, and there was an unquestionably high price for tampering with the orthodox economic mechanisms."[75]

The Market and Conservatism

Some conservatives, from Samuel Taylor Coleridge to Alexander Solzhenitsyn, have resisted close identification of the market ideology with conservatism of the broader, more inclusive kind, based on ideals of social order and transcendent purpose. Conservative critics of capitalism, like some socialists, have argued that the market, by pitting the individual against other members of his society and promoting material indulgence, tends to undermine social cohesion and to loosen attention to spiritual values.

Yet the system that was described, and to some extent invented, by Adam Smith was not intended to sanction an anarchic "war of each against all," but rather to provide a means, other than physical or social coercion, for meeting economic needs both of individuals and of society as a whole. The goal of capitalism, that is, was not merely individual enrichment, but an economic order operating through principles both more efficient and more humane than those of its chief alternative: government management of the economy backed up by force. Whether the market's reliance on individual incentives will in the end destroy the social harmony and discipline on which capitalism also depends, as Daniel Bell and others have predicted, remains to be discovered.

For Nixon and his principal economic advisers, the market ideology clearly possessed moral as well as theoretic authority—rooted in Protestant and Judaic concepts, among others, of human responsibility and accountability. Many of the policymakers seemed to react to the failure of controls and the explosion of inflation in 1973 and 1974 with a kind of grim moral satisfaction, which John Calvin or the Hebrew prophets would probably have understood. Herbert Stein wrote: "Just as it is necessary for the Jews to reread every year the story of their enslavement under the pharaohs and their subsequent deliverance, it is necessary to repeat the story of our 1971–74 price control experience, so that subsequent policymakers . . . will bear it in mind."[76] Or as George Shultz put it: "At least we have now convinced everyone else of the rightness of our original position that wage-price controls are not the answer."[77]

Not everyone was convinced, of course. But the experience of the United States with controls from 1971 to 1974 raised serious doubts about their potential effectiveness under political democracy, except in times of national emergency, and it went a long way, at least among conservatives, toward enhancing the prestige of the market as the best available means for allocating resources, establishing incentives, and making most economic decisions.

11

The Second Term:
Confronting the Bureaucracy

NIXON approached his second term with a tightfisted and caustic public attitude sharply different from the conciliatory temper he had displayed when he entered the presidency in 1969. "This country has enough on its plate in the way of huge spending programs, social programs, throwing dollars at problems," he told Garnett Horner in an interview a few days after the 1972 election.[1] Gone was the spirit of "Bring Us Together," the theme of Nixon's first inaugural. In its place appeared the assertive truculence of "the New Majority," which Nixon believed was fed up with social change.

The president's altered mood apparently sprang in part from the massive proportions of his 1972 victory. Nixon's popular majority—60.7 percent—was exceeded in modern history only by those awarded to Lyndon Johnson in 1964 and Franklin Roosevelt in 1936. In the electoral college, only the votes of Massachusetts and the District of Columbia deprived him of a unanimous verdict. Among groups giving majority support to Nixon were Catholics, manual workers, trade union members, southerners, and voters under thirty. Of the major elements that had made up the New Deal coalition, only Jews and blacks remained loyal to the Democratic candidate. Lack of confidence in George McGovern clearly contributed to the size of Nixon's victory. But the president believed, probably correctly, that the vote represented at least general approval by a large majority of Americans of his administration's performance during the first term and of the more conservative direction in which he had promised to lead the country if reelected.

232

In spite of this political success, however, Nixon's outlook on the future seemed somber, at times even depressed. On election night some aides found him strangely subdued. (He later speculated that "the melancholy that settled over me on that victorious night" might have been partly due to a sore tooth.)[2] On the day after the election, he startled his cabinet and staff by delivering orders, through H. R. Haldeman, that all appointed members of the administration should submit resignations and be prepared to accept new assignments.

A few days later the president, accompanied by Haldeman and Ehrlichman, flew by helicopter to Camp David. Living in semi-isolation for almost two months, the three men, with the help of a few aides, plotted a course for the second term. "I wished that Nixon would call me," Bryce Harlow, who had left the White House staff at the end of 1970, later said. "But he never did. They were up there planning the future of the administration as though they were in Berchtesgaden. I had the feeling they must be losing their bearings."[3] Cabinet members and presidential advisers who made the journey by helicopter to Camp David returned with impressions of an atmosphere both hectic and sullen. According to Elliot Richardson, who was to replace Laird at Defense in the new term, Nixon behaved "as though he were unable to realize the election was over and he had won."[4]

In a press conference held at Camp David on November 27, Nixon spoke of "the tendency for an administration to run out of steam after the first four years, and then to coast, and usually coast downhill." Even the size of his majority was viewed by the president as in some ways a burden: "Generally when you think of a landslide, you are submerged by it and you also think in terms of a landslide pushing you downhill." Nixon went on to say that he was determined to overcome these handicaps in his second term.[5] But his mood seemed the opposite of euphoric.

Part of the explanation for Nixon's evident uneasiness during the months between election and inauguration may lie in the deeper recesses of his personality and character. It may be true, as one former aide has said, that "there was a side of Richard Nixon that always believed the Nixon haters were right."

There were, however, more tangible and immediate problems to cause the president concern. The economy, he recognized, was headed for serious trouble as the effectiveness of wage and price controls crumbled. (The week before the inauguration, most controls were suspended.) The potential threat that Watergate, broadly defined, posed to the administration may have been ticking away at the back of his consciousness, although the cover-up at that time appeared to be succeeding. Probably most disturbing of all, the truce negotiations with the North Vietnamese, which in October had seemed on the verge of consummation, by December had broken down. On December 17 Nixon sent the bombers north in the most devastating raids of the war, which not only caused carnage in Vietnamese cities but resulted in many American casualties. Political and religious leaders throughout the world almost unanimously condemned the savagery of the new attacks. At the end of December, Nixon, having brought the North Vietnamese back to the negotiating table, and probably fearing the wrath of the returning Congress, at last stopped the bombings. By then, however, he must have known that the coming truce would be inconclusive, and that the pro-American regime in Saigon had only a limited chance for long-term survival.

A Liberal Bureaucracy

Partly to deal with some of these problems, and partly perhaps to escape them, Nixon began his second term with a sharp turn to the right. He aimed to bring an end, he told Garnett Horner, to "the whole era of permissiveness." The federal government, he said, had become "too fat, too bloated," and the time had come to "shuck off" and "trim down" some of the domestic programs set up in the 1960s.[6] In his second inaugural address, delivered on the cold, bleak afternoon of January 20, 1973, the president warned that the nation had "lived too long with [the] false promise" of a "purely governmental solution for every problem." This delusion had led "to inflated expectations, to reduced individual effort, and to a disappointment and frustration that erode confidence." It was time, he sternly recommended, consciously drawing a contrast with John Kennedy's rhapsodic invitation to "ask not what your country can do for you but what you can do for your country," for each American to ask "not just what will government do for me, but what I can do for myself."[7]

Rhetoric aside, Nixon's move to the right was chiefly carried out through two major policy initiatives: the effort to scale down the federal budget, planned by Shultz, Weinberger, and Stein; and, possibly even more important, a drive to achieve administrative mastery at last over the two and a half million person federal civilian bureaucracy. "I'll suggest that we're going to have a house cleaning," Nixon told Haldeman. "It's time for a new team. Period. I'm going to say we didn't do it when we came in before, but now we have a mandate."[8]

The view of the bureaucracy held in the Nixon White House has been to some extent shared by all modern presidents and their staffs. Arthur Schlesinger, Jr., after several years in the Kennedy White House, described the bureaucracy as "in bulk a force . . . with an inexhaustible capacity to dilute, delay, and obstruct presidential purpose."[9] John Gardner, Lyndon Johnson's secretary of HEW, concluded that on many issues of public policy, departmental bureaucrats join representatives of special interest groups in Washington and select members of Congress to form "not so holy trinities," which pursue their own goals, regardless of any administration's preferences.[10]

Under Nixon, the natural tension between the administration in the White House, elected by the voters, and the permanent civil service was further aggravated by ideological disagreement. A study of political attitudes among "supergrade" civil servants and high-ranking political appointees in the federal departments, carried out in 1970 by Joel Aberbach and Bert Rockman, found that among the political appointees, 66 percent were Republicans, 10 percent were independents, and 24 percent were Democrats (almost all holdovers from the Johnson administration, kept on because of special professional skills), whereas among the civil servants, 36 percent were independents, 47 percent were Democrats, and only 17 percent were Republicans. Aberbach and Rockman suspected, moreover, on the basis of responses to other questions in their interviews, that many of the civil servants who identified themselves as independents were in fact closet Democrats, adopting neutral political coloration to protect their jobs.[11]

Among the career civil servants, 54 percent favored "much more" of "some" additional government provision of social services; but among the political appointees, only 33 percent held these views (which the researchers classified as "left" and "left-center"). In the "social service agencies" (HEW, HUD, and the Office of Economic Opportunity), 92 *percent* of the administrators who identified themselves as Democrats favored the "left" option on the question of increasing social services, compared with only 11 percent of the Republicans. On the basis of these and other findings, Aberbach and Rockman concluded that the career bureaucracy had "very little Republican representation," and that the "social service bureaucracy" was "dominated by administrators ideologically hostile to many of the directions pursued by the Nixon administration in the realm of social policy" (a conclusion frequently cited with relish, after the study was published in 1976, by conservatives and defenders of the Nixon administration, including Nixon himself).[12]

Did the liberal ideology held by many of the civil servants affect their willingness to carry out the policies of the administration? Nixon and most members of the White House staff certainly thought so. A former Nixon aide has reported being told by a friend in the bureaucracy: "We send speeches up to the Hill attacking the administration's programs at the same time we send up the programs themselves." Nixon was "constantly thwarted," Raymond Price claimed, "by the bureaucracy nominally under his command."[13] Nixon, Ehrlichman, and particularly Haldeman, according to another former member of the White House staff, developed a deep hatred for the bureaucracy: "Nixon and Haldeman regarded the bureaucracy as a bunch of bastards. Haldeman felt, 'We should get those bastards.' Ehrlichman felt that too, though not so much as Haldeman. Haldeman's feeling and Nixon's were about the same, except that Nixon's was softer." From the time he entered the presidency, Nixon has written in his memoirs, he aimed to break the power of the "iron triangle," composed of the bureaucracy, the interest groups, and their allies in Congress.[14]

Antagonism toward the bureaucracy was not so strong among members of the administration who worked at one time or another in the departments. Nixon and Ehrlichman frequently complained that political appointees in the departments tended to "go native," taking on the interests and attitudes of the bureaucrats whom they were supposed to supervise. No doubt, this happened—as a means for achieving effective management, if for no other reason. But also many of the political appointees found that large numbers of their counterparts in the career civil service, regardless of personal ideologies, operated according to "professional" standards and were prepared, even eager, to carry out the policies of the administration, once these had been clearly communicated. Even orders to hold down staff and reduce spending were carried out without particular protest by many upper-grade civil servants (who, since their own jobs were not likely to be cut, could afford to wait for a greener season). John Whitaker, who became under secretary of interior in 1973 after spending four years on the White House staff, has said that he "never found the bureaucracy unresponsive—once they knew what the president wanted, they would rather help the president than fight him."[15] Frederic Malek, who could hardly be accused of having "gone native" during the year and a half he spent at HEW before joining the White House staff in 1970, found that "early in the administration there was some lack of responsiveness at HEW, but once I made clear to the civil service that the administration was really trying to help them do their jobs better, everyone got along very well."[16]

There seems to have been some tendency among Nixon appointees to believe that although bureaucrats in general were uncooperative with the administration, their *own* bureaucrats were for the most part loyal and responsive. George Shultz, for instance, has said: "I never had any major problem bringing the bureaucracy around, whether at the Labor Department, OMB, or the Treasury. It was probably different at places like HEW."[17] Even political appointees who experienced tension between the administration and the civil service often put much of the responsibility for dissonance on the administration. "I've come to the conclusion you can't say it's the damn bureaucrats," a political appointee in HEW told Hugh Heclo. "With some exceptions, that's not the problem. What's lacking is the political leadership."[18]

"Organization Is Policy"

Whatever their views on bureaucratic attitudes, members of the administration were almost united in the belief that the organization of the executive branch badly needed reform, to improve both responsiveness and efficiency. Nixon, while aiming to avoid what he regarded as the typical Republican overpreoccupation with structural change, always gave a high priority to government reorganization— an interest that seemed to rise as some of the administration's substantive problems grew intractable, and as his dislike for the bureaucracy increased.

Soon after the 1968 election, Nixon invited Roy Ash, chairman of the Litton corporation, a rapidly growing West Coast conglomerate, to the transition headquarters at the Pierre Hotel. At their first meeting, Nixon's greeting was almost abrupt: "I understand that you know something about management—we have a big management job to do!"[19] The president-elect asked Ash, whose favorite maxim was said to be "Organization is policy," to develop a management plan for the new administration.[20] Ash knew of a report containing broad recommendations for restructuring the executive branch that had been prepared for President Johnson by a commission headed by Ben Heineman, former chairman of the Chicago and Northwestern Railroad. Since the report had not been made public, Ash, through the Nixon transition team in Washington, asked the Johnson White House for a copy. Johnson's office denied that such a report existed. Ash nevertheless obtained a copy from one of the members of the commission. Drawing on this and other sources, he made some preliminary recommendations on structuring the White House staff and organizing the administration.[21]

On the day after Nixon announced his cabinet selections over television, Ash spoke to the new cabinet members and their wives in a meeting at the Mayflower Hotel in Washington. "I emphasized the distinction," he has recalled, "between effectiveness and efficiency—actually overstressing the difference in order to make the point. Efficiency, I told them, is doing things at the lowest dollar cost. Effectiveness is doing things in the way that will actually do the best job of solving the problems of the country."[22]

Nixon asked Ash to join the administration, even assigned an office to him in the White House, but the conglomerateur declined on the ground that his children, then in high school, were at the wrong ages for him to contemplate moving his family from California to Washington. Ash did agree to become chairman of a new council on executive branch reorganization. This council, composed of seven members, including John Connally and several leaders of the eastern business establishment, began its work in April 1969; within about a year it had submitted the last in a series of thirteen memoranda to the president.[23]

In his 1971 State of the Union message, Nixon, following recommendations made by the Ash council, proposed consolidating functions performed by eight existing departments into four new departments, dealing with human resources, community development, natural resources, and economic development. The president also asked for legislation to carry out recommendations made by the council for reducing the powers of some independent federal agencies. None of these proposals was given serious consideration by Congress.

The outcome was more favorable on the council's recommendations that the executive office of the president be restructured by establishing a Domestic Council, composed of cabinet members and others charged with major social service responsibilities, to coordinate domestic policies in much the way that the National Security Council was supposed to coordinate foreign and defense policies; and by expanding the Bureau of the Budget into a new Office of Management and Budget, which was to serve as the president's basic mechanism for administering the executive branch. In the spring of 1970, Nixon sent Congress a reorganization plan making these changes; it went into effect when neither house disapproved within sixty days.[24] John Ehrlichman was named to head the small staff assigned to the Domestic Council, and George Shultz became the first director of OMB.

The Domestic Council and OMB

From the start, neither the Domestic Council nor OMB operated quite as the Ash council had intended. Ash had thought of the Domestic Council as a forum in which leaders of the administration could deal conceptually with major problems of government and national life and make broad policy decisions, leaving the means for implementation to be worked out by OMB and the departments. Instead, Ehrlichman, assisted by an active staff, set out to take operational charge of those problems that at any given time seemed most urgently to require White House attention—including, as it later turned out, some concerns of the president not even remotely associated with domestic social issues. The full council rarely met, and the title "Domestic Council" quickly came to identify what was in effect an action agency comprising Ehrlichman and his staff. This change in role occurred in part because of Ehrlichman's ambition and extraverted personality. The experience of the National Security Council should have shown, however, that a planning body composed of busy cabinet members, in the Nixon White House at least, was likely to function chiefly as a base for the aims of its staff director. As John Kessel said in his book about the Domestic Council: "When busy men are given new responsibilities, it is well to inquire about the staff that is going to carry out these tasks."[25] Moreover, even if Ehrlichman had been less of a natural activist, he might well have concluded, as Kissinger did, that to be effective he must deal directly with the problems uppermost in the president's mind. The experience of presidential counsellors, from Burns through Moynihan and Finch, suggested that persons removed from the operational chain of command were likely to lose influence.

As time went on, some of the more thoughtful members of the Domestic Council staff developed a rationale for the role it was actually performing. Kenneth Cole, who became deputy director of the Domestic Council, said later: "The president needs a small staff that is equipped to present him with options on any given problem from an objective point of view. Obviously the departments and the cabinet members cannot be objective. It is true that OMB claims to be objective, but I would, first of all, doubt that they can be, and, second, doubt that they should be. OMB is basically a fiscal agency. It sees problems from the perspective of the budget. This is a very important perspective, often the most important, but not the only perspective. I would ask: if OMB submerges its budget perspective, who is going to present that point of view to the president? Some other agency is needed to referee disputes between competing interests within the government, including OMB. That was the Domestic Council's function."[26]

Raymond Waldman, who acted as Ehrlichman's chief liaison with OMB, came to view the council as a means for "gaining centralized political control over the executive branch for the president." It succeeded, Waldman wrote, "to a degree never before attempted. . . . John Ehrlichman was a name to be reckoned with in the federal government and the Domestic Council staff exercised enormous power in Washington."[27]

At the height of its influence, during the final two years of Nixon's first term, the Domestic Council had only about thirty professional staff members. A majority of these were lawyers, who were, according to Ehrlichman, "good brokers, seldom experts."[28] Many were assigned to oversee the activities of particular departments or agencies. They coordinated development of policies involving several departments and kept Ehrlichman informed on issues of White House interest.

When problems arose that required White House decisions, Ehrlichman often made them himself. If he felt the president should decide, he normally summarized the problem and alternative solutions in an "option paper," which he sent in to Nixon. Sometimes, but not always, Ehrlichman attached his own recommendations. Cabinet members, to their considerable chagrin, were not permitted to see the option papers in their final drafts. Nixon, who much preferred dealing with paper to dealing with people, often settled issues simply by checking one of the boxes beside the alternative decisions offered by the option paper. Ehrlichman has said that there were periods, particularly at critical stages in the Vietnam War, when he rarely saw the president face to face. At such times, the neat checks on the option papers exercised final authority over the domestic part of the government.[29]

The Domestic Council system was designed by Ehrlichman and Cole, but it certainly seems to have suited Nixon. Kenneth Cole told John Helmer and Louis Maisel: "Nixon needed not only a domestic advisor, but also a formal organization with formal procedures with a good idea of where it was going. I don't think that in the years 1971–1973 any better organization could have been put together and could have functioned. . . . The work got done, notwithstanding the barbs about the 'faceless assistants telling cabinet officers what to do.' . . . I think that relying on a powerful staff within the White House is the only good way to do it in a government organized as poorly as it is, even if it is somewhat insulting to the intelligence of the cabinet."[30]

The authority claimed by Ehrlichman for the Domestic Council was not strongly contested by OMB during George Shultz's tenure as director. Shultz emphasized the budgetary function of OMB—to the neglect of the newly added management functions, in Ash's opinion. In time, however, Shultz began to assert the role of OMB as "the president's own bureaucracy." The Domestic Council staff, he observed, was less interested in serious policy analysis than in "brokering the various contending views, dealing with the press, and negotiating directly with the Congress."[31] In his book on economic policy, Shultz wrote: "Budget making *is* policymaking, and OMB budgeteers remained participants in the White House policy process. The failure of the Domestic Council staff to fill the vacuum in White House policy analysis made it inevitable that the OMB staff would have to be consulted by the President and his closest aides if presidential decisions were to be made on the basis of facts and analysis rather than on advocacy views of the interested departments and on political judgments."[32] Despite his growing reservations about the effectiveness of the Domestic Council, Shultz as a rule continued to "avoid unnecessary differences of opinion" with Ehrlichman and his staff.[33]

Caspar Weinberger, Shultz's deputy, who became director of OMB when Shultz went to the Treasury in May 1972, appeared to be girding for a test of wills with Ehrlichman. But at the beginning of 1973, Weinberger, too, moved on, becoming secretary of HEW.

During the last year of Nixon's first term, Ehrlichman increasingly dealt with social policy in conceptual terms—somewhat as Ash had originally intended the full membership of the Domestic Council should do. When making policy decisions, or advising the president, Ehrlichman often referred to the philosophy of the New Federalism, in the version formulated by Richard Nathan. Raymond Waldman, sitting in as Ehrlichman's representative on budget-making sessions at OMB, sought to guide decisions on expenditures to conform to the philosophic prescriptions of the New Federalism.[34]

At this time a strain seems to have developed in relations between Haldeman and Ehrlichman. Perhaps Haldeman shared the view of many conservative fundamentalists that the New Federalism was a cover for irredentist liberalism. Or perhaps the White House chief of staff had begun to regard his old friend and protégé as a potential rival for power.

Changing the Team

By 1972 Nixon, Haldeman, and Ehrlichman had all decided that what Nathan has called the "counter-bureaucracy" operating out of the White House was an inefficient means for managing the executive branch.[35] Working along somewhat different tracks, Haldeman and Ehrlichman began to lay plans for gaining direct White House control over the entire bureaucracy. Their aim, according to Haldeman, was to strike, "for the first time, at the lower levels where the government is really run."[36]

Ehrlichman prepared a plan for imposing through executive order something resembling the new cabinet structure that Congress had failed to approve in 1970. Under Ehrlichman's plan, five presidential assistants would be responsible to the president for operations in broad functional areas: domestic affairs, economic affairs, foreign affairs, executive management, and White House coordination. At the next level of authority, three members of the existing cabinet would be given the rank of counsellor to the president, and made responsible to the assistant for domestic policy for overseeing broad areas of social policy: the secretary of agriculture would become counsellor for natural resources; the secretary of HUD, counsellor for community development; and the secretary of HEW, counsellor for human resources. These assistants and counsellors would act as a kind of supercabinet, enhancing the White House's ability, Ehrlichman believed, to exercise centralized control over the bureaucracy.[37]

"There shouldn't be a lot of leeway in following the President's policies," Ehrlichman told the *Washington Post*. "It should be like a corporation, where the executive vice presidents (the cabinet officers) are tied closely to the chief executive, or to put it in extreme terms, when he says jump, they only ask how high."[38]

Besides planning structural changes, Ehrlichman began ticketing key jobs in the departments to be awarded to some trusted members on the Domestic Council staff in the new term. The persons selected for these jobs were given the clear impression, according to one of them, that they were being "sent out to strengthen White House control over the departments."

Haldeman, meanwhile, assigned Frederic Malek, who had become director of the White House personnel office, to find replacements for all the departmental administrators subject to presidential appointment who had not been effective or responsive during the first term. By means of a thorough house cleaning, Haldeman believed, they would reach "a point where the Administration could, for the first time in decades, be controlled by a President." Nixon egged him on: "You've got to do it right after the election. You've got one week, and that's the time to get all those resignations in and say, 'Look, you're out, you're finished, you're done, done, finished.' Knock them the hell out of there."[39]

Malek, a successful young businessman who had come to Washington from South Carolina to work in the new administration at the beginning of 1969, had first attracted Haldeman's attention through his ability to get results from the supposedly recalcitrant bureaucracy at HEW. In the fall of 1970, Haldeman gave Malek the job of cleaning out the staff of Secretary of the Interior Walter Hickel, whom Nixon had just fired at the White House. (The previous spring, at the time of the Cambodia incursion, Hickel had written a letter to the president, which had been leaked to the press, urging that the White House should open lines of communication with young people protesting against the Vietnam War. Nixon had decided at once that Hickel should be fired, but had put off the dismissal until after the November elections.) Malek carried out his assignment with such dispatch— insisting, as Haldeman had ordered, that Hickel's staff should be out of their offices by the end of the day—that he acquired a reputation for brutality in the press. Such a reputation, however, strengthened his credentials with Haldeman—and with Nixon.[40] (The president confided to his diary in 1972 that another Haldeman protégé, John Dean, had "the kind of steel and really mean instinct that we need to clean house after the election in various departments and to put the IRS and the Justice Department on the kind of basis that it should be on.")[41]

In the summer of 1972, Malek moved from the White House to the Committee to Reelect the President, where he directed the use of government resources to boost Nixon's popularity in marginal districts. But he continued to work at putting together a "talent bank" of personnel to fill administrative posts in the departments for the second term. By the end of October, Malek was able to provide Nixon and Haldeman with a list of 200 candidates for important jobs, including cabinet positions, who had survived a rigorous screening process of background checks and interviews.[42]

Haldeman and Malek developed the idea for requesting resignations from all appointed officials on the morning after the election. "The plan was," Malek has explained, "that by the following day everyone would have heard from the White House who was to go and who was to stay. We would then put in place a full complement of people to fill the jobs of those who were being let go." On the day after the election, however, while Haldeman was stunning members of the cabinet and the White House staff with directions to submit their resignations, Nixon had second thoughts on the entire personnel selection process.[43]

"The president decided," Malek recalled, "that the election had shown that a 'New Majority' had formed in the United States, and that this New Majority should be represented throughout his administration in the second term. These had not been the criteria we had used for selecting people to fill positions in the second Nixon administration. We had not given consideration to geography or ethnic balance or anything like that. Being Italian or being Irish or being southern or being a member of a trade union or being a veteran had not been among the priorities we had used. If we had been told in March that we were to use these criteria, we could probably have come up with people who fitted these descriptions and also were highly qualified. But we had not been told. So when the president said these were considerations that must be used, we were back to square one. An entirely new recruitment process had to be set in motion. As a result, many weeks went by while nobody knew who was being replaced and who was being kept. In some cases, we finally settled for people who were not entirely qualified. I think now [in 1977] that it was a mistake to ask everybody for resignations on the day after election. But the whole thing would certainly have worked a lot better, with less pain for everybody, if we had gone through with the original plan."[44]

A Challenge to Battle

Roy Ash, his children having gone off to college, agreed to become director of OMB in the second term. Malek became his deputy. Ash and Malek soon developed doubts about the new structure of presidential assistants and counsellors that Nixon had set up following Ehrlichman's recommendation.[45] They viewed it, Malek has said, as a means for countering the influence of OMB in the White House. Ash produced an alternative plan for centralizing control over the executive branch in the White House through six staff officers, three dealing with areas of substantive responsibility (national security, domestic social policy, and economic policy), and three directing service functions (operation of the White House, congressional liaison, and OMB). Haldeman appeared favorably disposed toward Ash's plan.[46] Lines seemed to be hardening for a struggle within the White House between adherents of the Domestic Council and those who wished to strengthen the role of OMB.

The division within the administration was not clearly perceived by most participants in the various Washington establishments outside the White House—Congress, the departmental bureaucracies, the press, representatives of the interest groups. But even if these outside observers had been aware of the differences between Ehrlichman on one side and Ash, Malek, and probably Haldeman on the other, most of them would have regarded the varying approaches as simply alternative routes to the same unappealing goal: total centralization of control over the executive branch in the hands of the president and a few of his closest lieutenants. Coupled with the cutback in domestic programs called for in the 1974 budget, and Nixon's announced intention to impound funds voted by Congress beyond the levels he had requested, the move to impose reorganization through executive order sent signals of alarm through all the groups in Washington whose interests gave them a stake in maintaining effective influence or access within the executive branch.

Nixon seemed to be changing the rules. Most of the other players in the Washington game would probably have wished the administration well in achieving more efficient delivery of federal services. Some had supported Nixon for reelection. But all feared the development of a system in which most of the leverage would be held by a handful of technocrats and image makers, few of whom, except for the president, had risen through the traditional political structure. According to Haldeman: "Reorganization is the secret story of Watergate. That reorganization in the winter of [1973] . . . eventually spurred into action against Nixon the great power blocs in Washington. All of them saw danger as the hated Nixon moved more and more to control the Executive Branch from the White House, as he was constitutionally mandated to do."[47]

The background to Watergate was of course more complicated than that—and those whom the administration frightened could never have brought it down if Nixon and his lieutenants had not engaged in criminal activities, which, when made public, caused them to be driven from office. Yet the fears stirred up by the administration's attempt at unilateral reorganization certainly contributed to the atmosphere of confrontation in Washington, and this, at the least, produced an army of antagonists eager to take counteraction. "In this second term," Nixon has written, "I had thrown down a gauntlet to Congress, the bureaucracy, the media, and the Washington establishment and challenged them to engage in epic battle."[48] Not surprisingly, some of those so challenged responded in kind.

By the end of April, both Haldeman and Ehrlichman had left the administration, released by Nixon to make their own defenses against criminal charges. Kenneth Cole became executive director of the Domestic Council (after a brief period in which Melvin Laird returned to government as Nixon's chief domestic policy adviser), but the council staff shrank in size and influence. Helmer and Maisel have written: "As an effective staff institution, the Council's reputation was irretrievably lost as Ehrlichman and two assistant directors of the Council, Morgan and Krogh, were indicted for Watergate-related offenses."[49] The plan for a supercabinet of presidential counsellors was quietly abandoned a few months after it had been announced.

Under Ash's direction, the Office of Management and Budget became the dominant force in domestic administration. But the momentum of reorganization had been broken. Alexander Haig, Haldeman's successor as White House chief of staff, found it necessary to devote much of his time to defending the administration against charges growing out of Watergate. Instead of operating under centralized White House control, the departments became more autonomous than at any time in recent history. According to Stephen Hess: "Domestic planning, to the degree that presidential approval is necessary, seemed to come to a standstill."[50] Toward the end, Donald Santarelli, director of the Law Enforcement Assistance Administration, was quoted as saying: "There is no White House any more."[51]

The General Interest

Behind Nixon's drive to gain mastery over the bureaucracy, as well as behind his offensive to cut programs and costs in the 1974 budget, lay a view of his presidency as tribune for the "general interest" of the national public against the "special interests" championed by Congress, the bureaucracy, and the lobbies—John Gardner's "trinities." On his route to nomination and election in 1968, Nixon himself had skillfully played the game of appealing to the special interests. As president, however, he had increasingly become convinced that the combined influence of the liberal special interests was driving up government expenditures at a ruinous rate and smothering the economy through bureaucratic regulation. "The general interest of this country," he told a news conference on January 31, 1973, "whether it be rich or poor or old, is don't break the family budget by raising taxes or raising prices, and I am going to stand for that general interest."[52]

Franklin Roosevelt's New Deal coalition, Nixon told Raymond Price, had been "just that, a coalition . . . big city bosses, intellectuals, South, North." Roosevelt had kept the interests in check by "playing one against another." Since Roosevelt's time, however, the liberal interest groups—organized labor, minority groups, government workers, cause-oriented activists, some of the business lobbies—had learned that, in the absence of a coherent political force representing the public at large, they could win approval from politicians for their individual objectives, though these objectives might lack broad support or even be viewed unfavorably by a majority of Americans. The results were rapid expansion of government and rising federal expenditures. Nixon's New Majority, unlike the New Deal coalition, was to appeal "across the board—to Italians, Poles, southerners, to the Midwest and New York—for the same reasons, and because of the same basic values."[53] United, Nixon argued, the New Majority would prevail against the special interests, with resulting reductions in inflation, taxes, and government intervention.

Nixon's claim to speak for the general interest against the special interests gathered under the banner of liberalism seems to have contributed to his victory over George McGovern in 1972. Some members of the liberal interest groups themselves had begun to doubt whether modern liberalism possesses a sense of limit or a functioning principle of restraint.

One trouble with Nixon's version of conservatism, however, was that, by 1973 at least, it had become largely negative. Nixon was able to rally his New Majority against disruptive expansion of government. But he did not seem to offer positive goals by which legitimate uses of government, or other social instruments, could be measured. If the "general interest" lacked content, the special interests could not be expected to modify their individual demands, and over the long run would probably strengthen their holds over their beneficiaries and clients.

Perhaps because of this absence of positive standards around which to gather his majority, as well as for other reasons, Nixon, or some of his managers, did not trust lawful and accepted political practices to assure victory in 1972. (Nixon's demonstrated personal culpability in Watergate did not go beyond the cover-up. But one of his former aides has said, on the basis of recollection of the White House atmosphere at that time: "Even if he did not know what they were doing, they had reason to believe that if he had known, he would have approved.")[54] This raises an even more serious issue about modern conservatism: does it move inevitably toward its own brand of authoritarianism, as modern liberalism appears to move toward state-enforced collectivism? Was Watergate related, directly or indirectly, to the social values that the Nixon administration represented? Or did it grow wholly out of the ambitions and insecurities of a few political opportunists, who might have appeared in any administration, regardless of ideological inclination? Or some of both? I turn to these questions in my next and final chapter on the Nixon administration.

12

Watergate

AT ITS SIMPLEST, most tangible level, Watergate was nothing more than dirty politics. A gang of officeholders, unsure of their chances of winning the next election, set out through illegal means to shift the odds in their favor. Such behavior, however deplorable, has never been particularly unusual in American politics—is, in fact, common in many large cities, and present in many states.

There were, of course, certain distinguishing qualities about Watergate, even when it remained a "third-rate burglary" committed on the offices of the Democratic National Committee. For one thing, the prize at stake was the presidency of the United States. For another, among those participating in the meetings at which the crime was planned, or holding prior knowledge that it was to be committed, were the attorney general of the United States and members or former members of the White House staff. Finally, and most important in terms of immediate consequences, the burglars got caught; and one of them, under pressure from a ruthless and implacable "law and order" judge (just the kind Nixon most admired), proved willing to implicate the higher-ups.

Even at this point, Watergate, so long as nothing more than the planning and execution of the break-in was involved, would hardly have destroyed the Nixon administration or entered history as much more than an anecdote of bad judgment and low conduct in high places. If Nixon and his chief lieutenants had in no way interfered with the investigation and prosecution of the case after the Watergate burglars were arrested on the night of June 17, 1972, the costs to the administration and to some prominent individuals would still have been severe: more details of the background of the crime would have come out before the election; John Mitchell probably and Jeb Stuart Magruder almost certainly would have faced criminal charges; and the Democrats would have had an issue with which to hammer the administration during the fall campaign. *But* Nixon almost surely would have been reelected, though by a smaller majority; and Haldeman, Ehrlichman, Colson, and most of the others, probably even including John Dean, would have escaped prosecution, at least in connection with the Watergate break-in. Nixon would have begun his second term, much as he began his first, as a president subject to check by the "trinities"—Congress, the special interests, the bureaucracy—but able, through the tactical advantages available to the presidency and his own political skill, to move the country gradually in the direction that he wanted.[1]

Reasons for the Cover-up

Why then did Nixon try to intervene? Why did he set in motion efforts to use the government's own law enforcement and intelligence-gathering agencies, the FBI and the CIA, to forestall full investigation of the crime, and why did he give at least tentative approval to the secret payment of "hush money" to buy the silence of the conspirators already caught?

First, Nixon was apparently reluctant to sacrifice John Mitchell. Toy though he might with John Ehrlichman's idea of serving up a "big enchilada" to satisfy the prosecutors and the press, he shrank from abandoning his friend and adviser to probable imprisonment and disgrace. Whatever his faults, Nixon has always had the politician's virtue of loyalty to friends. (Witness his long attachment to Murray Chotiner, his repeated efforts to prop up Robert Finch, his resistance to dismissing Haldeman and Ehrlichman when their continued presence in the White House clearly had become a political liability.) Besides, to allow Mitchell to sink would be to acknowledge exceptionally bad judgment in appointing his former law partner to high office in the first place—not an easy concession for Richard Nixon, or for any president.

Second, reelection did not seem so safe in June, when the first and irretrievably damning decisions on how to handle Watergate were made, as it became later on. McGovern had scored an astonishing string of successes in the Democratic primaries. The Eagleton fiasco, which jelled public opinion against him, still lay ahead. As recently as December 1971, Nixon had led two possible Democratic candidates (Muskie and Kennedy) by only 3 percentage points in national polls.[2] Who could be sure that the huge Democratic lead in registration, coupled with a scandal touching some of the president's closest advisers, might not carry even a weak Democratic candidate to victory?

Third, the probable political outcome of allowing all the facts about the break-in to become public—a "limited hangout"—was simply not acceptable to Nixon. He wanted something more than four more years of frustration by the trinities. To carry out his concept of serving the "general interest," he needed a "mandate" in November, which would give him the political strength to cow the Congress, the interest groups, perhaps even the bureaucracy. The discovery of the full background of the Watergate break-in might not cause defeat, but it would probably produce a fairly close election. It must therefore be prevented.

Fourth, and most crucial, the chances that exposure could be limited to the immediate background of the burglary were never great. Nixon must have recognized that if his confidants and henchmen began to fall, other operations in which they had been involved would probably come to light (as ultimately happened). And there was, by that time, a great deal waiting to be uncovered: the break-in, authorized by Ehrlichman, at the office of Daniel Ellsberg's psychiatrist; the forgeries and staged assaults on private citizens hatched by the secret intelligence unit known as the "plumbers" in the basement of the Old Executive Office Building across from the White House; the taps placed on phones of critical journalists and suspected current and former members of the administration and even the president's brother; the attempts by John Dean to use the Internal Revenue Service to harass "enemies" of the administration; the conniving of members of the White House staff at "dirty tricks," low even by the permissive standards of recent presidential campaigns, against some of Nixon's potential Democratic opponents; and more—much more. Any one of these instances, or even several, would probably have been forgiven by much of the public, and even approved in cases involving national security. But the revelation of the entire pattern, the president could hardly have doubted, would earn him condemnation by the great majority of Americans.

Finally, Nixon allowed the cover-up to go forward because he thought it would succeed. Feeling threatened by Watergate, he at the same time believed himself invulnerable. Why pay the price that full disclosure would entail if the involvements of Mitchell, Magruder, and Dean could be kept hidden? As at several later critical points in the gradual unraveling of his defenses, Nixon chose to avoid immediate but limited loss because he underestimated the risk of ultimate disaster.

Authoritarian Tendencies

Of these reasons for Nixon's complicity in the cover-up, only the fourth—the connection of Watergate to a larger pattern of abuse of executive power—particularly touches the subject matter of this study. Did Watergate symptomize an underlying quality of authoritarianism within the administration? If so, was this quality related to the administration's substantive policies and ideological outlook?

A. James Gregor, in his book *The Fascist Persuasion in Radical Politics*, lists four characteristics of modern authoritarian regimes (as distinct from traditional forms of authoritarianism, which were usually based on domination by a property-owning aristocracy): radical rejection of democratic institutions; political organization around a charismatic leader and a "tutelary elite," supported by a "unitary mass movement of solidarity"; near-monopoly control by the state over means of mass communications and persuasion; and centralized state direction of the economy.[3] No reasonable person would contend that the Nixon administration displayed any of these characteristics in fully developed form. There were, however, *tendencies* within the administration that may fairly be interpreted as moving toward authoritarian modes.

The operations of the plumbers were carried out under direct White House supervision, and though absurdly incompetent in practice (almost always leading to "dry holes," as Nixon called them), they displayed chilling disregard for constitutional restraints. Attacks on major news media by leaders of the administration, particularly Vice-President Agnew, while raising some legitimate issues of bias and concentration of control, were clearly aimed at curbing independent criticism. The vast sums gathered through assessing business corporations to finance the 1972 campaign appeared to create a potentially dangerous imbalance of resources within the political system. Perhaps most threatening of all, the Nixon White House seems to have been engulfed, even before the exposure of Watergate began, by sentiments of fear and revenge that could justify almost any form of defensive or retaliatory action. John Dean is not a reliable source for anything, but his description, corroborated by others, seems to ring true: "The White House is another world. Expediency is everything."[4] In September 1972 Nixon told Dean: "We have not used the power in this four years, as you know. We have never used it. We have not used the Bureau and we have not used the Justice Department, but things are going to change now. . . . They are either going to do it right or go."[5]

Conceivably, the development of authoritarian attitudes and behavior in the Nixon administration might be traced almost entirely to the personality and moral character of one man, Richard Nixon. The election of Nixon to the presidency in 1968, some have argued, was brought about through his masterly political skill or through a sort of breakdown in the system or simply by chance—in any case, by a means that reflected little or nothing about the underlying values of either his party or the country at large. Once in the White House, this argument continues, Nixon assembled a band of political and public relations operators, who, because they were among the small minority who shared his values or because they succumbed to "blind ambition" or because he imposed on their innocence, were prepared to join him in moving toward a degree of political repression. In this interpretation—some version of which was held in the late 1970s by many liberals and conservatives within the various Washington establishments—the removal of Nixon and his closest associates from the White House ended, or largely ended, whatever danger there may have been of a drift toward authoritarian extremes.

The personalities and characters of Nixon and his associates undoubtedly contributed to the development of the pattern of attitudes and behavior brought to light by Watergate. The genesis of Watergate, Melvin Laird has said, lay in the fact that "these guys . . . didn't understand the difference between right and wrong."[6] But what caused this lack of moral judgment? Why did "these guys" seem to be so out of touch with values that most Americans claim to honor? To attribute the development of authoritarianism in the Nixon administration wholly to Nixon's personality, or to the accidental convergence of a group of low characters in the White House, seems to place too much weight on chance or the effects of individual idiosyncrasies.

Defenders of the Nixon administration have argued that the extraordinary measures the administration sometimes employed were largely responses to a pattern of flagrant lawlessness, amounting almost to civil war, carried on by part of the president's opposition.[7] Certainly, some of those who opposed Nixon's policies in Southeast Asia resorted to means that were both illegal and hard to control: more than 3,000 reported bombings, many of them by antiwar protesters, during 1970 alone; eruptions of violence on college campuses all across the country after the invasion of Cambodia by American ground forces; the theft and publication of the classified Pentagon Papers; the descent of tens of thousands of demonstrators on Washington in May 1971, with the announced purpose of "shutting down the government for a day." The issue became, Raymond Price later wrote, whether the nation's policies should be set through "the processes of representative democracy, or by mobs in the streets and bombers on the campus."[8] Faced by such challenges to lawful authority, any president of firm resolve would have drawn on the latent powers of the chief executive, claimed by many presidents, including Jefferson and Lincoln, to go beyond normal legal procedures and limits when fundamental issues of social survival are at stake.[9] Once off the reservation of constitutional restraint, however, Nixon and some of his lieutenants seemed to feel little compulsion to return. Illegal forms of harassment and surveillance were used not only to deal with violence or drastic breaches in security but also to explore mere suspicions of subversion—and finally just to achieve political ends. The tactics used by part of the opposition may have helped set the climate in which Watergate developed, but they do not provide an adequate explanation for the full range of abuses.

Politics, War, and Business

If Watergate, broadly defined, cannot be wholly traced to a combination of the malicious natures of Nixon and his associates and the need to maintain social order, some of its sources must have lain among more general attitudes and values operating in American society, or a part of American society. What were these attitudes and values and where did they come from?

The cynicism that has always pervaded a large sector of American politics unquestionably made some contribution to the moral atmosphere that produced Watergate. The many nonpoliticians involved in Watergate-related abuses seem to have absorbed this cynicism all too readily, and even to have gone beyond it, apparently under the impression that they were merely keeping up with the other side. Part of the reason they gained this impression was that Nixon, the politician most before their eyes, exhorted them to "come up with the kind of imaginative dirty tricks that our Democratic opponents used against us and others so effectively in previous campaigns."[10]

Prolonged acceptance of wartime standards of behavior also probably helped erode moral and ethical sensitivities. During the Second World War hundreds of thousands of Americans had died, and the United States had inflicted death and devastation on millions, to achieve victory over fascism. In the Korean War and again during the long and inconclusive struggle in Vietnam, this pattern of bloodshed and violence had been repeated, to check the spread of communism. From the Truman administration on, American agents all over the world had carried out covert operations against Communist opponents, and against unaligned parties thought to be serving Communist interests, in which "dirty tricks," sometimes deadly, were standard procedures. These procedures were praised and rewarded by government, glamorized and honored by what has probably become America's most influential arbiter of moral values, the mass entertainment media. If murder, violence, and all manner of double-dealing were not merely permissible but actually praiseworthy when carried out to advance the national interest abroad, why should one blanch at the violation of a few civil liberties on behalf of that same interest in domestic politics and government? The view that domestic political espionage simply carried on the fight for the good old cause in a new theater was particularly popular with Gordon Liddy and Howard Hunt, the actual field directors of the Watergate break-in who had formerly served, respectively, with the FBI and the CIA. It was also held, however, by others much higher within the administration. John Mitchell's bottom-line defense before the Senate Watergate com-

mittee was that his actions, or failures to act, had always been motivated by concern for his country's future.[11]

The business ethos of success also helped shape the values of some
of those responsible for Watergate abuses. Haldeman, Ehrlichman,
and others who came to government from the world of corporate
business brought with them a fierce dedication to the ideal of achieving
results, whatever the cost. Of his own role, Haldeman wrote: "I
drummed into them [members of the White House staff] the concept
that anything can be done if you just figure out how to do it and
don't give up. I wouldn't take 'no' for an answer. . . . I can see now
that I substantially over-reached in this approach. I put on too much
pressure, and in the process laid the groundwork for the mental
attitude that 'the job must be done.' "[12] Frederic Malek, who stayed
clear of Watergate-type behavior but observed the Nixon White House
from the inside, recalled: "It was generally understood that one did
everything possible to obtain results, and failure would not be tolerated. The results-at-any-price approach, with its attendant pressures, tacitly tolerated and even encouraged some within the Nixon
inner circle to operate on the fringes of the law and of moral behavior.
Watergate may well be regarded as a disaster that was just waiting
to happen."[13]

A Hamiltonian President

Watergate was also to some extent the consummation of a trend
toward authoritarianism that seems almost inherent in the modern
presidency—perhaps, as Acton suggested, in any institution possessing extremes of social power. Franklin Roosevelt and Lyndon
Johnson at times showed willingness to employ means of dubious
constitutionality to achieve their objectives. John Kennedy used the
FBI in 1962 to intimidate steel corporation executives who had raised
prices against his wishes (a precedent approvingly cited by Jeb Magruder to Haldeman).[14] Harry Truman, hero of latter-day populists,
seized the steel mills to end a strike in 1952 (an action later ruled
unconstitutional by the Supreme Court), and coolly told reporters
that "under similar circumstances" he would do the same thing with
the nation's newspapers and radio stations if he thought it were "for
the best of the country."[15]

Among postwar presidents from Truman to Ford, Eisenhower and Ford seem on the whole to have been most faithful in maintaining constitutional restraint over the use of executive power. That Eisenhower and Ford were also the most conservative of the postwar presidents in their substantive policies may suggest at least a mild correspondence between conservative emphasis on limited government and constitutional rectitude. (Ford also no doubt felt under pressure to observe a high standard as a means of distancing himself from Nixon and helping the nation get over the trauma of Watergate. But most who knew him, Republicans and Democrats, liberals and conservatives, agreed that he was conducting the office in the manner that he would in any case have believed proper.) Yet Nixon, also a conservative, though less conservative than Eisenhower or Ford, seems to have gone further in loose use of presidential power than any of the liberals (Truman, Kennedy, or Johnson). Nixon's personal character and the atmosphere of confrontation in which he had to govern explain part of this deviation. There is, however, a governmental strategy sometimes associated with conservatism, drawn upon by Nixon but for the most part avoided by Eisenhower and Ford, that helped legitimatize the administration's trend toward authoritarianism.

Since the rise of democracy in the eighteenth century, which began the shift of political power from the representatives of a dominant social elite to politicians able to win majority support among the general public, conservatives—political leaders who assign particularly high priority to the maintenance of social order, broadly conceived—have usually followed one of two governmental strategies. The first of these—the way of Madison (the Madison of the Constitution)—is to keep power within government so divided and inhibited by "checks and balances" that only large and enduring majorities have much chance of bringing about major social change. Eisenhower and Ford, except in foreign policy, as a rule represented this kind of conservatism. They viewed the expansion of central government authority, including the authority of the executive branch, as a threat to conservative institutions, such as the market and local community structures, which they aimed to protect. They were therefore relatively untempted to aggrandize the power of the presidency.

The second conservative strategy—the way of Hamilton—is to strengthen the executive branch as a means for using government positively to promote conservative values. This strategy assumes the possibility, even the likelihood, that a stable majority among the electorate can be won to the support of conservative parties and candidates, particularly candidates for the office of chief executive. This strategy was practiced in one form or another by such political leaders in the Western industrial nations as Disraeli, Bismarck, Theodore Roosevelt, and Charles de Gaulle. One might add Nelson Rockefeller.

Nixon in domestic policy largely pursued Madisonian social objectives with a Hamiltonian administrative strategy. While philosophically committed to returning some social power to the private sector and to local communities, he had concluded that the federal government and its special interest constituencies had grown so powerful that only a very strong president could "reverse the flow of power and resources from the states and communities to Washington."[16] To achieve his goals of devolution, therefore, he believed, it was necessary to become a Hamiltonian chief executive. "The central paradox of the Nixon administration," Leonard Garment has said, "was that in order to reduce *federal* power, it was first necessary to increase *presidential* power."[17]

Most of all in matters touching foreign policy and defense, where Eisenhower and Ford, too, were Hamiltonians, Nixon insisted on the president's need for broad operational leeway. Not surprisingly, it was in this area that the administration felt least constrained by law or constitutional limit. Many Watergate-related offenses, like the plumbers' illegal operations and the profligate use of wiretaps, were carried out in the name of national security. Nixon even justified the firing of Archibald Cox as Watergate special prosecutor at the time of the "Saturday night massacre," in October 1973, on the ground that continued toleration of Cox would make the president appear weak in the eyes of Brezhnev and other foreign leaders.[18]

A Heresy of the Right

Finally, the Nixon administration's espousal of conservative social values provided at least part of the rationalization for abuses of executive power. A political persuasion that especially values "law and order" must always run some risk that its leaders will ultimately be prepared to suppress individual human rights in the name of maintaining order.

The combining of "law and order" with political hubris, as occurred under Nixon, makes a drift toward authoritarianism probable. It tends to create a sort of Roman view of life and the world, with emphasis on order for order's sake. The main political objective becomes, not to keep social power contained and channeled through traditional institutions, but to make sure that those exercising power are on "our side." (In an interview a few nights before Nixon's second inauguration, Charles Colson argued that concentration of power in the White House posed no danger so long as the president was motivated by a philosophy like Nixon's.)[19]

Authoritarianism directed at maintaining social order has been a characteristic heresy of the right in modern democratic societies, as authoritarianism aimed at achieving equality in the distribution of social benefits (collectivism) has been a heresy of the left. In France, from the start of the Third Republic to the collaboration of the Vichy government with the Nazis during the Second World War, there were always some conservative politicians conspiring against democratic institutions—with particular flagrance at the time of the Dreyfus affair in the 1890s. Some Italian conservatives helped bring Mussolini to power, as some of their German counterparts later abetted the rise of Hitler. In the United States during the 1950s, many conservatives gave at least passive support to the assault on civil liberties carried out under the leadership of Senator Joseph McCarthy.

Conservatism does not, however, inevitably lead to authoritarianism, no more than liberalism is synonymous with left-wing subversion. Such characteristic American conservatives as Robert Taft and Dwight Eisenhower generally resisted authoritarian tendencies on both the right and left, and sought to maintain a balance between order and freedom.[20]

A Failure for Conservatism

Conservatism did not cause Watergate, or even exert a determining influence over the moral climate in which it developed. Yet Watergate represented a kind of failure for conservatism, because Nixon and his associates largely drew on conservative precepts, both to guide the administration's substantive policies and to rationalize their political tactics.

Throughout his presidency Nixon displayed exceptional skill at applying conservative principles to concrete problems of government. He had, moreover, won the support of a substantial majority of Americans for the policies and directions he believed the country should follow. Enemies he certainly had. Knowing that there were many among his political opposition and in the press and even in his own party who waited eagerly for a chance to bring him down, he might have chosen to govern on so high an ethical plane that they could have found few openings against him. Instead, he sought to combat them through political trickery, attempts at official intimidation, and a patchwork of lies. So doing, he fell—leaving to his successor not only substantive problems of enormous difficulty and complexity, but also a national consciousness so soured by disgust and disillusion as to threaten the minimums of civility and public trust on which any kind of cohesive social existence, let alone effective government, must depend.

The Ford Administration

13

Gerald Ford

WITH GERALD FORD, the character and personality of the president returned to the broad range that may be called "normal" for the small class of American chiefs of state. In this respect, therefore, the Ford administration offers a less eccentric base than Nixon's for examining the effects of ideology and other recurring influences on the governmental decisionmaking process.

This is not to say, however, that Ford's presidency was in any way typical or ordinary. The manner of his succession, and the fact that he served without election to any office by the voters outside the Fifth Congressional District of Michigan, were totally unique. His tenure was briefer than that of any but four presidents (William Henry Harrison, Taylor, Garfield, and Harding), and the shortest among the nine vice-presidents who have filled out the term of a president. Some of the problems he faced—like the Communist overrun of Vietnam, the gathering energy crisis, the most rapid inflation since the 1940s followed by the worst recession since the 1930s, a Congress overwhelmingly controlled by the opposition party, and the low level of public confidence in governmental institutions that was part of Nixon's legacy—were exceptionally severe.

To these challenges Ford brought traits of attitude and character that were in some ways representative of prevailing norms among the upper echelons of the American political community, particularly its more conservative branch. And that in some ways were quite his own.

In this chapter I trace the development of Ford's social and political values and assumptions, from his youth to the early months of his presidency, as a background for identifying (roughly) the effects of the president's personal values and attitudes on executive policy-making. My account will in general be chronological, but is not intended to provide a rounded treatment of Ford's pre-presidential life or career (for which the reader should turn to Ford's memoirs and to J. F. ter Horst's biography, *Gerald Ford and the Future of the Presidency*).[1]

Grand Rapids, Michigan, and Yale

The Grand Rapids in which Ford grew up was part of the old upper Midwest, settled before the Civil War and preserving a strong New England flavor—a culture more out of Booth Tarkington than Sinclair Lewis. The Ford family were of English descent and attended the local Episcopal church, which set them a bit apart from the numerically dominant Dutch Calvinists. (The area around Grand Rapids claims to have a heavier concentration of descendants of immigrants from the Netherlands than any other part of the United States. By Ford's time, however, local industries had attracted more recent immigrant groups, and the city had become fairly cosmopolitan.)

Gerald Ford, Sr., was the kind of man that Frank Nixon would probably have liked to have been: shrewd, austere, intensely self-disciplined, reasonably lucky. Having dropped out of school in the tenth grade to help support his family, the elder Ford, through hard work in the paint business and a knack for cultivating insiders, had made it to a modest but respected position in the Grand Rapids business community by the time he was forty. When the small paint manufacturing company he had started in 1929 ran into trouble during the depression, the Du Pont Company, his principal supplier, offered to keep on providing him with materials on no more than his promise to "work something out" as times improved. He told his employees that he could pay each of them five dollars a week, the same amount he planned to take out of the business for himself, if they would agree to the postponement for an indefinite period of the rest of their wages. The workers accepted, and the company survived.[2]

Despite financial worries, the Ford family environment appears to have been secure, orderly, and happy. The senior Fords neither smoked nor kept alcohol in the house, but do not seem to have been rigidly puritanical. Gerald Ford, Jr.—known as "Junie"—was separated from his three younger brothers by age gaps of five, eleven, and fourteen years. As the oldest son, he was given extra responsibilities and was expected to set a good example for his brothers.[3]

At school young Gerald was popular, though apparently somewhat shy. By the time he was in the seventh grade, he had concluded: "Everyone . . . had more good qualities than bad. If I understood and tried to accentuate those good qualities in others, I could get along much better."[4] According to one of his biographers, "he wore a suit and a tie [to school] most of the time instead of the casual shirt, slacks, and sweater that were so common"—which suggests a family determined to maintain the outward signs of middle-class respectability.[5] A former classmate remembered him in 1974 as having been "a rich boy—but a regular guy."[6]

From an early age Junie Ford displayed athletic ability, concentrating, at his father's urging, on football. His high school football coach, Clifford Gettings, whom Ford has credited as a major influence on his outlook, "lived to win and did not hesitate on the practice field to kick his players in the rear when they didn't try hard enough," but taught that there should be "no dirty tricks, no tampering with the rules."[7] Ford played the position of center, learning the difficult art, in pre-T-formation days, of snapping the ball smoothly and accurately so that it hit "the tailback who was in motion and in full stride," or enabled the punter to "kick it out of our backyard on time."[8]

His parents insisted that he work even harder at his studies than he did at football, and he finished in the top 5 percent of his high school class. After graduation his high school principal helped him obtain a full-tuition scholarship to the University of Michigan.[9]

Ford's childhood and youth were not without emotional traumas. The most painful of these, undoubtedly, was the discovery that Gerald Ford, Sr., was not his biological father, and that until he was two years old his name had been, not Gerald Ford, but Leslie King. In 1912 his mother, whose maiden name was Dorothy Gardner, at the age of twenty married an Omaha wool trader named Leslie King. The next year a son was born to the couple, and christened Leslie King,

Jr. Two years later, the marriage broke up. The young mother took her son to live with her parents in Grand Rapids. Soon she fell in love with and married Gerald R. Ford. The new husband took over the role of father for her son. Apparently to make the identity firm, the boy's name was changed to Gerald R. Ford, Jr. (although, Ford noted in his memoirs, formal adoption papers were not filed until "years later").[10]

When Ford was "twelve or thirteen," according to his memoirs, his mother told him that Gerald, Sr., was not his real father.[11] (On the Dick Cavett television show in 1974, he said that he did not know that he was adopted until he was "about seventeen."[12] Evidently he was thinking of a later experience, to be described shortly.) He also learned that Leslie King had failed to keep up the child support payments that had been ordered by the court in Omaha as part of the divorce settlement. Ford seems to have preserved no conscious memory of the time he spent in the King household, though he later heard that his "parents quarrelled all the time" and that "he hit her frequently."[13]

When Ford was seventeen, he took a part-time job making hamburgers in a diner in Grand Rapids. One day he was approached at the diner by a stranger who identified himself as Ford's real father, Leslie King. Over lunch with his son, King, who was driving from Detroit to Wyoming with his second wife in a newly purchased Lincoln sedan, chatted amiably about football and made no mention of the divorce. Before leaving, he gave Ford twenty-five dollars to "buy yourself something you want that you can't afford otherwise." That night, Ford has recalled, was "one of the most difficult of my life." His mother and stepfather, when he told them of the meeting, were "loving and consoling." But "nothing could erase the image I gained of my real father that day: a carefree, well-to-do man who didn't really give a damn about the hopes and dreams of his firstborn son."[14]

A lesser but perhaps significant problem was the fact that Ford was "left-handed sitting down and right-handed standing up." Following a practice common at the time, his parents and early teachers had tried to force him to become consistently right-handed. Eventually they gave up, and he remained "ambidextrous," throwing with his right and writing with his left. Ford has speculated that the effort to make him right-handed may have contributed to his tendency to

stutter—"some words gave me fits"—that he developed in childhood.
He got over the stutter when he was about ten.[15] (Ford's future vice-
president, Nelson Rockefeller, was also naturally left-handed. To
overcome this instinct, Rockefeller's father, John D., Jr., tied a string
to young Nelson's left wrist, which he yanked whenever the boy
attempted to feed himself with the forbidden hand.)[16]

Did these traumas, particularly Ford's discovery that he had once
been literally somebody else, damage his personality? They certainly
do not seem to have damaged it much. Through college, law school,
and wartime combat service with the navy in the South Pacific, Ford
proceeded with confidence and enterprise, though usually with a fair
amount of caution. He played football for four years at Michigan, and
he was selected in his senior year to participate in the Shrine college
all-star game in San Francisco. While in college, he became interested
in economics, but doubted whether he could make a good living as
an economist, and so decided to become a lawyer instead.[17] To support
himself after graduation, he took a job as assistant line coach for the
football team at Yale. After two years he managed to get himself
admitted to the Yale Law School. Though he continued to coach, he
finished in the top quarter of a law school class that included such
future luminaries as Potter Stewart and Cyrus Vance.[18] It seems fair
to speculate that the emotional blows experienced by Ford during
childhood may have caused some degree of underlying insecurity,
which, combined with parental urging and natural ability, motivated
him to run a good deal harder than most. But they seem not to have
impaired his performance, or to have left a significant residue of
bitterness of the kind that stuck with Nixon.

An incident that occurred while Ford was at Michigan throws some
light on his values and on his means of resolving value conflicts.
During Ford's senior year—when the Michigan football team was
doing poorly after two undefeated seasons—Georgia Tech, then an
all-white school, threatened to cancel an upcoming game unless the
Michigan administration promised not to play a black lineman called
Willis Ward. Michigan's athletic director, the famous Fielding ("Hurry
Up") Yost, agreed to keep Ward out of the game on condition that
Georgia Tech also bench one of its star players. Ford was friendly
with Ward and felt at first that he should not play, because the black
player's exclusion was "morally wrong." He called his stepfather,
who advised him: "I think you ought to do whatever the coaching

staff decides is right." Ford agreed to play, and Michigan won the game, 9 to 2—as it turned out the team's only victory that season.

Ford has recalled that he decided to play only after being urged to do so by Ward. When questioned about the incident in 1974, Ward, who went on to become a probate judge in Detroit, could not remember that Ford had told him he was considering not playing against Georgia Tech, but added: "It was just like Jerry. During orientation week he walked up to me on the campus, introduced himself and we were friends all the way through Michigan. . . . In my mind he was a decent guy."

Ford's way of dealing with the incident reveals several characteristics: a well-developed sense of fairness, apparently unclouded by racial prejudice; loyalty, when the chips were down, to the powers that be; and eagerness to combine the goals of the system with the ends of morality—in this case, defeat of the racist team. "That Saturday afternoon," according to Ford, "we hit like never before." Ford's recollection of the incident also suggests a quality valuable for a politician: belief that things in the end work out for the best. The team's reaction to the problem, Ford has written, gave "us a needed lift." Willis Ward's own recollection was different: "Dropping me from the lineup for racist reasons did something to team morale. . . . We just never got together as a close-knit team after that."[19]

Getting Started in Politics

During the summer of 1940, while home on vacation from law school, Ford decided to become active in the presidential campaign of Wendell Willkie (a decision made about the same time by young Richard Nixon in southern California). Ford's stepfather arranged an appointment for him to meet Frank D. McKay, a portly Grand Rapids insurance broker who had parlayed control of the Kent County Republican organization into a powerful, and profitable, role in the state's dominant political establishment. ("At one time," Gerald Ford has recalled, "Frank McKay sold every tire for every vehicle for every state agency from a little two-room building in Grand Rapids. He wrote bonds for almost all the state officials who needed them. I guess he left an estate of ten million dollars when he died.")[20] McKay kept the young law student waiting in his outer office for four hours, and then saw him for only a few minutes. Ford, who had come expecting "marching instructions," concluded that McKay "wasn't interested in my offer of help."[21]

After graduating from law school in 1941, Ford returned to Grand Rapids and established a law firm in partnership with Philip Buchen, a friend and college fraternity brother. Ford and Buchen were soon drawn into a group of lawyers and businessmen plotting to challenge the McKay machine within the Republican party. Ford was already contemplating a career in politics. He appears never to have thought of pursuing his goals as anything but a Republican. Republicanism was part of the Ford family heritage, and seemed to represent the values of hard work, moral behavior, and common sense in which he had been trained to believe. Besides, only Republicans in those days had much chance of being elected to office in Grand Rapids or western Michigan.[22]

Before the anti-McKay movement had developed very far, the Japanese attacked Pearl Harbor, and Ford joined the navy as an ensign. Until the United States was forced into the war, Ford had subscribed to the isolationist views expressed by midwestern Republican leaders like Senators Arthur Vandenberg and Robert Taft. (Vandenberg's home was in Grand Rapids, though he spent most of his time in Washington.) At Yale, which by 1940 was a hotbed of internationalist sentiment, Ford had spoken out against "entangling alliances." Like Vandenberg, however, he was converted during the war to the belief that "the United States . . . could no longer stick its head in the sand like an ostrich." Ford returned to civilian life in 1946 an "ardent internationalist." The United States, he had concluded, should "never again allow [its] military to be anything but the best"; and should "help the nations of Western Europe rebuild their shattered economies," so they could serve as "strong allies to resist the growing Communist threat"—a line of reasoning that placed him among the "tough" internationalists, like Truman, Dulles, and Vandenberg, who favored an aggressive role in world affairs so as to check communism and advance the national interest of the United States, rather than among the "soft" internationalists, like Henry Wallace, who sought to pursue humanitarian goals through cooperation with the Communist powers.[23]

While Ford had been in the navy, Buchen, kept out of the military service by the effects of childhood polio, had become a partner in a prominent Grand Rapids law firm. Ford now joined the same firm. During the war years the anti-McKay Republicans in Grand Rapids had won some victories. In 1944, as part of the drive to clean up the local party, Gerald Ford, Sr., had been persuaded by friends in the business community to accept election as Kent County Republican chairman. The next year McKay's power was further shaken when a scandal in the state legislature led to the apparent suicide of a state senator from Grand Rapids and the fatal shooting of another senator from a nearby county.[24] Some members of the old organization, however, still hung on to office. Most prominent among these was Bartel Jonkman, U.S. congressman from the fifth district, which included Kent County and an adjacent rural county. Originally elected in 1940 as a strong isolationist, Jonkman had not wavered in his views, and had become an embarrassment to Vandenberg, then cooperating with the Truman administration to champion the Marshall Plan through Congress. Encouraged by his parents and Buchen, Ford decided to run against Jonkman in the Republican primary in 1948.[25]

While testing the political waters, Ford had at the same time been courting a local beauty named Betty Warren—a recently divorced young woman, who had been a few years behind him in school, had gone off to New York to study dance under Martha Graham, and was now fashion coordinator for a Grand Rapids department store. Some of Ford's political advisers were worried that the morally conservative Dutch farmers might be put off by his association with a glamorous divorcée (known locally as "the thinking man's Rita Hayworth"),[26] and Buchen insisted that he keep his plan to run against Jonkman completely secret so that the incumbent would be taken by surprise. When Ford proposed marriage in February 1948, he therefore added: "But we can't get married until next fall, and I can't tell you why." Apparently not yet a feminist, the future Mrs. Ford raised no objection, and agreed that a fall wedding would be fine.[27]

The reformers expected an uphill fight against Jonkman, because of the supposed preference among the Dutch farmers for candidates of Dutch name and extraction, and the advantage of incumbency. Ford campaigned energetically across the district, giving short talks on the importance of European recovery and occasionally helping a farmer pitch hay. He challenged Jonkman to debate on foreign policy, but the incumbent ignored him. Leaving a campaign meeting one night in a little town north of Grand Rapids, Ford encountered Frank

McKay. "Hello, Mr. McKay, how are you, sir?" he inquired. "I like your style, young man," McKay answered, "but Barney Jonkman is going to stomp all over you."[28] McKay was wrong. Ford easily won the primary, attracting 62 percent of the vote. In November he polled a similar majority against his Democratic opponent.

Early Years in Congress

During his first term in Congress, Ford voted the Republican party line on 81 percent of the contested roll calls—a lower percentage than most of the other eleven Republicans serving in the House from Michigan, but about the same as Hugh Scott of Pennsylvania (82 percent), and higher than Richard Nixon of California (74 percent).[29] The aged Vandenberg, pleased to have a replacement for Jonkman, sagely advised Ford to concentrate on committee work and not to forget to service his district. Ford's most important associations, however, were in the House. In 1951, through the influence of tough old John Taber of upstate New York, a kind of living embodiment of stalwart Republican principles of fiscal conservatism, Ford was awarded a seat on the powerful Appropriations Committee after serving only a single term. Assigned to the Defense Subcommittee, he developed a close relationship with the subcommittee chairman, George Mahon, traditionalist Democrat of Texas, who was later chairman of the full committee for fourteen years. Working usually as a team, Mahon and Ford together shepherded the defense budget through the House during most of the 1950s and 1960s.[30]

In the struggle over foreign policy that divided the Republican party in the early 1950s, Ford aligned himself firmly on the side of the internationalists, and against the neo-isolationists led by Taft. In the winter of 1952, Ford joined seventeen other Republican congressmen in sending a message to Dwight Eisenhower urging him to return from Europe to run for president.[31] Ford's alignment with the internationalists separated him from most other midwestern Republicans in Congress, but had a precedent in Vandenberg, and was not displeasing to the auto magnates of Detroit, who had an interest in expanded foreign trade and had always maintained close financial ties with New York.

During the Eisenhower administration Ford warily associated himself with a group of younger Republicans in the House, like Melvin Laird of Wisconsin, Peter Frelinghuysen of New Jersey, and Robert Griffin of Michigan, who were critical of the "negative" image being projected by the House Republican leadership. Some of the rebels objected to what they regarded as the excessive conservatism of such leaders as Joseph Martin and Charles Halleck; but others, including Ford, were mainly concerned with the leadership's failure to offer effective challenge to the Democrats. In 1959 Ford participated in the coup through which Halleck replaced Martin as House minority leader. (Halleck, no less conservative on substantive matters than Martin, was expected to give more spirited leadership in floor debate against the Democrats.)[32]

In 1961, after the inauguration of John Kennedy, Ford became floor leader for a coalition of progressive and moderate Republicans and liberal Democrats fighting against deep cuts in foreign aid. To the surprise of both the Republican and Democratic leaderships, the full House narrowly approved an amendment offered by Ford to restore drastic reductions in aid that had been recommended by the Appropriations Committee.[33] In the 1961–62 session Ford's record for voting with the conservative coalition (Republicans and southern Democrats) fell to 64 percent—which made him the fourth most liberal member of the eleven-man Republican delegation from Michigan.[34]

At the beginning of 1963, Ford accepted the support of an insurgent faction calling themselves the "Young Turks"—led by Laird, Griffin, and two more recently elected members, Charles Goodell of upstate New York and Donald Rumsfeld of a suburban district outside Chicago—to oust a Halleck man as chairman of the House Republican Conference. The Young Turks selected Ford as their candidate, Griffin explained, because he was "electable—Jerry got along with all segments of the party."[35]

In the contest between Goldwater and Rockefeller for the Republican presidential nomination in 1964, Ford thankfully took refuge in supporting the favorite son candidacy of Michigan's governor, George Romney. At the Republican National Convention, however, Ford spoke against an amendment to the party platform offered by the moderates, including Romney, that would have repudiated some allegedly reckless remarks Goldwater had made regarding the use of nuclear weapons. Ford later criticized the Goldwater "zealots" for believing "that it was more important to nominate a candidate who was ideologically pure than to find someone who could win an election."[36]

After Goldwater's defeat, accompanied by the loss of thirty-six Republican seats in the House, the Young Turks decided that the time was ripe to replace Halleck with a leader of their choosing. Unable to get together behind one of their own number, the insurgent leaders turned again to Ford. "It wasn't as though everybody was wildly enthusiastic about Jerry," Goodell later said. "It was just that most Republicans liked him and respected him. He didn't have enemies."[37] Ford agreed to make the race against Halleck—and immediately flew off to vacation in the Caribbean, leaving Laird, Goodell, and the rest to round up votes among Republican members of the House. At the beginning of 1965, Ford was elected minority leader over Halleck by a vote of 73 to 67. The winning margin was provided by a young Kansas congressman, Bob Dole, who at the last minute brought four of Kansas's five Republican representatives to Ford's standard.[38]

Some commentators have suggested that Ford's rise through the House Republican leadership was largely accidental, resulting from his availability to front for the machinations of Laird, Rumsfeld, and others. It is true that all through his career Ford was carried forward by the plotting and exertions of persons with more identifiably Machiavellian skills. But avoidance of political infighting should not be mistaken for lack of subtlety or ambition. Ford seems to have sensed, probably more or less intuitively, that an appearance of blandness was likely to get him further than extreme belligerence or cunning.

House Minority Leader

As minority leader, Ford sought to present a "positive Republican" alternative to the Great Society programs being pushed through Congress by Lyndon Johnson. Particularly after the Republican gain of forty-seven House seats in the 1966 elections, the Republicans were frequently able to shape bills to suit their own philosophy. Often this took the form of enhancing the role of the states in the administration of federal programs. At Republican insistence, state departments of education were given a major say in allocating funds under the

Elementary and Secondary Education Act of 1965; and the Law Enforcement and Criminal Justice Assistance Act was amended to give
block grants to the states rather than categorical grants to local governments. As Charles O. Jones has written: "House Republicans were
notably successful in building majorities for their own proposals in
1967—a remarkable achievement for a minority party. On occasion
it appeared that the Republicans were the majority and the Democrats
the minority."[39] In January 1967 Ford gave his own State of the Union
message, calling for, among other things, enactment of federal revenue sharing, creation of an Industry Youth Corps to expand jobs in
private industry, restoration of the investment tax credit, increased
spending for defense, higher social security and veterans' benefits,
and cuts in "nonessential" federal spending.[40]

Ford largely discontinued Halleck's practice of coordinating legislative strategy with leaders of the bloc of conservative southern
Democrats. Collaboration with the southern Democrats to prevent
passage of liberal civil rights legislation, Ford believed, was propping
up conservative Democrats in the South and giving liberal Democrats
a free ride with blacks and civil rights activists in the North. Under
Ford's leadership a majority of House Republicans supported the
Voting Rights Act of 1965. (Before he became minority leader, Ford
had also voted for the Civil Rights Act of 1964.)

When civil rights legislation threatened the interests of business
allies of the Republican party, however, Ford stuck with business. In
1968, against vigorous opposition by the real estate lobby, the Senate
passed "open housing" legislation forbidding racial discrimination in
the sale or rental of housing. Although the open housing bill had
received active support from Everett Dirksen, Ford agreed to go along
with a plan devised by the real estate lobby to throw the bill into
conference between the Senate and the House—a move intended to
send the bill back for a second vote in the Senate, where the lobby
believed they could kill it through filibuster. Though Laird and most
of the House Republican leadership agreed with Ford's judgment,
Goodell joined with Congressmen Albert Quie of Minnesota and John
Anderson of Illinois to round up Republican support for immediate
passage of the Senate bill. When Ford discovered that he was about
to be deserted by about one-third of the Republican members of the
House, he capitulated, and voted on final passage for the bill in the
form it had passed the Senate. "On balance," he wrote in his news-

letter to fifth-district constituents, "the desirable portions were greater and more significant than the undesirable ones."[41]

Ford also differed with Dirksen on the issue of the Vietnam War. Whereas the Senate Republican leader consistently supported the Johnson administration's policies in Indochina, Ford by 1967 had decided that Republicans should begin taking an independent position on the war. In a speech to the House on August 8, 1967, Ford expressed "grave misgivings about the way the war in Vietnam is going." He criticized the administration for failing to make full use of conventional air and sea power against the enemy, while expanding the commitment of American ground forces. "What is especially dishonest," he said, "is secretly to forbid effective strategic action and publicly portray it as an honest try." He called for, at a minimum, a "Kennedy-type sea quarantine" against North Vietnam. "Why," Ford asked, "are we pulling our best punches in Vietnam? Is there no end, no other answer except more men, more men, more men?"[42]

In 1968 Ford was chosen to be permanent chairman of the Republican National Convention at Miami Beach. Before the convention he was mentioned as a possible candidate for vice-president. In his speech to the delegates, Ford proposed that the United States "rebuild [its] military power to the point where no aggressor would dare attack us." The Johnson administration, he charged, had "blundered into a war in Vietnam," and had created "the most dangerous military gap and the worst credibility gap in American history." (The speech was written by Robert Hartmann, former Washington bureau chief of the *Los Angeles Times*, who had joined the staff of the House Republican Conference in 1966, and had since become a key confidant and speechwriter for Ford.)[43]

When the Republican elders gathered after Nixon's nomination to give advice on the selection of a running mate, Ford recommended Congressman John Lindsay of New York—an odd choice, since Lindsay's voting record was much more liberal than Ford's, and Ford has been chagrined when the New Yorker surprisingly came down on the side of Halleck in the minority leadership contest in 1965.[44] Ford found Nixon's choice of Spiro Agnew so incomprehensible that he privately urged Goodell to arrange to have Lindsay's name placed in nomination for vice-president, even though Lindsay had declined to make the fight (had, indeed, agreed to second the nomination of Agnew).[45]

Floor Leader for Nixon

During Nixon's first term Ford, as was reported in chapter 5, effectively championed the administration's cause in the House. "On a number of issues," William Timmons, Nixon's second director of congressional relations, has said, "if Ford had had his druthers, he would have taken a different position, but out of loyalty to the president, he went along."[46]

Ford loyally helped push the family assistance plan through the House in 1970 and 1971, fended off efforts to undercut Nixon's strategy in Vietnam, led fights to uphold the president's vetoes on appropriations bills, and was instrumental in the passage of revenue sharing in 1972. His most important break with the administration came over Nixon's proposal in 1972 that some of the revenues accumulated in the highway trust fund, raised through the federal tax on gasoline, be diverted to subsidize mass transportation in the cities—again an issue on which the interest of a faithful benefactor of the Republican party, the highway lobby, was threatened. "Ford had some rather strong words with the White House on that issue," Timmons recalled. "He refused to go along. And on that issue, he had the votes to win."[47]

In April 1970 Ford launched an uncharacteristic attack on the integrity and character of Supreme Court Justice William O. Douglas. It was widely believed at the time that Nixon or Attorney General Mitchell had put Ford up to proposing that the House consider impeaching Douglas, to retaliate against the Senate's refusal to confirm Nixon's nominations of Clement Haynsworth and Harrold Carswell to the Supreme Court. Ford reported in his memoirs, however, that he had begun investigating Douglas in 1969, several months before the nomination of Haynsworth, and that Mitchell and the Justice Department gave him only "double-talk" when he asked for help. Ford's chief aide in the investigation, Robert Hartmann, wished to focus the case on the fact that Douglas for nine years had received a $12,000 annual retainer from the Albert Parvin Foundation, after helping Parvin, who had ties to the gambling industry, set up the foundation in 1960—an apparent violation of the federal law that prohibits federal judges from earning income from private sources. But Ford chose to concentrate on an article Douglas had written for

Evergreen Review suggesting that "violence may be the only effective response" when "grievances pile high" against "the establishment." Reportedly, Ford was particularly shocked and outraged that an associate justice of the Supreme Court would write for a magazine that specialized in pornography. The House Judiciary Committee, after a cursory inquiry, found no grounds for impeachment. (Later, Ford appeared to regret his campaign for Douglas's removal from the bench, but denied that he had been "irresponsible." When Douglas retired because of ill health in 1975, Ford, by now president, wrote, with no apparent sense of incongruity: "Your distinguished years of service are unequalled in all the history of the Court.")[48]

During the early 1970s Ford played an active role in efforts in Congress to curb court-ordered busing of schoolchildren to achieve racial integration. The political impact of the issue was particularly strong in Michigan, even causing many liberal Democrats from the Detroit area to join the antibusing phalanx. Ford, however, seems to have been moved by substantive as well as political considerations. "Ford's opposition to busing came from something he deeply felt," according to Hartmann, his closest confidant at the time. "It was not based on racism per se, at least not in his own mind. He was a product of neighborhood schools in Grand Rapids, and he thought that was a very positive experience that all American children should have. He believed that many blacks agreed with him. He felt that what he was doing was needed to preserve the neighborhood school."[49] Ford's position against busing further antagonized the civil rights community, which had not forgiven his efforts to dilute the open housing bill in 1968. At the House Judiciary Committee hearings on Nixon's nomination of Ford to be vice-president in 1973, Clarence Mitchell, director of the Washington office of the NAACP, testified that Ford had taken a "restrictive approach to civil rights."[50]

Before the summer of 1973, Ford firmly supported Nixon's military and diplomatic policies in Southeast Asia. During 1971 and 1972 a bipartisan coalition in the House, which Ford played a major part in holding together, repeatedly blocked efforts by the Senate to establish a fixed date for completion of American withdrawal from Vietnam. But when Nixon in the spring of 1973, after the conclusion of the Vietnam truce, ordered resumption of American bombing in Cambodia (to help prop up the pro-American government in Phnom Penh), the House, over Ford's opposition, joined the Senate in voting to prohibit continuation of the raids. On June 27 Nixon vetoed the appropriations bill to which the bombing halt had been attached. Later that same day the House upheld Nixon's veto, by a vote of 241 to override and 173 to sustain (276 needed to override)—with Ford leading the fight to sustain. After the vote Ford and Senate Minority Leader Hugh Scott decided, Scott has recalled, that "the time had come to end it." Under pressure from Ford and Scott, Nixon reluctantly agreed to sign a bill prohibiting use of appropriated funds to support American combat activities anywhere in Indochina after August 15, 1973.[51]

Ford did not entirely escape contact with the venal army of fixers and influence peddlers who swarm about the Capitol. The atmosphere on Capitol Hill is like that of a club in which nobody is ever sure of the identity of most of the members. In this environment—where even the recognizably criminal or demented can step into a picture or gain a handshake with one of the mighty—the more plausible or generous petitioners can quite easily establish an appearance of intimacy with the powerful, while possessing little or no actual influence. (Sometimes, of course, they *do* have influence.) One such, a free-lance lobbyist named Robert Winter-Berger, who briefly enjoyed access to Ford's office and person in the late 1960s, claimed in a 1972 exposé book that, besides in various ways abusing the confidence of Speaker of the House John McCormack, he had made an unrepaid loan of $15,000 to Ford and had channeled campaign contributions to the minority leader in return for political favors—and had introduced Ford to a New York psychiatrist, whose patient, he said, Ford later became. Ford denied all the lobbyist's allegations, while admitting he had known Winter-Berger. When Ford was nominated to become vice-president, the Senate Rules Committee interrogated Winter-Berger in closed session for an entire day, and concluded that the charges were baseless.[52] Investigations by the Senate Rules Committee, the House Judiciary Committee, and later the Watergate Special Prosecutor's Office produced no evidence that Ford had been involved in any scandal at any time during his public career.

An accusation of a different kind against Ford was made by John Dean, as part of the former Nixon aide's comprehensive confession on Watergate. Dean claimed that Ford, in response to a request from the White House, had helped cut off an investigation into the background of Watergate by the House Banking and Currency Committee (which claimed jurisdiction because of apparent violations of campaign financing laws) in the fall of 1972, a few weeks before the presidential election. Ford conceded that he had talked with the Republican members of the committee about stopping the probe (which subsequently was called off, through the votes of eight Republican and six Democratic committee members), but claimed he had done so on his own, out of concern that Congressman Wright Patman, the committee chairman, was "going about the matter in the wrong way . . . going on a fishing expedition."[53] Judging the matter comes down to choosing between the word of Dean, and the word of Ford, supported by two of Nixon's legislative assistants. In any case, it seems fair to say that anyone who thinks that a floor leader, whether or not solicited by his party's administration, would take no action to stop an investigation based on scant evidence by a hostile committee chairman six weeks before a presidential election simply does not know much about American politics.

The Vice-Presidency

During his career in the House, Ford generally chose the role of negotiator rather than that of heated partisan or trailblazing innovator. His voting record usually placed him in the category of Republicans that I have called stalwarts: the solid conservatives who made little effort to turn back the clock to the time before the New Deal, but as a rule fought each new expansion of the welfare state. He spoke often of the need to offer "positive alternatives" to the Democratic programs, but came up with few such himself. Like his stepfather long before in Grand Rapids, Ford sought to place himself among the "insiders"—not simply because he believed (as he no doubt did) that getting along well with insiders would help his career, but because he was deeply convinced of the moral rightness of government by insiders: the able, the competent, those who take the trouble to discipline themselves to the authority of facts. Leadership, he once said, should be based on "common sense—not just on intellectual capabilities but on how to evaluate, how to judge, how to read into something, whether it is on paper or the spoken word."[54]

Ford's highest ambition was to be Speaker of the House. "Quite frankly," he told John Osborne in 1977, near the end of his presidency, "I never aspired to any executive responsibility." He had felt, he said,

"overall non-interest in the executive branch of the government."[55]
When the Republicans failed to make significant gains in the House
in 1972 despite Nixon's landslide reelection (partly, Ford was convinced, because the managers of Nixon's campaign had refused to
give much help to Republican congressional candidates in close races),
he reluctantly concluded that his party was unlikely to win control
of the House in "the foreseeable future." Acceding to the wishes of
his wife, who over the years had made many personal and emotional
sacrifices to help sustain his career, Ford decided that he would run
once more for reelection, and then announce his retirement from the
House at the end of 1976.[56]

Why did Nixon nominate Ford to be vice-president? Though they
had served one term together in the House at the end of the 1940s,
and had often collaborated to promote Republican causes and programs, the two men were not personally close. Nixon reportedly did
not have a very high estimate of Ford's leadership capabilities. ("Can
you see," he is said to have asked Nelson Rockefeller, "Gerald Ford
sitting in this chair?")[57] When the vice-presidency opened up as a
result of Agnew's forced resignation in the fall of 1973, Nixon's first
choice was John Connally—the masterful political impresario whom
he had already chosen to carry on his grand design after 1976. He
was told, however, that Connally would be hard to get confirmed,
since he was opposed both by liberal Democrats and by Republicans
who resented the recency of his conversion from the opposition.
Facing growing troubles over Watergate, Nixon wanted no pitched
battle with Congress over his nomination of a replacement for Agnew.
After eliminating Rockefeller and Reagan because the selection of
either would split the Republican party, Nixon chose Ford, he has
written, because "Ford was qualified to be President . . . his views
on both domestic and foreign policy were very close to mine . . . and
there was no question he would be the easiest to get confirmed."[58]
Some commentators have suggested that not the least of Ford's at-
tractions to the incumbent president was that Nixon believed—
wrongly, as it turned out—that Congress would be reluctant to raise
Ford to the presidency. In the background Melvin Laird, briefly again
in Nixon's confidence, seems to have played an important role in
guiding the nomination toward his old friend Ford.

For his part, Ford was willing. Having given up hope of becoming

Speaker, he seems to have regarded the vice-presidency as a final elevation before retirement. "It would be a good way to round out my career," he told Joe Waggonner in the back of the House one night, while Nixon was making up his mind.[59]

On December 6, 1973, Ford was sworn in as the first vice-president selected through the procedure for appointment established by the Twenty-fifth Amendment. He was apparently convinced that talk of Nixon's impeachment would fade, and was resigned to carrying out his promise to his wife to retire from public life at the end of 1976. Eight months and three days later, he was president.

The Pardon

The most controversial act of Ford's presidency—the one that perhaps cost him election to a full term—occurred only four weeks after his administration began. On the morning of Sunday, September 8, 1974, after attending an early service at St. John's Episcopal Church, across Lafayette Square from the White House, Ford announced that he had granted a "full, free, and absolute pardon unto Richard Nixon for all offenses" he "committed or may have committed" while president of the United States.[60]

At the time Ford indicated that he believed that "Richard Nixon and his loved ones have suffered enough and will continue to suffer, no matter what I do, no matter what we . . . can do together to make his goal of peace come true."[61] In his memoirs, however, Ford maintained that his decision to pardon Nixon was largely based on his conclusion that any trial of the former president, which the special prosecutor estimated could not be completed in less than two years, would dangerously divide the nation and sap vital governmental energies, including his own. "My fundamental decision to grant a pardon," he wrote, "had nothing to do with any sympathy I might feel for Nixon personally or any concern I might have for the state of his health."[62] (Or he is not so sure. Elsewhere in his book he observed: "I wasn't motivated *primarily* by sympathy for his plight or by concern over the state of his health" [emphasis added].)[63] Hostile politicians and skeptical journalists (and taxi drivers) have suggested, without proof, that Ford must have made a commitment before he became president, to Nixon or to Alexander Haig, to grant the pardon if Nixon resigned before impeachment proceedings went forward in the House.[64] My own impression, based on talks with some of the aides whom Ford consulted before making his decision, is that he granted the pardon in part because he wanted to avoid the divisions and turmoil that a trial of Nixon would inevitably have produced, but also in very large part because, as he indicated on the day the pardon was announced, he believed that it was the decent thing to do—and if he was wrong, "ten angels swearing I was right would make no difference."[65]

Whatever Ford's motives in granting the pardon, it established an indissoluble link in the public mind between his presidency and that of his predecessor. During the first few weeks of Ford's term, a notion fostered by the media and apparently satisfying a deep yearning among some of the public, had developed that his entrance into the White House represented a totally fresh start—one unconnected with the political skulduggery and repressive tendencies of the Nixon administration or even with the whole structure of ideological assumptions and governmental goals that had underlain Nixon's substantive policies. This notion was now dispelled, never to return.

With or without the pardon, however, the ideological link between the two administrations would soon have become apparent. Nixon had selected Ford, and the former president was right that his successor's "views on both domestic and foreign policy" were very close to his own. In his memoirs Ford acknowledged identification with a series of "essentially conservative goals" attributed to him by James Naughton of the *New York Times:* reduced government intervention "in the affairs of citizens and corporations"; greater reliance on a free market economy; and shift of responsibility to local units of government "for overcoming adversity."[66] Nixon would have subscribed to the same list—and to Ford's preoccupations with strengthening national defense and combating inflation.

The two administrations began with similar assumptions about the nature of society and the state of the world and with similar underlying social values—all easily distinguishable from the assumptions and values of the two preceding Democratic administrations. But they differed in political style and administrative approach, and, perhaps most important, were led by presidents who differed widely in character and personality.

A Burkean Conservative

Early in Ford's administration, some of his aides became concerned that the president was not projecting to the nation his social "philosophy" or "vision." As one said: "The president has a philosophy, and we all act on it, but we don't seem to be able to tell what it is."

Either because they believed that some kind of presidential vision was needed to give internal coherence to the administration, or because they felt that the appearance of vision would be useful for public relations, Ford's aides regarded this lack as a problem, and tried to deal with it. Robert Goldwin, a political scientist who occupied the odd role of White House intellectual-in-residence (a position apparently created by Arthur Schlesinger, Jr., in the Kennedy administration) recalled spending a Saturday morning in the oval office with Richard Cheney, then White House deputy chief of staff, trying to elicit from the president some sketch of ideas from which a social philosophy or vision could be verbalized.[67] The effort failed, as did similar attempts made from time to time during the next two years, almost up to election day in 1976.

The assumptions and values on which Ford based his decisions, it appeared, resisted abstraction—or at least the president found it difficult to put them into words. In part, this resistance might have stemmed from his distaste for vague generalities, acquired during twenty-five years of listening to political bombast in the House. Essentially, however, it seemed to have grown out of his deep-seated doubt that theoretic generalizations can be usefully applied to much of experience. "We must take the practical problems that come before a President or before Congress as specific instances," Ford said, when asked at an American Enterprise Institute seminar in 1978 how he decided whether social problems required public or private solutions. "Among the wide variety of problems facing the responsible people in the federal government, no precise formula can determine what is the private or the public interest. The circumstances are totally different in almost every instance."[68]

Yet there *were* general principles, if not formulas, that underlay the practical decisions Ford had to make as president. Alan Greenspan, Ford's principal economic adviser, has said: "I found that I had a high degree of success at predicting how the president would decide on any given issue. That must have been because I was able to abstract a consistent line of policy from his concrete actions."[69]

In his memoirs Ford attempted to identify some of the principles on which his decisions were based. He proceeded, he wrote, on the beliefs that "the real purpose of government is to enhance the lives of people," and that "a leader can best do that by restraining government in most cases instead of enlarging it at every opportunity." Because of these "conservative" convictions, he tried to keep "the rate of growth of federal expenditures . . . below the rate of the economy as a whole," and "to inhibit the growth of income transfer payments." He gloomily commented: "I might not be able to reverse the process [of growing transfer payments], but at least I could point out the dangers in the trend." He went on to write, however: "Conservatism has always meant more to me than simply sticking up for private property and free enterprise. It has also meant defending our heritage and preserving our values." Ford associated his position with that set forth by Kenneth Clark at the end of his book *Civilisation:* "I reveal myself in my true colors as a stick-in-the-mud. I believe that order is better than chaos, creation better than destruction. I prefer gentleness to violence, forgiveness to vendetta. . . . I believe that in spite of the recent triumphs of science, men have not changed that much in the last two thousand years, and in consequence, we must still try to learn from history. Above all, I believe in the God-given genius of certain individuals, and I value a society that makes their existence possible."[70]

As he entered the presidency, Ford gave every sign of being the kind of conservative who relies on experience and inherited belief rather than on precisely formulated doctrines—a true Burkean. Apart from his switch from isolationism to internationalism, carried out while he was a young man under the impact of a world war, he had not moved far from the values and attitudes commonly held in the Grand Rapids of his youth. He maintained an inclusive Christian faith. On the night of the day he learned from Alexander Haig of the "smoking gun" tape that would soon make him president, he repeated with his wife a prayer from the book of Proverbs that he had learned in Sunday School: "Trust in the Lord with all thine heart, and lean not unto thine own understanding. In all thy ways acknowledge Him, and He shall direct thy paths." (He had said the same prayer years before on the night he discovered that his stepfather was not his real father.)[71]

He disliked "zealots" and "doctrinaire ideology," but he believed that a political party should operate within broad but definable principles. "We don't want people in the party just to pull a lever like the Democrats do," he told John Casserly, one of his speechwriters. "We want them in because they believe in traditional Republican principles." (Among traditional Republican principles, Ford included: belief in the free enterprise system; support for strong national defense; wide latitude for local and state governments to make their own decisions; and minimum government interference in business-labor relations and the conduct of individual lives.)[72]

Ford's conservatism sprang from a lifetime of personal and political experience, and from a deep stratum of social and religious beliefs. As the administration headed into the political, social, and economic storms that clearly were rising in the fall of 1974, the president's conservative principles faced enormous tests, both from the practical problems themselves and from the public's evaluation of his performance.

14

The Ford Team

A PRESIDENT raised to the White House through the normal election process has an eleven-week period between election day and inauguration during which he may recruit key personnel, as well as plan a legislative program and determine administrative priorities. Having just passed through a prolonged campaign, nowadays requiring almost as large and multiskilled a staff as that needed to run the White House itself, he is surrounded by experienced aides and advisers, most of whom are eager for government service. Even those presidents succeeding from the vice-presidency because of the death of an incumbent usually inherit active operations able to carry on current business while the new administration is finding its bearings.

Gerald Ford possessed none of these advantages when he entered the presidency on August 9, 1974. The White House for many months had been obsessed with Watergate and the threat of impeachment. Members of the White House staff, including many who had in no way been touched by Watergate, were viewed by much of the public as tainted through association with Nixon. Some members of the cabinet were tired and ready to leave. Others, particularly James Schlesinger at Defense and William Simon at the Treasury, had established their departments as almost autonomous baronies during the period of Nixon's political weakness, and seemed unlikely to welcome the reassertion of White House authority under the new president. Henry Kissinger, secretary of state as well as director of the National Security Council since July 1973, had achieved a national and international eminence that threatened to put even the president into the shade.

The delicacy of his position as vice-president had made it nearly impossible for Ford, or for his immediate staff, to make preparations for the succession until almost the end of Nixon's tenure. Until Alexander Haig told him on August 1 about the "smoking gun" tape, which revealed that Nixon had participated in the cover-up in the first week after the Watergate burglars were caught, Ford had continued to defend Nixon against impeachment. Such plans as had been made for the incoming administration were of necessity put together without Ford's approval, or even his knowledge—though not, perhaps, without his oblique intent.

The Transition

In March 1974 Ford had used a bit of patronage available to him as chairman of a White House commission on privacy rights to bring Philip Buchen, his old friend and former Grand Rapids law partner, to Washington. Buchen, installed as part-time executive director of the privacy commission, witnessed the apparently irreversible disintegration of the Nixon presidency. By May he had concluded that somebody had better begin preparing the underpinning for a new administration, and, recognizing the restraints imposed by the situation on Ford and his staff, he appointed himself to the job.

Buchen had clerked briefly in a Wall Street law firm (as it happened, the one in which Nixon and Mitchell later became partners) before returning to Grand Rapids, and during his legal career had developed extensive contacts within the eastern business and governmental establishments. But since he knew relatively little about the rules and folkways of the national government, he felt the need for a collaborator with broader Washington experience. For this purpose he turned to a young government official who happened to occupy an office down the hall from that of the privacy commission: Clay Whitehead, director of the White House Office of Telecommunication Policy (a Nixon administration creation that was supposed to coordinate the federal role in the technical aspects of broadcasting, but that could readily be converted to a political mission).[1]

Whitehead, who held a doctoral degree in management science from MIT, had gained passing notoriety in December 1972, when he made a speech attacking the television networks for inserting "ideological plugola" into their news broadcasts. Though an enthusiastic supporter of the administration's drive to build a national majority based on populist conservatism, he had grown disenchanted with Nixon, and without much hesitation agreed to help Buchen plan the initial steps a new president would have to take.

Buchen and Whitehead selected three more members for what they called the "transition team," all young men with some executive branch experience under Nixon: Brian Lamb, Whitehead's assistant at the Office of Telecommunications Policy; Lawrence Lynn, a former aide to Kissinger at the NSC, who had argued against the Cambodia incursion in the spring of 1970, but had not joined several colleagues in carrying dissent to the point of resignation; and Jonathan Moore, a former aide to Rockefeller, Romney, and Elliot Richardson. During the late spring and early summer, Buchen, Whitehead, and their associates met five times, discussing personnel changes that should take place at the start of the new administration. According to one account, Lynn and Moore stressed the need to clean out promptly all those who had directed Nixon's defense, particularly Haig. Reportedly, the team agreed to try to steer Ford away from the influence of Melvin Laird, who they believed was "an incorrigible schemer who would approach the new President . . . with grandiose plans."[2]

Buchen did not tell Ford what the group was up to until the night of August 6—only three days before Nixon's resignation. Ford, though he had carefully avoided any move that might be interpreted as disloyal to Nixon, was probably not much surprised to learn that somewhere in Washington there were persons making plans to facilitate his succession (as the Young Turks had plotted the overthrow of Halleck in 1964); he seems even to have been a bit disappointed that so little had been accomplished. In Ford's mind, Whitehead's name was associated only with the unfavorable publicity given to the young technocrat's attack on the networks in 1972; Moore, Lamb, and Lynn were "competent young men," but not, Ford felt, of the rank needed to manage a smooth transition.

Ford directed Buchen to expand the transition team to include some senior Washington figures: Robert Griffin, Michigan's junior senator since 1969; Bryce Harlow, just returned to his job as chief

Washington lobbyist for Procter and Gamble, after once more being recalled by Nixon to White House service in 1973; former Congressman John Byrnes of Wisconsin, a staunch conservative now practicing law in Washington; Secretary of the Interior Rogers Morton, former representative from the Eastern Shore district of Maryland and former chairman of the Republican National Committee; and "another old friend," William G. Whyte, vice-president in charge of governmental relations for United States Steel—in all, a revealing top slice of what might be called the corporate-political complex. Buchen, whose own political philosophy had always been a shade more liberal than Ford's, suggested the addition of William Scranton, former governor of Pennsylvania, still a leader in the progressive wing of the Republican party and a well-connected member of the eastern business establishment. Ford, whose law school class had overlapped with Scranton's at Yale in the 1930s, and who had come to know Scranton better when the latter served a single term in the House at the beginning of the 1960s, readily agreed.[3]

Buchen placed calls to the persons Ford had designated. Though he was a stranger to some of them, all agreed to meet at Whyte's home in suburban Bethesda on the night of August 7. At this meeting there was general agreement that Ford should clean out most of the White House staff as soon as he took office. (Some of those present had received their share of slights and rebuffs from Nixon's aides.) Some thought the purge should be expanded beyond the president's immediate staff to include Roy Ash and Frederic Malek, director and deputy director of OMB, who had increasingly carried on much of the actual administration of the executive branch.[4]

By the time Ford took office two days later, the transition team had again been altered. Buchen had become counsel to the president, charged with concentrating on such problems as how to deal with Watergate-related charges against Nixon and whether to grant some form of amnesty to young men who had evaded the draft during the Vietnam War. Whitehead and his young associates had fallen into the background. Whyte, Harlow, Griffin, and Byrnes continued in their roles as close friends to the new president, always available for advice, but for one reason or another were not included in the official inner circle.

The team that met with Ford in the Oval Office on the night of his swearing-in had been reduced to four men: Morton; Scranton; Donald

Rumsfeld, former congressman from Illinois, director of the Office of Economic Opportunity and chief of the Cost of Living Council under Nixon, and currently ambassador to NATO, who had been hastily recalled from Brussels to assist in the change in administrations; and John Marsh, formerly a Democratic congressman from Virginia, assistant secretary of defense in the Nixon administration, and a member of Ford's personal staff after Ford became vice-president. All four had served in the House with Ford. Scranton, Morton, and Rumsfeld were perceived as somewhat to the left of center on the ideological spectrum within the Republican party; Marsh, the Democrat, was deeply, but not dogmatically, conservative.

The ideological orientation of the transition team on August 9 was relatively more liberal than that of the group that had met at Whyte's home on August 7. Ford had decided that his responsibility to a national constituency obliged him to pursue a somewhat more progressive course than he had followed at earlier stages in his career. By designating Scranton to direct the recruitment of personnel for a reconstituted White House staff, the new president apparently aimed to call on some of the talent among Republican progressives that had been little used by Nixon (at least after 1969).

Rumsfeld was chosen to take Buchen's place as coordinator of the transition team; Morton was given charge of maintaining liaison with the departments and agencies; and Marsh was assigned to establish liaison with Congress. Ford directed the group to develop a structure for the White House staff that would "reflect my personal style by assuring openness and the free movement of people and ideas." Rumsfeld—"able, hard-driving," in Ford's description—proposed that the transition team swiftly wind up its work and pass out of existence in no more than thirty days, to avoid development of a dual structure of authority within the administration. The president and the other members of the team agreed.[5]

The Original Ford Staff

The new transition team renewed the recommendation of its two predecessors that Nixon's staff should be swept out of the White House as quickly as possible. It soon became apparent, however, that Ford intended to move more slowly. Ronald Ziegler, Nixon's press secretary, who had been a particularly visible symbol and apologist for the old administration, was immediately replaced by Jerald F. ter Horst, Washington correspondent for the *Detroit News* and a respected member of the capital press corps, who had covered Ford's first race for Congress in 1948. (Ter Horst did not last long at the job. Within four weeks, finding himself unable to defend Ford's pardon of Nixon, and perhaps having discovered he was not temperamentally suited for the position, he resigned. His post was taken by Ronald Nessen, a television news reporter with the National Broadcasting Company, who proved a resilient performer in the frequently uncivil atmosphere of the post-Watergate White House press room.) But except for Ziegler, most of Nixon's key aides, including Haig, remained for some time in place.

"I felt," Ford has said, "when I came into office that it would be wrong to clean out the Nixon appointees on a wholesale basis. Everyone, I felt, should have four or five months to give them a reasonable chance to find other jobs."[6] Besides humanitarian concern, Ford's slowness to remove Nixon's people grew out of his realization that in many cases qualified replacements were not quickly available. During his career in Congress, Ford had operated with a surprisingly thin staff. For advice and legwork he had largely relied on trusted colleagues like Laird, Goodell, and Rumsfeld. After 1969 he drew on the assistance of the White House congressional liaison staff. As a result, he had no extensive entourage of experienced political and governmental technicians to take with him to the executive branch.

When Ford became vice-president, he raised Robert Hartmann, his principal speechwriter, with whom he had developed a warm, confidential relationship, to the post of chief of staff. Hartmann was a lifelong Republican—he remembered having in his boyhood fastened posters to utility poles for Herbert Hoover. As a journalist, working for the *Los Angeles Times*, he had candidly identified with the Republican cause. His instincts were conservative, but, like Ford, he recognized the need for flexibility. He understood politics as a game, and through his work as a Washington bureau chief had acquired broad knowledge of the federal government. Yet Ford soon decided that making Hartmann his chief of staff had been "a dreadful mistake."[7]

Hartmann, it turned out, was a poor administrator. But what came to be known in the Ford White House as "the Hartmann problem" went deeper. Hartmann had grown up in the journalistic school that believes in developing a story as a string of beads, from which any one bead or group of beads may be cut without serious damage to meaning or coherence. Applying this style to speechwriting may produce punchy sentences, but it is not likely to lead to a reasoned argument or analysis. Robert Goldwin, who worked with Hartmann in the White House (or in Hartmann's view, against him), has said: "Hartmann saw no need for continuity in a speech. He felt that each sentence had to carry its own weight, and that no overall theme need be developed."[8] Applying this approach more generally, Hartmann seemed to see no need for overall themes in a political campaign or administration.

At the suggestion of Buchen, Ford invited a Grand Rapids friend of theirs, William Seidman, managing partner in the nationally active accounting firm of Seidman and Seidman, to come to Washington to organize his office. A graduate of Dartmouth and Harvard Law School, Seidman had been active in Michigan government and politics as an adviser on fiscal matters to Governor George Romney during the 1960s. Though representing a somewhat more progressive view within the Republican party than that with which Ford was identified, Seidman was sufficiently pragmatic in his politics and conservative in his economic outlook to hold Ford's confidence. His immediate assignment was to improve the operational efficiency of the vice-presidential office, but the breadth of his interests and his personal closeness to Ford made it likely that his influence would expand.

The third person of significant rank on Ford's vice-presidential staff was John Marsh, who, as a traditionalist Democratic congressman from the Shenandoah Valley of Virginia (stronghold of the conservative Byrd clan), had got to know Ford in the 1960s. Still a nominal Democrat, Marsh personified the institutional memory of the network of southern small-town lawyers and country gentlemen who for decades had dominated most of the major committees of Congress— by 1974, a waning force, but still maintaining useful connections in many federal departments and agencies as well as on Capitol Hill. Besides handling liaison duties with the Defense Department during the vice-presidential period, Marsh, though thirteen years younger than Ford, performed the function of sagacious Nestor offering detached counsel, somewhat as Clark Clifford had done for Lyndon Johnson, and Charles Kirbo was to do for Jimmy Carter.

These three—Hartmann, Seidman, and Marsh—plus Buchen and ter Horst were the principal members of the staff that accompanied Ford into the White House. He would need more, the president realized, to establish effective control over the executive branch. Either he would have to rely on many of Nixon's people, at least for a limited period, or he would have to find replacements who were both ideologically trustworthy and professionally qualified.

"The president," Donald Rumsfeld has recalled, "was subject to two tugs. On the one hand, he recognized that these people [the Nixon appointees] were overwhelmingly fine, decent human beings. Most of them had never thought of doing anything wrong. To fire them immediately would give the impression that he thought they were in some way connected with Watergate. In addition, they were skilled people. He needed them to operate the institutions of government. On the other hand, executive authority under Nixon had come to appear, both externally and internally, illegitimate. Things had reached a state in the government where if someone would say, 'Good morning,' others would think, 'What does he really mean by that?' This attitude had developed momentum, inertia, and had spread to the entire country. . . . So the first thing the president had to do was to restore a sense of legitimacy to the executive branch. There was a need for continuity, but also there was a need for change—or for a sense of change. The solution, Ford decided, was to make the minimal number of changes that would be needed to allow the critical mass that remained to become once more legitimate. His aim was to create a Ford presidency, rather than a Nixon presidency over which Ford was now presiding."[9]

During the period of transition, which in a sense continued right up to the end of the Ford presidency, the former Nixon people who were kept on and the new people who were appointed to the White House staff by Ford functioned together in uneasy harness. As Ford wrote: "Many of the Nixon holdovers on the White House staff were saying, 'Here comes Jerry Ford and his minor leaguers. Once we settle them down and show them how the game is played, everything will be all right.' And my own people were saying, 'As soon as we get rid of these Nixon appointees, the government will be legitimate again.'"[10] This description probably understates the tension that existed between the two camps—each of which contained a number of internal divisions. Meanwhile a formidable third force was moving toward the White House: on August 20 Ford had nominated Nelson Rockefeller to succeed to the vacant office of vice-president of the United States.

The New Vice-President

No one, except perhaps the Roosevelts and the Kennedys, has ever brought to American politics resources of organizational and intellectual talent comparable to those commanded by Nelson Rockefeller. The enormous Rockefeller family fortune, combined with the network of personal and professional connections maintained by the Rockefellers throughout the upper reaches of the business, governmental, academic, and scientific communities, gave him access to almost any kind of political, public relations, or research assistance. "My approach," Rockefeller said in an interview in the spring of 1978, about ten months before his death, "has always been to get the facts, analyze them, learn the different points of view on the issue, make myself aware of the social and economic problems involved, get the best minds available working on the problem, and then make a decision and go ahead."[11] Rockefeller could usually count on most of "the best minds available" being glad to share with him their conclusions—not simply because they would be well paid, but because of the courtesy and interest with which he received their recommendations, and, most of all, because Nelson Rockefeller, in or out of the government, possessed the magnet of social power: if the best minds influenced him, they had a good chance of having an impact on the real world of events.

In New York State politics the Rockefeller apparatus operated with superb efficiency in four successful gubernatorial campaigns. It helped produce notable social progress for the people of New York (a high-quality state university system, more accessible health care, increased state aid for the cities), if meanwhile dangerously undermining the state's fiscal stability. Yet in politics outside New York, the Rockefeller organization, and Rockefeller personally, always faltered. His campaigns for the Republican presidential nomination in 1960, 1964, and 1968 had all gone badly; they not only were unsuccessful, but projected images of arrogance and insensitivity, seemed to sink beneath their own weight, and failed to make much contact with the interests or aspirations of Americans who lived south of Staten Island or west of the Alleghenies.

The truth was that Nelson Rockefeller was to the tips of his toes a New Yorker—and New Yorkers have always been a special class within the broad genus Americanus. New Yorkers—capitalist financiers and entrepreneurs, silk-stocking liberals, social democrats, Marxists, Tammany Hall–type politicians—have been fascinated by power and have believed that the concentration of social power is both natural and necessary in a modern industrial society, whether for expanding industrial pro⁀ʰᵘction, succoring the poor, or democratizing economic opportunity. Since the nomination of Al Smith in 1928, some version of this view has usually prevailed within the national Democratic party. But among Republicans, many of whom have been master manipulators of power within their particular divisions of society or the economy, resistance to centralization of power, whether in New York or Washington, has been a dominant sentiment. New York, though it has provided the Republicans with two presidents (Chester Arthur and Theodore Roosevelt) and two unsuccessful nominees (Hughes and Dewey), as well as with Willkie, Eisenhower, and Nixon, who were New Yorkers during parts of their careers, has usually been regarded with distrust and even aversion by much of the national Republican party. An Illinois delegate to the 1860 Republican National Convention in Chicago complained that members of the New York delegation were "a class unknown to Western Republicans—drinking as much whiskey as any crowd of Democrats."[12] In 1928 Robert Taft wrote to a friend that the "discomfiture" of the New York "intelligentsia" gave him "as much pleasure as that of the radical farm leaders."[13]

By Rockefeller's time, some of the reality of power had shifted away from New York, to Washington and to new loci in the West and South, but the legend of power, and a substantial remnant of the reality, still clung to the banks, corporate headquarters, and national news media centers in Manhattan. This legendary authority imparted some advantages, but also heavy liabilities, to a politician who appeared to represent the combined influences of Wall Street and the great media empires—particularly if that politician were named Rockefeller, and particularly if he had been divorced in mid-life and had later married a beautiful younger woman, herself divorced and the mother of four children.

Even so, Rockefeller was probably right in thinking that he would very likely have been nominated and elected president if he had become a Democrat. He had chosen, however, to stay with the party of his father and his grandfathers (Nelson Aldrich of Rhode Island, Republican leader of the U.S. Senate in the early years of the century, as well as old John D.), a choice based on more than habit or accident of birth. At the roots of his being, Rockefeller held a view of order and a commitment to social continuity that prevented him from becoming a true liberal. "Nobody has more to conserve than I do," he liked to point out when trying to ingratiate himself with his party's right wing. But Rockefeller's social vision was more, too, than a rationalization of self-interest. "The Republican party, when it first held power in the nineteenth century," Rockefeller said in 1978, "was a party with a great national purpose. It supported agricultural expansion through the Homestead Act, set up the land grant colleges, encouraged the building of the railroads and the development of industry—all based on partnership between government and free enterprise. That was a very constructive relationship."[14]

Rockefeller aimed throughout his political career to infuse the Republican party of his own day with a similar purpose: economic progress and social amity based on active collaboration between business and government, with the great trade unions brought along as far as their internal political problems permitted. "I believe in partnership between the public and private sectors," he said. "Neither side should be dominant."[15] The Democratic party could not serve as vehicle for such a partnership, he was convinced, because the Democrats could never fully win the confidence of business or of the old middle class, still crucially influential in many parts of the country. The Republican party held the keys to social advance and orderly and constructive change—if only the Republican party could be persuaded to use them. "The federal government," Rockefeller said, "is like a glacier. Nothing is more difficult than changing its course." The Nixon and Ford administrations, he regretted, "sometimes did not seem to have clear objectives." In government, he had concluded, "it is not so necessary to have a systematic philosophy." But "a clear sense of direction" is essential. "In foreign policy," he said, "both Nixon and Ford, working with Henry Kissinger, developed ideas and direction. In domestic policy, they did not do as well."[16]

In his last years as governor of New York, Rockefeller appeared to grow more conservative: he tried to put ceilings on rising welfare

costs, resisted further increases in state spending, sponsored enactment of the nation's strictest (some said most repressive) law against
sale or use of prohibited drugs. Energy and inflation, he acknowledged, had become the nation's most pressing domestic problems.
Still, he felt, these challenges could be met, and progress made on
other national needs as well, if strong leadership called forth concurrent efforts from the public and private sectors. Rockefeller clearly
believed that he was uniquely equipped to provide such leadership.
But by 1974 he probably had recognized that the chances of his ever
achieving the presidency had become small. He was sixty-six, had
given up the governorship the year before, could not realistically
expect that the Republican party, grown even more conservative since
1968, was ever likely to nominate him for president. But he still had
ideas and energy, still had many of "the best minds" on call, and
still, he believed, had a clearer grasp of what the country needed than
any other national leader in either party.

When Ford offered him the vice-presidency, it seemed to Rockefeller that he might after all have an opportunity to apply his vision
and resources at the summit of national authority, even if not as
president. (And if he were the incumbent vice-president, who could
be sure what 1976 would bring?) He liked and respected Ford—"loved
the guy"—but he probably shared Nixon's view that Ford was not
likely to be a dynamic national leader. Rockefeller saw that the staff
Ford was bringing to the White House would need a great deal of
help in managing the executive branch. He anticipated a good working
relationship with Hartmann, whom he had first known as a journalist,
and who he assumed would remain Ford's closest personal adviser.
Buchen and Seidman were members of the Grand Rapids affiliate of
the eastern establishment that had always formed part of his constituency. He had also formed a friendly association with Haig, who he
thought might be staying on as chief of staff.[17]

Ford, Rockefeller understood, wished to move in a somewhat more
liberal direction. And Rockefeller could provide him with the planners,
the researchers, the conceptualizers who would design progressive
new programs, always staying within the bounds of fiscal soundness
and Republican concern for local self-determination and economic
freedom. Rockefeller probably genuinely did not care (very much)
who got the credit. Nothing would please him more than for Ford to
be remembered as a great, constructive president. But for that to
happen, Rockefeller quite naturally believed, it would be necessary

for Ford to govern along the lines that would be recommended by the new vice-president.

Delay in Rockefeller's Confirmation

Ford's reasons for appointing Rockefeller to the vice-presidency were both political and governmental. Within a few days after becoming president, Ford had narrowed the list of choices to five names: George Bush, former ambassador to the United Nations and currently Republican national chairman; Senator William Brock of Tennessee; House Minority Leader John Rhodes of Arizona; Rogers Morton; and Rockefeller. In a memorandum requested by the president, Bryce Harlow analyzed the strengths and weaknesses of the five. Bush, Morton, Rhodes, and Brock, Harlow observed, would all be acceptable to conservative Republicans. But they would not attract any great support from outside the regular Republican base. Rockefeller, on the other hand, was "anathema to conservatives," but his choice would indicate "that the new President will not be the captive of any political faction," and would "encourage estranged groups to return to the party." Moreover, Rockefeller was "professionally the best qualified by far" and would "make available superb manpower resources to staff the administration." Harlow concluded: "The best choice is Rockefeller."[18]

Ford, for the moment at least, was attracted by the vision of a great centrist coalition that moderate and progressive Republicans had always argued could establish the Republicans firmly in national power. No clearer signal could be given, as Harlow pointed out, of his intention to move toward the center than the selection of the symbolic leader of progressive Republicanism as vice-president. On the night of August 18, Ford broached the subject to Rockefeller in a phone call to the former governor's home in Seal Harbor, Maine. The next day Ford made the offer firm, and Rockefeller accepted.

Looking back, Rockefeller believed that if Congress had moved quickly to confirm him as vice-president, his relationship with the Ford White House, and perhaps the nature of the Ford presidency, might have been different. But Congress did not move quickly. Democratic liberals and some of Rockefeller's old enemies among Republican conservatives on the congressional committees reviewing the nomination took full advantage of the unprecedented opportunity to probe the size and reach of the Rockefeller fortune—not only Nelson Rockefeller's personal holdings, but also those of his brothers and other members of the Rockefeller family. "At one point," a former Rockefeller aide has said, "it appeared that Nelson would have to choose between doing terrible harm to his family or giving up the vice-presidency. He seriously considered withdrawing." A compromise was worked out, under which Rockefeller's own income and assets were reported in detail, and those of other members of the family were presented more generally. The examination of Rockefeller's tax returns revealed that over the years he had made large cash gifts and loans to Kissinger and other governmental aides and associates. As David Broder, political columnist for the *Washington Post*, put it, Rockefeller had been a politician, almost unique in American experience, "on the give."[19]

After the congressional elections in November produced the expected Democratic landslide, some liberal Democrats in the House began to talk seriously of defeating the nomination, or at least of holding it over until the new Congress, with a greatly enlarged Democratic majority, took office in January. Meanwhile, Speaker of the House Carl Albert stood first in the line of succession to the presidency—a job that he insisted he did not want, and that very few in Washington believed he was suited to fill. Finally, after four months of extended hearings and political maneuvering, the Senate on December 10 confirmed Rockefeller's nomination by a vote of 90 to 7. Voting in the negative were Barry Goldwater and two other Republican fundamentalists, and four Democratic liberals.[20] On December 19, the day before Congress was to adjourn, the House at last followed suit, approving the nomination by a vote of 287 to 128.

The distribution of the vote in the House by ideological groups was as follows (a yes vote being a vote to confirm):[21]

Republicans			*Democrats*		
	Yes	*No*		*Yes*	*No*
Fundamentalists	44	20	Traditionalists	26	12
Stalwarts	63	9	Centrists	46	26
Moderates	30	0	Regulars	44	28
Progressives	16	0	Liberals	18	33
Total	153	29	Total	134	99

The core of opposition to the nomination came from the Democratic liberals, including five from New York City. Besides those opposing the nomination, nine liberals did not vote, including three from New York. Substantial numbers of Democratic centrists and regulars took the opportunity to go on record against Rockefeller. These were joined by about one-third of the Republican fundamentalists, who were registering their continuing rancor against Goldwater's most stubborn opponent in the intraparty battle in 1964.

While confirmation of the nomination hung fire, Rockefeller felt it would not be appropriate for him to play an active role within the White House. When he finally took office at the end of December, it seemed to him that the outlook and direction of the administration had changed significantly since Ford had offered him the vice-presidency four months before. "When I was appointed," he later said, "Al Haig was still chief of staff. By the time I was confirmed, there had been a change of personnel in the White House. Don Rumsfeld had come in."[22]

Rise of Rumsfeld

The transition team had finished its work in less than a month after Ford's inauguration. Rumsfeld returned to his post in Brussels as ambassador to NATO; Morton went back to devoting full time to the Department of the Interior; Marsh took responsibility for congressional relations on the regular White House staff; and Scranton, after declining Ford's request that he take a full-time job in the new administration, became a member of the president's "kitchen cabinet," a group of old friends and advisers from private life who met at the White House about once a month.[23] Before disbanding, the transition team recommended that the White House staff be organized through a structure that gave several top aides equal access to the president. This accorded with Ford's thinking. "When I was in the House," Ford has said, "I observed how [different] Presidents seemed to organize the White House differently. President Nixon had had a very tightly held organization, with a chief of staff who ran the total operation. President Johnson seemed to have more intimate contact than President Nixon had with various people that reported from Defense and the domestic side. . . . When I became President . . . I initially felt that what I perceived as the Johnson organization was preferable, with seven or eight different people within the White House reporting directly to the President."[24]

Within a short time, however, Ford concluded that what he called the "spokes of the wheel" approach "simply didn't work." He found, he has said, "that a President needs one person who at least coordinates people such as the President's assistant for national security affairs, the head of the Domestic Council, the head of the Economic Policy Board, et cetera. Somebody had to organize the day's schedule and the flow of paperwork."[25]

By the beginning of September, Haig was again acting as chief of staff. Ford recognized, however, that Haig's "Nixon image" made it impossible for him to remain indefinitely at the White House.[26] On September 21 the president asked Rumsfeld, who was back in the country for his father's funeral, to consider taking Haig's place.

Rumsfeld at first resisted. The "spokes of the wheel" concept for organizing the White House staff, which the transition team had recommended, he now argued, was fine in theory, but would not work in practice. "I know you don't want a Haldeman-type chief of staff," he told Ford, "but someone has to fill that role, and unless I can have that authority, I won't be able to serve you effectively."[27] Ford said he had come to agree. When Rumsfeld continued to express doubt that he was the man for the job, the president asked Harlow (fast becoming as indispensable to Ford as he had been to Nixon) to talk with him. On September 30 Rumsfeld was named White House "staff coordinator"—in effect, chief of staff. A few days before, Haig had been designated the supreme commander of NATO forces in Europe.

When Donald Rumsfeld had first come to Congress in 1963, elected from the affluent North Shore suburbs above Chicago, he usually voted with the Republican fundamentalists; his record in the Eighty-eighth Congress was considerably more conservative than Gerald Ford's.[28] He had joined Laird and Goodell in the effort to oust Halleck as minority leader in 1964, not because he disagreed with Halleck's ideological orientation, but because he believed Halleck had become ineffective as a leader. Gradually, however, Rumsfeld's voting record became more moderate. In the Eighty-ninth Congress, elected in 1964, he moved a bit to the left of Ford;[29] and in 1968, his last full year in Congress, he voted with the conservative coalition on only 61 percent of the roll calls on which there was an ideological division—only six points more conservative than John Anderson of Illinois, the most visible Republican moderate in the House.[30] By 1969 Rumsfeld was generally regarded as a moderate, though more because of his open-mindedness and flexible style than because of the positions he took on issues.

Nixon's selection of Rumsfeld to direct the Office of Economic Opportunity in April 1969 appeared a brilliant stroke: the appointment of a promising young Republican, neither conspicuously liberal nor aggressively conservative, to direct an agency that Nixon had attacked during the campaign as a symbol of all that was wrong with the Great Society, but now was not quite prepared to liquidate. At the same time, Rumsfeld realized, the job could be a political dead end. "I decided several times not to go to OEO," Rumsfeld later said, "but I finally agreed to make the switch. The decision was about 51 to 49, with the 51 coming down on the side of OEO. . . . I did have an interest in the work of OEO, and the difficulties the agency was encountering. I thought I might be able to make it into an agency dealing with the problems of human beings, rather than simply a theoretic operation, which is what it had been. . . . I discovered no magic wand, but I think we developed some procedures that helped the poor, or at least stopped doing things that hurt the poor. . . . Directing OEO was not a high-morale activity. It was far outside the mainstream in the Nixon administration. But I tried to operate in a sensible and humane way, following policies that the public, if you could drop a plumb line through the country measuring public opinion, would favor."[31]

During his two years at OEO, Rumsfeld for the most part won the respect of liberals without antagonizing conservatives. To bring him more closely into the inner circle, Nixon gave him the rank of counsellor to the president, with an office in the White House. (At one point, Haldeman decided to move the offices of Rumsfeld and his fellow counsellor, Robert Finch, to less exalted locations in the Executive Office Building. Finch moved; Rumsfeld insisted on staying in the White House and got his way.) When Nixon imposed wage and price controls in August 1971, Rumsfeld became director of the Cost of Living Council. In 1973, before the controls program had totally disintegrated, he was off to Brussels as ambassador to NATO.

Rumsfeld advanced steadily through the Nixon administration and appeared to enjoy Nixon's confidence, yet never became identified as a "Nixon man." Clearly ambitious, he was a highly effective administrator, an organization man who equated the welfare of the organization with his own advancement. His absorption in work was accompanied by an almost ascetic avoidance of sensual indulgence. Robert Goldwin, who served under Rumsfeld at both NATO and the White House, has remarked with astonishment: "Even when Rumsfeld goes to Paris, he lives off peanut butter sandwiches!"[32] In Benjamin Franklin–like fashion, he would jot down aphoristic observations from time to time. These reflected a turn of mind both skeptical and enterprising. For example: "When an idea is being pushed because it is 'exciting,' 'new,' or 'innovative'—beware. An exciting, new, innovative idea can also be foolish"; and, "Every day is filled with numerous opportunities for serious, if not fatal, error—enjoy it"; and, "Each [member of Congress] managed to get there, and there is a reason—discover it, and you will have learned something important about our country and its people."[33]

During the period they served together in the House, Rumsfeld had won the admiration, and even the affection, of Ford. Rumsfeld was not exactly a younger version of the president—Ford had never been so single-minded—but he personified qualities that Ford had been taught to admire: industry, drive, self-discipline. In the limited universe of former House colleagues from which Ford chose much of his administrative and political team (Marsh, Morton, Scranton, Bush, Howard Callaway, Bob Dole, and at least half a dozen others, as well as Rumsfeld), only Rumsfeld had direct White House experience. He was therefore a natural choice for the position of chief of staff, a job that he probably hesitated to accept only because he already hankered for command of one of the major line departments.

Spokes to the Wheel

Even after Rumsfeld took over as chief of staff, Ford's White House continued to be a much more open operation than Nixon's had been. In part this reflected Rumsfeld's intention. "A President needs multiple sources of information," Rumsfeld wrote in a note to himself.

"Work to assure adequate access. Avoid overly restricting the flow of paper, people, or ideas to the President, even as you strive to avoid wasting his time. If you over-control, it will be your 'regulator' that controls, not his."[34] He encouraged Goldwin, a political scientist from the University of Chicago whom he had brought with him to the White House, to set up a series of seminar meetings between Ford and respected scholars, of varying ideological persuasions, on subjects like crime control and the world food shortage. He also approved Alan Greenspan's practice of bringing panels of leading economists, including some who had served in Democratic administrations, to talk with the president.

The lack of structure, however, went well beyond what Rumsfeld would have preferred. Some of the "spokes to the wheel" accepted direction only from the president.

Robert Hartmann, for instance, who was now counsellor to the president (a title invented six years before by Nixon for Arthur Burns), continued to maintain a special relationship with Ford. Although Hartmann probably felt few real regrets over having been displaced as Ford's chief of staff in 1974, he had no intention of giving up his privileged place at the president's elbow. The speech he had composed for Ford's swearing-in ("Our long national nightmare is over") had struck just the right note. Other speeches written by Hartmann, and particularly by members of his staff, usually fell flat, in the opinions both of Ford's other advisers and of the press and the political community. This failure was caused in part by Ford's uninflected delivery (the product, one friend has suggested, of years of trying to make himself heard over the constant babble of the House), but also in part by the speechwriters' pedestrian prose.

Ford, however, trusted Hartmann. Their social and political outlooks were similar, and they shared the view that political discourse, including most presidential addresses, should aim at a fairly low denominator of public acceptance. (The nadir was perhaps reached in a speech Ford made to the Future Farmers of America in October 1974, in which he was caused to utter, among other homely observations: "Some have said that instead of asking Congress and the nation to bite the bullet, I offered only a marshmallow. Congress wouldn't even chew the marshmallow. But if they don't like the menu, I may be back with some tough turkey.")[35] Ford realized that Hartmann did not write speeches that rang with eloquence or conveyed even moderately complicated ideas, but felt that he could be depended on to keep the language simple and to avoid boring and possibly divisive discussions of political or economic principles.

In preparation for Ford's first State of the Union message in January 1975, Rumsfeld, assisted by Greenspan, Seidman, and Richard Cheney, produced a draft that attempted to confront the issues more sharply than the version turned out by Hartmann. Both drafts reached Ford on the night before the speech was to be given. When the two sides proved unable to reconcile their differences, the president had to weave the two versions together himself.[36] The incident represented a partial victory for Rumsfeld, in that it enabled him to gain a foothold in the speechwriting process. But it ended whatever chance there may have been for a reasonably harmonious relationship between Rumsfeld and Hartmann.[37]

Buchen and Seidman, Ford's old friends from Grand Rapids, usually agreed with Rumsfeld that the president's speeches should contain more substance. But they shared an interest with Hartmann in preserving a looser staff structure than Rumsfeld would have preferred. Buchen had become counsel to the president, and Seidman was named director of the new Economic Policy Board—a more broadly constituted successor to Nixon's triad. In general, their views were a bit more liberal than the prevailing outlook of the Ford White House.

The "kitchen cabinet," too, formed a channel of influence that was not controlled by Rumsfeld. Composed of a few old friends—Laird, Harlow, Scranton, John Byrnes, William Whyte, and one or two others—who met with the president about once a month, the kitchen cabinet offered candid advice on both political strategy and governmental policy. Except for Scranton, whose views tended to be relatively liberal on issues ranging from Vietnam to reform of the food stamp program, the members of the group were moderate conservatives, protective of the interests of corporate big business (which they identified with the interest of the United States), but not noticeably moved by ideological passions.

Rockefeller versus Rumsfeld

By far the most serious potential challenge to Rumsfeld's authority in the White House at the beginning of 1975 was the new vice-president and his staff. Ford had proposed that Rockefeller take responsibility for coordinating the administration's domestic policy, presumably through the Domestic Council, which had maintained a low profile since Ehrlichman's departure in 1973. "You've been studying these issues," the president told Rockefeller when asking him to become vice-president. "This is one area where you can be very helpful to me."[38] Rockefeller enthusiastically accepted the assignment, and began laying plans to reinvigorate the Domestic Council after he was confirmed.

"It was my intention," Rockefeller said in 1978, "to make the Domestic Council a parallel operation to the National Security Council, as a means of serving the president." The Domestic Council, he believed, should coordinate both long-range planning and day-to-day decisions. "The two," he said, "are closely related. When you come to the crossroads and look fifty miles down the road, a decision you make today may have effects five or ten years in the future."[39] While recognizing the need for the federal government to proceed with fiscal caution, Rockefeller also believed that the administration could not succeed, politically or governmentally, if it did not come to grips with pressing national social problems, like rising health care costs and spreading decay within the core areas of many cities. "It was Rockefeller's view," James Cannon, a former *Newsweek* editor who had joined the Rockefeller staff in 1969, has said, "that the administration should be prepared to take humanitarian risks. He believed that this might reduce the president's chances for getting the Republican nomination in 1976, but that, if he were nominated, it would increase his chances for winning the election."[40]

After Rockefeller was sworn in, Ford, over Rumsfeld's objection, made good his promise to give the vice-president control of the Domestic Council. The president had decided, however, to limit the council's role in policymaking. He used the council staff, Ford later said, to "staff out issues" and "make recommendations" on current problems, rather than to "organize policy around long-range planning."[41] Cannon was made director of the council, and several other Rockefeller people were added to the council staff. But Rockefeller soon concluded that the council was to be used mainly to "put out brushfires" that developed in domestic policy areas.[42]

This diminution of the council's function, Rockefeller felt, was largely due to Rumsfeld's influence. He could not be sure, he said in

1978, if there had been an ideological basis for the resistance he encountered from Rumsfeld. "It was hard to tell what his ideology was," Rockefeller said. "You couldn't read it on his sleeve." More likely, Rockefeller thought, the problem had grown out of personal antagonism. Rockefeller said he could not tell why, since he had never met Rumsfeld before he joined the Ford administration—in fact, had never heard of him.[43] (Actually, Rockefeller and Rumsfeld had met. In 1971 Nixon had sent Rumsfeld to a meeting on revenue sharing in Albany. Rockefeller repeatedly referred to Rumsfeld as "Ruckelshaus," apparently confusing him with William Ruckelshaus, Nixon's appointee as director of the Environmental Protection Agency. After Rockefeller had made this error for about the fifth time, Rumsfeld stepped forward and said: "Governor, my name is Donald Rumsfeld, and I think you should remember that." Rockefeller, evidently, did not remember.)

Rumsfeld's own view of the adversary relationship that developed between him and the vice-president was that it "need not have happened, should not have happened." But Rumsfeld was not sure how he could have avoided it. The truth was, he said in 1978, that Rockefeller had found that the president sometimes did not agree with him. Not wishing to recognize that he and Ford had somewhat different points of view, Rockefeller, like others in the administration who did not always get what they wanted, had, in Rumsfeld's view, taken out his anger on the president's chief of staff. He understood that, Rumsfeld said. "Part of my proper function," he believed, "was to serve as a lightning rod for the president."[44]

Rumsfeld's assessment no doubt contains at least part of the truth. But it leaves unanswered the question why Ford, between August 1974 and January 1975, moved from the moderate direction he had seemed to be pursuing during his first few weeks in office (exemplified by his offer of conditional amnesty to draft evaders and other early decisions as well as by his nomination of Rockefeller) back toward a more conservative approach. This shift probably resulted in part from his reaction to the alarming deterioration of the national economy during the fall of 1974; in part from the growing influence of conservative White House advisers, particularly Alan Greenspan; and in part from his own natural integrity, which made it difficult for Ford to depart far from the course he had generally followed for twenty-five years in the House. In addition, Rumsfeld's influence, exercised during the crucial hours when the president and his chief of staff were alone in the Oval Office, undoubtedly played some part, just as Rockefeller suspected. ("Have an understanding with the President," Rumsfeld wrote, "that you are free to tell him what you think, on any subject, 'with the bark off.'")[45] Rumsfeld did not usually publicize the views he imparted privately to the president. But on issues where his position became known, such as Rockefeller's proposals for a more extensive domestic social program and for a federal Energy Independence Authority to provide government-backed loans for private sector energy projects, Rumsfeld was almost always found on the side of the vice-president's conservative opponents within the administration.

Why did Rumsfeld, who usually had sided with the moderates in the Nixon administration, lean to a more conservative position under Ford? Partly, no doubt, because times had changed. In the depressed atmosphere created by Watergate, Vietnam, and the economic reverses of late 1974 and early 1975, Rumsfeld was drawn back toward the conservative position he had held when he first came to the House in 1963. Also, he had fair grounds for arguing that on some of the more visible issues, like the Energy Independence Authority, common sense was on the side of the conservatives. Quite apart from substantive considerations, however, Rumsfeld was probably inclined to cast his weight against any general approach that Rockefeller favored.

There is no reason to doubt the sincerity of Rumsfeld's avowal that he "respected and admired the way Rockefeller pitched in and helped the president."[46] He wrote, in another note to himself: "A vice president has a very difficult set of relationships. Do your darndest to make things work well for him. It will take everything you have, and you still may fail."[47] Nevertheless, Rumsfeld seems to have proceeded from the start on the assumption that Rockefeller represented a natural obstacle that he must overcome.

Rockefeller, Rumsfeld knew, was one of the great superstars of American politics—far better known nationally than Ford before Ford became vice-president, and on the basis of past experience alone perhaps the best qualified of all Americans to be president. The resources that Rockefeller brought with him could be of great value, but they also gave him the means to overshadow Ford, even against his own intent. If Rockefeller dominated, or even appeared to dominate, the administration, Ford would sink—and Rumsfeld would

sink with him. The widely held assumption that Kissinger was running foreign policy was damaging enough; if it were also assumed
that Rockefeller had taken over domestic policy, Ford would seem an
amiable cipher, as Truman had at first seemed in 1945. Rumsfeld, at
that point in his career, was Ford's man. He could not, even if he had
been so inclined, become Rockefeller's man. Nor was he equipped
by temperament or positioned by role to play the part of middleman
between Ford and Rockefeller, as Cannon tried to do, with limited
success, after becoming director of the Domestic Council. For Ford
to appear master in his own house, and for Ford's chief of staff to
maintain authority over that house, it was necessary, Rumsfeld seems
to have concluded, for Ford to move in a different direction from that
prescribed by Rockefeller. If a conservative with status roughly comparable to that of Rockefeller, like Barry Goldwater or Ronald Reagan
had become vice-president, Rumsfeld might have shifted to the left.
In fact, he did so in response to a lesser challenge from Secretary of
the Treasury Simon. But confronted with the threat, or perceived
threat, represented by Rockefeller, Rumsfeld instinctively leaned toward the conservatives. ("Following your instincts," Rumsfeld wrote,
"should not necessarily be avoided.")[48]

Management Problems

One effect of Ford's decision to restrict the role of the Domestic
Council was that the Office of Management and Budget continued
to operate as the chief coordinating agency for domestic policy within
the executive branch, a function it had begun to perform under Ash
and Malek during Nixon's second term. Ash and Malek had soon
returned to private life, but their places were taken by two equally
effective conservative technocrats: James Lynn, an Ohio lawyer and
Nixon's last secretary of HUD, became OMB director; and Paul
O'Neill, a career budget officer who had first joined the staff of the
old Bureau of the Budget in the Johnson administration, became
deputy director. Both were fiscally tightfisted, but pragmatic and
innovative in their approaches to administration and governmental
structure. O'Neill, who during his years at BOB and OMB had acquired enormously detailed understanding of the budget and the way
the government works, in particular quickly gained Ford's confidence.

A ranking member of Ford's White House staff has said: "Ford liked Jim Lynn's personality, and he enjoyed having him around to make peppery comments. But he relied at least as heavily for actual guidance on Paul O'Neill. He was constantly on the phone to O'Neill for advice and facts."

Lynn and O'Neill allied themselves with the Rumsfeld faction within the White House, as did Alan Greenspan, the new chairman of the Council of Economic Advisers (appointed by Nixon, but not actually installed until Ford had taken over). The three together, along with Rumsfeld's deputy, Richard Cheney, a young political scientist from Wyoming who had early hitched his wagon to Rumsfeld's career, formed a quadrumvirate of conservative advisers, not only well situated, but also equipped to invoke what George Shultz had called "the authority of knowledge."

By the early months of 1975, the most visible Nixon White House appointees—Haig, Ash, Malek, Timmons, Price, Buchanan—had left the government. Just beneath the top level, however, key positions were still held by veterans of the Nixon administration. Rumsfeld kept them on, though often at different jobs, largely because he could not easily find replacements who matched their qualities of government experience, administrative talent, and ideological reliability. As a result, Rumsfeld, and later Cheney, when he took Rumsfeld's place after Rumsfeld became secretary of defense in November 1975, had at their disposal what remained of the Nixon secretariat—still the most effective network of political operators and governmental technicians in the Republican party.

Despite the gradual evolution of the White House toward a more hierarchical structure, neither Rumsfeld nor Cheney ever exercised the kind of authority that had been held by Haldeman or Haig under Nixon. Hartmann, Marsh, Buchen, and to some extent Seidman continued their special relationships with the president. Henry Kissinger, besides being secretary of state, kept an office at the White House as director of the National Security Council until the major shakeup of November 1975, when he was required to give up responsibility for the NSC to his deputy, General Brent Scowcroft. Inevitably, Scowcroft continued to be regarded by many as Kissinger's man. William Baroody, Jr., a Laird protégé, who had worked closely in the House with Ford before going to the Pentagon with Laird in 1969, directed an office maintaining liaison with various private sector groups, like labor unions and ethnic organizations, which operated somewhat outside the direct chain of command. Press Secretary Nessen, while generally identified with Rumsfeld, kept lines out in several directions. Some of Rockefeller's people on the Domestic Council established an informal alliance with the Grand Rapids contingent, claiming the bond of being "substantive," as distinguished from "political," practitioners.[49]

Some of these individuals, groups, and subgroups carried on running battles for status and place, unusually bitter even by the standards of earlier White Houses. These undermined efficiency and eventually caused Ford embarrassment when some of the participants began carrying tales to the press. "Throughout my political career," Ford wrote, "nothing upset me more than bickering among members of my staff. It was time-consuming, distracting, and unnecessary. I had told my aides that I wouldn't tolerate it. But it continued, even accelerated . . . and—given the ambitions and personalities of the people involved—there didn't seem any way to put an immediate stop to it."[50]

Besides being troubled by internal feuds, the Ford White House, in the experience of many who dealt with it, had difficulty arriving at firm decisions and sticking to them. Attorney General Edward Levi, who took office in February 1975, has said that he developed a "rule of three"—a White House decision had to be affirmed three times before it could be regarded as final.[51]

Ford's problems as a manager, some who observed or participated in the Ford administration have suggested, stemmed in part from the fact that the president had spent most of his career in a legislative environment, where decisions are arrived at through consensus, and found it difficult to adapt his style to executive decisionmaking. "Training as an executive in either business or government," Nelson Rockefeller said, "is helpful background for the presidency. Life in Congress is entirely different. . . . As minority leader, President Ford had learned to bring together, with great patience, many different points of view without alienating any of them." In the presidency, Rockefeller suggested, a different kind of leadership is needed. "The president must be prepared to take positions, even if some people become alienated."[52]

Robert Hartmann, looking back in December 1977 on his years with Ford, was inclined to agree that the president's style had caused

problems in administering the executive branch. "Ford's style worked
superbly in his dealings with congressmen," Hartmann said. "In the
White House, it did not work as well. . . . Ford never came down
hard on the way he wanted the White House to operate. He did not
like a highly structured military kind of staff. He did not want chan-
nels. He delegated responsibility, but he did not delegate authority,
which caused a great deal of frustration among some of his staff.
. . . Ford did not want to have a true chief of staff—someone who
could cast his vote except under direct instructions from the president.
. . . When clashes developed, Ford used to complain about them. He
used to demand that they be straightened out. But he never really
did anything to straighten them out himself."[53]

Rockefeller and Hartmann were among the relative losers in the
struggle for power within the Ford White House. Rumsfeld, a relative
winner, has argued that Ford's style was well suited for the time in
which he was called to govern—or in fact for any time in a democratic
society: "When Ford entered office, executive authority had to a great
extent disintegrated within the government. The question was: How
do you change it? Under our system, the president cannot command.
The country responds like a wet noodle if the president tries to
command the United States. . . . Through his service in the House,
Ford had come to understand the things that make this country go.
It's true that his congressional experience led him to seek a synthesis
of opinion. But that is the proper way for the president to behave
under our system of government. . . . Ford understood that under
our system all the marbles are not given to the president. He sought
a product that was representative of the country. He had respect for
the genius of the system. . . . There is no particular difference between
executive leadership and legislative leadership. Both are aimed at
bringing matters to fruition. Getting a congressional staff to function
or a congressional committee to function requires leadership of people,
of much the same kind that is required to get the executive branch
to function. Ford's approach to leadership was more collegial than
that of most recent presidents. But that is the approach under which
our system works best."[54]

Even Ford and Rumsfeld have conceded that there was room for
improvement in the way the White House operated. They have
argued, however, that the problems were largely due to the abrupt
way in which the administration took office, and to the brief time

they had to build an administrative framework before the 1976 presidential campaign was upon them. "After all," Ford said in an interview in March 1978, "we only had thirty months. I never was able to get the West Wing [of the White House, containing offices of the chief presidential aides] fully reorganized in the way I would have liked. Issues sometimes were not adequately staffed out. We were not well enough set up for dealing with long-range problems." If he had been elected to a full term, Ford suggested, with time to carry out a reorganization that Cheney was planning, many of the administrative problems he had encountered would have been straightened out.[55]

A Strong Cabinet

Ford and Rumsfeld agreed in the fall of 1974 on the desirability of moving some of the authority that had been concentrated in the White House under Nixon back to the departments. "When I came into office," Ford has said, "I made a deliberate effort to make better use of cabinet people. Particularly after I got my own cabinet in place, I tried to give more authority to cabinet members, both in the planning and the execution of policy, than had been the case under the former administration."[56]

To some extent this dispersion of authority was carried out in response to the charge that Watergate had resulted in part from the overcentralization of executive power under Nixon and Haldeman. But Ford and Rumsfeld also believed there were positive advantages to decentralization, both within the executive branch and between levels of government. "We did not believe," Rumsfeld has said, "that it was necessary to draw all the threads through a single needle head. People in the departments and agencies must deal directly with Congress and the public. They are therefore less insulated from interaction with the people outside government than people in the White House. Also, people in the departments tend to be more experienced than those working in the White House. So the president decided to place greater reliance on the cabinet."[57]

By the end of March, Ford had in place a cabinet widely judged to be stronger than any of those that had served under Nixon. Kissinger, Simon, and Schlesinger—strong men all, whatever other qualities they might possess—remained at State, Treasury, and Defense. Edward Levi, former president of the University of Chicago and a distinguished legal scholar, had been appointed, at Rumsfeld's suggestion, to rebuild the morale and reputation of the Department of Justice. William Coleman, a highly successful Philadelphia lawyer, was secretary of transportation—the second black to serve in a cabinet, and the first under a Republican president. Carla Hills, a young California attorney who had worked her way up through the Justice Department under Nixon, had taken James Lynn's place at HUD— the first woman in the cabinet since Oveta Culp Hobby under Eisenhower. John Dunlop, a Harvard economist who had won the confidence of George Meany and other leaders of organized labor as chairman of Nixon's committee on wage stabilization in the construction industry, was secretary of labor. Rogers Morton was preparing to move to Commerce, to be replaced at Interior by former Governor Stanley Hathaway of Wyoming. Earl Butz, popular with the more conservative segments of the farm community and a close personal friend of the president, remained at Agriculture. Caspar Weinberger, although he had indicated his desire to leave, would be staying for a few months longer at HEW.

The administration had a fresh and vigorous look. Ideologically, the top posts were about equally divided between moderate and stalwart Republicans—with Secretary Simon thrust out to the right, and Vice-President Rockefeller to the left. It was an administration that appeared well equipped to unite the Republican party. Whether it would appeal much to the rest of the public—disenchanted by Watergate, frightened by rising unemployment and continuing inflation, and shocked by the apparently uncheckable Communist advance in Vietnam—remained to be seen.

15

Ford and the Ninety-fourth Congress: The Veto Strategy

THE CONGRESSIONAL ELECTIONS held in November 1974, three months after Nixon's resignation, produced, as expected, large Democratic gains. The Democrats won 46 additional seats in the House of Representatives, and, ultimately, added 4 in the Senate. (The contest for succession to the New Hampshire Senate seat from which Norris Cotton was retiring was not finally decided until September 15, 1975, when a rerun of a disputed election gave victory to the Democratic candidate, John Durkin.) When the Ninety-fourth Congress convened in January 1975, the Democrats had majorities of 23 in the Senate and 147 in the House—the largest Republican deficit in the latter since the Congress elected in 1936, during the heyday of the New Deal. In the House the Democrats, if all voted together, held one vote more than the two-thirds majority needed to pass bills over the president's veto. In the Senate the partisan advantage, though less overwhelming, was more than enough to dominate ordinary legislative business.

The Congress that confronted Ford in 1975, moreover, was determined to reclaim some of the authority that the legislative branch had been losing rather steadily to the executive since Franklin Roosevelt's first term. Nixon had given congressional leaders a decided scare at the beginning of 1973. By unilaterally refusing to spend funds appropriated for programs that he aimed to terminate or curtail (impoundment), by setting out to reorganize the executive branch along lines that Congress had refused to approve, and by excluding Con-

317

gress from participation in important military and foreign policy decisions, Nixon had seemed to give notice that he intended to govern on the basis of his 1972 electoral mandate, without much regard for congressional preferences or prerogatives.

Such presidential boldness, followed swiftly by the decay of Nixon's real political strength, had moved Congress to take the offensive. In 1973, after cutting off funds for the continuation of bombing raids against Communist forces in Indochina, Congress enacted the War Powers Resolution, directing the president to "consult" with the legislative branch "in every possible instance" before committing troops to military combat, and requiring congressional approval if such actions continued for longer than sixty days. The following year Congress passed legislation requiring the president to give notice of any further impoundments of appropriations, which could be over-ruled by majority vote by either house. Recognizing that its loss of power had resulted in part from failure to check its own spending proclivities, Congress set up a new budgetary procedure requiring that individual appropriations be fitted into an established limit on total expenditures. Finally, Congress, through its designated com-mittees, doggedly pursued the trail of Watergate, breaking through repeated attempts by Nixon to invoke executive privilege, until its great adversary was at last brought to ground in August 1974. At the beginning of 1975, congressional leaders, armed with new powers and expanded Democratic majorities, made clear their intention to deal firmly with the recently installed president, whose own political legitimacy still appeared exceptionally shaky.

Ford, however, held some cards of his own. First, he possessed the tactical advantages inherent in the presidency, such as high public visibility and capacity for quick and dramatic maneuver. Second, Ford understood the internal politics of Congress better than any postwar president except Lyndon Johnson—and maintained warmer personal relationships, on both sides of the aisle, than those enjoyed by John-son. Third, and perhaps most important, the memory of the 1972 presidential election, in which the voters had overwhelmingly sup-ported a relatively conservative administration against a forthrightly liberal challenge, lingered in the political atmosphere. Watergate ap-peared to have reversed the shift toward the Republicans. But might the underlying trend toward conservatism be continuing? The Dem-ocratic leaders of Congress could not be sure.

Ideological Groups

The ideological distribution of the Ninety-fourth Congress, besides registering the shift in party strengths, reflected some other trends at work within the national polity. In the three Congresses elected in 1968, 1970, and 1972, party strengths had remained fairly stable. But within the parties the relative strengths of ideological groups, measured by the adherence of members to the conservative coalition, had undergone significant alterations (see table 15-1). In the new

Table 15-1. *Distribution of Strength among Ideological Groups in Congress, 1969–76*

Group	Ninety-first Congress (1969–70)	Ninety-second Congress (1971–72)	Ninety-third Congress (1973–74)	Ninety-fourth Congress (1975–76)
Senate Republicans				
Fundamentalists	17	20[a]	16	16
Stalwarts	10	11	11	10
Moderates	7	6	7	3
Progressives	9	7	8	9
Total	43	44	42	38
Senate Democrats				
Traditionalists	12	10	8	10
Centrists	9	14	11	12
Regulars	19	13	21	25
Liberals	17	18	18	15
Total	57	55	58	62
House Republicans				
Fundamentalists	72	87	64	71
Stalwarts	48	57	75	48
Moderates	44	24	32	15
Progressives	25	15	16	11
Total	189	183	187	145
House Democrats				
Traditionalists	56	47	40	44
Centrists	49	73	75	80
Regulars	66	68	73	106
Liberals	72	64	58	59
Total	243	252	246	289

Sources: *Congressional Quarterly Almanac*, vol. 26 (1970), pp. 1147–49; vol. 28 (1972), pp. 68–70; vol. 30 (1974), pp. 994–96; vol. 32 (1976), pp. 1010–12.

a. Senator Karl Mundt of South Dakota was absent because of illness throughout the Ninety-second Congress and therefore is not included here.

Congress elected in 1974, most of the ideological trends observable during the previous six years continued or accelerated.

Broadly speaking, the two middle groups among the Democrats, the centrists and the regulars, increased their strength during the 1969–74 period; among the Republicans there was a gradual drift to the right, interrupted, perhaps by Watergate, in the Ninety-third Congress.

In both houses, Democratic traditionalists (mainly from the South) declined in number through this six-year period. In the Ninety-second Congress this decline among the traditionalists was more than matched by gains among the Democratic centrists. But in the Ninety-third Congress some Democratic centrists, perhaps motivated to maintain greater party unity through the climactic struggle with Nixon, moved from the centrist to the regular category, actually producing a net loss among centrists in the Senate. The strength of Democratic liberals remained uniform in the Senate throughout the six-year period, but suffered gradual erosion in the House, partly compensated by some increase among Democratic regulars.

Republican fundamentalists gained strength after the 1970 midterm election, when Nixon and Agnew had tried to draw a clear ideological line, but suffered losses in the Ninety-third Congress, perhaps owing to defections caused by Watergate. Republican stalwarts increased their numbers in both houses in the 1970 and 1972 elections. Republican progressives and moderates suffered only small losses in the Senate. But in the House both progressives and moderates lost more than one-third of their strength after the "law and order" election of 1970, the moderates recovering slightly in the Ninety-third Congress.

In the Ninety-fourth Congress, which took office in 1975, the partisan swing toward the Democrats produced no corresponding increase in strength among purist liberals. Indeed, the number of Democratic liberals in the Senate declined by three, owing to the more moderate voting records compiled by senators like Cranston of California, Stevenson of Illinois, and Williams of New Jersey. The great gain, particularly in the House, came among Democratic regulars, typified by the House majority leader, Thomas P. O'Neill of Massachusetts. Democratic traditionalists and centrists also made small gains, mainly because of a post-Watergate Democratic resurgence in southern states like Florida, North Carolina, and Tennessee.

On the Republican side the loss of party strength generally continued the erosion of representation among progressives and moderates, particularly in the House. From the Ninety-first to the Ninety-fourth Congress, Republican progressives lost more than half, and Republican moderates almost two-thirds, of their strength in the House. The combined representation of progressives and moderates, which had been 37 percent of the Republican total in the Ninety-first Congress, had fallen to 18 percent in the Ninety-fourth. Republican fundamentalists, by contrast, actually achieved some absolute gain in numbers in the Ninety-fourth Congress, and rose to 49 percent of the Republican total, as against 38 percent in the Congress elected in 1968.

In both houses the base of the conservative coalition, composed of Republican fundamentalists and stalwarts and Democratic traditionalists, was weaker than it had been in 1969—declining from 38 to 35 in the Senate, and from 176 to 163 in the House. The base of the somewhat less cohesive liberal coalition, composed of Democratic liberals and regulars and Republican progressives, on the other hand, rose from 46 to 49 in the Senate, and from 163 to 176 in the House. The liberal coalition therefore needed the support of only two Democratic centrists or Republican moderates in the Senate to command a majority, but still required more than 40 votes from centrists or moderates to assure passage of bills in the House. For the purpose of sustaining vetoes, the conservative coalition unaided could produce just 1 vote more than the 34 votes needed to avoid override if all members voted in the Senate; in the House it had a more comfortable margin of 17 above the necessary one-third plus 1.

Of the traditionalist southern Democrats who had dominated most of the major congressional committees in 1969, only a few were gone— notably Richard Russell of Georgia from Senate Appropriations, and William Colmer of Mississippi from House Rules. Among the more doughty who remained were Eastland of Mississippi at Senate Judiciary (also the successor to Russell as president pro tem of the Senate), McClellan of Arkansas at Senate Appropriations, Stennis of Mississippi at Senate Armed Services, and Mahon of Texas at House Appropriations. Some of these were less vigorous than they once had been, but they were still able to place their imprint on legislation or hold up bills of which they disapproved. As before, they were often joined by Long of Louisiana, a centrist, at Senate Finance. Mills of Arkansas, after a bout with alcoholism and a highly publicized spree with an exotic nightclub dancer, had yielded House Ways and Means to Al Ullman of Oregon. Also a centrist, Ullman was almost as conservative as Mills on fiscal issues, but was considerably less dominant within the committee.

Liberal Democrats, however, had increased their leverage within the power structures of both houses. They still held comparatively few chairmanships: two of the seventeen in the Senate, and three of twenty-two in the House. But three of these chairmanships were key posts, held by well-respected members: Muskie of Maine at Senate Budget, Rodino of New Jersey at House Judiciary, and Reuss of Wisconsin at House Banking, Currency, and Housing. Moreover, the Democratic regulars who chaired many of the important committees, like Madden of Indiana at House Rules and Jackson of Washington at Senate Interior and Insular Affairs, and regulars within the Democratic leadership, like House Majority Leader O'Neill and Senate Majority Leader Mansfield, were generally eager to cooperate with the liberals. At the beginning of 1975, Congressman Phillip Burton of California, a liberal and former chairman of the Democratic Study Group, was elected chairman of the House Democratic Caucus. On the whole, the Democratic leadership that confronted Ford in 1975 was considerably more aggressive, and more oriented toward programmatic goals, than that which Nixon had faced in 1969.

The administration also felt concern over the evident restlessness and independence of recently elected Democratic members, many of whom had won office because of public reactions against Watergate or the Vietnam War. These were not inclined to defer to the established Democratic leadership, either within committees or on the floor. On the other hand, many of the freshman and sophomore Democrats came from fairly conservative districts, recently represented by Republicans, and in general were not anxious to be identified as extreme liberals. (For more detail on the regional and social compositions of the ideological groups in the Ninety-fourth Congress, see appendix B.)

The Veto Strategy

"When I was in Congress myself," Ford has written, "I thought it fulfilled its constitutional obligations in a very responsible way, but after I became President my perspective changed. It seemed to me that Congress was beginning to disintegrate as an organized body."[1] Ford's response to what he regarded as Congress's growing irresponsibility was to dig in his heels and defend his conception of the national interest, as opposed to the narrow aims of the "single-issue special interest groups" that he believed were coming to dominate the legislative branch.

The administration had positive legislative objectives in areas like defense, energy, deregulation of the economy, and tax policy, for which it sought majority support in Congress. But Ford's main legislative effort was devoted to achieving what he viewed as the highest governmental priority of the age: restraint of the growth of federal spending. "The basic philosophy of my administration," Ford has said, "was embodied in the economic plan that I recommended to Congress in January 1975, calling for tax reductions and a 50 percent cut in the rate of growth in federal spending."[2] To secure these objectives, while spending more for defense, which he also believed was necessary, Ford called for more drastic cuts in the growth of domestic social programs than had ever been attempted by Nixon, even during the budgetary offensive of 1973. In the battle that followed, Ford's chief legislative weapon was the presidential veto, which gave him formidable power so long as he held the support of one-third plus one in either the House or the Senate.

Max Friedersdorf, a soft-spoken Indiana Hoosier, who had been a member of Nixon's congressional liaison staff, and who stayed on under Ford to direct day-to-day congressional relations, has recalled: "The Ford administration really had two legislative strategies: one, a strategy for legislation that we hoped to pass, mainly dealing with energy; and second, to deal with legislation that the administration found objectionable, which included most of the other legislation that Congress was moving at that time. On a number of occasions, President Ford was forced to veto bills that the administration opposed. Then the legislative team would have to go to work at sustaining those vetoes. I would say that we were quite successful."[3]

Ford delivered more vetoes, relative to time in office, than all but three other presidents in American history. (In total vetoes, he ranks eighth.) As seen in table 15-2, Ford's 66 vetoes average to 26.4 vetoes a year—behind Grover Cleveland, the all-time champion, with an average of 73 a year; Franklin Roosevelt, with 53; and Harry Truman,

Table 15-2. *Presidential Vetoes, 1932–76*

President	Total vetoes	Average vetoes a year	Overrides
Franklin Roosevelt	635	53.0	9
Harry Truman	250	31.3	12
Dwight Eisenhower	181	22.6	2
John Kennedy	21	7.0	0
Lyndon Johnson	30	6.0	0
Richard Nixon	43	8.0	7
Gerald Ford	66	26.4	12

Source: *Presidential Vetoes, 1789–1976*, compiled by the Senate Library (Government Printing Office, 1978), p. ix.

with 31.3; and a bit ahead of Dwight Eisenhower, with 22.6. Ford's average was far above that of Kennedy, Johnson, or Nixon.

Probably more important than the quantity of vetoes is the significance of the measures rejected. Most presidents have vetoed at least a few bills.[4] But the overwhelming majority of vetoes, including most of those delivered by Cleveland, F. D. Roosevelt, Truman, and Eisenhower, were used against private bills, usually passed by Congress at the request of individual members to provide special immigration privileges, pensions, or monetary settlements to constituents pressing claims against the federal government. Even among vetoed bills with some public policy content, many have dealt with minor federal government matters, like designation of national historic monuments, or with local government concerns of the District of Columbia.

Only a few presidents have used the veto to combat Congress on major national issues. Important examples are Andrew Jackson's veto of the renewal of the charter of the second Bank of the United States and of items in the program for public improvements pushed through Congress by Henry Clay; Andrew Johnson's vetoes of parts of the civil rights and reconstruction programs enacted by the Republican Congress after the Civil War (mostly overridden); Herbert Hoover's vetoes of economic measures passed by the Democratic Congress to fight the depression; Truman's vetoes of the Taft-Hartley Labor-Management Relations Act in 1947 (overridden) and the bill to give control over tidelands oil to the states in 1952; and Eisenhower's vetoes of items in the liberal program enacted by Congress after the Democratic landslide of 1958. Even in these cases, presidents have generally used the veto weapon selectively, rejecting only measures on which they thought the opposition was most vulnerable. Eisenhower, for instance, during eight years in office vetoed only about thirty bills involving nationally important substantive issues, seventeen of them after 1958.[5]

Nixon, though confronted throughout his tenure by opposition Congresses, did not sharply increase the rate of vetoes above those maintained by Kennedy and Johnson, and stayed well below Eisenhower's average. But Nixon made more use of the veto on broad public issues than most of his predecessors. Of Nixon's forty-three vetoes, only three were of private bills. Beginning with his veto of the Labor-HEW appropriations bill in 1970, Nixon rejected thirty appropriations bills or budget authorizations—more than two-thirds of his total. Most of his other vetoes were delivered against bills dealing with significant public matters, like the War Powers Resolution and a bill to require Senate confirmation of the director and deputy director of OMB. In only five instances—four spending measures and the War Powers Resolution—was Congress able to muster the two-thirds majorities in both houses needed to overcome Nixon's vetoes of public bills.[6]

Ford, who had played a key role as House minority leader in sustaining most of Nixon's vetoes, made even greater use of the veto as an instrument of policy. Of Ford's sixty-six vetoes, only five were of private bills. All the rest involved national policy issues, except a bill, passed soon after he became president, to rename the federal courthouse in Grand Rapids the Gerald R. Ford Federal Office Building, and a bill to exempt congressmen from paying state and local income taxes in the Washington suburbs. No fewer than thirty-nine of Ford's vetoes were against bills that would have significantly and directly affected the federal budget. Most of the others dealt with foreign policy, energy, or general economic policy. During his brief tenure Ford undoubtedly vetoed more bills raising important substantive issues than any previous president.[7]

Coalition Building

The veto barrage began only three days after Ford became president, with his rejection on August 11, 1974, of a relatively minor bill to increase the pay of U.S. marshalls. Congress made no effort to override the veto. On October 15, however, the House easily overrode, by a vote of 360 to 12, Ford's veto of a bill to use general revenues to make up a projected $7 billion deficit in the railroad retirement fund. The next day the Senate followed suit, by a vote of 72 to 1. By the end of the year, Ford had delivered vetoes against eighteen public bills, four of which had been overridden.[8]

"It was often a very difficult task to assemble the strength needed to sustain a veto," Max Friedersdorf recalled. "But more often than not, the administration team was able to do it. In the House there were 140 to 145 Republicans, but the administration usually would lose from 20 to 40 of these, so it was necessary to pick up from 20 to 30 Democrats to sustain a veto. In the Senate the problem was the same. There were about 38 Republican senators, but normally we could count on only about 30 of those. So the battle was to hold the Republican base, and then pick up enough Democrats to win."[9]

In the early part of Ford's administration, holding the support of moderate and progressive Republicans was as difficult as it had been under Nixon. "Appealing to party loyalty was not a very effective argument," according to Friedersdorf. "On one occasion, I literally got down on my knees in the Republican cloakroom to Senator Mathias [of Maryland], asking him for his vote on an issue that would have helped the administration and would not have hurt Mathias. But he would not give it. . . . The tendency of the moderates to oppose the administration was partly just to show independence from the White House—to prove they were not rubber stamps. The individual issues sometimes didn't matter so much as their wish to be able to go home and say they had shown themselves to be independent. Some congressmen also used key votes as a way of paying back slights, real or imagined, they had received from the administration. . . . It was my approach, and President Ford's approach, never to ask a congressman or a senator to vote for the administration if it would hurt him in his own campaign, except on a very small number of very high priority issues. Ford's philosophy was not to ask a man to do something that might damage his chances of coming back. Don't hurt yourself, was his constant advice, both as minority leader and as president. . . . I would try to show the moderates, on each issue, how they could vote with the administration without hurting themselves."[10]

In seeking support from the Democrats, the administration usually turned first to the southern traditionalists. "Waggonner, Mahon, and 'Tiger' Teague [Congressman Olin Teague of Texas] were the key figures [in the House]," Friedersdorf explained. "Waggonner was the best head counter in the House. Through Waggonner, I sometimes had access to the Democratic whip check, which was very helpful in planning strategy. Depending on the issue, from twenty to sixty southern Democrats would follow Waggonner. A philosophic issue generally would carry the group. But on an issue involving pure pork, the southern members would vote on the basis of the goodies being offered for their own districts. Despite the general conservatism of southerners, I found there is nobody more anxious to look out for their own districts when it comes to appropriations. . . . The new breed of Democrats from the South—senators like Nunn [of Georgia], Johnston [of Louisiana], and Morgan [of North Carolina]—had pretty much the same political backgrounds and attitudes as the older conservatives, but they could not be counted on as much to vote for conservative positions. In the House the old boll weevil group was gradually passing away. . . . At times, I worked as closely with the southern Democrats as I did with my own people. There was resentment among some Republicans about the amount of attention the administration devoted to southern Democrats. Many Republicans resented the amount of time and attention given to senators like Sparkman, Stennis, and Eastland. The Republicans felt they were being taken for granted, and there was some justice to that view. But I had limited resources, and had to put my time and resources where I thought they would do the most good. John Rhodes [the House minority leader] was very understanding about the problem, but there was resentment among the rank and file."[11]

Unlike Nixon, Ford made a definite effort to keep lines open to liberal Democrats. "I began seeing people in the White House I had not seen there before," Friedersdorf recalled. "Frank Church [senator from Idaho, a regular Democrat], for instance, began appearing in the White House. Ford had a close relationship with Hubert Humphrey. Humphrey came to the White House frequently, and Ford would call him on the phone frequently. Humphrey would communicate to Ford the liberal viewpoint on a given issue. Ford also had a good relationship with Phil Burton. . . . Ford got along better with the Democrats in Congress than Carter so far has done [in 1977]. This was partly because the Democrats did not expect too many favors from a Republican administration and were always pleased with what they got. But from Carter, the Democrats expect a lot, and because there are so many more Democrats than there are Republicans, there just isn't enough to go around."[12]

Showdown Votes

The first important test of the administration's ability to sustain vetoes in the Ninety-fourth Congress came on June 4, 1975, on a $5.3 billion appropriation bill intended to create more than one million new jobs. With unemployment approaching 9 percent, the House had passed the bill on May 14 by a vote of 293 to 109 (25 more than the majority needed to override) and the Senate had given its approval on May 16 by voice vote. Through intensive lobbying, the administration was able to reduce the majority in the House voting to override to 277 to 145—5 votes short of the needed two-thirds. The distribution by ideological groups of the vote to override was as follows:[13]

Republicans			*Democrats*		
	Yes	No		Yes	No
Fundamentalists	0	69	Traditionalists	26	17
Stalwarts	8	39	Centrists	71	4
Moderates	5	10	Regulars	103	1
Progressives	6	5	Liberals	58	0
Total	19	123	Total	258	22

Under heavy pressure from the White House and both party leaderships, House members came close to dividing along party lines. The labor unions and other liberal interest groups were able to shake loose only five Republican moderates and six progressives, as well as eight stalwarts, mainly from areas suffering from very high unemployment. On the other hand, about three-fifths of the Democratic traditionalists and almost all the centrists voted on the liberal side.

Who were the members who gave the administration the extra votes it needed to overcome the deficit it faced when the bill passed on May 14? Members who either changed sides or were absent on one vote but recorded on the other distributed their votes as follows:

	Voting yes on June 4	*Voting no on June 4*	*Absent on June 4*
Voting yes on May 14	. . .	32	7
Voting no on May 14	2	. . .	1
Absent on May 14	21	7	. . .

As these figures show, supporters of the emergency jobs bill were highly successful at rounding up members who were not recorded on May 14 to vote in favor of the override in the showdown with the administration on June 4. All twenty-one members absent on May 14 but voting to override on June 4 were Democrats, including eight southerners who had skipped the original vote. Among the added yes votes was that of Speaker Carl Albert, who took the unusual step of descending from the rostrum to cast his vote with the majority. Two Democrats, both centrists who had voted against the bill on original passage, were persuaded to switch over to vote for the override.

Still, it was not enough. The administration and the Republican leadership, besides bringing in seven members who had been absent on May 14 to vote against overriding the veto, were able to convert thirty-two members who had voted yes on the original bill to vote against the override. The group of converts consisted of five Republican fundamentalists, fourteen stalwarts, five moderates, and four progressives, plus three Democratic traditionalists and one centrist. In addition, there were seven members who voted for the bill on May 14, but were unrecorded on June 4: one Republican stalwart, one moderate, one Democratic traditionalist, three centrists, and one regular. It seems reasonable to suppose that not all those absences were unavoidable.

Three months later, on September 9, the opposition at last managed to override a veto in the House. On July 25 Ford had vetoed the education appropriation bill for fiscal 1976, which Congress had increased $1.5 billion above the amount requested in the president's budget. Confronting not only the Democratic leadership but also the highly efficient education lobby, representing schoolteacher and school board associations with memberships in every congressional district, the administration's tactical defenses collapsed. The House overrode the veto by a vote of 379 to 41. Voting to sustain were only twenty-seven Republican fundamentalists and nine stalwarts (including Minority Leader Rhodes), plus five Democrats (three traditionalists, one centrist, and one regular). The next day the Senate completed the override by a vote of 88 to 12. Voting to sustain were ten fundamentalists, one stalwart (Griffin of Michigan), and one Democratic regular (Proxmire of Wisconsin, who treasured a reputation for fiscal frugality).[14]

Ford finished the year with a record of twenty-one vetoes (of public bills), of which four, containing appropriations for popular education, health care, and school lunch programs, were overridden. "On 'motherhood issues,' like education and child nutrition," Friedersdorf has said, "it was hard to make the point that, while these were good programs, and spending more on any one of them might not seem too damaging, collectively the [increased] expenditures that were being passed were very inflationary."[15]

Effects of the Presidential Campaign

In the second session of the Ninety-fourth Congress, the approaching presidential election increased pressure for party unity on both sides of the aisle. "Picking up Democrats became more difficult in 1976," Friedersdorf recalled. "Often the Democratic leadership aimed to override the president just to make him look bad, and they would argue this with other Democratic members. On the other hand, it was easier to maintain the Republican base in support of the administration. Once the run for the presidency began, the moderates and progressives were more inclined to support the president. The Reagan challenge before the convention helped maintain Republican solidarity in Congress. Even the congressmen who were backing Reagan felt they could not desert the president on the kind of issues that were being voted on. And the moderate and progressive Republicans were more prepared to support Ford to strengthen his hand against Reagan. John Anderson and Senator Javits and Senator Percy, for instance, lined up with the president, and became much more open to administration influence. Also, the Republicans began to sense that the vetoes were becoming popular with the voters, and this helped keep them in line."[16]

None of Ford's vetoes in 1976, of which there had been eleven by the end of July, was overridden until July 22. On that day the House, following action by the Senate the day before, overturned the president's veto of a bill authorizing $3.95 billion for public works employment and antirecession aid to financially strapped state and local governments. Ford's veto of an even more expensive bill for public works and antirecession aid in February had been overridden in the House, but sustained by the Senate by a vote of 63 to 35—3 votes short of two-thirds. But on July 21 the Senate voted to override the second public works veto by a vote of 73 to 24—8 more than the needed margin. Seven Democrats and four Republicans who had voted to sustain the president's veto in February voted to override in July; three Republicans and no Democrats switched the other way. (The remaining difference between the two votes was caused by the effect of absentees.)[17]

Several factors may have influenced senators who changed their positions between the first and second public works vetoes: pressures coming from the presidential campaign; concern over the recession, which had gone on for five more months, though moderating somewhat by July; the Democratic leadership's decision to reduce the extent of the combined public works and antirecession program from $6.1 billion to $3.95 billion (though Ford insisted, "Bad policy is bad whether the inflation price tag is $4 billion or $6 billion"). Another factor, unrelated to the bill itself, may also have altered the outcome: Ford's decision to close or reduce work forces at obsolete military bases in the United States, to produce a projected annual saving of $150 million.

Three days before vetoing the second public works bill, Ford had vetoed the fiscal 1977 military construction authorization, passed by Congress in June with an amendment requiring one year's notice before any closing or significant work force reduction at a military base anywhere in the United States. Ford's veto of the military construction bill was sustained in the Senate on July 22 by a vote of 51 to 42. But ten of the eleven senators who switched from supporting the president's veto of the first public works bill to voting to override the second—including four Democratic traditionalists (Eastland, Stennis, Allen, and Johnston) and one centrist (Long)—were also among those who voted to override the veto of the military construction authorization.[18]

"The administration's decision to cut back on military bases made my work much more difficult," Friedersdorf recalled. "I argued strongly against closing some of the bases, at least until after the election. But President Ford stood absolutely firm. Don Rumsfeld [by then secretary of defense] had recommended a list of closings, and the president took the position that it was the right thing to do, and he would not budge. I discussed the matter very thoroughly with Jack Marsh, and told him the administration was losing a number of votes in the Senate that we would not lose if only the president would modify his position on the base closings. We were able to get a number of groups [opposing the closings] in to see the president, but he was absolutely adamant on the issue itself. I argued that the president should at least delay the closings until Congress adjourned, but with no success. The president took the position that the bases had been obsolete for a long time, and now was the time to save the government some money. If Ford had still been the minority leader, I feel sure he would have been arguing the other way, urging the president to delay the closings. But as president, he felt that he had to stand for the national interest."[19]

Despite resentment stirred by the base closings, and the increased pressure for Democratic party unity, Ford completed the year with a record of twenty vetoes of public bills and four overrides. The significant overrides, besides that on the second public works bill, were on a bill establishing stricter leasing provisions for coal lands owned by the federal government, and on the Labor-HEW appropriations bill, which exceeded the administration's budget request by $4 billion.

During Ford's entire tenure, twelve of his sixty-six vetoes were overridden and fifty-four were sustained. Twenty-six of the vetoes were of appropriations bills or budget authorizations, most of which were sustained. Ford succeeded reasonably well in achieving his stated aim of using the veto "to force Congress to recognize fiscal restraint and to keep the economy on track."[20]

"Ford Was Trusted"

Despite frequent and fundamental differences with Congress over substantive issues, Ford maintained reasonably friendly relations with the legislative branch. "Ford never allowed an atmosphere of confrontation to develop," John Marsh, who exercised overall responsibility for congressional relations, has said. "He always kept his lines of communication open."[21]

Looking back in the fall of 1977 or the winter of 1978, congressmen of all ideological persuasions agreed almost unanimously that relations between the White House and Congress had been much better under Ford than under Nixon. According to John Anderson: "Nixon was never accepted by Congress. His approach was arrogant and heavy footed. With Ford, it was entirely different. Ford was well liked, and had high credibility in both houses of Congress, and in both parties." Congressman Richardson Preyer of North Carolina, a Democratic centrist, recalled: "Democratic congressmen, at least, felt a physical dislike toward Nixon. Ford, in contrast, was trusted, even among those who strongly disagreed with him." Congressman Abner Mikva of Illinois, a Democratic liberal and chairman of the Democratic Study Group while Ford was president, said: "President Ford and the Ford administration had a very supportive relationship with Congress. He did not want the right things—in fact, he did not want very much at all. But there was a warm feeling in Congress toward Ford. [Majority Leader] Tip O'Neill gave a speech to Democratic congressmen beating the pants off Ford, and it did not sit well. That was not the way most Democratic congressmen felt toward Ford." Congressman Barber Conable of upstate New York, a Republican stalwart, recalled that, though he was a member of the House Republican leadership, he had never been invited into the Oval Office while Nixon was president. He went there regularly under Ford. "President Ford brought Congress deeply into his confidence," Conable said. "He worked closely with Congress. The White House staff was very responsive to the needs of Congress." Congressman Joseph McDade of Pennsylvania, a Republican moderate, remembered: "We had a president who welcomed congressmen to the White House. The hard-knuckled business was gone."[22]

Ford did not, of course, lack critics in Congress. Most of these, however, based their disapproval on differences over ideology or policy, rather than on complaints against the administration's approach to Congress. In the view of Senator Birch Bayh of Indiana, a Democratic liberal: "Ford's positions on the issues went beyond conservatism almost to the point of irresponsibility. But at least he never succumbed to the imperial presidency." Congressman Frank Thompson of New Jersey, a Democratic liberal who became chairman of the House Administration Committee during Ford's presidency, said: "There was more personal acceptance of Ford, because people in Congress were very fond of Jerry Ford. But in the end, it came down to the same thing—Ford was at least as conservative as Nixon, if not more conservative." Senator Charles Mathias of Maryland, a Republican progressive, said that he had enjoyed a good personal relationship with Ford, but complained: "He let the right wing of the Republican party buffalo him too much." Congressman Louis Stokes of Cleveland, a Democratic liberal, said: "The Ford administration was much more open with Congress than Nixon had been. I found myself being invited to White House social functions, which had not been my experience with Nixon. At bottom, though, there was not much difference in their social philosophies. Both administrations were totally unresponsive to the problems expressed to them by the Black Caucus. Both were insensitive to the needs, problems, and concerns of the cities. The only difference was that in Nixon's case, this was the result of personal insensitivity, as well as of conservative philosophy."[23]

At the opposite end of the ideological spectrum, Congressman Philip Crane of Illinois (representing Rumsfeld's old district), a Republican fundamentalist who supported Reagan for the Republican presidential nomination in 1976 (and ran for president himself in the early primaries in 1980), said that Ford had been "more accessible" than Nixon, and conceded that the Ford administration had "followed a course slightly to the right of center," but complained that Ford's policies "were not grounded in a set, of philosophic convictions." Crane said that he was "more troubled by people like Ford than by actual liberals, because at least you know where liberals are coming from, but with people who are not grounded in philosophic principles, you cannot be sure in a crisis which way they will go." Congressman Jack Kemp of upstate New York, a Republican fundamentalist and coauthor of the controversial Kemp-Roth bill (proposing a 30 percent tax cut over a three-year period without an equal cut in federal spending), said that he had liked Ford personally, but regretted that "Ford failed to heed the free-enterprise doctrine preached by Adam Smith. When he insisted on a dollar-for-dollar cut in spending to match cuts in taxes, he repeated the same error made by Hoover in 1931 when he failed to lower tax rates."[24]

Members of Congress, both friends and foes, who had found Nixon hard to categorize, seem to have felt more comfortable with a type they regarded as familiar: a traditional Republican, allied with business and representing conservative values. In Congressman Preyer's view: "Ford was less adventurous than Nixon. I doubt that he would have proposed Nixon's welfare reform plan. Ford was a conventional Republican president, sticking to the traditional principles of his party."

Senator Bob Dole of Kansas, who was Republican national chairman during part of the Nixon administration, and ran with Ford for vice-president in 1976, recalled: "Nixon believed he could build a new national majority, including Democrats and independents as well as Republicans, based on the so-called sunbelt strategy [Kevin Phillips' theory that a majority party could be formed around conservative populists in the South and West]. Ford's objective was more simple. He aimed to be a good Republican President, moving within the traditional Republican philosophy."[25]

Ford's approach to Congress fitted logically with his underlying social attitudes and beliefs. Much though he disapproved of many of the policies commanding majority support in Congress, Ford seems never to have considered, as Nixon did, the option of trying to govern almost without reference to the legislative branch. In part, this self-restraint may have reflected an acceptance of post-Watergate political realities. Primarily, however, Ford's approach was the result of a deep commitment to the federal system of shared powers and checks and balances ordained by the Constitution. His social philosophy had developed more from an attachment to institutions than from a dedication to political theories or programmatic goals. So long as the federal system functioned in the way he believed the founders had intended, he felt confident that basic social values would be secure. "I know well the coequal role of the Congress in our constitutional process," he told Congress the week after he became president. "As President, within the limits of basic principles, my motto toward Congress is communication, conciliation, compromise, and cooperation."[26]

While respecting the role of Congress in the federal system, Ford was also determined to maintain the proper authority of the president. "When Ford came into the presidency," Marsh has recalled, "the executive power was very much under attack. If Ford had given in to Congress, the executive branch might simply have been overwhelmed within the federal system."[27]

Perhaps long-range social and political trends common to all the industrial democracies would have prevented much enduring reduction in executive authority. Perhaps, over the long run, the legislative will still turn out to be the more imperiled branch. But for the immediate post-Watergate period, at least, Ford maintained the effectiveness of the presidency by establishing and forcefully upholding an independent point of view for the executive branch. By promoting the policies growing out of this point of view in a spirit of amity and civility, rather than through attempted intimidation or aggression, Ford advanced the healing, not only of the executive, but of the entire governmental system.

16

Foreign Policy: Conservative Internationalism

ALTHOUGH he had served for fourteen years on the Defense Subcommittee of the House Appropriations Committee, and had often traveled abroad on official inquiries and goodwill missions, Ford entered the presidency without a sure grasp of either the substance or the procedures of foreign policy. Among his first acts when he knew that his succession was inevitable was to ask Kissinger to stay on. ("Sir," the secretary of state reportedly replied, "it is my job to get along with you and not yours to get along with me.")[1] To the end of his term, Ford relied heavily on Kissinger's counsel. As time went on, however, other voices began to exert strong influence—particularly those of Rumsfeld and Scowcroft. And the president himself gained increasing confidence in his ability to deal with the intricacies of international problems and relationships.

It happened that the three most important European allies of the United States were at that time led by tough-minded political pragmatists: Helmut Schmidt of the Federal Republic of Germany, Valéry Giscard d'Estaing of France, and James Callaghan of Britain. All had been called upon to tidy up after more visionary predecessors. They got on well with Ford, and he with them—man to man, as the president liked to say. "When I became president," Ford has recalled, "I found that our friends were apprehensive about the reliability of the United States as a partner. I set out to reassure them, through both bilateral and multilateral meetings."[2] Leonid Brezhnev was essentially the same type of leader—shrewd, stubborn, realistic—governing through stamina and managerial skill rather than charisma or

337

prophetic insight. All—even the elegant Giscard, a career politician—were men who would have been at home among the likes of Melvin Laird or T. P. O'Neill. They were, therefore, leaders to whom Ford felt he could relate.

Ford never conceptualized his foreign policy goals or strategies in the systematic way that Nixon had attempted. "He lacked a clear sense of architecture," according to one of his chief foreign policy advisers. Nevertheless, he proceeded on the basis of tenaciously held values and beliefs, adapting these as best he could to changing domestic and international conditions.

Defeat in Vietnam

The Ford administration had been in office for only a few months when the Communists launched a major new offensive in Vietnam. In January 1975 the North Vietnamese for the first time won secure control of a province in the South. On January 28 Ford asked Congress for $522 million in emergency military aid for South Vietnam and Cambodia. The majority in Congress, however, feared that such assistance might draw the United States back into direct combat involvement in Southeast Asia. On March 12 the House Democratic caucus voted 189 to 48 against further aid for either South Vietnam or Cambodia.

By the end of March, the Communists had gained control of fourteen provinces in South Vietnam and were encountering little organized resistance as their armies swept south. In Cambodia the end appeared near. Kissinger urged Ford to charge that "Congress was solely to blame for the debacle in Southeast Asia."[3] Instead, the president on April 10 went before Congress with a new request for $722 million in emergency military aid for South Vietnam, and a proposal that Congress "clarify immediately its restrictions on the use of U.S. military forces in Southeast Asia for the limited purposes of protecting American lives, by ensuring their evacuation, if this should be necessary." Responding to growing disenchantment with the containment doctrine that had guided American foreign policy for more than a quarter-century, Ford acknowledged: "It has been said that the United States is overextended, that we have too many commitments far from home, that we must reexamine what our truly vital interests are and shape our strategy to conform to them. I find no fault with this as a theory, but in the real world such a course must be pursued carefully. We cannot, in the meantime, abandon our friends while our adversaries support and encourage theirs."[4]

Ford's request for increased military aid for South Vietnam was overtaken by events. On April 16 Phnom Penh surrendered to the Communists, and resistance ended in Cambodia. Five days later Nguyen Van Thieu resigned as president of South Vietnam. The American government, Thieu charged, had failed to honor pledges made by Nixon that "if North Vietnam renewed its aggression, the United States would actively and strongly intervene." On the night of April 23, Ford, in a speech at Tulane University in New Orleans, conceded that the war in Vietnam "is finished as far as America is concerned." The next day the House passed by a vote of 230 to 187 a bill authorizing the use of American troops for evacuation purposes and providing $150 million for humanitarian and evacuation programs. The ideological distribution of the vote on the bill—the last expression of Congress before the end of the Vietnam War—was as follows:[5]

Republicans			Democrats		
	Yes	*No*		*Yes*	*No*
Fundamentalists	50	17	Traditionalists	27	16
Stalwarts	42	3	Centrists	52	21
Moderates	15	0	Regulars	35	70
Progressives	4	6	Liberals	5	54
Total	111	26	Total	119	161

Only Republican stalwarts and moderates still gave almost solid support for even a minimum of continued action in Vietnam. Approval had eroded among Democratic centrists, and even among Republican fundamentalists and Democratic traditionalists. Although some Democratic regulars representing ethnic constituencies in places like Chicago and Jersey City supported the administration, a large majority of the regulars joined T. P. O'Neill to vote two to one in the negative. Democratic liberals were almost unanimous in opposition.

By the time House and Senate conferees reached agreement on the aid bill, the North Vietnamese army had entered Saigon. On April 29 South Vietnam formally surrendered to the Communists. When the evacuation of American personnel by helicopters from Saigon was completed on the evening of April 29, Ford stated simply: "This action closes a chapter in the American experience." On May 1 the House rejected the conference report on the aid bill, which the president argued was still needed to help care for Vietnamese refugees, by a vote of 162 to 246—only 90 Republicans and 72 Democrats voting to fulfill this remaining obligation of the Vietnam War.[6]

Moynihan, Kissinger, and the Third World

One of the flaws in the international strategy Nixon and Kissinger had been trying to develop at the beginning of Nixon's second term was that it seemed to assume continued political impotence or passivity among the peoples of the third world, located mainly below the northern hemisphere's thirtieth parallel. Nixon believed that most international problems would be solved if the United States, the Soviet Union, China, Western Europe, and Japan entered into a "pentagonal" relationship based on mutual accommodation. This strategic concept was rudely upset when the Arab countries embargoed the flow of oil to the United States in retaliation for American aid to Israel during the Yom Kippur War in the fall of 1973, and the Organization of Petroleum Exporting Countries (OPEC) roughly quadrupled the price of oil between the middle of 1973 and the end of 1974, setting off inflationary explosions in most of the industrial nations. Early in 1975 Kissinger went so far as to warn that the United States might use military force to break the oil cartel if there were "some actual strangulation of the industrial world."[7] The price of oil, however, continued to rise.

Although the non-oil-producing countries in the third world suffered even more grievous economic hardship than the industrial nations as a result of the oil price rise, OPEC's success in defying the West, coupled with the defeat of the United States in Vietnam, produced general elation among the former subjects of political or economic colonialism in Asia, Africa, and Latin America. A sense was developing in the third world, clearly shared by many political leaders and intellectuals in the industrial democracies, whether with enthusiasm or foreboding, that the West had had its day, and that the future belonged to peoples recently repressed, including some, like the Arabs, with exciting memories of earlier roles as conquerors.

At the beginning of 1973, Nixon had appointed Daniel P. Moynihan, who had returned to Harvard after Congress rejected the family assistance plan, as the U.S. ambassador to India. During his final weeks at this post at the end of 1974, Moynihan composed a long essay in which he argued the need for a more forceful response by American spokesmen to third world challenges. The third world countries, Moynihan claimed, with an eye on the example of India before him, were conceptually dominated by the ideology of British Fabian socialism, imbued by the years of British tutelage through which many of them had passed, or impressed during the early decades of the twentieth century by the commanding model of British culture. Because of addiction to the exceptionally complacent brand of socialism preached by the Fabians, Moynihan argued, most of the third world countries had fallen into the error of believing that economic redistribution rather than increased production was the key to broadly shared prosperity; they had thereby missed out on the actual prosperity achieved by the few developing countries, such as Singapore, Brazil, and Taiwan, that had built their economies on the capitalist model. Moreover, the third world had inherited from British socialism an anti-American bias, reflecting the view that "America was both capitalist *and* vulgar."[8]

As the third world countries had proliferated, Moynihan continued, the United States and its allies, which had commanded numerical majorities in most international bodies during the early postwar years, had found themselves increasingly outvoted. Countries that had once lined up with the West, like some in Latin America and among the Arab nations, had joined the third world alignment, competing with one another to heap abuse on the United States. American diplomats had failed to recognize the changed situation. Acting as though the West still led the majority, and sometimes paralyzed by personal guilt over perceived shortcomings of American democracy, spokesmen for the United States had tended to turn the other cheek. The time had come, Moynihan proposed, to change all that—the sensible course for the United States was to recognize its minority status, and, like members of the minority in a representative assembly, "go into opposition."[9]

First, Americans should call attention to the errors in the economic assumptions on which most third world countries were proceeding. "It is time," Moynihan wrote, "we asserted that inequalities in the

world may not be so much a matter of condition as of performance."
Then, even more important—and more satisfying—Americans should
remind the governments of the third world countries of their frequent
lapses from the political and civil liberties called for by their own
ideologies. "It is time . . . that the American spokesman came to be
feared in international forums for the truth he might tell." Despite
present differences, Moynihan maintained, the United States need
not accept permanent divergence from the third world, as it must
from the "totalitarian powers." Different though their ideologies
might be, the United States and the third world were, after all, joined
in attachment to political and civil liberties, through which they could
hope to reach "an accommodating relationship at the level of principle."[10]

When a revised version of the essay appeared in the March 1975
issue of *Commentary*, after Moynihan had returned once more to
Harvard, it attracted much favorable attention—partly because it was
both anti-British *and* antisocialist, neither sentiments likely to want
for audiences in the United States, but largely because it set forth
with refreshing confidence and clarity a course of action to deal with
what obviously was becoming a serious problem for American diplomacy. Among its appreciative readers was Kissinger, a colleague of
Moynihan's at Harvard before they both had gone to work for Nixon.
On March 23—as the North Vietnamese armies rolled toward Saigon—
the secretary of state asked Moynihan to return to government service
as ambassador to the United Nations. Three weeks later, after an
interview with the president (of whom he wrote: "a decent man, he
inspired decency in others"),[11] Moynihan accepted.

At the United Nations Moynihan soon concluded that the driving
force behind third world hostility to the United States was not so
much ideology as childish arrogance. His analysis had been based on
experience with South Asia, where ideology, he continued to believe,
mattered. But the six nations of South Asia, though containing a
quarter of the world's population, were overshadowed within the
third world caucus by the fifty-one nations of Africa, though all these
together had only half the population of India. In most of Africa, he
observed, colonial administrators had been succeeded not by earnest
Fabian socialists, steeped in the works of Sidney and Beatrice Webb,
but by swaggering dictators, concerned mainly with personal ag-
grandizement and survival. "The newest of the new nations were

hardly Fabian. . . . The legacy of Portuguese fascism was a cluster of Stalinist dictatorships in its former colonies. Nothing very good was going on in Africa, and it was there that the numerical majority of the Third World would be found."[12]

The petty dictatorships of the third world, Moynihan discovered, had generally allowed themselves to become cat's-paws for the Russians or the oil-rich Arabs or both together—particularly when the interests of the two coincided on a project like the defamation of Israel. American diplomats feared to attack this alliance: "Our diplomats had no ideas left. Communism was near to nothing to them: fascism only a word Communists used."[13] The new ambassador planned to follow a different course.

In a speech before the UN general assembly on October 1, 1975, President Idi Amin of Uganda, then taking his turn as chairman of the Organization of African Unity, called for "the expulsion of Israel from the United Nations and the extinction of Israel as a state"; and alleged that Israel continued to exist only because "the United States of America is in the hands of the Zionists." Representatives of Communist and third world countries interrupted Amin's speech several times with applause, and gave him a rousing ovation when he had finished. Moynihan, who had been away from the floor when Amin spoke, responded two days later in an address before the national convention of the AFL-CIO by endorsing a newspaper description of Amin as a "racist murderer." He found it "no accident" that Amin should be "head of the Organization of African Unity," and charged that the United Nations had in thirty years "done damn little for democracy."[14]

When a coalition of Communist and third world countries in November pushed a resolution through the general assembly equating Zionism with racism, Moynihan rose in opposition. "The terrible lie that has been told here today" he predicted, "will have terrible consequences. Not only will people begin to say, indeed they have already begun to say, that the United Nations is a place where lies are told. Far more serious, great and perhaps irreparable harm will be done to the cause of human rights. . . . The idea has not always existed in human affairs. It is an idea which appeared at a specific time in the world, and under very special circumstances. It appeared when European philosophers of the seventeenth century began to argue that man was a being whose existence was independent from that of the state. . . . That was the idea from which the idea of domestic and international rights sprang. But most of the world does not hold with that philosophy now. Most of the world believes in newer modes of political thought, in philosophies that do not accept the individual as distinct from and prior to the state. . . . If we destroy the words that were given to us by past centuries, we will not have words to replace them, for philosophy today has no such words. . . . The United States of America declares that it does not acknowledge, it will not abide by, it will never acquiesce in this infamous act."[15]

Reaction in the United States to Moynihan's performance at the United Nations was mixed. Among that part of the public that had always viewed the United Nations with hostility or suspicion, the new ambassador's lambasting of the Communist–third world coalition was naturally a hit. For others, who had formerly regarded the United Nations with hope, but now were revolted by the anti-American and anti-Israel postures of the majority in the general assembly, Moynihan seemed to be striking pretty much the right note. But within the foreign policy community—diplomats, scholars, journalists—many began to argue that his belligerence was likely to drive the third world more deeply into the arms of the Russians. Kissinger, and to a lesser extent Ford, began to develop doubts.

On November 16 Britain's ambassador to the United Nations, Ivor Richards, speaking to the United Nations Association in New York, while not mentioning Moynihan by name, said that he personally did not approve of approaching the United Nations "as a confrontational arena in which to 'take on' those countries whose political systems and ideology are different from mine. . . . Whatever else the place is, it is not the OK Corral and I am hardly Wyatt Earp."[16] Moynihan suspected that Kissinger, through the British government, had put Richards up to it. Kissinger denied involvement (truthfully, Moynihan later came to believe). Ford and Kissinger expressed continued confidence in Moynihan. But a distance was opening between the secretary of state and the UN ambassador.

Moynihan became convinced that his difference with Kissinger went beyond tactics, and was rooted in the secretary's lack of deep commitment to liberal values, which, in Moynihan's judgment, formed the essence of the American tradition. Liberalism, Moynihan believed, was now under attack from the left, and therefore a consistent liberal must become to some degree an operational conservative. "It was no longer possible," he wrote, "at this point in the twentieth century to be truly a liberal without enemies on the left."[17] But Kissinger, proceeding from the "coldest calculations of power," was conservative to the core—the sort of person against whom liberals of the seventeenth and eighteenth centuries had rebelled.[18]

Kissinger's philosophic point of view, set forth in many books, articles, and speeches, was indeed distinguishable from the strain of liberalism defended by Moynihan in his current manifestation. Kissinger valued freedom, but only as one part of the complicated heritage of Western civilization, built on foundations more varied and complex than the single tradition derived from the theories of Locke and Bayle. For Kissinger, the cardinal value was order, because without order there could be no organized society—therefore, no freedom, no economy, no morality, no basis on which to sustain life itself. If world stability required some toleration of violations of civil liberties, as it might in Chile or Saudi Arabia or Iran, or, in a different context, in the Soviet Union, then Kissinger would take a raincheck on freedom— just as Moynihan suspected. If more could be gained through diplomatic courtesy toward third world dictatorships than through public indictment of their behavior, Kissinger was willing.

Moynihan acknowledged some merit in Kissinger's approach. "I was forty," he has written, "before I had any real idea what Burke was about; Kissinger knew in his cradle." But the principle of freedom, he believed, remained the United States' most effective diplomatic weapon: "On the other hand, I knew what [Woodrow] Wilson was all about. . . . I knew that the world over, and especially in the new countries, [pursuit of political and civil liberties] was a tie we had, a claim we had, that could be put to our purposes."[19]

By the beginning of 1976, Moynihan's departure had become inevitable. The triggering incident was publication by the New York Times on January 27 of a rather innocuous memorandum by Moynihan complaining against "a large faction [in the State Department] which has an interest in our performance being judged to have failed."[20] A column by James Reston in the Times three days later reported: "Mr. Kissinger agrees with Moynihan's defense of American interests, but not with his style, his provocative rhetoric, his rambling off-the-cuff debating tactics, his self-concerning appeals to the rest of the U.S. Foreign Service, his vicious attacks on the State Department bureaucracy."[21] Moynihan submitted his resignation. When he had offered to resign two months before, after Ivor Richards's speech, Ford, while dissuading him, had urged him to try to get along better with Kissinger. This time Ford did not refuse.

At the least, Moynihan had helped bring the role of moral values in foreign policy to the forefront of the administration's attention. For some time Kissinger had been troubled that American foreign policy lacked sufficient moral content. Moynihan was right, he recognized, that unless the United States stood for something in the world beyond its own self-interest, it would have little appeal to ordinary citizens, on whom the attitudes of governments must ultimately depend, in either the developed or the developing nations. In a speech in Bloomington, Minnesota, in July 1975, the secretary of state had warned: "Because of history and moral tradition, we cannot live with ourselves as an island of plenty in a world of deprivation."[22] The United States, he said, could not afford to choose "between morality and pragmatism. We cannot escape either, nor are they incompatible." When Jimmy Carter began raising the human rights issue in the 1976 presidential campaign, a former State Department official has recalled, "Kissinger [privately] made fun of Carter's remarks, but also was bothered by them."

In April 1976 Kissinger, who had earlier accepted the existence of white minority rule in southern Africa as an unalterable fact, committed the United States, during a visit to Lusaka, Zambia, to support of "self-determination, majority rule, equal rights, and human dignity for all the people of Southern Africa—in the name of moral principle, international law, and world peace."[23] The secretary's proposal of a "constitutional structure," to "protect minority [white] rights" somewhat dampened the appeal of his statement for his African hosts. Nevertheless, the "Lusaka doctrine," delivered with Ford's approval, appeared to place the United States on the side of change in the world's last stronghold of white minority rule.

Tension between the interests of the United States and those of the third world were always inevitable. In material development the United States has ranked near the top throughout the postwar years, whereas many of the third world countries have been at or close to the bottom. It has naturally been tempting for third world statesmen to believe that their countries' problems may be solved by "redistributing" wealth from the industrial nations. Just as naturally, the

United States and its industrial allies have tended to look upon the more militant third world nations as threatening rascals. Chances have never been strong for achieving "an accommodating relationship at the level of principle," through common attachment to liberal ideas, as Moynihan had hoped while he was in India. The best that can be said is that during the 1970s there was recognition, perhaps growing, among some within both the developed and developing countries that we share at least the interests of a common planet—and a common humanity. Perhaps cautious diplomacy of the kind practiced by Kissinger, which pursues multiple values, will finally prove most adept at finding common purposes. In any case, it had become clear by 1976 that the third world would remain high on the United States' foreign policy agenda. The world would be more than pentagonal—OPEC, whatever its offenses, had made sure of that.

Cracks in Détente

One objective that Nixon had hoped to achieve through détente was to preserve security despite the cuts in the military budget that he had concluded were politically inevitable.[24] During Nixon's first term, expenditures for national defense fell, in constant 1972 dollars, from $98 billion in fiscal 1969 to $70 billion in fiscal 1973. By fiscal 1975 the decline had reached $67 billion in constant dollars. Though some of this reduction resulted from the ending of the Vietnam War, the percentage of GNP going for defense declined from 8.2 percent in fiscal 1964, the last year before heavy American involvement in Southeast Asia, to 5.2 percent in fiscal 1975. From fiscal 1969 to fiscal 1975, military expenditures for purposes unrelated to Southeast Asia fell in constant dollars by about 10 percent.[25]

The Russians, unfortunately, did not reciprocate. Soviet military expenditures, according to American intelligence estimates (not, to be sure, an unprejudiced source, but usually accepted within the defense community as reasonably accurate), increased in constant values an average between 4 and 5 percent a year from 1970 to 1975. In 1975 about 12 percent of total Soviet GNP went for military spending, compared with little more than 5 percent in the United States. In fiscal 1975 the dollar cost of matching Soviet military expenditures by the United States would have been almost a third greater than the actual American military budget. Through these increased expenditures the Soviet leaders by 1975 had at their disposal almost 50 percent more intercontinental ballistic missiles than the United States, about four times as many tanks, and about 20 percent more large surface warships—though in some areas, such as total nuclear warheads and manned bombers, the United States continued to lead.[26]

As House minority leader and as vice-president, Ford had grown increasingly alarmed over the shifting military balance between the United States and the Soviet Union. While favoring détente as a means for defusing tensions between the superpowers, he shared with his old friends in the Pentagon the view that the United States could not safely allow development of even the appearance of Russian superiority in overall military strength. When he entered the presidency, Ford has said, he "recognized that the nation's security required that the decline in defense spending be reversed."[27] To achieve this end, he was prepared to cut popular domestic programs and, if necessary, to risk provoking the Soviet leaders.

Ford's general assessment of military needs was fully shared by James Schlesinger, secretary of defense since 1973. Schlesinger, a former RAND corporation economist (with a Harvard Ph.D.) who had joined the Nixon administration as assistant budget director with responsibility for national security in 1969, was a cold war intellectual with an almost Wagnerian view of the rivalry between the United States and the Soviet Union. "History," he later wrote, "has destined this American nation to be a superpower—indeed the single great superpower among the free nations. . . . If the American people choose to turn their backs, History would not forgive us."[28] His cool nerve and analytic skill had attracted Nixon, who promoted him first to head the Atomic Energy Commission, then the Central Intelligence Agency, and finally the Defense Department, when Elliot Richardson was shifted to Justice in April 1973. Though a proponent of massive arms expansion, Schlesinger was the opposite of bellicose when faced with actual operational decisions. In the discussions that preceded Nixon's decision to replenish the battered Israeli army during the Yom Kippur War in 1973, as later during the confrontation over the seizure of the American ship *Mayaguez* by the new Communist government of Cambodia in 1975, he favored the most limited possible use or commitment of American forces.[29]

Distrust of Soviet intentions—coupled, no doubt, with the normal tendency of the secretary of defense to argue for expansion of his department's budget—led Schlesinger to a dire view of international affairs. The continuation of current trends, he warned at the beginning of 1975, would produce Soviet "preponderance" by 1978. To maintain military balance with the Russians, the administration proposed that defense outlays for fiscal 1976 be increased by $8.7 billion—a growth of about 10 percent. If Congress chose not to approve this increase, Schlesinger told the Senate Armed Services Committee, it should act "in clear recognition that we [the Defense Department] will not be able to fulfill our responsibilities."[30]

Though they both favored expansion of the military budget, Ford and Schlesinger differed on strategic approach and political style. Besides, they simply did not like each other. While he was vice-president in 1974, Ford had been appalled when Schlesinger sided with Congressman Edward Hébert of Louisiana, chairman of the House Armed Services Committee, against Ford's old ally George Mahon, chairman of the House Appropriations Committee, in a jurisdictional dispute over which committee should determine the level of American aid to South Vietnam, because Hébert favored the higher figure. Schlesinger, the vice-president told John Osborne, in an interview not for attribution, "doesn't understand Congress and doesn't know how to deal with Congress." The feud between Hébert and Mahon, Ford said, was a problem "Schlesinger simply didn't know how to handle and wasn't equipped to handle."[31]

When he became president, Ford decided to keep Schlesinger at the Pentagon "to emphasize to allies and adversaries alike the continuity of our foreign and military policies." But he continued to find Schlesinger "aloof, frequently arrogant."[32] The defense secretary, for his part, made little attempt to conceal the fact that he did not regard Ford as his intellectual equal. As one of Ford's advisers has said: "It is basically a mistake to talk down to the president of the United States."

Ford was somewhat annoyed by Schlesinger's reputation as a hawk, which he believed was undeserved. During the *Mayaguez* confrontation, the president noted critically, Schlesinger "didn't seem to want any bombing at all," in contrast to Kissinger, who was "adamant about the need for a strong response."[33] Toward Congress, on the other hand, Schlesinger was resolutely pugnacious. When Mahon's Appropriations Committee reduced the Defense Department's budget request for fiscal 1976 by about $7 billion (including, however, the elimination of $1.3 billion in aid for the by then defunct government of South Vietnam), the secretary told the press that the cut was "arbitrary and vicious."[34] Viewing the reduction as one skirmish in an extended battle, Ford believed that Schlesinger's language was intemperate—and certain to offend Mahon, whose support the administration badly needed to help hold down spending in other areas.

While laid up with a cold and severe sinus infection at the White House in October 1975, Ford mulled over a number of personnel problems that had been bothering him. Apparently consulting no one except Bryce Harlow, he put together the series of job changes that later became known as the "Sunday morning massacre." Schlesinger, the president decided, had to go. Into the secretary's slot at the Pengaton, he would move the faithful Rumsfeld. Cheney would take Rumsfeld's place as chief of the White House staff. George Bush, whom Ford had made U.S. representative in Peking, would come home to replace William Colby, a Schlesinger ally, as director of the Central Intelligence Agency. Elliot Richardson, whom he had recalled to public service as ambassador to Great Britain, would succeed Rogers Morton, already ill with the cancer that would kill him three years later, as secretary of commerce. Since Schlesinger had become a favorite among conservative fundamentalists, who regarded him (wrongly according to Ford) as their champion against dovish tendencies fostered by Kissinger, the president would compensate for Schlesinger's fall by giving Kissinger's job as national security adviser in the White House to Brent Scowcroft—which would have the incidental effect of shrinking Kissinger's appearance of dominance over foreign policy. Finally, he would carry out the painful task of accepting removal from the 1976 Republican ticket of Nelson Rockefeller, whose unpopularity among the fundamentalists he believed threatened his renomination.[35]

When the changes became public, after Ford fired Schlesinger and Colby in the Oval Office on the morning of Sunday, November 2, 1975, many governmental analysts at first thought they recognized the Machiavellian influences of Rumsfeld or Kissinger or both. The two, however, have insisted that they knew nothing of the president's plan until he presented it to them on the afternoon of October 25; and both have maintained that they then urged him to reconsider.

Rumsfeld has said: "I felt it was too late for the president to change his cabinet. I told him that he had passed the point when cabinet changes should appropriately be made. But the president was very stubborn. He would not be moved. I particularly objected to placing Bush and myself in positions where we could not participate in the [1976] campaign. We both had backgrounds in politics, and we should have been in positions where we could be helpful to the president. By placing us at the CIA and Defense, he effectively took us out of politics. Putting Bush at the CIA also effectively ruled him out of consideration for the vice-presidency, which I also thought was a mistake. I thought that the president should preserve his options on the vice-presidency. The only part of the package that I favored was making Elliot Richardon secretary of commerce. This placed Richardson in a position where he could be selected for vice-president, and where he could be helpful to the president in a political year."[36]

Kissinger said that he did not mind giving up the job of national security adviser, but feared it might be misunderstood in foreign capitals.[37] Also, he opposed the firing of Schlesinger, with whom his differences were more over personal style than over substance—and whom he probably, on balance, would prefer at the Pentagon to the politically more astute Rumsfeld. But the president, as Rumsfeld put it, "would not be moved."

Schlesinger's dismissal was seized upon by hawks in both parties, particularly Ronald Reagan and Henry Jackson, who were preparing their own bids for the presidency, as evidence that Ford was fearful of confrontation with the Russians. In a farewell address on the steps of the Pentagon, the departing secretary warned of a "national mood of skepticism" and a "vacuum of the spirit" that he said were sapping the strength and will of the nation. In 1976 Schlesinger became an international policy counsellor to Reagan. After Reagan's defeat by Ford at the Republican National Convention, he moved on to become an adviser to Jimmy Carter (who later made him secretary of the newly established Department of Energy, from which job he departed in yet another cabinet shakeup in 1979).

Besides promoting an increased military budget, Ford in 1975 sought to check the expansion of Russian influence in southern Africa. In an effort to counter the introduction of Russian arms and Cuban

combat troops into Angola, the administration began covertly sup-
plying arms and equipment to two non-Marxist factions fighting in
the civil war for control of the former Portuguese colony. This effort
was halted because of action by Congress, where many members
were fearful of risking a repetition of Vietnam. On December 18, 1975,
the Senate passed, by a vote of 54 to 22, an amendment offered to
the defense appropriation bill for fiscal 1976 by Senator John Tunney,
liberal Democrat of California, prohibiting use of appropriated funds
"for any activities involving Angola directly or indirectly." The following month, despite strong objection from the administration, the
House approved the Tunney amendment by a vote of 323 to 99. Ford
commented after the House vote: "Congress has stated to the world
that it will ignore a clear act of Soviet-Cuban expansion by brute
military force into areas thousands of miles from either country.
. . . The consequences of this action can only result in serious harm
to the interests of the United States."[38]

In the vote in the Senate on the Tunney amendment, the administration was supported only by a few Republican fundamentalists
and stalwarts and Democratic traditionalists, plus one Republican
moderate (Hugh Scott of Pennsylvania), and two Democrat centrists
(Long of Louisiana and Morgan of North Carolina). Even among the
fundamentalists, three senators identified with the so-called New
Right (Jesse Helms of North Carolina, Jake Garn of Utah, and William
Scott of Virginia) voted for the amendment. Among the three more
liberal groups (Democratic liberals and regulars and Republican progressives), not a single senator voted against cutting off aid to the
purportedly pro-Western factions in Angola. (Henry Jackson, a regular, was paired against the amendment.)[39]

At the Pentagon Rumsfeld quickly became even more outspoken
than Schlesinger had been in proclaiming the reality of the Russian
challenge. "Before going to Defense," Rumsfeld has said, "on the
basis of my work at NATO and participation in National Security
Council meetings, I had opinions but I did not have convictions. After
a short period at Defense, in which I did almost nothing except review
budget matters and receive intelligence briefings—except for some
time spent on SALT—I became absolutely convinced that the United
States was falling behind the Soviet Union, and there was no doubt
in my mind that we would have to increase our budget substantially
in order to preserve an effective defense system."[40]

At the beginning of 1976, the administration proposed a military budget for fiscal 1977 $14.4 billion above what Congress had approved for the previous fiscal year. "I certainly would state without doubt," Rumsfeld told the House Armed Services Committee in January, "that given what has taken place in the last 20 to 15 years with respect to the relationship between the Soviets and the United States, there has been a tremendous shift. If these trends are allowed to continue, it would be a great mistake for this country and the stability of the world."[41] To suggestions from liberals that the important question was not the exact level of Soviet military capabilities but whether the Russians in fact intended to use these capabilities to attempt world hegemony, Rumsfeld responded: "Intentions can change." In any case, he argued, hegemonic ambitions were inherent in Communist doctrine: "If one looks at their literature and their doctrine, it is rather clear that [Communists] do not believe in freedom, that they are committed to their philosophy, and that they have it in their minds that they will prevail in the world. . . . They have not been inhibited from attempting to spread their philosophy throughout the world. We believe in freedom and the God-given rights of man, and they don't."[42]

While Rumsfeld railed publicly against the Russians to gain support for the increased defense budget, Kissinger was pressing quietly on the diplomatic front for the conclusion of a more comprehensive treaty limiting production and deployment of nuclear weapons (SALT II). The two objectives, though not necessarily incompatible, were soon pulling in opposite directions. Kissinger and Scowcroft became concerned that Rumsfeld's rhetoric was needlessly antagonizing the Russians. Scowcroft has said: "Rumsfeld's briefings to Congress pictured the Soviets as a dark menace which inevitably had the effect of undermining negotiations with the Soviet Union."[43]

Ford was of two minds. On the one hand, he agreed with Rumsfeld that the growth of Soviet arms required a strong American response. On the other, he was convinced that a new SALT treaty would "be in the best interests of the United States militarily," and would help him win election to a new term in 1976.[44] The tipping factor appears to have been the growth of opposition to détente within the Republican party, generated by Reagan's campaign for the presidency. Ford has said: "I never backed away from détente as a means for achieving a more stable relationship with our Communist adversaries. But the situation that developed in connection with the presidential primaries and the fight at the convention made it necessary to deemphasize détente."[45] Under strong challenge from Reagan in the presidential primaries, Ford reluctantly went along with "highly technical" objections by Rumsfeld and the hawks at the Pentagon against a compromise SALT agreement that Kissinger was close to working out with the Russians.[46] As a result, further negotiations on SALT had to be left for the next administration.

For Ford, détente was never much more than a strategic move in the continuing struggle to thwart Soviet ambitions for world domination. He shared little of Nixon's hope that the Russians could be drawn into a traditional power game relationship, based on limited national objectives—partly because he had observed the continued expansion of Soviet military capabilities after the first SALT agreement in 1972. Ford did not return to the clear ideological distinctions of the cold war. American courtship of Communist China continued, and efforts were made to improve relations with some of the Communist-bloc countries in Eastern Europe (which contributed to the president's famous blunder in finding "no Soviet domination of Eastern Europe" during his 1976 foreign policy debate with Carter). But the Soviet Union remained a fundamental antagonist—deterred, according to a statement issued by the White House in August 1976, from "military adventurism" and "expansionism" mainly by countervailing American strength.[47]

At the urging of Ford and Rumsfeld, Congress in 1976 increased military spending in constant dollars for the first time since 1967. According to Senator Henry Bellmon, Republican stalwart of Oklahoma, the fiscal 1977 defense budget marked "the end of détente." It did not quite do that. But the administration and Congress, by reversing the decline in expenditures for defense, gave notice of deepening national concern over Soviet behavior and intentions.

Conservative Internationalism

Ford's foreign policy ideology was a compound of nationalist goals and internationalist strategies. Like Hamilton, Theodore Roosevelt, Eisenhower, and Nixon, Ford believed that the national interest of the United States could best be served through active participation in international affairs. The objectives of such participation, however, were to be limited to the nation's clear economic and security interests, rather than aimed at any Wilsonian program for remaking the world in the image of American democracy. From his isolationist youth Ford seemed to retain a distaste for meddling in the governmental arrangements or social policies of other nations.

Moynihan has marveled that Ford did not take up the defense of international human rights before Carter hit upon it as a campaign issue in 1976.[48] Actually, according to Scowcroft, Ford did, through quiet diplomacy, achieve progress against specific human rights violations in such places as the Soviet Union, South Korea, and Syria.[49] But it does not seem to have entered Ford's mind that the United States might have some responsibility for promoting *institutional* reforms outside its own governmental jurisdiction.

Ford viewed the Soviet leaders as antagonists, not because they denied human rights to their people, or imposed their rule on other nations, but because he regarded the military and territorial expansion programs upon which they had embarked as threats against the future security of the United States. He was therefore easily guided by Kissinger, for whom the success of policy was tending to become its own reward, into ignoring the visit of Alexander Solzhenitsyn to Washington in the summer of 1975. According to his own account, Ford considered inviting Solzhenitsyn to the White House in order to improve his political "standing with conservatives," but decided against it because he thought it might "jeopardize" the success of upcoming negotiations with Brezhnev. The idea that there might be intrinsic moral or ideological value in honoring Solzhenitsyn seems hardly to have occurred to him. Likewise, the slip about "no Soviet domination of Eastern Europe" in the debate with Carter, though partly the result of jumbled semantics, also reflected a tendency to think in terms of formal governmental arrangements rather than of the underlying conditions of peoples. Beneath the yards of internationalist rhetoric served up for him by the State Department, Ford seems to have stuck pretty closely to the old American view that the nation's most important, perhaps only, international moral responsibility is to serve as a "city upon a hill," inspiring others through the example of our own success.

While avoiding aggressive or highly visible advocacy of international human rights, Ford at the same time, on grounds of economic, political, and military realism, rejected any thought of returning to isolationism. The administration, in short, pursued policies based on classic tenets of conservative internationalism: a pragmatic doctrine that aims at tough-minded promotion of national interests through a global system of treaties and alliances.

What were the available alternatives? It suited the administration's purposes to warn from time to time against a resurgence of isolationist sentiment in Congress and among the public. National opinion polls, particularly those taken immediately after the Communist victory in Vietnam, did show some decline in public support for an activist foreign policy and some loss of interest in world problems.[50] A few actions by Congress indicated a more cautious approach to international involvements. But there was little real isolationism of the old Taft variety, prescribing withdrawal from most foreign entanglements, among the nation's political leaders or prospective leaders during the middle years of the 1970s.

The alternative to the administration's approach offered, in somewhat different forms, by Ronald Reagan and Henry Jackson, and identified with James Schlesinger, was far from isolationist. Indeed, it called for a policy more aggressively interventionist than that practiced by Ford and Kissinger, though to be carried out with less attention to the views or interests of allies. The policy advocated by Moynihan while he was at the United Nations, and later when he campaigned for Jackson for president and in his own campaign for the Senate, was supposed to be based on broadly conceived moral principles, but in practice appeared to be more narrowly nationalistic than the administration's approach, and fully as belligerent as that favored by Reagan or Jackson.

The "liberal alternative" to Ford's policies, rather vaguely set forth by leaders like Hubert Humphrey and Frank Church, placed somewhat greater emphasis than the administration on self-interested cooperation and moral altruism. Yet on the whole it appeared to aim at achieving Ford's goals through strategies quite similar to those pursued by Ford, though at a lower price—nationalism on the cheap.

The challenger who actually won the Democratic nomination and was elected president in 1976, Jimmy Carter, seemed at times closer in foreign policy approach to Jackson and Moynihan than to Ford, but shied away from the belligerence and indifference to allies that the Jackson-Moynihan position implied. Carter effectively attacked the lack of moral content in Ford's policies, but seemed unwilling to face the potential costs, such as causing irritation among America's allies and burdening arms negotiations with the Russians, that a more moralistic approach was likely to entail. Carter also took up Zbigniew Brzezinski's criticism that the administration's policies were based more on "acrobatics" than on "architecture"; but he gave no very clear sense of what his own architectural system might be, particularly since he made a point of consulting with advisers identified with very different ideological points of view.

The long-lived postwar consensus on foreign policy continued to erode, as was shown by the vote on the Tunney amendment barring aid to non-Marxist factions in Angola, among other incidents. But no new consensus, or even a clear choice between competing policies, had appeared to take its place. Nixon dealt with this situation through a series of brilliant foreign policy maneuvers, which served the old goal of containment, while establishing a political atmosphere in which a new ideological synthesis for Western policy became feasible. Had he remained president, he might have woven a broad ideological framework appropriate to American and world needs and opportunities in the final quarter of the twentieth century (though his indicated preference for John Connally as a successor suggests that he was moving toward a narrow and belligerent form of nationalism). Neither Ford nor Kissinger was up to this conceptual task. They administered foreign policy around the goals and strategies that had been developed by Nixon (with Kissinger's assistance)—a structure that produced some practical results, but offered few clear guides to the future.

17

Energy Policy:
The Fight for Decontrol

AMONG THE CHALLENGES with which Nixon and Ford administrations had to deal, none was more vexing, or potentially more momentous, than the shortage of energy resources that became critical in the fall of 1973.

The energy shortage was not entirely unanticipated. Everyone knew that supplies of oil and natural gas, upon which both industry and private households had become increasingly dependent, were not inexhaustible. Informed persons in government and industry had noted that oil production within the United States had peaked at 3.5 billion barrels in 1970, and then begun to fall. The share of American oil consumption supplied by imports had risen from 22 percent in 1968 to 29 percent in 1972.[1] Proven domestic reserves of natural gas reached their high point in 1967, and then slid into decline.[2] As early as 1965, James Schlesinger told his friend Charls Walker that the nation would soon be facing an energy crisis.[3]

Yet for most Americans, the day of reckoning, if there was to be one, seemed far in the future. Oil prices increased only 10 percent from 1960 to 1970—less than the rate of inflation. Natural gas prices actually fell, chiefly because of federal regulation of the price of gas sold in interstate commerce.[4] For more than fifty years, proven reserves of oil and natural gas had usually seemed to be in danger of running down—but were always replenished by new discoveries in time to keep ahead of rising demand. Long before supplies of oil and gas were finally exhausted, the public had been led to believe, nuclear power would be harnessed to meet most energy requirements. Even

358

if snags occurred in the development of nuclear energy, the nation would still have at its disposal enormous reserves of coal, which had met most fuel needs, except for automotive transportation, before the Second World War.

Consequently, the severe energy shortages that began in the winter of 1972–73, and reached crisis proportions after the Arab oil embargo in October 1973, took the public and the nation's political leaders largely by surprise. Gas lines, limited supplies of electricity, chilly offices and homes, and potential threats to American economic and military security were suddenly major national concerns. The United States, Nixon warned, faced "the most acute shortage of energy since World War II."[5] In January 1973 the Gallup poll found that 46 percent of the public, a large plurality, regarded the energy shortage as the United States' most serious national problem.[6]

Clearly, the nation urgently needed a coherent and effective energy policy. Americans would have to consume less, or find new sources of supply, or both. The development of such a policy could not go very far, however, without some decisions on fundamental issues of social equity and economic feasibility—decisions that, as it turned out, the governmental system, in its currently divided state, was poorly equipped to make.

Origins of the Problem

Before the 1970s the problem of oil had usually been viewed as one of potential glut rather than shortage. Under the authority of the Interstate Transportation of Petroleum Products Act, pushed through Congress in 1935 by Senator Tom Connally and Congressman Sam Rayburn of Texas, state regulatory bodies systematically limited oil production, purportedly for conservation, but actually to keep up prices. (E. O. Thompson, dominant member for more than twenty years of the mighty Texas Railroad Commission, which controlled about 40 percent of domestic oil production, explained that there was "more incentive for conservation in the recovery of oil bearing a good profit.")[7] When cheap oil from Venezuela and the Middle East began invading the domestic market during the 1950s, Congress in 1955 authorized President Eisenhower to impose quotas on oil imports, on the ground that national security would be threatened if domestic producers were driven out of business. After experimenting with a program of voluntary quotas, Eisenhower established a complicated mandatory quota system in 1959.[8]

By the time of Nixon's election in 1968, political pressure was growing, particularly from New England, where the costs of the quota system were felt most heavily, to permit more foreign oil to enter the country. Besides, quotas were viewed with ideological distaste by free traders within the new administration. Soon after taking office, Nixon ordered a study of the oil import issue by an internal administration task force, headed by George Shultz, whom the president presumably knew was a convinced free trader. After extensive study Shultz's task force concluded that import quotas were inflating oil prices in the United States about 50 percent above the world market, and making the "world oil industry less efficient." In February 1970 the task force recommended that the quota system be replaced by a tariff that would permit "a more careful and calibrated approach to the control of imports." (Dissents were filed by Secretary of Commerce Stans and Secretary of the Interior Hickel, who favored continuation of the quota system.) Nixon, who had been generously supported by the oil industry throughout his political career, took no action, except to appoint another internal study committee, with Shultz not included among its members.[9]

During the 1950s and the 1960s, the major oil companies, based in New York and London, set prices in the world oil market pretty much as they pleased. When competition brought down prices in the domestic market in the late 1950s, Jersey Standard, the world's largest oil company, cut payments to its foreign producers without even bothering to negotiate. Responding to this affront, five oil-producing countries joined to form OPEC in 1960. During its first decade OPEC was unable to halt the decline of oil prices in the world market, which reached a low of about $1 a barrel in the Persian Gulf in 1969. By the end of the 1960s, however, the peaking of oil production in the United States and the continued rapid increase in demand in all the industrial countries had placed the OPEC nations in a potentially strong market position.[10]

The turning point came in May 1970, when Colonel Muammar el-Qaddafi, the newly installed dictator of Libya, demanded a substantial increase in the price paid by American companies for Libyan oil. Because a break in the pipeline carrying oil from the Persian Gulf to the Mediterranean had caused a temporary shortage, the companies felt they had to comply. An American oil company executive said at the time: "Everybody who drives a tractor, truck, or car in the Western world will be affected by this."[11]

Nixon's Response

In December 1970 Nixon, faced by rising petroleum prices in the domestic market that were helping to fuel inflation, ordered the first breach in the quota system by permitting more Canadian oil to enter the United States. Two months later OPEC, emboldened by Qaddafi's success, pushed through a general price increase of about fifty cents a barrel—the cartel's "first clear-cut victory over the West."[12] On August 15, 1971, Nixon, still wrestling with inflation, imposed general wage and price controls, including controls on the price of petroleum—the true source, Milton Friedman was later to argue, of most of the energy problems that followed.[13]

Since controls were imposed in summer, prices were high for gasoline but low for fuel oil. As a result, even as winter approached, refiners were able to make a better profit producing gasoline than fuel oil. Fuel oil shortages therefore developed in many northern cities during the particularly severe winter of 1972–73, causing hardship for householders and some school closings. Henry Jackson, who had done poorly in the Democratic presidential primaries in 1972 but already was planning to try again in 1976, warned that the development of a national energy policy was "the most critical problem facing the nation." Aiming to head off future shortages, Nixon in April 1973 finally suspended the entire system of oil import quotas. Imported oil immediately poured into the country.[14]

In October 1973, after Nixon's decision to reequip the beleaguered Israeli army during the Yom Kippur War, the Arab nations embargoed the supply of oil to the United States. Prices paid to countries that continued to export oil, such as Iran and Nigeria, rose to more than ten times what the world market price had been when the war began. Meeting in Tehran in the middle of December, OPEC, following the leadership of the shah of Iran, decreed a price of $7 a barrel, up from $1.77 three months before.[15] "What they did was based on pure raw power," Charls Walker, who had become a private Washington consultant in 1973, lamented before the Senate Budget Committee. "I am sure 40 years ago or less it would have been answered on the basis of pure raw power, in internationalization of the oil fields."[16] But the days of gunboat diplomacy seemed to have passed. The price increase held.

Nixon responded to the embargo by calling on Congress to give him emergency powers to control the production and use of energy, and to approve a $10 billion program for the development of new energy technologies, which he had first called for the previous June, and which he now said would make the United States "self-sufficient" in energy by 1980. As he had done in proposing the New Federalism four years before, Nixon invoked "the spirit of Apollo" in launching what he called "Project Independence."[17]

Congress quickly granted authority to impose a national 55-mile-an-hour speed limit, and to establish year-round daylight saving time (revoked the following year in response to protests by parents concerned about sending their children to school in the dark). But the overall energy emergency bill, which would have empowered the president to ration petroleum and to intervene directly in the operations of the oil industry, became enmeshed in congressional efforts to limit oil company profits.

Riding along with OPEC price increases, profits of the major oil companies were rising in 1973 at a median rate more than 50 percent above that of 1972.[18] The companies claimed that such increases were needed to compensate for a series of lean years, and to provide funds for investment in new resource development. These arguments were not well received among motorists sitting in gas lines or householders shivering in minimally heated homes. In December the House added a windfall profits tax to the energy emergency bill. When oil-state senators led by Russell Long successfully filibustered against the windfall profits tax in the Senate, the House refused to pass the bill before the end of the 1973 session.[19]

While wrangling over the energy emergency bill, Congress promptly passed legislation, at first opposed but ultimately accepted by the administration, requiring the president to allocate petroleum to assure balanced distribution among geographic regions and economic sectors, and providing authority to continue price controls over petroleum products. Nixon, who had become convinced that controls were inhibiting investment in the development of increased domestic supply, proceeded, after signing the bill on November 27, 1973, to remove all controls on the price of oil produced from newly drilled wells or from old wells in excess of the 1972 volume (which became known as "new oil"), and to permit a $1 a barrel increase in the price of oil from old wells up to 1972 volume ("old oil"). Not surprisingly, production of new oil rose sharply, while production of old oil fell, causing proponents of controls to suggest that "something is going on in the oil industry that is not in the best interest of the American people."[20] Spokesmen for the industry replied that the two-tier price system gave producers little incentive to strive for maximum recovery from old wells, and that, in any case, old wells tend naturally to produce declining yields.[21]

Simon as Energy Czar

To direct the new oil allocation program, Nixon selected Deputy Secretary of the Treasury William Simon. A successful Wall Street bond promoter, Simon had come to the Treasury at the beginning of Nixon's second term. On the recommendation of George Shultz, Nixon soon made him chairman of an interdepartmental Oil Policy Committee, because, knowing nothing about oil, he was "a man without any built-in prejudices or vested interests."[22] In this role, Simon was drawn into conflict with John Love, the affable former Republican governor of Colorado, whom Nixon had appointed director of the Energy Policy Office.

Simon seems to have viewed with contempt members of the old Republican squirearchy, like Rogers Morton and Love, who held high posts in the Nixon administration. He was astonished to overhear Morton tell Love on a Friday afternoon in October 1973, at the height of the oil crisis, of plans to "go out and get me some quail" over the coming weekend. Love said that sounded like a good idea, and he thought he would do the same. Love, Simon believed, "never fully grasped the magnitude of the emergency."[23] Nixon, apparently, soon agreed. After the Arab oil embargo, the president fired Love and designated Simon czar of the administration's energy program. He would have authority, Nixon told Simon, like "that of Albert Speer in the Third Reich when he was put in charge of German armaments."[24]

Though an unsparing critic of what he called "bureaucratic moles and bag carriers" in the executive branch, Simon quickly grasped that "without a bureaucratic base of my own, I would be cooked."[25] Within a few months he had expanded Love's staff of twelve to a thriving bureaucracy of eighteen hundred. (Speaking in 1976 in Houston, Simon, then secretary of the treasury, called the growth of the energy bureaucracy "a striking example of the cancer of big government.")[26]

Simon's later judgment on the allocation program that he administered was unequivocal: "The kindest thing I can say about it is that it was a disaster. . . . The normal market distribution system is so complex, yet so smooth that no government mechanism could simulate it. All we were actually doing with our so-called bureaucratic efficiency was damaging the existent distribution system." Yet the program, he conceded (or boasted), was not a total failure. By his own account, his decision at the end of January 1974 to pour gasoline reserves into "all the pockets of shortages in the country" helped end panic buying and take some of the pressure out of demand. But whatever success the program achieved, Simon insisted, resulted from his having remained an "*anti*bureaucrat"—an internal antagonist of the governmental system. "In the crunch," he wrote, "I had used the decisive methods that had served me well in the marketplace. They were not the methods admired or desired in Washington. . . . That is how I ultimately realized the profundity of the difference between the businessman and the government bureaucrat. The businessman's standard of efficacy is a solution to the problem, and the more responsive he is to external reality, the better. The bureaucrat's standard of efficacy is obedience to the rules and respect for the vested interests of the hierarchy, however unyielding of a solution; response to external reality is often irrelevant."[27]

In February 1974 Congress passed the energy emergency bill that had been left hanging at the end of the 1973 session. To avoid a resumption of the oil-state filibuster in the Senate, the windfall profits tax had been dropped. But in its place had been put a requirement mandating the restoration of controls over new oil, at a level substantially below the current market price. On March 6 Nixon vetoed the bill, on the ground that the price rollback provision would "cut the supply of gasoline and other oil products, and make compulsory rationing of gasoline much more likely."[28] In the immediate aftermath of the Arab oil embargo, gas rationing had seemed almost inevitable, and the president had asked for standby rationing authority in his energy message to Congress in November 1973. On November 15 an amendment to the energy bill requiring that rationing be put into effect no later than January 15, 1974, had been defeated by a vote of only 40 to 48 in the Senate. By the beginning of March, however, with the worst of the winter behind him and a good prospect that the embargo would soon be lifted, Nixon had come to believe that rationing, which he viewed with holy dread, might be avoided after all—one of the reasons he did not much mind losing the energy bill. An effort led by Henry Jackson to override the president's veto in the Senate fell far below the needed two-thirds majority.[29]

The Arab embargo was lifted on March 18, 1974, and the flow of oil resumed—though at much higher prices. An effort in the House on May 21 to revive the energy emergency bill, no longer supported by the administration, was defeated by a vote of 191 to 207. A Republican representative who voted against the bill, though he had supported the energy bill the first time around in the fall of 1973, explained that his earlier vote had been cast "in a different year and a different time and under different circumstances than exist today."[30]

Ford's Drive for Decontrol

So matters stood when Gerald Ford became president in August 1974. There were no significant current shortages. But imports had risen to 38 percent of American consumption (up from 29 percent in 1972).[31] The United States was clearly becoming increasingly dependent on the politically volatile Middle East for its energy needs. During 1974 OPEC, now following the supposedly moderate leadership of Saudi Arabia, dictated further increases, bringing the price to about $10 a barrel—ten times what it had been only five years before.[32]

Though at first preoccupied with pressing problems of inflation and foreign policy, Ford by the middle of the fall had concluded that action must be taken to deal with "an energy crisis that was growing more acute every day."[33] He began by changing the leadership of the administration's energy team. John Sawhill, who had become director of the newly established Federal Energy Administration (FEA) in June 1974, irritated Ford by publicly arguing that the best way to reduce consumption was to increase the excise tax on gasoline by twenty cents a gallon—a course that the president regarded as politically and economically unfeasible. When Sawhill declined to recant, Ford fired him at the end of October.[34]

Energy policy then became the joint responsibility of a triumvirate, composed of Simon, who had succeeded Shultz as secretary of the treasury in May 1974; Rogers Morton, then still secretary of the interior; and Frank Zarb, an aggressive young New York investment banker who took Sawhill's place as director at FEA.[35] Of the three, the most visible at first was Simon, though his regular departmental duties had least to do with energy.

Morton and Zarb agreed with Simon that decontrol was needed to clear the market and increase production. Both, however, were prepared to approach this goal gradually, if political realities so required. Zarb, in addition, regarded decontrol as only one part of a larger agenda, which should include strong government encouragement for conservation, and development of new energy technologies, supported, if necessary, by government subsidies.

The program developed by the administration's energy team for the president to present to the new Congress at the beginning of 1975 had two main objectives: to raise the price of petroleum products enough to check consumption, and to provide producers with economic incentives to seek new sources of supply. Ford himself was most interested in expanding supply. "My emphasis," he has said, "was on stimulating production of domestic oil and gas through increased price levels, which also hopefully would bring some conservation."[36]

In his State of the Union message on January 15, Ford announced that he would lift controls on the price of all domestic oil on April 1, and proposed enactment of a $2 a barrel tax on petroleum imports, aimed at reducing demand for foreign oil. As a goad to congressional action, the president announced that, under the authority given him by the 1955 oil import act, he would temporarily increase import fees by $3 a barrel on all imported crude oil and petroleum products, with the first $1 to go into effect on February 1, and subsequent increases to follow on March 1 and April 1. Through these steps, Ford promised, the United States would achieve energy "independence" by 1985— five years after the target year set by Nixon fourteen months before. As a result of his program, the president acknowledged, "gasoline and oil will cost even more than they do now." But higher costs to consumers would be partly offset by a windfall profits tax on oil producers, the revenue from which Ford proposed to return to the economy through tax cuts and direct subsidies to low-income families.[37]

The Democratic leadership in Congress, apparently taken by surprise, sought to gain time by quickly pushing through legislation to nullify the first of the oil import fee increases. On March 4 Ford vetoed the nullification bill, but agreed to hold up imposition of the second and third increases for sixty days, on the understanding that the Democrats in Congress would present counterproposals within that time.[38] Ford also announced that he would not for the time being go ahead with his plan for full deregulation of domestic oil.

The Democrats responded during March with their own plan for encouraging conservation and increasing supply, based on the work of task forces headed by Senator John Pastore of Rhode Island and Congressman Jim Wright of Texas. Congressional Democrats, the leadership announced, had rejected the administration's alleged premise that "the only way to achieve energy conservation is deliberately to raise the price of all petroleum products to all American consumers by heavy, indiscriminate additions in taxation." The Democratic program called for a relatively mild five cents a gallon increase in the federal tax on gasoline, and tax incentives to automobile manufacturers to motivate production of more fuel efficient cars.[39]

However, Democratic members of the House Ways and Means Committee, led by their new chairman, Al Ullman, seemed to be in a mood for sterner stuff. On March 2 Ullman, claiming to speak for the Democratic majority on the committee, proposed a much more drastic tax increase on gasoline of up to forty cents a gallon phased in over a five-year period, and the reimposition of a direct quota system on oil imports.[40] On May 12 the Ways and Means Committee sent to the floor, by vote of only 19 to 16, a bill providing for reimposition of quotas; a gas tax increase of up to twenty-three cents a gallon fully effective by 1979; and a tax on automobiles with low fuel efficiency (the so-called gas guzzlers) to go into effect on 1978 models.[41]

On June 11 the House, by a vote of 345 to 72, stripped from the bill all but three cents of the proposed gas tax increase; and then, by a closer vote, knocked out the remaining three cents. The next day the House replaced the gas-guzzler tax with a provision for civil enforcement of fuel efficiency standards, said to be preferred by the automobile companies. By the time the bill passed the House on June 19, on a largely party-line vote of 291 to 130, it contained few incentives either to encourage conservation or to expand supply. Forwarded to Russell Long's Senate Finance Committee, it sank without a trace.[42] The problem faced by the Democrats, apparently, was that, while preferring to deal with the problem through conservation rather than by giving the oil companies economic incentives to increase production, they shrank from imposing the added costs on consumers that most conservation measures necessarily entailed.

The 1975 Compromise

The Democrats' alternative program having effectively self-destructed, attention shifted back to Ford's proposal for achieving both increased supply and conservation through oil price decontrol. The administration was in a fairly strong tactical position, since authority for controls would lapse on August 31 if no new law were signed by the president. As the 1976 presidential campaign approached, however, Ford began to develop second thoughts about the effects of instant decontrol. A sudden surge in prices resulting from total decontrol, producing even fatter oil company profits, the president reasoned, would provoke such bitter public reaction that Congress would no doubt whip through a price rollback and a new control program, which he would come under heavy political pressure to sign. Choosing the course of political prudence, Ford on July 16 submitted to Congress a program, designed by Zarb, for phased decontrol over a thirty-month period. This proposal was rejected by the House on July 22 by a vote of 262 to 167. On July 25 Ford submitted a second decontrol plan, proposing a rollback on existing prices to $11.50 a barrel on all domestically produced oil, followed by a gradual phaseout of controls over a thirty-nine month period. This plan, too, was rejected by the House on July 30 by a vote of 228 to 189.[43]

Before acting on the president's second decontrol plan, the House took up an amendment to an energy bill then on the floor, offered by Congressman Robert Krueger, centrist Democrat of Texas, which in effect would have approved the president's plan, while delaying its effective date until Congress enacted an excess profits tax on resulting oil company windfalls. The rejection of the provision for gradual decontrol in the Krueger amendment carried by a vote of only 218 to 207—the negative votes probably representing the maximum vote then available in the House for some kind of decontrol.

The distribution of the vote by ideological groups on the motion to reject Krueger's plan for gradual decontrol was as follows (a yes vote being a vote in favor of continuing controls):[44]

Republicans	Yes	No		Democrats	Yes	No
Fundamentalists	1	69		Traditionalists	5	34
Stalwarts	4	44		Centrists	48	32
Moderates	4	10		Regulars	92	13
Progressives	6	5		Liberals	58	0
Total	15	128		Total	203	79

Party lines were unusually firm on the issue, Democrats favoring continued controls and Republicans opposing, except for three groups: Democratic traditonalists and centrists and Republican progressives. Democratic traditionalists voted overwhelmingly along ideological rather than party lines. The handful of Republican progressives broke about equally for and against, suggesting a stronger than usual tug for party regularity. Democratic centrists divided three to two in favor of continued controls. Of the thirty-two centrists who voted against controls, sixteen represented districts in the seven major oil-producing states (Texas, Louisiana, California, Oklahoma, Wyoming, New Mexico, and Alaska).

As authority for controls was about to lapse, Congress passed a bill extending controls for six months—which would lead to revival of the issue just as the 1976 presidential primaries were getting under way. Ford vetoed this legislation, but announced he would accept a forty-five-day extension, during which a compromise plan could be worked out, if his veto were sustained. On September 10, with controls already technically in limbo, the Senate defeated an effort to override Ford's veto by a vote of 61 to 39—6 less than the necessary two-thirds.

The distribution of the vote by ideological groups on the attempted override was as follows (a yes vote being a vote to override, and therefore to continue controls):[45]

Republicans	Yes	No		Democrats	Yes	No
Fundamentalists	0	16	Traditionalists		8	2
Stalwarts	1	9	Centrists		10	4
Moderates	0	4	Regulars		21	1
Progressives	6	3	Liberals		15	0
Total	7	32	Total		54	7

Democratic solidarity on the move to override extended even to the Democratic traditionalists, perhaps because both parties viewed the vote as having tactical bearing on the coming presidential election, or perhaps because the current unpopularity of the oil companies caused even conservative Democrats like Senators Allen, McClellan, Talmadge, and Stennis to avoid appearing to take their side. (A month later, an amendment to break up the big oil companies through vertical divestiture lost in the Senate by a vote of only 45 to 54. Earlier in 1975, Congress had revoked the famous oil depletion allowance, except for small producers, which the industry had enjoyed since 1926.) The four Democratic centrists and one regular (Gravel of Alaska) who voted to sustain the president's veto all represented one of the seven major oil-producing states. The Republican party line also held firm, except for one stalwart (Cotton of New Hampshire, where alarm over the price increases that were expected to follow decontrol was particularly strong) and six of the nine progressives. Of the four Republicans elected from New England, all but one (Weicker of Connecticut) voted to override the veto.

On September 26 Congress cleared a temporary extension of controls to November 15, which Ford, true to his promise, signed. When no bill had been produced by the middle of November, the administration and congressional leaders agreed to one last temporary extension to December 15.

On December 17, two days before adjournment, Congress finally sent to the president a compromise energy bill, rolling back all domestic oil prices to an average of no more than $7.66 a barrel, substantially below current market levels for new oil (which Nixon had decontrolled), but giving the president authority to carry out gradual decontrol over a forty-month period. Simon strongly urged Ford to veto the bill, thereby, since statutory authority for controls had once more expired, ending all price controls on oil for the first time since August 15, 1971. Zarb, on the other hand, having represented the administration in negotiations with congressional leaders over the final compromise, recommended that the bill be signed. A veto, Zarb pointed out, would set up another confrontation with Congress in 1976, and quite possibly produce a less acceptable bill. "Phased deregulation," he argued, was "better than no deregulation at all." In addition, Zarb maintained, the bill contained other desirable provisions, such as its grant of emergency powers to the president in the event of another foreign oil embargo, which on balance warranted its approval.[46]

On December 22 Ford announced that he would sign the bill. The secretary of the treasury was outraged. The decision, Simon believed, was "the worst error of the Ford administration," ideologically inconsistent and economically indefensible. "After long years of battling for a sensible energy policy," he later wrote, "Ford caved in. . . . It may have got him a few votes in New Hampshire, but it lost him a great deal of moral support in his own party and was in part responsible for the conservative rebellion against him."[47]

Be that as it may, Ford and Zarb were able to carry out a good deal of deregulation during 1976 under the terms of the 1975 compromise. In succeeding "energy actions," the FEA sent Congress plans to end price controls on residual fuel oil, home heating oil, diesel fuel, and naphtha jet fuel. The 1975 act gave Congress power to block such actions through majority vote by either house within fifteen days. None of the administration's deregulation plans, however, was turned down, Congress apparently being prepared to accept decontrol so long as no positive action on its part was needed. By the end of 1976, more than half the products of a barrel of fuel oil had been decontrolled—without any significant price increases, according to the FEA.[48]

On January 19, 1977, the day before leaving office, Ford submitted a final energy action to end controls on gasoline, which, had it taken effect, would have almost completed deregulation. This action, however, was quickly rescinded by the incoming administration, and the stage cleared for yet another round of presidential proposals and congressional intransigence on the issue of controls.

The Natural Gas Problem

The economic arguments for deregulating natural gas were even stronger than those for decontrolliing oil prices. Natural gas, which in 1973 supplied 31 percent of all American energy consumption (against 42 percent from petroleum, 18 percent from coal, and 9 percent from other sources),[49] came under controls in the first place almost by accident. In 1954 the Supreme Court ruled that the 1938 Natural Gas Act gave authority to the Federal Power Commission (FPC) to establish a "just and reasonable price" for natural gas sold in interstate commerce—while leaving gas sold within the state in which it was produced free to be sold at market prices. Congress promptly moved to overturn the Supreme Court decision. In 1956, legislation to deregulate the price of natural gas, supported by the Eisenhower administration, passed both houses. During the debate in the Senate, however, Senator Francis Case, Republican of South Dakota, disclosed that he had been offered what he interpreted as a bribe of $2,500 by a lobbyist for the natural gas companies to vote for the bill. Eisenhower, denouncing the "arrogant" gas lobby, vetoed the bill, so there would be no "doubt among the American people concerning the integrity of governmental processes." As a result, regulation of natural gas was locked into place.[50]

By 1975 the average price permitted by the FPC for newly discovered natural gas was 57 cents a thousand cubic feet, whereas the average market price at which gas was sold within the gas-producing states was $1.40 a thousand cubic feet—a difference of 145 percent! Predictably, producers sold as much gas as possible in the intrastate markets. By 1970 two-thirds of natural gas reserves were dedicated to intrastate sales.[51] The result was shortages in regions with little internally produced natural gas, especially New England. Perhaps partly because federal price controls discouraged exploration for new sources of supply, natural gas reserves in the United States fell 20 percent from 1967 to 1973.[52]

In April 1973 Nixon, having observed the decline in gas reserves, proposed decontrol, except for gas sold in interstate commerce under existing contracts. Congress, however, took no action.

Shortly after his inauguration in 1974, Ford repeated Nixon's proposal, warning that the decline in reserves was approaching a perilous level. Congress, fearful that decontrol would bring steep price rises in non-gas-producing states, still did not act.

Finally, in September 1975 the Senate Democratic leadership, alarmed by predictions that natural gas would be in short supply during the coming winter, placed on the Senate calendar, without going through committee, an emergency measure to permit partial decontrol for a 180-day period. When this bill reached the floor late in September, Senators James Pearson, moderate Republican of Kansas, and Lloyd Bentsen, centrist Democrat of Texas, offered an amendment, supported by the administration, calling for permanent deregulation of most natural gas by the end of April 1976. Still resisting permanent decontrol, the Democratic leadership moved on October 2 to kill the Pearson-Bentsen amendment. This motion was defeated by a vote of 45 to 50. The Senate then went on to pass the entire bill by a vote of 58 to 32—the first legislation passed by either house for deregulation of natural gas since 1956.[53]

The distribution of the vote by ideological groups on the leadership attempt to kill the Pearson-Bentsen amendment was as follows (a yes vote being a vote to kill the amendment and therefore to continue controls):[54]

Republicans			Democrats		
	Yes	No		Yes	No
Fundamentalists	0	16	Traditionalists	1	9
Stalwarts	0	9	Centrists	6	7
Moderates	0	4	Regulars	21	0
Progressives	5	4	Liberals	12	1
Total	5	33	Total	40	17

The Senate divided on the issue largely on ideological lines, with party loyalty and sectional economic interests exerting some cross-cutting effects. As on the issue of decontrolling oil, Republican moderates lined up solidly with the administration, and a high proportion of progressives (Weicker, Percy, Mathias, and Hatfield) also took the side of deregulation. The one Democratic liberal (Tunney of California) and four of the seven centrists who voted on the side of deregulation represented major natural gas–producing states.

The House took no action on deregulation until February 1976, when a bill was passed lifting controls on small producers, but actually broadening regulation of the major producers by extending controls to intrastate as well as interstate gas. Proponents of decontrol in the Senate resisted going to conference because they feared that Senate conferees would accept the House approach, and the bill died at the end of the 1976 session.[55]

Rockefeller's Proposal

Deregulation of oil and natural gas would provide market incentives that might temporarily increase available domestic energy supplies. Permanent solution or even adequate short-run response to the nation's energy problem, however, would require some combination of improved conservation techniques, expanded use of nuclear energy or coal, production of synthetic fuels from oil shale or liquefied coal, and development of new technologies to utilize the energies of the sun, the winds, the tides, or the earth's internal heat. But many of these longer-run approaches were either so costly or so economically risky that private industry was hesitant about taking them on. (An additional factor, according to some enthusiasts for solar heating and other new technologies, was that banks and corporations with large economic stakes in conventional fuels were resisting deployment of innovative approaches.) At the same time, most governmental decisionmakers, in both parties, opposed direct government involvement in energy production.

Seeking a way around this dilemma, Vice-President Rockefeller in 1975 submitted to the president a plan for creating a $100 billion government corporation, which he called the Energy Independence Authority (EIA), to provide loans and guarantees over a ten-year period to private companies engaged in developing new domestic energy sources. "The American enterprise system," Rockefeller later told a congressional committee, "has shown itself to be the most efficient and capable producer in the world. By providing financial assistance to take those risks which are beyond the capacity of the private sector, the Government would act as a catalyst in getting the energy independence program into motion."[56]

Shortly after Rockefeller's plan was presented to the president, Rumsfeld circulated it for comment among the administration's top economic policymakers. Responses ranged from passionate opposition to prudent ambiguity. To Secretary of the Treasury Simon, the EIA was "a gargantuan welfare boondoggle for the energy industries, lifted right out of the taxpayer's wallet, an inflationary scheme that would additionally put serious strains on the capital markets."[57] CEA Chairman Greenspan warned that the scope of the proposed corporation would be "virtually unconstrained."[58] OMB Director Lynn was also strongly negative. William Seidman and Rogers Morton saw both strengths and weaknesses in the plan. Frank Zarb, according to an account written for the *Wall Street Journal* by Dennis Farney, "was an enigma . . . seeming to oppose the scheme on some occasions, seeming to support it on others."[59]

Rockefeller accused Rumsfeld, the latter has recalled, of "trying to sandbag the idea" before it got off the ground. "The truth is," Rumsfeld has said, "that the president himself asked me to circulate the proposal, so naturally I did. . . . It seemed natural to me that the people who would have to budget for such an agency and the people who would have to testify on it before Congress should be given an opportunity to comment on it before it was proposed by the president. I thought the president should be exposed to many different points of view before making up his mind." Rumsfeld himself opposed the EIA, partly, he has said, because he was concerned that association with such a grandiose scheme would cause the president political embarrassment.[60]

Despite the strong disapproval of some of his chief advisers, Ford on September 22, 1975 (as it happened, the day on which he was shot at by an eccentric woman named Sara Jane Moore outside the St. Francis Hotel in San Francisco), proposed the EIA, in a speech before the AFL-CIO Building and Construction Trades convention, as a means to "stimulate economic growth" and to "give us control over our own destiny."[61]

Ford has explained his decision to go for the EIA on the ground that it offered a means to promote energy research and development without much immediate impact on the budget.[62] (Three-quarters of the corporation's $100 billion was to be raised through government-financed bonds; the remainder would be made available through appropriation as needed to cover defaults.) It seems likely that the EIA appealed to Ford—somewhat as the family assistance plan had appealed to Nixon—as a way to make a splash for an administration that, partly because of budgetary constraints, had up to that time made few positive recommendations for dealing with domestic problems. Rockefeller's determined and enthusiastic advocacy also no doubt influenced the president's judgment. (During discussion of the proposal within the administration, one of Ford's conservative economic advisers reportedly said at one point: "Mr. Vice President, there is not one redeeming feature in your plan." Rockefeller cheerily replied: "Glad to have you aboard.")[63] And it may be that the president, as some of his aides have speculated, simply felt that it was time for the vice-president "to win one."

Some of the administration's policymakers who fought the EIA while it was under consideration at the White House dropped their opposition after the president announced his decision. James Lynn, for instance, has said: "It is my philosophy to fight like hell before the president takes a position, but once the president has decided, to go along with the team and try to sell the administration's position— or, if I can't do that—to resign."[64] But others, particularly Simon, made no secret of their continued opposition. Rockefeller later said: "I welcomed opposition within the White House while the president was making up his mind. A free exchange of views should lead to the best possible judgment. But when the president has made his decision, he should have been able to count on support from the entire administration. At that point, any one who feels he cannot support the president's decision should resign. But it didn't work out that way."[65] In October Rockefeller publicly suggested that Simon leave the administration if he could not support the EIA. But Ford, perhaps taken aback by the fire storm of criticism from both liberals and conservatives that the proposal had raised, had by then decided not to push for its enactment. Rumsfeld has recalled: "The president finally decided to send the Energy Independence Authority to Congress. But he never actively supported it—at least, not so far as I know."[66]

Many conservatives opposed the EIA on the grounds that it was "simply the first step on an energy equivalent to the Post Office" (regarded as a notorious bureaucratic wasteland), and that it would siphon out of the economy "enormous amounts of capital that are badly needed for other purposes." Liberals regarded it as a "giant rip-off" for the energy companies that would be eligible for the loans.[67] The EIA, Senator Edward Kennedy charged, would subsidize big business "without any evidence that these rich profits can be justified by benefits in other ways to the American economy."[68] Even some of those who were supposed to benefit from the alleged "rip-offs" had strong reservations. The American Petroleum Institute, representing the oil industry, announced: "We share the concern of economic experts . . . who have cautioned against the inflationary and other adverse economic impacts that could evolve from a government-financed and backed program on the magnitude of $100 billion."[69]

After the "second energy shock," following the Iranian revolution in 1979, proposals similar to the EIA were revived both within the Congress and by the administration. But in 1976, with shortages temporarily in remission, the idea attracted few supporters. "The administration did not give the idea strong support," Rockefeller later said. "But even if it had, Congress was not then in the mood to accept a proposal of that kind."[70]

A Cutting Issue

During most of Nixon's tenure, ideology had relatively little effect on the administration's energy policy. Though theoretically opposed to price regulation, Nixon initiated controls on the price of petroleum as part of his overall price control program in 1971, and continued them in modified form in 1974. The Nixon administration made no effort to do away with controls on natural gas before 1973. Up to the time of the Arab oil embargo, such opposition to controls as existed came mainly from conservative economists and publicists and from elected representatives of the oil- and gas-producing states.

Under Ford's presidency, however, the fight to end price controls on oil and gas was carried on mainly along ideological and party lines—which in these cases were unusually similar—except among representatives from areas where economic interests were heavily on one side or the other. Ford, supported by most Republicans in Congress, pushed for decontrol, to promote consumer conservation and increase supply. There was debate within the administration, and among Republicans generally, over the political feasibility of wiping out controls with one bold stroke, as the ideological purists recommended. But on the desirability of doing away with controls completely in a relatively short time, there was practically no disagreement. Democrats in Congress, on the other hand, except those representing the major oil- and gas-producing states, and some southern traditionalists, overwhelmingly favored continuing controls, and indeed rolling back prices below current levels, on the grounds that decontrol would push up inflation, further increase the "obscene" profits being reaped by the giant oil companies, and cause extreme hardship among the poor, particularly those who had to drive to their jobs.

Why did the struggle over controls become more ideological under Ford than it had been under Nixon? There were four main reasons. First, Ford was instinctively more of a free-market true believer than his predecessor had been (though not so much so—or at least not so willing to proceed without concern for the political costs—as Simon or Greenspan). Second, the shortages of oil and gas, and growing dependence on Middle East oil, made the economic and national security costs of controls seem heavier and more obvious, at least to conservatives. Third, rival constituency groups exerted increasing pressure on political representatives who had received their support: the oil companies, and other business groups with economic interests in decontrol, on Republicans and conservatives; the labor unions and consumer groups, which favored continuation of controls, on Democrats and liberals. Finally—and perhaps most important—the issue, once Ford had defined it sharply (though he later smudged it again somewhat as the political stakes rose), brought into play differing beliefs about the way the economic system works and about social justice, which are among the fundamental distinctions between contemporary conservatives and liberals.

Conservatives were convinced that controls, by forcing producers to sell their goods for prices below what the market would bring, had the inevitable effects of drying up supply, misallocating resources, and creating artificial and unnecessary shortages. Domestic oil shortages, moreover, helped lead to potentially disastrous dependence on Middle Eastern suppliers. If controls were lifted, conservatives conceded, prices would rise. But this would moderate demand by discouraging uneconomic consumption and motivate domestic producers to increase supply, which in turn would eliminate shortages and perhaps end up balancing the market at prices not much above controlled levels.

Candid conservatives were prepared to admit that decontrol would enable the oil companies to make a lot more money, and would cause some hardship among low-income earners, who would be forced not only to use their resources more carefully but also to curtail some forms of consumption that most Americans regard as necessities. Indeed, if decontrol did not have these effects, it could not achieve the results that conservatives were aiming for: if the oil companies did not make more money, they would not be motivated to seek and develop new sources of supply; if consumption were not discouraged, inevitably including some consumption among the poor, pressure on available supply would not be relaxed. Enrichment of the oil companies and discomfort among low-income consumers could to some extent be moderated by "windfall" profit taxes and tax cuts or direct subsidies to consumers. But these would represent further tinkering with the market mechanism, which would perhaps be justifiable on social policy grounds, but which always involves some economic costs and therefore should be employed with restraint.[71]

The fact that decontrol would make the oil companies richer did not cause most conservatives grave concern. The economic system envisioned by conservatives depends for its motivating force on material rewards and punishments. If these are not real—if there are not real winners and real losers—the system will not work. Persons (or companies) efficiently producing goods for which the system has established high demand can expect to prosper beyond their fellows—sometimes far beyond. But everybody who shares in the output of the system will ultimately benefit—even the poor (those whose skills or goods are in low demand), who, though they will always have relatively less than the more efficient or more fortunate, will gradually be able to increase their absolute consumption as the system's total output expands.

Conservatives regard this state of affairs either as inherently just (increased rewards for increased production), or, if perhaps not particularly just in its distribution of rewards and punishments (the rich and poor after all not being wholly responsible for their respective conditions), as economically efficient (producing more goods for everybody) and morally superior to any other system so far devised for a large-scale society. Human nature being what it is and the world at best imperfect, conservatives argue, every large society will distribute its rewards unevenly. Under a market system this distribution reflects the successes or failures of free individuals (free in the sense of being unhampered by government coercion) pursuing economic incentives. In all other known systems distribution is carried out on the basis of assigned status, established, in the last resort, by force.

The intrusion of the OPEC cartel into the market, conservatives admitted, disrupted the normal interchange between supply and demand for petroleum. But the sensible response to OPEC was not to establish artificial restraints over domestic oil prices, which had the effect of driving domestic supply off the market, but rather to leave the market free to develop incentives for increased domestic production. As an additional remedy, reluctantly accepted, the flow of high-priced imports might be inhibited through trade barriers, preferably a levy on imports of the kind proposed by Ford in his 1975 State of the Union message.

Liberals saw matters differently.[72] For liberals, the market may be a useful economic tool for allocating some goods and providing incentives. But when the market rewards some individuals or companies exorbitantly or causes other individuals undeserved hardship—particularly when such effects have been produced by unnatural forces like OPEC—its operations must be brought into conformance with the dictates of social policy. The aim of social policy, most contemporary liberals believe, should be movement toward a more equitable distribution of economic and social benefits, based on the standard of rough equality among individuals, with some provision for added rewards for extra effort, special training, unusually difficult jobs, years of service, and redress to correct the effects of past inequalities of treatment. Liberals, too, recognize that the world is by nature imperfect, and would not go so far as, for instance, socialists in suppressing natural differences to achieve forced equality. But when the market produces or is likely to produce extreme disparities—as would result, it was held, from the sale of oil or natural gas at market prices—these must be corrected through intervention by government. If such intervention is met by recalcitrant behavior by private interests—as many liberals (and many ordinary citizens, according to public opinion polls) believed the oil companies were doing in allegedly holding back their product to wait for higher prices—the system is headed toward a constitutional crisis, which the private interests would be well advised to avoid.

Underlying the liberals' attitude toward the market is a rather vaguely held form of the old medieval belief that there exists a "fair price" for any given product, justified by the material costs, effort, and perhaps risk that go into its production. If the market price greatly exceeds the "fair price," government intervention may well be warranted. For conservatives, the fair price for goods exchanged in a genuinely free market is simply the price established through interplay of supply and demand: goods are worth whatever consumers are willing to pay for them in a competitive market. (Most conservatives concede that the market may be rigged through monopoly, which government must therefore either break up, or, when this is impossible as in the case of most utilities, regulate. But the domestic oil and natural gas industries are not controlled by monopolies or even, by most definitions, oligopolies.) One of the great merits of the market system, its proponents claim, is that it removes the question of price from the subjective influences necessarily affecting any abstract estimate of "fairness."

In the political context established by conflicting conservative and liberal beliefs in the middle of the 1970s, Vice-President Rockefeller's proposal for a government-backed corporation to make loans to companies developing new energy techniques was an ideological nonstarter. Conservatives regarded the idea as an unjustified intrusion into the market system, and liberals distrusted its linkage of private profit to public welfare. At some earlier times—and perhaps at a later one—the Energy Independence Authority might have found its way onto either conservative or liberal agendas. But during Ford's presidency, both sides were tacking toward strict construction of ideological principles. Rockefeller's personal political situation and association in the public mind of his energy plan with the kind of grandiose spending schemes that were currently causing fiscal difficulties for both New York City and New York State probably contributed to the hostile response given to the EIA. But even if these added handicaps had not existed, it was probably true, as Rockefeller suggested, that the political system was "not then in the mood to accept a proposal of that kind."

Ideology powerfully influenced, though it did not by itself determine, both the Ford administration's energy policy and the responses offered to it by liberals in Congress. Ideological positions were compromised—hopelessly so in the views of purists on each side—to accommodate perceived political realities, and to meet concerns of politicians on both sides that national unity and the image of governmental effectiveness not be too deeply fractured. But both camps stuck stubbornly to the essentials of what they believed. The perhaps inevitable result, given the ideological gulf between the president and the majority in Congress, was the enactment of only short-run remedies and partial solutions, leaving important aspects of the energy problem for future presidents and future Congresses to resolve.

18

Economic Policy: Changing Direction

"AS WE CELEBRATE our Bicentennial and the success of our Revolution," Alan Greenspan wrote in a memorandum to some of his White House colleagues in November 1975, "we need to do more than merely revel in our accomplishments. We should use this period to take stock of where we stand as a people, how we got here, and what we can learn from our past to guide us in the years ahead."

Greenspan later felt that the fundamental stocktaking he recommended had not been fully carried out. But the desire he expressed for a return to neglected basic principles underlay much of what the Ford administration set out to accomplish—particularly in the crucial area of economic policy.

The Nixon administration had generally approached economic policy on the assumption that the mixed public and private economic system developed by and since the New Deal was basically sound, though liable to abuse when liberals controlled the governmental machinery. For Nixon and his economic advisers, the economic problem was essentially one of administration: through conservative management, they believed, a mixed system could be made to operate with reasonable efficiency for the public good. (Not all members of Nixon's economic team were so sanguine. But those who believed that more fundamental change was needed usually felt constrained, either by internal administration pressure or by their assessments of current political realities, to play down their misgivings.)

The Ford administration, by contrast, proceeded on the conviction that the mixed economic system in the form it had reached by the

382

middle of the 1970s was inherently, probably inevitably, predisposed to produce rising waves of inflation alternating with worsening troughs of recession, which would lead in the end to economic collapse, followed no doubt by some form of political repression. What was needed, therefore, was not merely prudent management of the role of government, but a return to the economic and social principles on which the republic had been founded.

"Our prosperity and greatness," Greenspan said in his memorandum, "have not come automatically or by accident. They are a consequence of a very solid foundation, our Constitution, and the inevitable progress that a free people will generate once government sets the legal framework through which citizens unencumbered by repressive government can flourish and prosper. . . . Starting in the 1930's, regrettably, a whole new approach to government and politics emerged, flowing from acceptance of a view that government should have a program to 'solve' every 'problem' identified by our society."

The tendency of this approach to expand government beyond what the economy can afford, Greenspan argued, was for some time restrained "by the prevailing view that the federal budget should generally be balanced, except in times of war." But with the coming of "the so-called New Economics of the 1960's," resistance to budget deficits became passé. As a result, there had been a "transfer payments explosion," quintupling domestic spending by the federal government from 1961 to 1975. "If we are to be honest with the American people," he warned, "we must end this game of making it appear that government can create benefits to some without imposing costs to others. . . . Somehow we must counter the idea that the 'federal government' is able to live outside the rules that apply to individuals and other institutions."

Secretary of the Treasury Simon was—characteristically—even more outspoken. "Americans did not turn their backs on reality 200 years ago," he said in a speech in San Francisco in the spring of 1976, "and there is less reason to do so today. . . . What is at stake is not just the future of this or that industry. At stake is the survival of the private sector, and the individual liberties which have never long survived the collapse of a society's free enterprise system."[1]

President Ford—also characteristically—instinctively thought of the administration's objectives in operational terms. "The fight against inflation," he said in an interview in 1978, "provided the basic theme of my administration."[2] Ford shared, though in more moderate terms, the belief of Greenspan, Simon, and other influential members of the administration that a basic change in national direction was needed to avoid economic and social disaster. "In the recent past," the president sternly recalled in his 1976 State of the Union address, "we sometimes forgot the sound principles that guided us through most of our history. . . . We unbalanced our economic system by the huge unprecedented growth of Federal expenditures and borrowing. And we were not totally honest with ourselves about how much these programs would cost and how we would pay for them." The time had come, Ford said, for "a fundamentally different approach"—a "new realism" in economic policy based on "the great principles upon which this Nation was founded."[3]

The Economic Policy Board

Ford took to economic policy with genuine relish. In college he had thought about becoming an economist, but had turned to the law as a better way to earn a good living. His years on the House Appropriations Committee had given him a firm grasp of the intricacies of the federal budget. As president, he enjoyed probing cabinet members about obscure details of the fiscal operations of their departments. His briefings of the press on the budget amazed OMB technicians, who claimed that he spoke as knowledgeably as they could have on each of their specialties. He liked fitting together the pieces of economic policy, somewhat as Nixon had enjoyed plotting international strategy. Moreover, he could not help finding some satisfaction, mixed with concern, in the way that current economic troubles seemed to confirm long-standing conservative warnings.

To help bring about the change in economic direction that he believed was necessary, Ford established a policymaking apparatus more broadly based than Nixon's had been. In place of Nixon's "triad" (the secretary of the treasury, the chairman of the Council of Economic Advisers, and the director of the Office of Management and Budget), Ford shortly after taking office set up the Economic Policy Board, designed by William Seidman, who had become his chief economic adviser while he was vice-president. The full board, which included all members of the cabinet except the attorney general and the secretary of defense, met about four times a year. The real policy-shaping body, however, was the board's executive committee, at first composed of the secretary of the treasury, the chairman of the CEA, the director of the OMB, the executive director of the Council on International Economic Policy, and Seidman. Other cabinet members were invited to participate in executive committee meetings when subjects affecting their departments were up for discussion. When Ford appointed John Dunlop secretary of labor early in 1975, Dunlop, a professional economist, insisted as a condition for taking the job that he be made a member of the executive committee. In June 1975 the committee was further expanded to include the secretary of state (Kissinger) and the secretary of commerce (Rogers Morton). Kissinger rarely attended meetings, but was represented by one of his deputies.[4]

Ford named Secretary of the Treasury Simon chairman of the Economic Policy Board, and Seidman its executive director. In practice, Simon left the development of the executive committee's agenda largely to Seidman and his assistant, Roger Porter. The executive committee met most weekday mornings at 8:30 in the Roosevelt Room (a conference room a few steps from the Oval Office). Under Seidman's guidance the committee functioned more as a forum for clarification and discussion of policy options than as an instrument for final decisionmaking. "We took a multiple advocacy approach," Seidman has said. "We did not try to achieve a consensus. All of the views represented at the committee meetings went in to the president as part of my summary. . . . The summary was circulated among members of the committee before I gave it to the president. Each member had the right to make corrections."[5] When there was disagreement within the committee, final decisions were made by the president, usually after a meeting with Seidman and the chief disputants.

Cabinet members found the board a useful means for advancing their particular interests. For instance, Carla Hills, secretary of HUD after March 1975, has recalled that if she could "get a split of, say, six [in favor] to two [against] from the Economic Policy Board, that would put me in a much stronger position when the issue went to the president."[6] William Coleman, secretary of transportation, discovered that he "could get more things done through Simon and Seidman's Economic Policy Board than through the Domestic Council."[7]

Opinion in the executive committee, though not monolithic, usually gathered around the conservative point of view represented by Simon and Greenspan. The secretary of the treasury and the chairman of the CEA did not always totally agree. Greenspan believed, for instance, that Simon rather overstated the immediate danger of federal government borrowing "crowding out" private capital needs.[8] As a rule, however, the two took common positions in favor of checking federal spending and reducing the role of government in the economy. OMB Director James Lynn, another influential figure on the executive committee, was also generally conservative, though he tended, according to one who participated in most of the committee meetings, to favor fiscal policies a few degrees more expansionary than those approved by Simon and Greenspan.

Arthur Burns, who was in his fifth year as chairman of the Federal Reserve when Ford became president, was kept informed about the policy board's agenda, and attended meetings of the executive committee when items that interested him were up for discussion. When present, Burns often took positions somewhat more liberal than those of the committee's majority. "Burns held the view that government should be the employer of last resort, which was not a very popular position in the Ford administration," Seidman has recalled. "He was also very interested in social issues. But at the same time he was a strong advocate of fiscal stability, which put him in basic agreement with the administration."[9] Among regular members of the executive committee, John Dunlop was most inclined toward more liberal positions. Burns and Dunlop were sometimes joined by Elliot Richardson after he was named secretary of commerce in November 1975. On issues touching their departments, Hills and Coleman were effective advocates for their constituencies. Seidman also sometimes argued that Simon and Greenspan were too rigid in their conservatism. "My approach," Seidman has said, "was more pragmatic, and in fact more political."[10]

However, the ideological spectrum represented on either the full board or the executive committee, from Simon and Greenspan on the right to Dunlop on the left, was not very wide. Richardson, Hills, and Coleman fully supported the administration's decision to bring unemployment down gradually in the 1975 recession rather than risk rekindling inflation. In Coleman's view: "While 7 percent unemployment was very bad, nevertheless it would not have been reasonable to take actions to help the 7 percent who were unemployed if those actions would have harmed the other 93 percent who were still holding jobs."[11] Even Dunlop's relative liberalism was muted by his agreement with the conservatives that increased private capital formation was the best way to create more jobs.[12]

"The Ford administration was philosophically fairly homogeneous," Greenspan has said, "which was not a bad thing. There is a strong argument to be made that the people around the president should have a common philosophy, and that their philosophy should be close to that of the president—provided the president is kept in touch with a wide range of opinion from outside the administration."[13] According to one who participated in the work of the Economic Policy Board: "There were no deep differences of the kind that I have heard occurred in the Nixon administration between George Shultz and John Connally."

In Greenspan's opinion Seidman probably had more influence on economic matters with the president than anybody else, because "Ford had known him the longest and trusted his judgment."[14] According to most other members of the administration's inner circle, the adviser who contributed most to shaping the president's decision was Greenspan himself.[15]

Greenspan's Thesis

Greenspan, like Simon, had achieved substantial success in the New York money markets. The personal styles of the two men, however, were very different: Greenspan, reserved and scholarly; Simon, pugnacious and flamboyant. Early in the Ford administration, Simon developed an antagonistic relationship with Donald Rumsfeld, whom he believed coveted his job.[16] (At various times, Rockefeller, Kissinger, and Simon all believed that Rumsfeld was out to replace them.) The secretary of the treasury also let it be known through the press when he disagreed with administration policy. Greenspan, by contrast, was the classic insider: he attached himself almost as a crony to Rumsfeld, whom he correctly identified as the likely winner in the struggle for power within the White House; and made himself indispensable to the president and Rumsfeld (and later to Richard Cheney) through his ability to respond quickly to requests for politically relevant economic facts and arguments.

During the hearings on Greenspan's confirmation as chairman of the CEA in August 1974, considerable fuss was made over his association with Ayn Rand, a philosopher-novelist and New York right-wing cult figure. Rand espoused a Nietzschean survival-of-the-fittest brand of individualism.[17] Greenspan recalled that before he met Rand in New York in the 1950s, he had been "a free enterpriser in the Adam Smith sense—impressed with the theoretical structure and efficiency of markets," but that she had led him to realize that "capitalism is not only efficient and practical but also moral." His philosophic views, Greenspan acknowledged, led him to oppose antitrust laws and the progressive income tax, which he regarded as limitations on competition and freedom. But these opinions, he said, would not affect his performance with the CEA, which he regarded primarily as a staff agency providing the president with "research" and information on "basic economics."[18]

Greenspan's actual role in the administration turned out to go far beyond "research" or "basic economics." More than anyone else, including Simon, who was more an evangelist than a conceptualizer, Greenspan gave an underlying intellectual texture to the administration's economic policies. His social attitudes seemed closer to those of his old teacher at Columbia, Arthur Burns, than to the timber-wolf ideology identified with Ayn Rand. Like Burns (and, for that matter, like Adam Smith), he recognized the need for government in a complex industrial society to fill some social needs. Where he differed from Burns was in setting a lower limit on the responsibilities that government could safely undertake without endangering the health of the general economy.

Greenspan's basic thesis was that government spending was growing more rapidly than the total national economy, thereby causing high taxes and contributing to inflation by creating greater "entitlements" (rights to income) than there were goods to purchase. If permitted to continue unchecked, Greenspan argued, this rate of increase would lead ultimately to government control of the entire economy.

Stated in the simplistic form that was sometimes used by administration spokesmen in political speeches, this argument had some apparent flaws, which were quickly pointed out by liberals. *Federal* government outlays as a percentage of GNP had grown only from 18.5 percent in 1960 to 19.8 percent in 1974. During the same period federal debt as a percentage of GNP actually declined from 58.5 to 35.7. In 1975 federal outlays did jump to 22.4 percent of GNP—but this was chiefly due to the recession, which liberals argued was caused in part by conservative economic policies.[19] State and local government expenditures had risen somewhat more rapidly, going from 12 percent of GNP in 1960 to 17.6 percent in 1975, which might in part be attributable, as conservatives claimed, to lures held out by federal programs. But this growth, too, by the middle of the 1970s seemed to have leveled off.[20] *Total* government revenues in 1975 took 30 percent of gross domestic product in the United States,· a lower percentage than in most of the European democracies—not only Sweden (46 percent) and Britain (37 percent), but also France (37 percent) and West Germany (35 percent)—though a higher one than in Japan (20 percent).[21]

Going behind these figures, Greenspan was able to show that the slow growth of overall federal expenditures as a percentage of GNP during the previous fifteen years concealed a trend that, he claimed, threatened in the near future to drive the share of total national product taken by government far beyond acceptable limits. Although total spending had been relatively stable in relation to GNP, Greenspan pointed out, spending on social service programs like medicare, medicaid, and food stamps had been going up much faster than general economic growth. The expansion of these programs had been financed out of reductions in the defense budget (figured in constant dollars). From 1960 to 1975, spending on "human resources" programs rose from 5.1 percent to 11.7 percent of GNP. During those same years, military spending as a share of GNP fell from 9.3 to 5.9 percent.[22] In 1956, Greenspan reported, social service programs accounted for 17 percent of the federal budget; by fiscal 1976, they took 55 percent of all federal outlays.[23] Paul O'Neill, deputy director of OMB and Greenspan's close intellectual collaborator, pointed out that in 1971 federal expenditures for transfer payments and grants to state and local governments had for the first time exceeded the federal government's expenditures for its own goods and services—which meant, O'Neill contended, that in that year "the federal government's predominant business became the transfer of income and wealth between individuals and institutions."[24]

The time had come, Greenspan and his colleagues argued, when further growth of social service programs could no longer be paid for by spending less on defense. Indeed, if Congress accepted the president's recommendation to increase the defense budget, either the trend toward increasing expenditures on "entitlement" programs would have to be turned back, or government would inevitably take a rapidly increasing share of total GNP. "It is quite apparent," Greenspan said in a speech to the Missouri Industrial Development Conference on March 23, 1976, "that unless we as a country are willing to allow real defense expenditures to continue to decline or are willing to raise taxes we cannot continue to expand 'entitlement' programs at anywhere near past rates."

Given a choice framed in these terms, Ford had no difficulty determining where he stood. The chickens that conservative prophets had long been expecting were at last coming home to roost. The president saw it as his duty to apply conservative corrective remedies—though not so quickly or so broadly as some of his advisers prescribed. Inflation, Ford was convinced, was the nation's number-one domestic enemy. The first and most essential step in conquering inflation, he believed, was for government to break the trend toward increased spending on social programs. Achieving this goal would be made more difficult, he soon discovered, by the onset of the worst recession to hit the American economy since the Great Depression of the 1930s.

Fighting Inflation and Recession

When Ford entered the presidency in August 1974, most economists were predicting that the recession then expected would be relatively mild. Economic production in the third quarter, in constant dollars, was slowing at a somewhat lower rate than it had during the first two quarters.[25] Unemployment in August rose to 5.5 percent—not much higher than it had been running during most of the year.[26] "I did not perceive [in September]," Greenspan recalled in 1978, "the extent of the recession that was to break on us within a few months. I was concerned that inventories were high, and I said publicly that the economy would be vulnerable if it were not for the continued demand for capital goods. In July [before joining the administration] I had predicted a mild recession, but I did not expect it to be as severe as it turned out to be. Some economists now say that they were calling for tax cuts at the time. But these were the people who are always calling for tax cuts, so they really do not deserve any more credit for foreseeing the extent of the recession than the rest of us. Once the recession got under way, I had a clear understanding of what was going on in the economy. But that is different from being able to foresee it in advance."[27]

The economic danger that everyone agreed was growing at the end of summer was inflation. During the first eight months of the year, the economy had entered the frightening area of double-digit inflation for the first time since the 1940s.[28]

On September 23 Ford presided in Washington over a "summit conference" on inflation (called for in his first speech to Congress in August), which was attended by leading economists, members of Congress, and administration officials. Each of the economists spoke in his accustomed vein: John Kenneth Galbraith proposed returning to wage and price controls; Milton Friedman recommended indexation of federal tax rates to reflect the effects of inflation; Arthur Okun suggested that workers be motivated to restrain wage demands through enactment of a tax credit to offset real wage losses due to inflation; and so forth.[29]

After pondering these and other suggestions, Ford proceeded on October 8 to propose an orthodox conservative program, including a one-year, 5 percent surcharge on corporate taxes and personal income taxes for families with incomes over $15,000, and a cut in federal spending to bring expenditures for the year below $300 billion ($4.4 billion less than Nixon's last budget and far below the actual rate of current spending being authorized by Congress). Since these recommendations were soon overtaken by events, Ford's October 8 speech was best remembered for his suggestion that concerned citizens begin wearing WIN ("Whip Inflation Now") buttons[30]—an idea that Robert Hartmann's rivals never permitted Hartmann or the president to forget originated in the White House speechwriting shop.

In the fourth quarter of 1974, GNP suddenly fell 7.5 percent in constant dollars (compared with a drop of 2.3 percent the quarter before). Unemployment rose to 6.7 percent in November and to 7.2 percent in December.[31] "We are going to be in serious economic trouble in the next four to six months," Greenspan told Ford in the Oval Office in December 1974. "You are going to be under very heavy pressure to open up the taps and let federal money flow out to try to spend our way out of the recession." Greenspan conceded that some stimulation was required, but said that heavy additional spending would be "very shortsighted," leading inevitably to more inflation, which in time would produce an even deeper recession. Ford said that he thoroughly agreed. "It took a great deal of guts on Ford's part," Greenspan said later, "but he stuck to that decision, which laid the basis for the stable recovery that followed."[32]

In his 1975 State of the Union message to Congress, Ford reported: "The state of the union is not good." To help overcome the recession, the president recommended, in place of his proposal for a tax surcharge a few months before, a $16 billion tax cut: $12 billion in rebates to individual income tax payers, and $4 billion to business. To offset the increased federal deficit that would result from the tax cut, Ford proposed a moratorium on new federal programs, except for energy, and a ceiling on domestic spending.[33]

Congress responded, as unemployment rose toward a May peak of 8.9 percent, by pushing through appropriations for domestic programs far in excess of those called for by Ford, and enacting a $22.8 billion tax cut—$6.8 billion more than the president had asked for. Through use of the veto (as was described in chapter 15), Ford was able to turn back some of the appropriations increases. Federal outlays for fiscal 1976 nevertheless ended up $17 billion above what the administration had proposed.[34]

In October Ford, clearly aiming to turn the Democrats' flank on the tax-cut issue, while at the same time promoting fiscal economy, suddenly proposed a permanent tax reduction of $28 billion ($16 billion more than would result from a Democratic plan to extend the 1975 tax cut beyond its scheduled expiration date at the end of December), provided that Congress agree to a $395 billion ceiling on expenditures for fiscal 1977. The recommendation of a combined reduction in taxes and a curb on spending was regarded as a great budgetary and political coup by the administration leaders who had worked it out over a period of several months—principally Ford, Rumsfeld, Lynn, O'Neill, Greenspan, and Cheney.

"We set out in a very methodical way," James Lynn has recalled, "to look at everything the federal government does, and to make cuts wherever we legitimately could. We worked in secret. . . . I was very proud that there were no leaks out of OMB on the work we were doing. . . . We could have gone even deeper, but I think the president was right to feel that there were only so many interest groups that we could take on at any one time. The cuts we proposed were both reasonable and politically realistic. . . . We were not totally pure. The Energy Independence Authority, which I opposed as long as it was under consideration by the president, was certainly not a conservative program. Also, there were some things that the president felt he had to do for middle-income people, for Middle America . . . [like] his proposal for new housing assistance, and his endorsement of a tax credit for college education . . . that violated his philosophy of fiscal conservatism. . . . But in general the president stuck to his philosophy of cutting taxes after the government had met its essential spending needs. . . . There was much less pragmatism in the Ford administration than there had been under Nixon, much less concern about whether or not something would go over in Peoria."[35]

In December, with the fight over decontrol of oil prices also approaching a climax, the administration and Congress headed toward confrontation on the tax-cut issue. On December 16—the day before passing the energy bill—Congress cleared a six-month extension of the 1975 tax cut, but without the ceiling on expenditures that Ford had demanded. (Democratic leaders in Congress took the position that approval of Ford's mandatory ceiling on spending would undercut Congress's own new budgetary procedures, in operation for the first time in 1975.) On December 17 Ford vetoed the tax cut, warning that the lack of an accompanying ceiling on expenditures would leave "the Federal cash register wide open for whatever spending Congress wants to take out in an election year."[36] The following day the House sustained Ford's veto by a vote of 265 to 157—17 fewer votes in favor of the override than the necessary two-thirds.

The distribution of the vote by ideological groups on the attempted veto override was as follows (a yes vote being a vote to override, and therefore to put into effect the tax cut without the ceiling on expenditures called for by the president):[37]

Republicans			Democrats		
	Yes	No		Yes	No
Fundamentalists	0	70	Traditionalists	18	25
Stalwarts	8	40	Centrists	70	6
Moderates	4	11	Regulars	100	1
Progressives	7	4	Liberals	58	0
Total	19	125	Total	246	32

The Democratic leadership had been counting on attracting a considerable number of Republicans, fearful of voter resentment if the tax cut were lost, to vote for the override. In the showdown, however, the overwhelming majority of Republicans stood by the administration—either out of party loyalty or out of belief that the president was right in demanding fiscal restraint. Even so, the administration would have lost without the help it received from Democratic traditionalists, who presumably were voting their ideological convictions.

On the same night that the president's veto was sustained, with adjournment only hours away, Russell Long negotiated compromise language on the expenditure ceiling with Republican congressional leaders and Joe Waggonner, representing the conservative Democrats. "Neither the President nor Congress," Long suggested, "wants to be accused of being the grinch that stole Christmas."[38] On the following day both houses voted overwhelmingly to pass the compromise bill, which included the same tax cut that Ford had vetoed, plus a vaguely worded commitment by Congress to seek a "reduction in the level of spending" if tax revenues declined in fiscal 1977. Though the compromise language hardly met the president's stated criteria, Ford agreed to sign the bill, and so, according to Long, put "Santa Claus back in his sleigh."[39]

During 1976 Congress showed little disposition to stay within the expenditure limit Ford had proposed, and the battle of the vetoes resumed. In the end, outlays for fiscal 1977 amounted to $402.7 billion—$8.5 billion more than had been requested by Ford, but $10.4 billion less than was authorized by Congress.[40] "I soon realized," Greenspan has said, "that dealing with Congress on the budget was essentially a labor negotiation. Whatever the president proposed, Congress was bound to add to. If you wanted to stay anywhere near expenditure levels that were sound and sensible, you had to start with a position that was considerably below what you wanted. There is no doubt in my mind that the budget cuts we recommended in the fall of 1975 fended off much heavier expenditures by Congress, which, if they had been enacted, would have seriously increased inflation and led to renewal of the recession."[41] Ford himself has said that he "sincerely hoped" that Congress would approve his 1977 budget as submitted, but that he had "realistic doubts that Congress would bite the bullet to make all the cuts" he recommended.[42]

Common-Situs Picketing

Along with the tax cut, the energy bill, and the prohibition against further aid to anti-Marxist forces in Angola passed by the Senate, Congress at the end of 1975 left Ford a bill legalizing so-called common-situs picketing, which would permit unions to picket an entire construction site in a dispute involving only a single contractor—a practice prohibited by the Supreme Court in 1951. Vigorously promoted by organized labor, and just as vigorously resisted by organized business, the proposed legalization of common-situs picketing had become not simply an economic issue but an ideological shibboleth, arousing deeply held concerns and grievances on both sides.

The previous summer John Dunlop believed he had worked out an agreement, under which the contracting industry would accept legalization of common-situs picketing in return for approval by the unions of a statutory prohibition against wildcat strikes. The issue, Ford later said, "was not adequately staffed out by the [White House] West Wing."[43] The president, who placed great confidence in his secretary of labor, and was then hoping to receive some support in 1976 from the building trades unions, committed himself, through Dunlop, to sign the bill if it were passed by Congress.[44]

By December, however, the construction industry had retreated from the agreement. Most segments of the business community and all shades of conservative activists joined to demand rejection of the bill. More than 700,000 communications poured into the White House, most of them urging a veto.[45] "Ford really had no choice," John Marsh later said. "The sentiment in his national constituency was so strong that he just could not go in the face of it."[46] The president, moreover, no longer could count on a secure conservative base: a Gallup poll released on December 12 showed Ronald Reagan favored by 40 percent of Republicans for the 1976 presidential nomination, and Ford by only 32 percent.[47]

On December 22 Ford announced that he would veto the common-situs bill. He explained that his "earlier optimism that this bill provided a resolution which would have the support of all parties was unfounded."[48] Three weeks later Dunlop, feeling that his relationship with the leaders of organized labor had been compromised, resigned. Even members of the Economic Policy Board who had not shared Dunlop's relatively liberal position regretted the loss of his political acumen on economic issues. "I will not criticize John Dunlop for anything that he did," Ford later said. "This was a case in which the White House staff did a less than adequate job."[49]

Failure to Articulate Direction

While the president was preoccupied with the stack of controversial legislation passed by Congress in the final days of the 1975 session, a tug of war was going on within the White House over the 1976 State of the Union message, to be delivered by the President before Congress in the third week of the new year. Greenspan, Lynn, and Cheney, joined by David Gergen, Nixon's talented last chief speech-writer who had moved over to the Treasury to work for Simon after Nixon resigned, and then returned quietly to the White House at Cheney's invitation in 1975, "implored" (Gergen's word) the president to use the State of the Union message to help establish the administration's philosophic direction. "The administration had a philosophy," Greenspan has said, "but it was not being well articulated."[50] Simon, approaching the president on a separate track, also urged that the State of the Union message contain a declaration of philosophic principles instead of being limited to a "laundry list" of administration programs.[51] But Hartmann, who still controlled the speechwriting process, insisted on avoiding what he regarded as ideological abstractions.

Just as in 1975, this difference of view brought two very different draft speeches to the president's desk. Once more, Ford found himself working over the final draft with disputing aides on the day before the message was to be given. The final speech contained a few conceptual observations about the need for a "new realism" in governmental approach, but in general followed the format that Hartmann had favored. As a result, in Gergen's opinion, the administration "lost whatever chance it may have had to set a clear philosophic direction."[52]

Many members of the administration felt that Ford's failure to articulate underlying principles was in the end politically costly. "The president," Lynn has said, "never succeeded in establishing the link between tax reduction and more jobs. . . . His program was to make the [economic] pie bigger. He was never able to make clear that he realized that the country has many unmet needs, but that his way of meeting those needs was economically the most sensible."[53]

The Humphrey-Hawkins Bill

The economy, meanwhile, was slowly coming out of the recession. Growth had resumed in the second quarter of 1975, and moved forward at a steady rate through the early months of 1976. Unemployment in January fell to 7.8 percent—still higher than in any postwar year before 1975. Inflation, reflecting the effects of the recession as well as of the administration's policy, had slowed during 1975 to an increase of 7 percent in the consumer price index.[54]

While the administration continued to emphasize the need to restrain inflation, liberal Democrats in Congress approached the nation's economic troubles from quite a different angle. Supported by organized labor and many leaders of the black community, liberals pressed for enactment of the famous Humphrey-Hawkins "full employment bill," first introduced in 1974 by Senator Humphrey and Congressman Augustus Hawkins, liberal Democrat of California. Though it passed through many drafts, Humphrey-Hawkins consistently proposed guaranteeing that "adult unemployment" (variously defined) would not rise above 3 percent within a stated period after the bill's enactment. To make good this guarantee, Humphrey-Hawkins would require the federal government to become "employer of last resort" for all those who could not otherwise find jobs. Passage of Humphrey-Hawkins, Senator Humphrey promised in March 1976, would "reject the discredited economic doctrine of the present administration and replace it with a new economics that puts all of America's resources back to work."[55]

The administration's spokesmen, and conservatives in general, attacked Humphrey-Hawkins as a particularly splendid example of the liberal propensity for attempting to repeal the law of gravity through government fiat. Appearing before a subcommittee of the House Committee on Education and Labor in April 1976, Greenspan predicted that "millions of jobs would have to be funded under large scale public employment projects in order to reduce the unemployment rate" to the level called for by Humphrey-Hawkins. Public service jobs of the kind envisioned by the bill, Greenspan claimed, "by taking a worker out of the labor market, may actually inhibit the normal processes of job search and productive employment." Even worse, "the heavy budget costs of funding the programs would likely interfere with capital investment," and therefore slow the creation of additional productive jobs in the private sector.[56]

Conservatives were not alone in expressing concern over the probable economic effects of Humphrey-Hawkins implementing mechanisms. A study by the Congressional Research Service of the Library of Congress concluded that enactment of Humphrey-Hawkins would cause "difficulty in recruiting skilled workers for critical tasks, adversely affecting production," and "greatly accelerate the inflationary spiral."[57] Probably the most serious single blow given to the bill's chances in 1976 was testimony before a subcommittee of the Senate Committee on Labor and Public Welfare in May by Charles Schultze of the Brookings Institution, director of the Bureau of the Budget in the Johnson Administration (and later chairman of the CEA under Carter). Humphrey-Hawkins in its current form, Schultze warned, "threatens to make the inflation problem worse." The bill's requirement that persons hired under its public service jobs program be paid at local prevailing wages for government employees, he argued, would inevitably act as a magnet, attracting workers holding low-paying jobs in the private sector to the government payroll. As a result, there would be an "exodus from private industry," and overall wage rates would rise, leading to further inflation. Schultze concluded: "The concept of government as employer of last resort is not a workable method of pushing the overall unemployment rate down to very low levels."[58]

In late April Jimmy Carter, who had up until then resisted joining most of the other Democratic presidential candidates in supporting Humphrey-Hawkins, came under heavy pressure from the unions and his supporters in the black community to endorse the bill. Apparently at least in part to offset adverse reactions to his remark during the Pennsylvania primary campaign favoring "ethnic purity" in urban neighborhoods, Carter at last complied. The bill was also endorsed (though not by name) in the 1976 Democratic platform.

Early in the fall campaign Ford and other Republican spokesmen made some efforts to debate the merits of Humphrey-Hawkins. Soon, however, campaign attention focused on such items as Carter's concession to *Playboy* magazine that he had "lusted" for women other than his wife, and a scatological remark about blacks made by Ford's secretary of agriculture, Earl Butz. In the closing weeks of the campaign, neither side showed much inclination to discuss significant issues. The Democrats were therefore relieved of a potential liability (assuming that the public opinion polls were correct in showing that most voters regarded inflation as a more fundamental danger than unemployment).[59]

Deregulation

As part of his effort to restore the long-range vitality of the private economy, Ford proposed greatly reducing government regulation of business. The real effect of many of the regulations that had been enacted over the years, many economists argued, was to limit competition, which in turn drove up prices. In February 1976 the administration achieved passage of an act authorizing some deregulation of the economically stagnant railroad industry. Ford also sent legislation to Congress for deregulation of the aviation and trucking industries, and for systematic assessment and revision of all federal regulatory activities.

Ford's interest in deregulation was apparently stimulated by Roderick Hills, a young California lawyer with a background in progressive Republican politics, who joined the White House staff as counsel to the President at about the same time that his wife, Carla, was becoming secretary of HUD.[60] Hills persuaded first Seidman, and then Ford, that deregulation should form an important part of the administration's economic program. "The president did not have a conservative knee-jerk reaction to regulation," Hills has said. "He recognized that some regulation is valuable and needed. . . . Our approach was not to eliminate all regulation, but to rationalize the regulatory process."[61] Hills was made cochairman with Paul Mac-Avoy, a brilliantly iconoclastic member of the CEA, of a regulatory reform task force, composed of representatives from the Domestic Council, OMB, the CEA, the Justice Department, the Treasury, and several other departments and agencies with regulatory responsibilities.

Opposition to deregulation quickly developed, both within and from outside the administration. "The president," Philip Buchen has said, "did not realize how difficult regulatory reform would be. He was surprised to find that many free-enterprise businessmen, who in principle were against regulation, actually welcomed government regulation in their own industry, and reacted in a very hostile way when the president proposed reform. The president came to feel that business is not a very trustworthy supporter for a Republican president."[62]

Edward Schmults, a Wall Street lawyer who took Hills's place as cochairman of the regulatory reform task force after Ford appointed Hills chairman of the Securities and Exchange Commission at the end of 1975, has recalled: "The president was determined to push ahead with deregulation, but many of his advisers believed it was a political loser."[63] Rogers Morton argued that the Republican party had traditionally received substantial support from the transportation industry, both the companies and the unions. This support, Morton said, was being jeopardized by the president's proposals for deregulation. Seidman, too, began to develop doubts about the political effects of the drive for deregulation. In the opinion of Vice-President Rockefeller, deregulation had "about as much political sex appeal as a sick alligator." (Rockefeller said in 1978 that he had favored "systematic simplification of regulations," but had been concerned that "sudden deregulation would produce chaos in many industries.")[64]

Deregulation stood high on the list of things that Ford aimed to accomplish if he had been elected to a full term. A report filed with the president by Schmults's task force at the beginning of 1977 concluded: "Thirty to forty years of government regulation cannot be changed in a few months or even a few years. . . . Much remains to be done. We hope that the efforts of the past two and a half years provide a beginning."[65]

Economic Policy and the 1976 Election

Ford resolved in the fall of 1975 not to follow Nixon's 1972 example of pumping up federal expenditures to assure economic prosperity in an election year. "I never in any serious way considered increasing spending in 1976," Ford later said. "For one thing, I was not sure that any great increase in spending would produce a significant reduction of unemployment. More important, I had a concern that any wild increase in spending, even if it won the election, would regenerate inflation, which would not lead to a very happy outcome for the country. Basically, I believed that a balanced, responsible economic policy would lead to success in the election. It almost worked."[66]

Greenspan has recalled that there was "real pressure" within the administration to increase spending at the beginning of 1976, "but it did not come from the president." Those within the administration who wished to increase spending were not, according to Greenspan, "Machiavellian," but they did favor relaxing fiscal restraints to speed the recovery. "But we could not be sure," Greenspan maintained in 1978, "that increased spending would have a positive effect in the short run, and then we would have to deal with the effects of having unleashed inflationary pressures into the economy. . . . Actually, the extent to which economists can predict the effects of economic decisions is really quite limited."[67]

According to William Seidman: "Consideration was given to increasing spending on public works in 1976. If the administration had gone ahead with this, we would have gained the support of construction workers, who lean toward the Republicans, and we would have avoided the pause in the economy that took place a month or so before the election. Whether or not it would have been good [in the long run] for the economy is a different question. Anyhow, the president decided against it. He believed that the country had been subjected to enough of that kind of manipulation, and he refused to go along with it one more time."[68]

Ford's decision against artificial stimulation was probably made easier by his belief that recovery without extra stimulation would restore a reasonable amount of prosperity in time for the election. "To the extent that Alan Greenspan could be understood," Robert Hartmann has said, "he seemed to be forecasting that the economy would continue to improve. Economists are very skillful at hedging everything they say, and he would probably be able to point to reservations that would indicate that he was not being unduly optimistic. Nevertheless, the impression he gave the president was that things would continue to get better."[69]

Unemployment fell according to plan during the first five months of 1976, reaching 7.3 percent in May. But during the summer it began to rise again. By the time of the Republican National Convention in August, Greenspan has said, he "expected the economy to slow down [in the fall], but not to slow down as much as it did."[70]

At a meeting of the president's advisers the week after the Republican convention at the Fords' vacation home in Vail, Colorado, Vice-President Rockefeller, according to Greenspan, "argued in favor of pumping up the economy to get us through the election." Ford has recalled that "the vice-president to some extent urged increases in spending, although in most areas he was not for any sizable increases over what the budget called for."[71]

Rockefeller's own recollection was that he had "not favored spending more than the administration had authorized," but that he did argue for "commitment of all that had been authorized." Actual federal spending was at the time reported to be running about $12 billion below what the president and Congress had approved. A large part of this "shortfall" was in the Defense Department. "I can't believe that any system could fail in that way if someone had not wanted it to fail," Rockefeller said in 1978. "Nothing doesn't happen unless somebody wants it not to happen. Somebody had to know. The administration had been alerted three or four months in advance that the funds were not being committed. It was a major factor in Ford's failure to win the election."[72]

Ford, too, was angered and alarmed by the shortfall. Greenspan has recalled: "The major shortfall was in the Defense Department, and Rumsfeld was told to get all authorized expenditures rolling. But we never did get a really satisfactory answer as to why expenditures were not being kept up to authorized levels."[73]

(An analysis prepared in 1977 by Sidney Jones, assistant secretary of the treasury for economic policy under Simon, found that the "alleged shortfall" was mostly due to "larger-than-expected-revenues which are treated as negative expenditures" from offshore oil leases, sale of government-held mortgages, and the like. Only about $3 billion of the total resulted from "administrative and appropriations delays" in the Defense Department and other agencies. In percentage terms the fiscal shortfall for 1976, 1.7 percent, was about average for recent years—more than in 1975 and 1973, but less than in 1974.)[74]

Artificial stimulation at the beginning of September, Greenspan argued, could rekindle inflation, and would be of no political help.

"In order to use federal expenditures to pump up the economy for political purposes in 1976," Greenspan has said, "the decision would have had to be made late in 1975. The president had moved in exactly the opposite direction. Once the budget decisions were made at the end of 1975, there was really not much we could do, even if we had wanted to."[75]

In the third quarter the pace of economic growth slackened. Unemployment went up to 7.9 percent in August and reached 8 percent in November. "The pause in the economy," Ford later said, "could not have come at a more inauspicious time."[76]

Many members of the administration concluded after the election that the slowdown in the economy had caused Ford's defeat. "In the spring," Hartmann has said, "there was a feeling that things were getting better. But it didn't pan out that way, and that was why Ford lost the election."[77]

Another of the president's counsellors, John Marsh has said: "Ford's whole appeal to the country was based on the promise that he would get the economy under control and growing again. That was the bottom line for the Ford administration. Things were going well until the check in September and October. Once that happened, people felt that Ford had not lived up to his promise, and the election was lost. The ironic thing is that the pause was caused by the election. People were waiting to see how the election would come out before making economic decisions." In Marsh's view, additional stimulation might have prevented the September pause. "But it would have been totally inconsistent with the man, with his integrity. If he had done such a thing, he probably would have lost out politically as well. Ford's whole appeal was on being a consistent conservative. It was unheard of for a president to say, 'No new spending,' in an election year. If he had changed direction in the middle of the campaign, he would have lost the support of many of the people who believed in him."[78]

Ford himself, looking back in 1978, had no regrets. "It would have been politically as well as economically unwise," he said, "for me to have gone on a big spending spree in 1976."[79]

Departing from office in January 1977, Ford had the satisfaction of leaving an economy far healthier than the one he had found in 1974. When the final figures were in, inflation in 1976 was found to have gone up only 4.8 percent. Moreover, by inauguration day the recovery was back on track. GNP surged 7.5 percent during the first quarter of 1977, and in May unemployment at last fell below 7 percent. The economy's restored vitality could be attributed in part to the boost in public confidence caused by the election of a new president. But in large part, Ford could convincingly argue, it reflected the fact that his plan for gradual recovery without inflation had been working after all.

Conservative Gradualism

Ford entered the presidency at a time when democratic governments all over the world were encountering severe economic strains. The period of almost continuous rapid expansion that had followed the Second World War seemed at last to be coming to an end. Growth might continue, most economists maintained, but probably at less dynamic rates than during the immediate postwar decades. While rates of economic growth declined, demand for steady increases in material benefits among the peoples of the industrial democracies remained at least constant. To meet these pressures, without taking benefits from one economic group to give to another, governments in most democratic countries, including the United States, adopted economic policies that helped fuel inflation. "Inflation," Fred Hirsch wrote, "has served as a vent for distributional strife, an escape hatch through which excess demands are automatically channelled."[80]

For this essentially political and social problem, Keynesian economics, which had been adopted by most governmental leaders in the industrial democracies by the end of the 1960s—even Nixon!— did not provide a satisfactory solution. The tactic of accepting a certain amount of inflation to preserve high employment proved during the middle years of the 1970s to be self-defeating. Inflation created consumer resistance and uncertainty among investors, leading to business contraction, and resulting unemployment. "Whatever may have been true in the past," Arthur Burns told an audience at the University of Georgia in 1975, "there is no longer a meaningful trade-off between inflation and unemployment."[81]

For Alan Greenspan, William Simon, and other admirers of the pure laissez-faire model, the solution appeared relatively simple (in theory if not always in application): return to minimum government involvement in the economy and minimum federal support for social services, as was supposed to have existed before the New Deal. In this way, the laissez-faire purists believed, the tendency of democratically chosen governments to generate inflation would be moderated, and economic equilibrium would be restored—not, to be sure, to the satisfaction of all individuals or all interest groups, but with optimal results for the nation as a whole, and therefore for most citizens.

Ford did not go that far. The president, as James Lynn suggested, was "not totally pure," measured against the laissez-faire standard. For better or worse, Ford believed, the federal government had become committed to maintaining reasonable levels of economic activity and providing some measure of support for social services like education, health care, income maintenance for the elderly and disabled, housing, and even recreation. In the process of developing these commitments, he agreed with Simon and Greenspan, government had overextended its resources and overburdened the economy. But the most that a responsible administration should now do, Ford maintained, was to limit further expansion of domestic services, remove government regulations that served no useful purpose, and channel as much federal aid as possible into revenue sharing and broad block grant programs that gave state and local governments primary responsibility for administration and planning.[82]

Ford regarded as frivolous Ronald Reagan's proposal in the fall of 1975 that the federal budget for human services be cut by $90 billion—more than one-third of the total.[83] In 1976 the administration strongly supported renewal of revenue sharing (authorized originally for a five-year period), which some fundamentalist conservatives opposed, because they regarded it as a means for continuing programs that they thought should be cut out altogether. While encouraging Lynn, O'Neill, and Greenspan to find new ways to cut the federal budget, Ford at the same time installed activists like Coleman, Hills, Richardson, and Dunlop as secretaries of major service departments. He fully expected these department heads to argue for the reasonable interests of their constituencies (unlike Nixon in 1973, who had sent Weinberger to HEW and Lynn to HUD to resist constituency pressures), and he often ruled in their favor when they got into disputes with OMB.[84] When inflation was brought under control, Ford even favored gradual expansion of federal support for some social services. During his vacation at Vail after the Republican convention in 1976, the president, partly because of advice from his campaign pollster, Robert Teeter, announced that in a new term he would give increased attention to "quality of life" concerns, such as housing, education, health care, protection against crime, job training, and recreation.[85] Ford said little about the "quality of life" issues during the remainder of the campaign, but he appeared to maintain at least an open mind on how large a role the federal government should play, given favorable economic conditions, in helping to fill social needs.

Ford's lack of laissez-faire "purity" no doubt to some extent stemmed from his willingness to make political compromises, as Simon later charged. But to some extent, too, it seems to have reflected the president's own brand of conservatism, based on practical experience and belief in the complexity of social reality rather than on narrowly defined theoretic models. (In practice, Greenspan, too, was less of a purist than some of his arguments implied. When recession struck in the fall of 1974, the CEA chairman asked not *whether* to stimulate, but *how much*—not, of course, an insignificant question.) If Ford feared and resisted the destabilizing effects of continued rapid increases in government spending, he also viewed as unacceptable the social and economic upheavals that would result from a radical contraction of government.

Public opinion polls in the fall of 1976 indicated that even among industrial workers, many people had come to share Ford's view that inflation was a more fundamental danger than unemployment.[86] As David Broder has said: "The Republicans won the argument, but lost the election." Unfortunately for Ford, the Democrats' choice of Jimmy Carter—according to numerous liberal authorities, the most conservative candidate to be nominated by the Democratic party for president since John W. Davis in 1924, and the most conservative Democrat elected since Grover Cleveland—somewhat offset the appeal to the electorate of the administration's conservative approach.

Ford carried into the 1976 campaign the burdens of his identification with Nixon, the continued high level of unemployment, the relatively low attracting power of the Republican party (which had more to do with historic antagonisms than with current ideology), and persistent doubts among the public that he was quite up to the job of being president. Against these liabilities, he hammered away at the administration's success in bringing down inflation, the sense of moral steadiness and decency that he had restored to the presidency, and the alleged inconsistency and inexperience of his opponent. As Ford said: "It almost worked."[87]

19

Ideology and Policy

IN THE FOREGOING chapters I have identified some of the social values, beliefs, and attitudes, such as support for free-market capitalism, conservative internationalism, and preference for state or local administration of social programs, that influenced policy formation in the Nixon and Ford administrations. Questions to be dealt with in this final chapter include: How important were these social ideas in their actual effects on policymaking? Do these social values, beliefs, and attitudes add up to a "distinct and broadly coherent" ideology called conservatism? And, finally, what is the likely future role of this ideology in American politics?

Major Policy Themes

Among the social values, beliefs, and attitudes that influenced the policies of the two Republican administrations, as described and analyzed in earlier chapters, were the following:

1. In foreign policy, both the Nixon and Ford administrations derived many of their strategic directions from the structure of ideas I have called "conservative internationalism." This structure was founded on beliefs that (a) "national interest" is the self-evident goal of foreign policy, and (b) effective pursuit of this interest requires active international involvement. National interest was interpreted by Nixon, Ford, and their advisers, among whom Kissinger was certainly the most influential, to comprise not only military security but also

407

access to foreign resources and markets, the maintenance of a world atmosphere hospitable to American capitalism, and, at a considerably lower level of urgency, an international climate conducive to democratic values. Both administrations felt constrained in their applications of this activist approach by their evaluations of American capabilities and their judgments of the limits set by domestic politics.

Leaders of both administrations regarded the Soviet Union as the United States' chief antagonist in world affairs. They believed that communism is intrinsically evil, smothering economic enterprise and taking away fundamental human rights from people unlucky enough to be caught under its rule. Nevertheless, they based policy toward Communist countries, including the Soviet Union, primarily on calculations of interest and power, rather than on any passion for liberty. Both administrations were prepared to make deals with Communist governments, and to aid and support non-Communist authoritarian regimes, when such arrangements appeared to serve the national interest of the United States. The newly discovered common security interests of the United States and Communist China were held to supersede all ideological differences.

Nixon, more than Ford or Kissinger, seemed at times to glimpse a future in which the rivalry between the United States and the Soviet Union might no longer be the single dominating focus of American foreign policy. Neither administration made much serious effort to move, or look, beyond a context in which irreducible national sovereignty is the main organizing principle of the world system.

2. In economic policy, both administrations subscribed to the belief that as a general principle free-market competition produces the best overall results. Both, however, were prepared to undertake or maintain substantial government intervention to deal with short-run economic problems, and to mitigate social inequities not responsive to market forces. Nixon, partly for political reasons and partly because of more flexible economic assumptions, departed more readily than Ford from the pure laissez-faire model. Ford sought to eliminate some government regulations that he and some of his advisers believed were impeding the efficiency of the market.

Both presidents regarded inflation as a more dangerous problem than unemployment. Ford's economists developed with considerable sophistication the argument that rising inflation in the long run *causes* unemployment, so that efforts to combat unemployment by permitting inflation are bound to be self-defeating. Both administrations, in accord with this view, were prepared to accept some temporary rise in unemployment in order to bring down inflation—Ford being willing to go further along this route than Nixon. Both administrations held that large deficits in the federal budget contribute to inflation, and both therefore sought to keep government expenditures in balance with revenues—at least at "full employment," or over the period of an entire business cycle. Here, too, Ford followed theory more strictly than Nixon (although with no greater success at avoiding deficits).

3. In domestic policy, both administrations accepted some form of the national welfare state that had evolved since the New Deal. During his first term, Nixon in some areas, notably income maintenance and environmental protection, proposed substantial expansion, along with structural reform, of domestic programs. At the beginning of his second term, Nixon set out to cut back on some aspects of the welfare state, but became engaged in the Watergate controversy before he had made much headway. Ford proposed reduction in at least the rate of growth of federal social programs—but stopped well short of the kind of massive cutbacks demanded by some fundamentalist conservatives.

Both administrations promoted the decentralization of administrative control over social programs and the delivery of federal aid to state and local governments through general purpose revenue sharing or "block grants" rather than through narrowly defined "categorical" programs. Nixon favored decentralization because he believed it would lead to more effective management and would give more weight to community values. Ford approved it for these reasons, too, and also because he thought that block grants could more easily be brought under budgetary discipline.

4. Both administrations supported the elimination of vestiges of government-enforced segregation by race. Nixon and Ford disassociated themselves from Lyndon Johnson's announced goal of "equality of result," but claimed commitment to equality of opportunity— "an equal chance at the starting line."[1]

Both administrations sought to overcome the effects of past discrimination, particularly by requiring affirmative action in favor of blacks and women in employment and higher education. Both, however, strongly opposed busing of schoolchildren to achieve racial integration, except for limited times in areas directly involved in former deliberate segregation. Their opposition to busing appeared to spring in part from political considerations, but also from convictions that busing violated individual human rights and threatened the solidarity of neighborhoods and communities.

5. Both administrations were determined to maintain social order and to protect the internal security of the executive branch, especially on matters affecting national defense. Nixon allowed these concerns to carry him and some members of his administration into numerous illegalities and improprieties. In Nixon's view, all such acts were legitimate, because "when the President does it, that means that it is not illegal."[2]

6. Most leaders of both administrations regarded the federal departments and agencies, particularly those dispensing domestic services, as undisciplined governmental monsters, wallowing in waste and inefficiency, and supporting vast armies of parasitic bureaucrats. Both administrations made some efforts at structural reform of the executive branch. Neither felt it achieved much success.

The Role of Social Ideas

The preceding list does not include all the social values, beliefs, and attitudes that the Nixon and Ford administrations applied to national problems, but it does give a fair sample of those that entered most directly into policy formulation. How important a role did these ideas play in the actual development of policy?

Governmental practitioners and political commentators often claim that American administrations deal "pragmatically" with the nation's social, economic, and geopolitical problems, working out responses on the basis of examination of the relevant "facts" in each case as it comes up. But facts do not provide their own interpretations, nor do problems automatically suggest possible solutions. For these it is necessary for presidents and their advisers to turn, at least in part, to the beliefs, values, and attitudes on which they depend for their understandings of social reality.

Nixon did not get his policies for dealing with the Russians, or for sharing federal revenues with state and local governments, or for reorganizing the executive branch simply by following the news or studying the Gallup poll. Nor did Ford arrive at his plan for bringing down inflation, or his energy policy, or his decision to increase military expenditures on the basis of statistics alone. A mix of factors, political and personal as well as substantive, affected the development of all these policies. But at some point all required the introduction of *ideas*—about how the economy works, how nations relate to each other, what the value is of trying to maintain local communities in a modern industrial society, and so forth.

Besides dealing with objective national problems, every administration must be concerned with maintaining a high level of voter support. In many cases, perhaps most, this interest reinforces rather than undercuts the influence of social beliefs and attitudes in the policymaking process. Presidents assume that governmental approaches based on their substantive beliefs will ultimately serve the good of the national public. (If they did not, they could hardly be said to hold such beliefs.) They naturally expect, therefore, that at least over the long run these approaches will win voter approval: "Good government makes good politics." Nixon's China policy, Ford's program for fighting inflation, and the revenue-sharing program championed by both administrations are examples of policies that, while undertaken as responses to objective problems, were expected to produce favorable political results—for the very reason that administration leaders believed these policies would serve the public good.

Sometimes, of course, presidents and their advisers conclude that policies they favor on substantive grounds clash with the administration's short-run political interests. When such conflicts occur, presidents sometimes go ahead with the policies anyhow—as when Nixon ordered the mining of Haiphong harbor in the spring of 1972, though he expected this action would probably cause the Russians to cancel the upcoming Moscow summit, and would therefore undermine his image as a master diplomat and peacemaker going into the 1972 campaign; or when Ford even in 1976 held out against what he regarded as excessive stimulation of the economy, though increased federal spending might have brought down unemployment in the short run, without putting much further pressure on inflation until after the election.

At other times presidents stick up to a point with policies they believe in substantively, but compromise or change direction when they decide the political price has become too high—as when Nixon imposed wage and price controls in 1971, though he and almost all his advisers (Connally being the principal exception) foresaw that controls over the long run would have bad economic effects; or when Ford gave up on SALT II in 1976, though he believed a treaty that would serve American interests might have been achieved. At still other times presidents violate their substantive principles simply to take out political insurance—as when Nixon pumped up federal spending to create an artificial economic boom before the 1972 election.

A given president's willingness to take political risks for policies that he believes are right may depend to some extent on the amount of background and interest he has in a particular policy area and on the degree of confidence he feels in his own judgment about substance. Nixon was more willing to risk political damage for substantive goals in foreign policy than in economic policy. With Ford it seems to have been the other way around. Neither Republican president was prepared to take large political risks to advance domestic social policy goals. (Nixon proposed the controversial family assistance plan during the first year of his first term, but backed away from it as the 1972 election approached.)

Abandoning substantive positions for political reasons does not necessarily free presidents or their advisers from dependence on social ideas. As a rule, even policies that are undertaken mainly for political purposes must be at least rationalized through some kind of substantive arguments and theories. When Nixon decided in 1971 that the political costs of continuing the economic policies favored by Shultz and McCracken had become too high, he turned to the differing theories suggested, through Connally, by Volcker and Weidenbaum. When Ford concluded that Reagan's attack on his right flank made it impossible for him to go ahead with SALT II in 1976, he embraced, at least temporarily, the geopolitical outlook of the Pentagon. Nixon's pumping up of the economy before the 1972 election perhaps was carried out with less attempt at theoretic rationalization or justification; but even this departure was probably made easier by the existence of Keynesian doctrine, which Nixon interpreted as recommending stimulation.

When presidents for political purposes compromise or abandon positions they believe in substantively, they often argue, probably to themselves as well as to those who share their beliefs, that such tactical change is justified in order to keep them available to fight on these and other issues another day. Sometimes when the political situation changes, they do indeed return to positions given up out of fear of the electoral consequences: Nixon pursued conservative budgetary policies with a vengeance after his reelection in 1973; Ford had laid the groundwork for renewing efforts to achieve an understanding on nuclear arms with the Russians in 1977 if he had been elected to a full term.

Besides serving the dual goals of developing workable solutions to the nation's objective problems and maintaining the administration's political strength, every administration's policymaking process is conditioned by the same kinds of personality factors that affect all group activities. Political and governmental practitioners themselves sometimes claim that policy formulation is in fact "all a matter of personalities"—who gets along with whom, or, sometimes even more important, who is out to get whom. Former members of the Nixon and Ford administrations interviewed for this study usually stressed the influence of personal relationships on policy formulation, particularly within the White House inner circle.

Participants in day-to-day policy development are likely to be more conscious of their colleagues' personalities than of their underlying beliefs and values, and therefore probably tend to exaggerate the effects of personality alone. Nevertheless, personal relationships undoubtedly play an important part in the evolution of policy: Nixon approved the family assistance plan in part because Moynihan was more adept than Burns at playing up to the president's self-image; Ford replaced Schlesinger with Rumsfeld as secretary of defense in part because he felt more comfortable with Rumsfeld.

Over time, however, political ideology is a major factor in determining who gets and who stays in the administration's inner circle, and therefore who is available to participate in intragroup relationships. Indeed, ideological agreement may be indispensable in most prolonged intimate political relationships. The Nixon administration at first included representatives drawn from a fairly broad range on the ideological spectrum (though never so broad as has sometimes been suggested); but most of those who did not share the administration's prevailing ideological direction, like Moynihan or George Romney, eventually either were isolated or dropped away. The Ford administration was ideologically more homogeneous from the start (partly as a legacy from Nixon's last phase), and became increasingly more so during its short time in office. Nelson Rockefeller's loss of influence in the Ford White House was due not only to the play of personal relationships, but also to the fact that the vice-president held social and economic attitudes that were significantly, though not radically, different from those that prevailed within the administration's inner circle.

Some commentators hold that social values, beliefs, and attitudes are no more than rationalizations for economic interests or, alternatively, inner personality drives, which are held to be the real determining forces in governmental policy formulation. Marxists, for instance, maintain that all ideologies (except their own) are simply masks for economic interests, which themselves reflect changes in the means of production. Freudians, on the other hand, assign the chief generative role to instinctual drives and early psychological traumas that have affected individual policymakers. Economic interest and inner personality obviously influence social values and beliefs. But so, apparently, do other factors not easily reduced to simple economic or psychological determinants, such as moral and cultural traditions, political opportunity, the shock of world events, views gathered from books or friends, even deliberate thought—or, as Keynes suggested, "the gradual encroachment of ideas" affecting politicians "who think they hear voices in the air."

Nixon's apparent need for self-justification and his economic situation as a struggling young lawyer might easily have contributed to the formation of a liberal Democrat. But the combined influences of family tradition, reaction against big government during wartime, and exposure to conservative ideas in southern California and Washington helped guide Nixon to the conservative side of the ideological divide. Rockefeller's political ambition and economic background might have produced a conservative fundamentalist (like the Buckley brothers) or a patrician liberal (like Averell Harriman). But ideas about social responsibility and economic effectiveness, acquired during his formative years, induced Rockefeller instead to channel his personal drives into leading the progressive wing of the more conservative party. Kissinger's passion for order was given philosophic direction by his reading of Kant and Burke during his undergraduate years at Harvard. His association with Rockefeller no doubt gave Kissinger an interest in maintaining alignment with the Republicans. But shared beliefs, in strong executive leadership and a tough but flexible foreign policy, were the chief factors that brought Kissinger and Rockefeller together in the first place. Ford's beliefs perhaps seem to have risen more inevitably out of his personality and economic situation—but even in Ford's case, there was enough inner flexibility to permit conversion from isolationism to internationalism during the Second World War, as a result of experience and reflection.

Social values, beliefs, and attitudes do not by themselves determine the formulation of any administration's policy. Neither does any other single set of influences, so far as has ever been demonstrated. But social ideas permeate the entire policymaking process, affecting not only substantive judgments but also political strategies and personal relationships.

Conservatism in America

Were the social ideas that influenced policy in the Nixon and Ford administrations related within a "distinct and broadly coherent" ideology called conservatism? Writers like Louis Hartz and Samuel Beer have argued that what goes by the name of conservatism in the United States is in fact merely a variant of Lockean liberalism promoted by businessmen, and is little related to the conservative tradition represented by figures like Burke, Disraeli, Bismarck, and de Gaulle.[3] This view rests primarily on two observations: first, that American conservatives align themselves with market capitalism; and, second, that most contemporary conservatives accept the values of political democracy.

Capitalism, however, as was pointed out in chapter 1, early became separated from democracy and secularism, the other two elements in the original triad of liberalism. The natural affinity of conservatism, both positional and ideational, for the institution of private property, and the dependence of capitalism on social order helped forge an entente during the nineteenth century, not only in the United States but throughout the West, between conservatism and capitalism. The productive energies unleashed by capitalism, conservatives soon argued, bring economic benefits for entire societies as well as enrichment for the capitalists. Particularly after government welfare and insurance programs had softened the harsher aspects of capitalism during the early decades of the twentieth century, conservatives maintained that the market system provides a means for balancing a high degree of personal autonomy with the order and discipline needed to achieve economic plenty; and that it is far more compatible with the values of traditional conservatism than its collectivist rivals on either the left or right. Conservatives, therefore, adopted capitalism as the best available means for dealing with the economic side of life. Modern liberalism, on the other hand, reacting against the social and economic inequality that are endemic to capitalism, has turned increasingly to government regulation of the economy to advance the liberal goal of equality of condition. The original positions of conservatism and liberalism on economic freedom have therefore been largely reversed.[4]

Conservatism originally moved to an acceptance of representative democracy for a more pragmatic reason: once democracy was established, continued resistance against democratic forms by conservatives would only assure loss of elections (assuming that conservatives were not prepared to support right-wing seizures of governmental power). Over time, however, most conservatives have come to regard democracy operating within a framework of constitutional limits as a positive good in itself. Democracy bestows more legitimacy on social authority than could usually be achieved through the mumbo jumbo of absolute monarchies or feudal nobilities. Popular majorities, moreover, have turned out to be more reliable supporters of traditional social values than social elites—a discovery expressed by William Buckley's crack that he would rather be governed by the first hundred names in the Boston telephone book than by the Harvard faculty. Conservatives continue to insist that large areas of economic life and personal relationships be kept beyond the reach of democratic governments—but more out of fear of government bureaucracies than of the voters themselves. On many social issues, like the busing controversy and abortion, conservatives, as was shown in chapter 9, have turned to the democratically chosen branches of government to defend traditional values, whereas liberals have sought to advance their objectives through the nondemocratic institution of the courts.

American conservatism, moreover, goes far beyond support for market capitalism and constitutional democracy. Both Nixon and Ford aligned themselves firmly with social order, patriotic nationalism, local control of social services, and cultural and moral traditionalism—

all properties of modern conservatism, as was observed in chapter 1. Nixon's landslide victory over George McGovern in 1972, Theodore White has argued, was won largely because of broad support for Nixon's conduct of foreign policy, and for his aim "to let the ethnic communities and local governments of the United States lead their own lives with minimal interference by the federal government."[5] Republican publicists in 1972 effectively contrasted Nixon's traditionalism with McGovern's identification with the "three A's: amnesty [for deserters and draft evaders in the Vietnam War], acid, and abortion." American conservatism in the 1970s was not, of course, identical with British conservatism in the 1830s, or with traditional European conservatism of the kind identified with Bismarck and Disraeli, or even with conservatism in the United States during the era of McKinley. Despite much change in the surrounding social environment, however, the essential values of conservatism remained much as they have always been: church, family, personal responsibility, order, country.

It is true that some liberals find worth in some, or even all, of these values. But taken together, they represent a view of life very different from the standard liberal vision.

None of which is to say that the thesis advanced by Hartz and Beer, among others, is wholly wrong. Conservatism has taken over elements of liberalism, both traditional and modern, and these elements alter conservatism's approach to objective problems of government. They also create tensions within conservatism itself—some of which contribute to the differences among fundamentalists, stalwarts, moderates, and progressives, described in chapter 2 and succeeding chapters. Fundamentalists and stalwarts derive much of their economic philosophy from the libertarian strain of traditional liberalism. Progressives and moderates, on the other hand, go along part way with modern liberalism's belief in using government to deal with many social problems. Contact with both kinds of liberalism has helped broaden and modernize conservatism. But this very broadening and modernization have created risks that conservatism will lose some of the moral strength that is its legacy from Burke, the Adamses, Lincoln, Disraeli, Theodore Roosevelt, Taft, Eisenhower, and other, more ancient forebears.

Nevertheless, American conservatism, as it was practiced under

Nixon and Ford, and as it continues to be practiced today, surely qualifies as an expression of a distinct social ideology.

WHAT IS the likely future role of conservatism in American politics? Positional conservatism, most commentators of all political persuasions agree, performs the useful function of maintaining checks against too rapid or unconsidered social change. In addition, positional conservatism may act as a political rallying point for social order—in Hegelian terms, a thesis of order opposed by an antithesis of dissent, from which presumably may issue the synthesis of a free and stable society.

The electoral fortunes of the party most closely identified with positional conservatism—for the foreseeable future, no doubt the Republicans—will depend, first, on whether the public is more concerned with maintaining the existing social and economic system than with achieving further equalization in the distribution of social benefits; and, second, on whether the party is willing to pursue policies sufficiently moderate to attract the middle-of-the-road voters who are likely to continue to hold the balance of power in national politics.

The goals of ideational conservatism are more ambitious than those of positional conservatism—and, partly for that reason, also more controversial. Claiming to represent the deep mainstream of Western values, in contrast to ideologies like liberalism and socialism that conservatives contend reflect distorted fragments of the Western tradition, ideational conservatives aim to establish the basic cultural and constitutional framework within which various forms of positional conservatism, radicalism, and moderation play out their political differences.

Given the seeming exhaustion of liberal and socialist ideologies at the beginning of the 1980s, an enduring resurgence of ideational conservatism, adapted to meet contemporary needs and conditions, seems possible—not only in the United States, but throughout the democratic world. This apparent trend is reflected not only in the recent electoral successes of conservative parties in many of the industrial democracies, but also in the growing conservatism of leadership groups in many liberal and even socialist parties who seek solutions to pressing problems common to most democratic countries, such as economic inflation, the drying up of sources of cheap energy, social dissonance, personal alienation, rampaging hedonism, institutional corruption, and the renewed danger of Soviet aggression.

A decisive shift toward conservatism will not, however, occur, or at least will not last very long, if conservatism is no more than a rationalization for organized greed, or a soapbox for belligerent nationalism. If conservatism's roots are in the essential tradition of the West, and even in the fundamental nature of humanity, its contemporary expression should possess a breadth and nobility that reflect such origins. To approach this standard, conservatism will have to include a capacity for change as well as foundations for stability; it will have to represent the aspirations of the human spirit, as well as the hard-won lessons taught by experience about the limits imposed by the human condition. Whether conservatism, or any other contemporary political philosophy, is able to meet this kind of challenge is a question that remains to be answered.

APPENDIX A

The Demographic Distribution of Ideological Groups in the Ninety-first Congress

THE DISTRIBUTION of ideological groups in Congress has, as one would expect, a strong regional basis. Any division of the United States by political regions must to some extent be arbitrary. The scheme I have used seems to me to make the most analytical sense and to follow the categories most frequently used by the politicians themselves.

The South, in my system of classification, is composed of the eleven states that joined in 1861 to form the Confederacy. The Northeast consists of the six New England states, New York, Pennsylvania, and New Jersey. The border states—the least satisfactorily and least internally cohesive "region"— consist of six states that did not belong to the Confederacy but have strong cultural affinities with the South: Delaware, Maryland, West Virginia, Kentucky, Missouri, and Oklahoma. The Great Lakes states are the six states west of Pennsylvania that touch the Great Lakes, plus Iowa—in other words, the part of the Middle West most affected by industrialization. The Rocky Mountain–Great Plains region comprises the twelve sparsely populated states that occupy the entire western half of the United States except the Pacific coast. The Pacific region comprises the four West Coast states and Hawaii.

Some regional attributes of the Ninety-first Congress can be observed in table A-1. Republican fundamentalists in the Senate were drawn mainly from the South and the Rocky Mountain–Great Plains region, and in the House from those regions plus the Great Lakes region. Republican stalwarts, who at the beginning of 1969 included Senate Minority Leader Dirksen and House Minority Leader Ford, were concentrated in the Great Lakes region in the House and were rather evenly distributed in the Senate. The Republican moderates in the House were drawn mainly from the Northeast and Great Lakes region and in the Senate represented states in the Pacific, Northeast, and border regions. Republican progressives in both the Senate and the House were largely concentrated in the Northeast.

On the Democratic side, the traditionalists came mostly from the states that had belonged to the Confederacy; a few representatives came from the

421

Table A-1. *Distribution of Strength among Ideological Groups in the Ninety-first Congress, by Region*

Group	South	Border	Northeast	Great Lakes	Rocky Mountain–Great Plains	Pacific
Senate Republicans						
Fundamentalists	3	0	1	0	12	1
Stalwarts	1	3	2	3	1	0
Moderates	0	2	2	0	0	3
Progressives	0	1	5	2	0	1
Total	4	6	10	5	13	5
Senate Democrats						
Traditionalists	11	0	0	0	1	0
Centrists	4	2	1	2	0	0
Regulars	3	1	3	1	6	5
Liberals	0	3	4	8	2	0
Total	18	6	8	11	9	5
House Republicans						
Fundamentalists	22	3	7	24	11	5
Stalwarts	2	5	9	20	4	8
Moderates	2	2	13	15	5	7
Progressives	0	1	15	6	1	2
Total	26	11	44	65	21	22
House Democrats						
Traditionalists	50	5	0	0	1	0
Centrists	23	14	3	4	1	4
Regulars	5	5	24	15	5	12
Liberals	1	2	37	18	0	14
Total	79	26	64	37	7	30

Sources: Based on *Congressional Quarterly Almanac*, vol. 25 (1969), pp. 1052–64; and vol. 26 (1970), pp. 1144–54.

border states (and one senator and one representative were from the Rocky Mountain–Great Plains region). The Democratic centrists comprised most of the Democrats from the southern and border states who were not traditionalists, plus a small number from all the other regions (only one from the Rocky Mountain–Great Plains region). Among the centrists were House Majority Leader Albert and House Majority Whip Hale Boggs of Louisiana, as well as Senator Russell Long and Congressman Wilbur Mills.

The effects of urban-suburban-rural differences have almost as much effect on congressional politics, particularly in the House, as regional attachments. (Most senators, except those from a few overwhelmingly rural states in the

South and West, must represent all three kinds of constituencies.) The ideological distribution of members of the House in the Ninety-first Congress by urban-rural characteristics is shown in table A-2.

As "mega-metropolitan" districts I have included only those in the twelve truly massive conurbations that had total populations above 2 million in 1970: New York, Los Angeles, Chicago, Philadelphia, Detroit, San Francisco–Oakland, Washington, Boston, St. Louis, Pittsburgh, Baltimore, and Cleveland. Of the 116 congressional districts in these metropolitan areas, 44 lay wholly within the boundaries of central cities, 45 were wholly suburban, and 27 were divided between city and suburbs. The 43 districts classified as "middle-sized metropolitan" were those, other than mega-metropolitan districts, that did not reach beyond the bounds of a single metropolitan area— including districts in and around such cities as Houston, Atlanta, Phoenix, Milwaukee, and Dayton—ranging in population from about 600,000 to almost 2 million. Most of these included both central city and suburban constituencies. The 190 districts classified as "mixed urban-rural"—the largest single category, comprising almost half the total membership of the House—were districts containing both metropolitan and nonmetropolitan constituencies. Typically, these included a city of considerable size, like Harrisburg, Pennsylvania; Grand Rapids, Michigan; Peoria, Illinois; and Greensboro, North Carolina; along with adjoining suburbs and rural hinterland. The 86 "rural" districts were those located wholly outside any metropolitan area. They were mainly in the South, the border states, and the Rocky Mountain–Great Plains region, plus a few in the Great Lakes region and upstate Pennsylvania and New York.

Examination of table A-2 shows that Democrats in 1968 represented more than twice as many districts in the mega-metropolitan areas as Republicans. Only one Republican represented a district wholly within the limits of a major city (Seymour Halpern of New York, elected from a district in Queens bordering suburban Nassau County). In the 45 purely suburban districts, Republicans outnumbered Democrats two to one. In the 27 districts that include some city and some suburban areas—usually, of course, the portion of the suburbs closest to the city—Democrats were almost as predominant as in the districts wholly inside city limits. In the 43 middle-sized metropolitan districts, Democrats led Republicans by seven. The 189 urban-rural districts and the 86 purely rural districts were almost evenly divided between the two parties.

Within the parties, Republican fundamentalists came mainly from the urban-rural and rural districts, though with a few from mega-metropolitan suburbs. Republican stalwarts and moderates were elected chiefly from the urban-rural districts (Grand Rapids, Peoria, Harrisburg), whereas progressives were significantly represented only in the mega-metropolitan suburbs.

On the Democratic side, traditionalists and centrists were elected chiefly from urban-rural and rural districts. Regulars came from urban-rural, middle-sized metropolitan, and mega-metropolitan districts, including five from the Chicago metropolitan area and three from New York City. Liberals comprised

Table A-2. *Distribution of Strength among Ideological Groups in the House of Representatives, Ninety-first Congress, by Urban-Rural Characteristics*

	District						
	Mega-metropolitan				*Middle-sized metropolitan*	*Mixed urban-rural*	*Rural*
Group	*Total*	*City*	*Suburbs*	*Mixed*			
Republicans							
Fundamentalists	7	0	6	1	6	39	20
Stalwarts	10	0	10	0	4	23	11
Moderates	8	0	7	1	6	23	7
Progressives	10	1	7	2	2	9	4
Total	35	1	30	4	18	94	42
Democrats							
Traditionalists	0	0	0	0	4	32	20
Centrists	5	2	1	2	3	24	17
Regulars	24	10	5	9	9	26	7
Liberals	50	29	9	12	9	13	0
Total	79	41	15	23	25	95	44

Sources: See table A-1.

five-eighths of all Democrats elected from mega-metropolitan districts—including fourteen from New York City, six from Los Angeles County, and five from the Detroit metropolitan area—and a scattering from middle-sized metropolitan and urban-rural districts. Almost two-thirds of all Democrats elected from mega-metropolitan suburbs were liberals.

APPENDIX B

The Demographic Distribution
of Ideological Groups
in the Ninety-fourth Congress

As SHOWN in table B-1, the regional origins of the ideological groups in the Ninety-fourth Congress were generally similar to those in the Ninety-first Congress (see table A-1). But some changes had occurred, reflecting, among other things, the results of the 1970 census.

As in 1969, Democratic traditionalists were drawn almost entirely from the South. In the House, however, the traditionalists had lost strength to a rising breed of centrists, like Congressmen Wright and Krueger of Texas and Preyer of North Carolina. Democratic regulars had substantially increased their representation from the Northeast and Greak Lakes states, dominating delegations from Boston, Detroit, Chicago, and Cleveland, and holding many of the seats that had been taken from Republicans in upstate and suburban districts in New York, Pennsylvania, Michigan, Indiana, and Illinois. Democratic liberals, on the other hand, had barely managed to hold their own, exercising dominance only in delegations from New York City, Los Angeles, and the San Francisco Bay area.

Severe Republican losses in the House from the Great Lakes states had come mainly among the fundamentalists and the moderates, with the stalwarts holding their own. In the Northeast the progressives had lost badly in the House, but had actually added one member in the Senate (Stafford of Vermont and Weicker of Connecticut more than making up the loss of Goodell of New York). In the Pacific states, fundamentalists more than doubled their representation in the House, but had lost their one member in the Senate (Murphy of California). In the Rocky Mountain and Great Plains states, all six moderates or progressives in the House had gone, but a moderate had been added in the Senate, through the movement of Pearson of Kansas from stalwart to moderate. Fundamentalists had strengthened their dominance among Republican delegations from the South and the border states.

Among all Democrats in the House, the share of the total from the South and the border states had fallen from 43 percent in 1969 to 37 percent in 1975;

426

Table B-1. *Distribution of Strength among Ideological Groups in the Ninety-fourth Congress, by Region*

Group	Region					
	South	Border	Northeast	Great Lakes	Rocky Mountain– Great Plains	Pacific
Senate Republicans						
Fundamentalists	4	1	0	0	11	0
Stalwarts	2	2	2	2	0	2
Moderates	0	1	0	0	1	1
Progressives	0	1	6	1	0	1
Total	6	5	8	3	12	4
Senate Democrats						
Traditionalists	10	0	0	0	0	0
Centrists	5	4	0	0	3	0
Regulars	1	3	6	3	7	5
Liberals	0	0	4	8	2	1
Total	16	7	10	11	12	6
House Republicans						
Fundamentalists	25	5	5	14	11	11
Stalwarts	2	1	12	22	7	4
Moderates	1	1	9	3	0	1
Progressives	0	1	7	2	0	1
Total	28	8	33	41	18	17
House Democrats						
Traditionalists	38	5	0	0	1	0
Centrists	33	15	11	8	5	8
Regulars	7	4	34	36	5	20
Liberals	2	3	26	15	1	12
Total	80	27	71	59	12	40

Source: Based on *Congressional Quarterly Almanac*, vol. 32 (1976), pp. 1010–12.

the share from the Pacific, Rocky Mountain, and Great Plains states had risen from 15 to 21 percent; and the share from the Northeast and Great Lakes states had remained stable at 42 percent.

Among the shrunken total of Republicans, the share representing the South and border states had risen from 19 percent to 25 percent, and the share from the Pacific, Rocky Mountain, and Great Plains states had gone up from 12 percent to 24 percent, whereas the share representing the Northeast and Great Lakes states—the old Republican heartland—had fallen from 69 percent to 51 percent.

Table B-2 shows the rising Democratic dominance among House members elected from what I have called mega-metropolitan areas, along with signif-

Table B-2. Distribution of Strength among Ideological Groups in the House of Representatives, Ninety-fourth Congress, by Urban-Rural Characteristics

Group		District					
		Mega-metropolitan			Middle-sized metropolitan	Mixed urban-rural	Rural
	Total	City	Suburbs	Mixed			
Republicans							
Fundamentalists	9	0	8	1	6	35	21
Stalwarts	7	0	7	0	6	26	9
Moderates	5	0	4	1	1	5	4
Progressives	7	0	6	1	1	3	0
Total	28	0	25	3	14	69	34
Democrats							
Traditionalists	0	0	0	0	2	25	17
Centrists	8	2	3	3	10	44	18
Regulars	39	8	18	13	16	38	13
Liberals	42	26	4	12	5	10	2
Total	89	36	25	28	33	117	50

Source: See table B-1.

icant Democratic gains in old Republican strongholds among the urban-rural and rural districts (cf. table A-2).

By 1975 all House members representing districts entirely inside city limits from the mega-metropolitan areas were Democrats, and most of these were liberals. From the wholly big city districts, regulars were well represented only among the delegations from Chicago and Philadelphia. (The two centrists from wholly big city districts, Delaney and Zefretti, were from New York City.) From mixed city-suburban districts, however, regulars were numerous in delegations from Boston, Cleveland, Detroit, St. Louis, and Los Angeles. In wholly suburban districts, liberal representation fell by more than 50 percent, whereas representation among regulars more than tripled. Regular gains were particularly large, mainly at the expense of Republicans, in the suburbs of New York, Detroit, and Washington, D.C. Suburban districts continued to produce significant numbers of progressive and moderate Republican representatives, chiefly from the Northeast; and representation of the suburbs by fundamentalist Republicans actually rose from six to eight, including such articulate conservative spokesmen as Congressmen Crane of Illinois and Rousselot of California.

From middle-sized cities, Democratic representation increased by two-thirds, with centrists and regulars the big gainers, elected from cities like Denver, Louisville, and Atlanta. The largest Democratic gains of all were made among urban-rural districts, which elected twenty-two more Democratic representatives in 1974 than they had in 1968. Included among these were such traditionally Republican districts as those based on Jamestown, New York (formerly represented by Charles Goodell); Lafayette, Indiana (formerly represented by Charles Halleck); Aurora, Illinois (formerly represented by Leslie Arends)—and even Grand Rapids, Michigan! Here, too, regulars and centrists were the major gainers. Finally, Democrats made a net increase of six seats, mainly won by regulars, from totally rural districts, in areas like central Illinois, western Iowa, central Indiana, and northern Wisconsin.

Notes

Chapter 1 (pages 1–21)

1. Albert H. Cantril and Charles W. Roll, Jr., *Hopes and Fears of the American People* (Universe Books, 1971), pp. 15–30.

2. Tom Wicker, "Introduction," in John Osborne, *The First Two Years of the Nixon Watch* (Liveright, 1971), p. x.

3. George H. Gallup, *The Gallup Poll: Public Opinion 1935–1971* (Random House, 1972), vol. 3, pp. 2107, 2128, 2151, and 2158.

4. John Gardner, "Godkin Lectures" (Harvard University, 1969), lecture 1, p. 1.

5. Philip B. Converse, "The Nature of Belief Systems in Mass Publics," in David E. Apter, ed., *Ideology and Discontent* (Free Press, 1964), p. 207.

6. Ibid; Jerrold S. Schneider, *Ideological Coalitions in Congress* (Greenwood Press, 1979), pp. 11–12; Martin Seliger, *Ideology and Politics* (Free Press, 1976), p. 119. Seliger gives a useful account of the evolution of the term *ideology* since it was first coined in France during the Napoleonic era (pp. 28–62).

7. *The Oxford English Dictionary*, s.v. "conservative"; Robert Blake, *The Conservative Party from Peel to Churchill* (London: Eyre and Spottiswoode, 1970), p. 26.

8. *Niles' Register* (Baltimore, Md., May 26, 1832), p. 236. The platform was adopted by an "assembly of young men," which met in response to a resolution by the National Republican Convention, held in December 1831. Many historians regard the Democratic platform of 1840 as the first true party platform.

9. See, for example, Robert G. McCloskey, *American Conservatism in the Age of Enterprise* (Harvard University Press, 1955), p. 22; and Michael Walzer, "In Defense of Equality," in Lewis A. Coser and Irving Howe, eds., *The New Conservatives* (Quadrangle, 1973), p. 107.

10. Robert Michels, *Political Parties* (Free Press, 1962), p. 44; Hugh Cecil, quoted in William A. Orton, *The Liberal Tradition* (Yale University Press, 1945), p. 14; Karl Mannheim, *Ideology and Utopia* (Harcourt, Brace, 1936), p. 118; Daniel Bell, *The End of Ideology* (Free Press, 1962), p. 28; Michael Oakeshott, *Rationalism in Politics* (Barnes and Noble, 1962), p. 188; Samuel P. Huntington, "Conservatism as an Ideology," *American Political Science Review*, vol. 51 (June 1957), p. 460.

11. Seliger, *Ideology and Politics*, pp. 92–94.

12. In the mountain of literature on the Western tradition, see particularly Crane Brinton, *Ideas and Men: The Story of Western Thought* (Prentice-Hall, 1950), pp. 105–210; Carl J. Friedrich, *Constitutional Government and Democracy: Theory and Practice in Europe and America* (Little, Brown, 1941), pp. 3–35; George H. Sabine, *A History of Political Theory* (Holt, 1937), pp. 198–433; Arthur O. Lovejoy, *The Great Chain of Being: A Study of the History of an Idea* (Harvard University Press, 1936); Frederick Watkins, *The Political Tradition of the West: A Study in the Development of Modern Liberalism* (Harvard University Press, 1948), pp. 3–89; William H. McNeill, *The Rise of the West: A History of the Human Community* (University of Chicago Press, 1963), pp. 547–59; Henri Pirenne, *A History of Western Europe* (Doubleday, 1956), vol. 2, pp. 221–307; John Herman Randall, Jr., *The Making of the Modern Mind: A Survey of the Intellectual Background of the Present Age* (Houghton Mifflin, 1940), pp. 9–106; J. Huizinga, *The Waning of the Middle Ages* (Doubleday, 1954), pp. 9–31, 56–67; Isaiah Berlin, *Against the Current: Essays in the History of Ideas* (Viking Press, 1979), pp. 1–129; Robert Nisbet, *History of the Idea of Progress* (Basic Books, 1980), pp. 3–167.

13. Thomas Hobbes, *Leviathan* (Dutton, 1950), pp. 101–44.

14. John Locke, "An Essay Concerning the True Original, Extent and End of Civil Government," in *Of Civil Government* (London: Dent, 1924), pp. 117–82.

15. George H. Sabine, *A History of Political Theory* (Holt, 1937), p. 529.

16. Progressive authoritarian nationalism, of the kind developed by Fichte and Hegel, also has some of its roots in ideational conservatism.

17. M. Ostrogorski, *Democracy and the Organization of Political Parties*, vol. 1: *England* (Doubleday, 1964), p. 54.

18. Karl Marx, *Essential Writings*, ed. Frederic Bander (Harper and Row, 1922), p. 66.

19. For a discussion of Hamilton's view, see John C. Koritansky, "Alexander Hamilton's Philosophy of Government and Administration," *Publius*, vol. 9 (Spring 1979), pp. 99–122; for the English Tories, see Blake, *Conservative Party*, pp. 10–59; and Boyd Hilton, *Corn, Cash, Commerce: Economic Policies of Tory Governments, 1815–30* (Oxford University Press, 1977).

20. See McCloskey, *American Conservatism in the Age of Enterprise*; and Louis Hacker, *The Triumph of American Capitalism* (Columbia University Press, 1940).

21. Milton Friedman, *Capitalism and Freedom* (University of Chicago Press, 1963), p. 2; Edmund Burke, *Reflections on the Revolution in France* (London: Dent, 1910), p. 93.

22. Louis Hartz, *The Liberal Tradition in America* (Harcourt, Brace, 1955), p. 153.

23. For an extended evaluation of capitalism in the light of traditional conservatism, see Irving Kristol, *Two Cheers for Capitalism* (Basic Books, 1978). See also Edward R. Norman, "Denigration of Capitalism: Current Education and the Moral Subversion of Capitalist Society," in Michael Novak, ed., *The Denigration of Capitalism* (American Enterprise Institute, 1979), pp. 7–23.

24. *The Federalist: A Commentary on the Constitution of the United States* (Modern Library, 1937), p. 339.

25. Ostrogorski, *England*, p. 127.

26. Gordon A. Craig, *Germany: 1866–1945* (Oxford University Press, 1978), pp. 150–57.

27. Malcolm Moos, *The Republicans* (Random House, 1956), p. 77.

28. Quoted in Hacker, *Triumph of American Capitalism*, p. 279.

29. In the nine presidential elections from 1948 to 1980, Republican candidates averaged 49.8 percent of the popular vote and Democrats averaged 46.4 percent. Republicans were victorious in five elections, and Democrats in four. In the 1980 election, Republicans won a majority in the Senate for the first time since 1952, but remained a minority in the House.

30. See F. A. Hayek, *The Constitution of Liberty* (University of Chicago Press, 1960), p. 29. Hayek's view that planned economies are bound to fail because of "the inevitable ignorance of all of us concerning a great many of the factors on which the achievement of our ends and welfare depends" is a libertarian argument that fits well with the skeptical view of detailed social planning characteristic of traditional conservatism.

31. For the relationship between nationalism and liberalism, see James H. Billington, *Fire in the Minds of Men: Origins of the Revolutionary Faith* (Basic Books, 1980), pp. 57–71, 146–66.

32. Craig, *Germany*, pp. 39–43.

33. Quoted in John Gunther, *Inside U.S.A.* (Harper, 1946), p. vi.

34. L. B. Namier, *England in the Age of the American Revolution* (Macmillan, 1930), p. 210.

35. Clinton Rossiter, *Parties and Politics in America* (Cornell University Press, 1960), p. 114.

36. Some members of the liberal community have continued to support pluralism, but there seems to have been a drift among liberal pluralists toward the standard of "neoconservatism."

37. John Osborne, *White House Watch: The Ford Years* (New Republic Books, 1977), p. 167. While covering the 1968 campaign, I often heard Nixon use this line.

38. See, for instance, Harvey Cox, *The Secular City* (Macmillan, 1965).

39. For an eloquent expression of this view, see Reinhold Neibuhr, *Christian Realism and Political Problems* (Scribners, 1953), particularly pp. 53–74 and 105–18. See also James V. Schall, "Religion and the Demise of Capitalism," in Novak, ed., *Denigration of Capitalism*, pp. 32–38.

40. Richard Nixon, *RN: The Memoirs of Richard Nixon* (Grosset and Dunlap, 1978), p. 354.

41. *Public Papers of the Presidents: Richard Nixon, 1971* (Government Printing Office, 1972), p. 934.

Chapter 2 (pages 22–37)

1. The best account of the Republican party on the eve of the 1968 campaign is Stephen Hess and David S. Broder, *The Republican Establishment: The Present and Future of the G.O.P.* (Harper and Row, 1967). For other relevant discussions of various aspects of Republican politics during the 1960s, see Kevin P. Phillips, *The Emerging Republican Majority* (Arlington House, 1969); Richard M. Scammon and Ben J. Wattenberg, *The Real Majority* (Coward-McCann, 1970), especially pp. 200–11; John H. Kessel, *The Goldwater Coalition: Republican Strategies in 1964* (Bobbs-Merrill, 1968); Theodore H. White, *The Making of the President, 1960* (Atheneum, 1961); White, *The Making of the President, 1964* (Atheneum, 1965); White, *The Making of the President, 1968* (Atheneum, 1969); Richard J. Whalen, *Catch the Falling Flag: A Republican's Challenge to His Party* (Houghton Mifflin, 1972); Lewis Chester, Godfrey Hodgson, and Bruce Page, *An American Melodrama: The Presidential Campaign of 1968* (Viking Press, 1969); James L. Sundquist, *Dynamics of the Party System: Alignment and Realignment of Political Parties in the United States* (Brookings Institution, 1973), pp. 308–73; Samuel H. Beer, "In Search of a New Public Philosophy," in Anthony King, ed., *The New American Political System* (American Enterprise Institute, 1978), pp. 15–33; Norman H. Nie, Sidney Verba, and John R. Perrocik, *The Changing American Voter* (Harvard University Press, 1976), pp. 194–209; Henry Fairlie, *The Parties: Republicans and Democrats in This Century* (St. Martin's Press, 1978), pp. 11–125; Everett Carll Ladd, Jr., with Charles D. Hadley, *Transformations of the American Party System from the New Deal to the 1970's* (Norton, 1975), pp. 232–48; Jules Witcover, *The Resurrection of Richard Nixon* (Putnam, 1970); Robert D. Novak, *The Agony of the G.O.P., 1964* (Macmillan, 1965); and James M. Perry, *The New Politics: The Expanding Technology of Political Manipulation* (Potter, 1968). For the earlier history of the Republican party, see Malcolm Moos, *The Republicans* (Random House, 1956); George H. Mayer, *The Republican Party 1854–1964* (Oxford University Press, 1964); Charles O. Jones, *The Republican Party in American Politics* (Macmillan, 1965); Sundquist, *Dynamics of the Party System;* Leonard D. White, *The Republican Era 1869–1901* (Macmillan, 1958); Louis Hartz, *The Liberal Tradition in America* (Harcourt, Brace, 1955), pp. 203–24; Richard Hofstadter, *The American Political Tradition* (Knopf, 1948), pp. 93–314; Walter Dean Burnham, *Critical Elections* (Norton, 1970); William Allen White, *Masks in a Pageant* (Macmillan, 1928); and Matthew Josephson, *The Politicos* (Harcourt, Brace, 1938). Besides the above sources, the descriptions and analyses in this chapter are based on information and impressions gathered while preparing articles for *Fortune* magazine on the Republican party and national politics in general during 1967 and 1968. See A. James Reichley, "Ronald Reagan Faces Life," *Fortune,* July 1967; "Here Come the Republicans," *Fortune,* September 1967; "How

Nixon Plans to Bring It Off," *Fortune*, December 1967; "The Last Stand of Accommodation Politics," *Fortune*, October 1968.

2. Taft was not himself, except in his foreign policy isolationism, a representative stalwart, and indeed held more progressive views on many social issues than his great rivals Dewey and Eisenhower. Many of the stalwarts seem to have sensed that he viewed public affairs from a different perspective than theirs, but this did not reduce, and may even have enlarged, the extraordinary devotion with which they followed him. See James T. Patterson, *Mr. Republican: A Biography of Robert Taft* (Houghton Mifflin, 1952).

3. Nathaniel Hawthorne, *The Complete Novels and Selected Tales* (Modern Library, 1937), p. 122.

4. Brand Whitlock, *Forty Years of It* (Appleton, 1914), p. 27.

5. Daniel Walker Howe, *The Political Culture of the American Whigs* (University of Chicago Press, 1979), pp. 150–80; Ronald P. Formisano, *The Birth of Mass Political Parties: Michigan, 1827–1861* (Princeton University Press, 1971), pp. 128–64. See also Lee Benson, *The Concept of Jacksonian Democracy: New York as a Test Case* (Princeton University Press, 1961), pp. 198–207.

6. See Richard Jensen, *The Winning of the Midwest: Social and Political Conflict, 1888–1896* (University of Chicago Press, 1971), pp. 58–88.

7. Interview with Clarence Brown, Jr., September 13, 1977.

8. Scammon and Wattenberg, *Real Majority*, pp. 35–44.

9. A reader of this book in manuscript pointed out that controversy over the causes of the Communist takeover in China in 1949 also contributed to the fundamentalists' special interest in Asia.

10. Phillips, *Emerging Republican Majority*, pp. 437–43.

11. Scammon and Wattenberg, *Real Majority*, p. 333.

12. White, *Making of the President, 1968*, appendix B.

13. For Disraeli's view, see M. Ostrogorski, *Democracy and The Organization of Political Parties*, vol. 1: *England* (Doubleday, 1964), p. 127.

14. For a classic description of the program of the first Republican administration, see Louis Hacker, *The Triumph of American Capitalism* (Columbia University Press, 1940), pp. 361–73. The thirteenth amendment, abolishing slavery, was not approved by the states until the end of 1865, but had been passed by Congress before Lincoln's assassination.

15. Edmund Burke, *Reflections on the Revolution in France* (Dutton, 1910), p. 20.

16. Moos, *Republicans*, p. 279. Roosevelt's conservatism, though it fluctuated during his career, was not late-blooming. Roosevelt always took delight in pummeling William Jennings Bryan and the populists. During the 1896 campaign, while canvassing for McKinley, he refused to meet Governor John Altgeld of Illinois, a liberal Democrat, because, Roosevelt said, he might some day "have to fire on the Governor at the head of a regiment." Mayer, *Republican Party*, p. 252. See also Edmund Morris, *The Rise of Theodore Roosevelt* (Coward, McCann, and Geoghegan, 1979), pp. 547–55.

17. After losing the Republican nomination for mayor in 1969, Lindsay ran and was reelected on the Liberal line. During his second term he had no

real political base. In 1971 he became a Democrat and waged an abortive campaign for the Democratic presidential nomination in 1972.

18. Kirk H. Porter and Donald Bruce Johnson, *National Party Platforms, 1840–1968* (University of Illinois Press, 1970), p. 735.

19. *Republican Platform, 1968* (Republican National Committee, 1968), p. 1. The platform, prepared by the committee on resolutions, chaired by Senator Dirksen, was approved by acclamation at the Republican convention and may be viewed as at least minimally acceptable to all major Republican groups.

20. Ibid., pp. 14–15.

21. Porter and Johnson, *National Party Platforms*, pp. 734–36.

22. *Nixon on the Issues* (Nixon-Agnew Campaign Committee, 1968), p. 86.

23. *Republican Platform, 1968*, p. 6.

Chapter 3 (pages 41–58)

1. Quoted in Richard Neustadt, *Presidential Power*, rev. ed. (Wiley, 1976), p. 61.

2. Arthur Schlesinger, Jr., *The Imperial Presidency* (Houghton Mifflin, 1973), p. ix.

3. Richard Nixon, *RN: The Memoirs of Richard Nixon* (Grosset and Dunlap, 1978), pp. 3–15; Earl Mazo and Stephen Hess, *Nixon: A Political Portrait* (Harper and Row, 1968), p. 30.

4. Most attempts at a psychohistory of Nixon are highly speculative or belong to the genre of political polemic, or both. One exception is Bruce Mazlish, *In Search of Nixon* (Basic Books, 1972), which is scholarly in its approach, though sometimes farfetched in its conclusions.

5. Interview with Elliot Richardson, January 9, 1978.

6. Nixon, *RN*, p. 5.

7. Ibid., p. 14.

8. Ibid., pp. 6–7.

9. Mazlish, *In Search of Nixon*, p. xi.

10. Nixon, *RN*, p. 27.

11. Digby Baltzell has brilliantly contrasted the passive attitude of the Quakers toward politics with the activist zeal of the New England Puritans in *Puritan Boston and Quaker Philadelphia* (Free Press, 1979). Since Methodism in some ways carries on the Puritan tradition, perhaps Nixon owed more than has been recognized to the Methodist strain inherited from his father.

12. Nixon, *RN*, pp. 14–15.

13. Ibid., p. 21.

14. Interview with Harry Dent, April 3, 1978.

15. Nixon, *RN*, pp. 21–22.

16. Ibid., p. 25.

17. Ibid., p. 26.

18. Ibid., p. 35.

19. Ibid., pp. 35–42.

20. *Congressional Quarterly Almanac*, vol. 3 (1947), pp. xxviii–xxxi.

21. Ibid., pp. xxii–xxiii.

22. Nixon, *RN*, p. 51.

23. *Congressional Quarterly Almanac*, vol. 6 (1950), pp. 60–61.

24. Theodore H. White, *Breach of Faith: The Fall of President Nixon* (Atheneum, 1975), p. 65.

25. Nixon, *RN*, pp. 44–45.

26. Alistair Cooke, *A Generation on Trial: U.S.A. v. Alger Hiss* (Knopf, 1950).

27. A. James Reichley, *States in Crisis* (University of North Carolina Press, 1964), pp. 172–73.

28. *Congressional Quarterly Almanac*, vol. 8 (1952), pp. 67–183.

29. Dwight D. Eisenhower, *Mandate for Change* (Doubleday, 1963), pp. 46–47; Nixon, *RN*, pp. 83–89. The other four names on Eisenhower's list were Congressmen Charles Halleck of Indiana and Walter Judd of Minnesota, and Governors Dan Thornton of Colorado and Arthur Langlie of Washington.

30. Eisenhower, *Mandate for Change*, pp. 65–69; Nixon, *RN*, pp. 92–110.

31. Nixon, *RN*, p. 112.

32. A. Robert Sobel, *The Worldly Economists* (Free Press, 1980), pp. 39–52.

33. Richard Nixon, *Six Crises* (Doubleday, 1962), pp. 309–10; Rowland Evans, Jr., and Robert D. Novak, *Nixon in the White House* (Random House, 1971), pp. 13, 179–80.

34. Nixon, *RN*, p. 139.

35. Interview with Nelson Rockefeller, March 24, 1978.

36. Eisenhower, *Mandate for Change*, p. 46.

37. Nixon, *RN*, pp. 219–21; Theodore C. Sorensen, *Kennedy* (Harper and Row, 1965), pp. 205–06.

38. Nixon, *RN*, p. 226.

39. Ibid., p. 241.

40. Ibid., p. 268.

41. Ibid., pp. 263–64.

42. Ibid., p. 268.

43. Interview with Richard Nixon, September 28, 1967.

44. *Nixon Speaks Out* (Nixon-Agnew Campaign Committee, 1968), pp. 11–12.

45. Ibid., p. 37.

46. Ibid., pp. 20–27.

47. Interview with Richard Nixon, July 5, 1968.

48. Kevin Phillips, *The Emerging Republican Majority* (Arlington, 1969), p. 436.

49. Lewis Chester, Godfrey Hodgson, and Bruce Page, *An American Melodrama* (Dell, 1969), pp. 549–50.

50. Interview with Bryce Harlow, November 3, 1977.

51. Nixon, *RN*, p. 352.

52. William Safire, *Before the Fall* (Doubleday, 1975), p. 690.

53. Ibid., p. 230.

54. Nixon, *RN*, p. 581.

55. Raymond Price, *With Nixon* (Viking Press, 1977), p. 47. Admittedly, this passage sounds a bit more like Price writing for Nixon than Nixon speaking in his own voice. Price concedes that some of the notes from which he takes his quotes are not verbatim. On the other hand, several former Nixon aides have mentioned Nixon's capacity for adjusting his manner of speech to his immediate audience, even in casual conversation. One aide who worked closely with Nixon for many years says he never heard Nixon swear.

56. *Nixon Speaks Out*, pp. 31–32.

57. Nixon, *RN*, p. 354.

58. Safire, *Before the Fall*, p. 218.

59. John Gardner, "Godkin Lectures" (Harvard University, 1969), lecture 1, p. 4, and lecture 2, p. 15.

60. Interviews with Robert Finch, March 8, 1978, and John Veneman, September 12, 1977.

Chapter 4 (pages 59–78)

1. Rowland Evans, Jr., and Robert D. Novak, *Nixon in the White House* (Random House, 1971), p. 11.

2. Earl Mazo and Stephen Hess, *Nixon: A Political Portrait* (Harper and Row, 1968), p. 314.

3. A. James Reichley, "How Nixon Plans to Bring It Off," *Fortune*, December 1967.

4. Theodore H. White, *Breach of Faith: The Fall of President Nixon* (Atheneum, 1975), pp. 92–94; H. R. Haldeman, with Joseph DiMona, *The Ends of Power* (Times Books, 1978), pp. 45–58.

5. White, *Breach of Faith*, p. 96.

6. Richard J. Whalen, *Catch the Falling Flag* (Houghton Mifflin, 1972), p. 223.

7. Haldeman, *Ends of Power*, pp. 48–49, 74.

8. Interview with Martin Anderson, January 3, 1978.

9. John Kessel, *The Domestic Presidency* (Hemel Hempstead, England: Duxbury Press, 1975), p. 114.

10. Interview with Leonard Garment, October 19, 1977.

11. Interview with William A. Madison, September 5, 1969.

12. A. James Reichley, "Elm Street's New White House Power," *Fortune*, December 1969.

13. Interview with John Mitchell, September 18, 1969.

14. Evans and Novak, *Nixon in the White House*, p. 28.

15. Interview with Robert Finch, March 8, 1978.

16. Interview with John Sears, August 26, 1978. Sears left the administration at the end of 1969. He later gained celebrity as manager of Ronald Reagan's presidential campaigns of 1976 and 1980. His association with

Reagan was terminated when he was fired by the candidate, after a struggle for power inside the campaign, on the day of the 1980 New Hampshire primary.

17. Interview with Alan Greenspan, January 28, 1978.

18. Evans and Novak, *Nixon in the White House*, p. 11.

19. Stephen Hess has pointed out to me that Nixon also resented Dillon's willingness to serve in the Kennedy administration.

20. Interview with William Rogers, September 28, 1967; Evans and Novak, *Nixon in the White House*, p. 23.

21. Evans and Novak, *Nixon in the White House*, p. 24; interview with Melvin Laird, March 31, 1978; letter from Henry Jackson to the author, April 4, 1980.

22. Whalen, *Catch the Falling Flag*, pp. 30-31.

23. *Nixon Speaks Out* (Nixon-Agnew Campaign Committee, 1968), pp. 242-43.

24. Interview with Richard Allen, October 27, 1977.

25. Allen served briefly as deputy director of the National Security Council under Kissinger, but resigned when he realized that Kissinger was shutting him out of a substantive role. In 1980 Allen reappeared as chief foreign policy adviser to Ronald Reagan, and in 1981 became director of the National Security Council—Kissinger's old job—in the Reagan administration.

26. Henry Kissinger, *White House Years* (Little, Brown, 1979), p. 12.

27. Ibid., pp. 10-16; Marvin and Bernard Kalb, *Kissinger* (Little, Brown, 1974), pp. 17-30; Evans and Novak, *Nixon in the White House*, pp. 19-21. I have also drawn on interviews with several of Kissinger's former colleagues at the State Department and National Security Council.

28. Interview with Arthur Burns, September 21, 1977; Evans and Novak, *Nixon in the White House*, p. 14.

29. Daniel P. Moynihan, "Where Liberals Went Wrong," in Melvin R. Laird, ed., *Republican Papers* (Praeger, 1968), p. 132. Moynihan's article had first appeared in *Newsday*, where it was seen by Laird.

30. *Nixon Speaks Out*, p. 22.

31. Interview with Daniel Patrick Moynihan, July 13, 1978.

32. Interviews with Burns and Anderson.

33. Richard Nixon, *RN: The Memoirs of Richard Nixon* (Grosset and Dunlap, 1978), pp. 424-25; interview with Moynihan. Nixon also quotes Moynihan as saying, "The urban ghettos will go up in flames" if Great Society programs were cut too fast. Moynihan denies having said that.

34. Raymond Price, *With Nixon* (Viking Press, 1977), pp. 44-45.

35. Henry J. Aaron, *Politics and the Professors* (Brookings Institution, 1978), pp. 158-59.

36. Daniel P. Moynihan, *The Politics of a Guaranteed Income* (Random House, 1973), p. 53.

37. Interview with Moynihan; Peter Drucker, "The Sickness of Government," *The Public Interest*, no. 14 (Winter 1969), p. 3.

38. Moynihan, *Politics of a Guaranteed Income*, pp. 50-64; interview with

440

Moynihan. For a fuller discussion of Moynihan's ideological evolution, which makes some of the same points mentioned here, see Peter Steinfels, *The Neoconservatives* (Simon and Schuster, 1979), pp. 108–60.

39. Moynihan, *Politics of a Guaranteed Income*, p. 215; interview with Moynihan.

40. William Safire, *Before the Fall* (Doubleday, 1975), p. 33.

41. Interview with Charls Walker, October 4, 1977; Evans and Novak, *Nixon in the White House*, pp. 25–26.

42. Interview with Robert Mayo, January 24, 1978.

43. Paul W. McCracken, "The U.S. Balance of Payments Problem and Domestic Prosperity," in McCracken and Emile Benoit, eds., *The Balance of Payments and Domestic Prosperity* (University of Michigan, 1963), p. 29.

44. Paul W. McCracken, "What Our Society Should Be All About," *Across the Board*, vol. 14 (July 1977), pp. 5–10.

45. Hearings before the Joint Economic Committee, 91 Cong. 1 sess. (Government Printing Office, 1969), pt. 2, pp. 284–304.

46. Interview with George Shultz, January 19, 1973.

47. Interview with Milton Friedman, March 9, 1978.

48. Interview with Paul McCracken, October 5, 1978.

49. Interview with Richard Nathan, August 4, 1977.

50. Interviews with Burns and Anderson. The characterization of Nixon's campaign pronouncements as "sketchy" is mine, not theirs.

51. Quotations from the Burns report are from an unpublished memorandum, January 18, 1969.

52. Ibid.

53. Ibid.

54. Interview with Bryce Harlow, November 3, 1977.

55. Interview with Burns.

56. Interview with Moynihan.

57. Nixon, *RN*, p. 339.

Chapter 5 (pages 79–97)

1. Interview with Bryce Harlow, November 3, 1977.

2. Morris Fiorina, "The Case of the Vanishing Marginals: The Bureaucracy Did It," *American Political Science Review*, vol. 71 (March 1977), pp. 177–81, argues that incumbents have benefited from increased emphasis on the role of congressmen as emissaries to the federal bureaucracy. John Ferejohn, in "On the Decline of Competition in Congressional Elections," ibid., pp. 166–75, contends that the decline of the parties has made challenge to incumbents more difficult. The huge increase in expenditures by Congress for its own staff and public relations facilities has also undoubtedly contributed to the growing importance of incumbency, at least in the House. See *National Journal*, February 4, 1978, p. 182.

3. Malcolm Jewell and Samuel Patterson, *The Legislative Process in the United States*, 3d ed. (Random House, 1977), pp. 391–92.

4. Based on *Congressional Quarterly Almanac*, vol. 25 (1969), pp. 1052–64; and vol. 26 (1970), pp. 1144–54.

5. Quoted in David Vogler, *Politics of Congress* (London: Allyn and Bacon, 1977), p. 114.

6. Ibid., p. 113.

7. Julius Turner, *Party and Constituency: Pressures on Congress*, revised by Edward V. Scheier, Jr. (Johns Hopkins Press, 1970), p. 180.

8. During the period of the Nixon and Ford administrations, two senators, Harry F. Byrd, Jr., of Virginia and James Buckley of New York, were not strictly aligned with either of the major parties. Buckley, elected as a Conservative from New York in 1970, participated in the Republican caucus and is included in this study with the Republicans. Byrd switched from Democrat to Independent in 1970, but continued to receive his committee assignments from the Democrats, and is included here among the Democrats.

9. See, for instance, Samuel H. Beer, "Adoption of General Revenue Sharing," *Public Policy*, vol. 24 (Spring 1976), pp. 176–77.

10. Interview with William Timmons, November 29, 1977. For a description of Nixon's congressional liaison operation, see Stephen J. Wayne, *The Legislative Presidency* (Harper and Row, 1978), pp. 155–58.

11. Interview with Timmons.

12. Interview with Richard Cook, September 16, 1977.

13. Interview with Gerald Ford, June 20, 1967.

14. Interview with Timmons.

15. Interview with Cook.

16. Interview with Timmons.

17. Ibid.

18. Interview with Harlow.

19. Interview with Cook.

20. Interview with Harlow.

21. Interview with Joe Waggonner, February 8, 1978.

22. Interview with G. V. Montgomery, November 9, 1977.

23. Interview with Timmons.

24. Based on *Congressional Quarterly Almanac*, vol. 26, pp. 2-H, 3-H.

25. Interview with Cook.

26. Based on *Congressional Quarterly Almanac*, vol. 26, pp. 16-H, 17-H.

27. Interview with Charls Walker, October 4, 1977.

28. Based on *Congressional Quarterly Almanac*, vol. 25, pp. 26-H, 27-H.

29. Interview with Harlow.

30. Interview with Eugene Cowen, October 5, 1977.

31. Interview with Timmons.

32. Interview with Harlow.

33. Ibid.

34. For a detailed account of the antiballistic missile controversy, see Alton Frye, *A Responsible Congress: The Politics of National Security* (McGraw-Hill, 1975), pp. 17–37.

35. Interview with Kenneth BeLieu, September 13, 1977.

36. Based on *Congressional Quarterly Almanac*, vol. 25, p. 13-S.

37. Interview with John Sears, August 26, 1977; Rowland Evans, Jr., and Robert D. Novak, *Nixon in the White House* (Random House, 1971), pp. 110–14.

38. Interview with Sears.

39. Interview with Hugh Scott, December 6, 1977.

40. Interview with Cowen.

41. Interview with Scott.

42. Ibid.

43. Evans and Novak, *Nixon in the White House*, pp. 159–64.

44. *Public Papers of the Presidents: Richard Nixon, 1969* (Government Printing Office, 1971), pp. 814–20.

45. Based on *Congressional Quarterly Almanac*, vol. 25, p. 29-S.

46. Interview with Cowen.

47. Interview with Charles Mathias, September 22, 1977.

48. Based on *Congressional Quarterly Almanac*, vol. 26, p. 21-S.

Chapter 6 (pages 98–129)

1. *Public Papers of the Presidents: Richard Nixon, 1972* (Government Printing Office, 1974), p. 198.

2. Richard Buel, Jr., *Securing the Revolution: Ideology in American Politics, 1789–1815* (Cornell University Press, 1972), especially pp. 28–49; William Nisbet Chambers, *Parties in a New Nation: The American Experience, 1776–1809* (Oxford University Press, 1963).

3. Robert W. Tucker and William Watts, eds., *Beyond Containment* (Potomac Associates, 1973), pp. xiii–xxxix.

4. Richard Nixon, *RN: The Memoirs of Richard Nixon* (Grosset and Dunlap, 1978), p. 45.

5. Ibid., pp. 150–55; Chalmers M. Roberts, "The Day We Didn't Go to War," *The Reporter*, September 14, 1954, pp. 31–35.

6. Nixon, *RN*, p. 235.

7. *Proceedings of the American Legion National Convention* (Washington, D.C.: American Legion, 1966), p. 63.

8. Nixon, *RN*, p. 282.

9. Richard Nixon, "Asia after Vietnam," *Foreign Affairs*, vol. 46 (October 1967), p. 121.

10. Nixon, *RN*, p. 289.

11. Interview with Richard Nixon, July 5, 1968.

12. *Public Papers of the Presidents: Richard Nixon, 1969* (GPO, 1971), p. 3.

13. John P. Leacacos, "Kissinger's Apparat," in Tucker and Watts, eds., *Beyond Containment*, p. 189; Marvin and Bernard Kalb, *Kissinger* (Little, Brown, 1974), p. 80.

14. The discussion of the role of the National Security Council is based on interviews with several former staff members, particularly William Watts on September 21, 1977. Henry Kissinger has described the early operations of the reconstituted council in *White House Years* (Little, Brown, 1979), pp. 38–48.

15. Leacacos, "Kissinger's Apparat," pp. 184–89; Kissinger, *White House*

Years, pp. 46–48. For good discussions of Nixon's foreign policy system, see I. M. Destler, *Presidents, Bureaucrats, and Foreign Policy* (Princeton University Press, 1972), pp. 118–53; and Wilfrid L. Kohl, "The Nixon-Kissinger Foreign Policy System and U.S.-European Relations," *World Politics,* vol. 28 (October 1975), pp. 1–43.

16. Nixon, *RN,* pp. 382–85; Kissinger, *White House Years,* pp. 316–21.

17. William Shawcross, *Sideshow: Nixon, Kissinger, and the Destruction of Cambodia* (Simon and Schuster, 1979), p. 102.

18. William Safire, *Before the Fall* (Doubleday, 1975), p. 486.

19. Nixon, *RN,* p. 457; Tad Szulc, *The Illusion of Peace* (Viking Press, 1978), p. 279.

20. Interview with Melvin Laird, March 31, 1978.

21. Ibid. Kissinger was skeptical about Vietnamization on the ground that "withdrawals would become like 'salted peanuts' to the American public; the more troops we withdrew, the more would be expected." *White House Years,* p. 284.

22. Interview with Laird; letter to the author from Paul C. Warnke, June 4, 1980.

23. Nixon, *RN,* p. 289.

24. Interviews with former NSC staff members, some of whom wished to remain anonymous; Kalb and Kalb, *Kissinger,* p. 157; Roger Morris, *Uncertain Greatness: Henry Kissinger and Foreign Policy* (Harper and Row, 1977), p. 135.

25. Safire, *Before the Fall,* p. 396.

26. "Kissinger: Action Biography," ABC Television Network, June 14, 1974, pp. 1–2; quoted in Bruce Mazlish, *Kissinger* (Basic Books, 1976), p. 19.

27. *New York Times,* November 14, 1971.

28. Mazlish, *Kissinger,* p. 38.

29. Ibid., p. 225.

30. My analysis of the psychological sources of Kissinger's conservatism generally follows Mazlish.

31. See Stephen R. Graubard, *Kissinger: Portrait of a Mind* (Norton, 1973), p. 8.

32. Henry A. Kissinger, *A World Restored* (Grosset and Dunlap, 1964), p. 204. This is a slightly revised version of his 1954 dissertation.

33. Ibid., pp. 193–95.

34. Henry A. Kissinger, "Reflections on American Diplomacy," *Foreign Affairs,* vol. 35 (October 1956), p. 37.

35. Mazlish, *Kissinger,* pp. 120–21; Graubard, *Kissinger,* pp. 176–77. In *White House Years* Kissinger recalls that Bundy "tended to treat me with the combination of politeness and subconscious condescension that upper-class Bostonians reserve for people of, by New England standards, exotic backgrounds and excessively intense personal style" (pp. 13–14).

36. Henry A. Kissinger, *The Troubled Partnership* (McGraw-Hill, 1965), p. 250.

37. Henry A. Kissinger, "Central Issues of American Foreign Policy," in Kermit Gordon, ed., *Agenda for the Nation* (Brookings Institution, 1968), pp. 588, 614, 602.

38. Henry A. Kissinger, "The Vietnam Negotiations," *Foreign Affairs*, vol. 48 (January 1969), pp. 234, 230, 232.

39. Kissinger, *White House Years*, p. 256.

40. Graubard, *Kissinger*, p. 253.

41. Szulc, *Illusion of Peace*, p. 112; Mazlish, *Kissinger*, p. 244. Early spade work on the new China policy was done by Under Secretary of State Elliot Richardson, who was to play many roles in the Nixon administration.

42. Kissinger, *White House Years*, pp. 65–70, 191–94.

43. Kissinger, *White House Years*, pp. 226–30; *Public Papers of the Presidents: Richard Nixon, 1973* (GPO, 1975), p. 377.

44. *Public Papers: Nixon, 1973*, p. 347.

45. Szulc, *Illusion of Peace*, pp. 150–56.

46. Kissinger, *White House Years*, p. 288.

47. *The Gallup Opinion Index*, no. 60 (June 1970), p. 4.

48. Nixon, *RN*, p. 457.

49. Based on *Congressional Quarterly Almanac*, vol. 26 (1970), pp. 33–35.

50. Nixon, *RN*, p. 468.

51. *Public Papers of the Presidents: Richard Nixon, 1970* (GPO, 1971), p. 826.

52. Nixon, *RN*, p. 757.

53. Safire, *Before the Fall*, p. 412.

54. Nixon, *RN*, pp. 588–89.

55. Ibid., p. 579.

56. *Public Papers: Nixon, 1973*, pp. 355, 364.

57. *Public Papers of the Presidents: Richard Nixon, 1971* (GPO, 1972), pp. 806–07.

58. Henry A. Kissinger, *American Foreign Policy*, 3d ed. (Norton, 1977), p. 105.

59. Transcript of television interview with David Frost,*Washington Post*, May 26, 1977.

60. Daniel Patrick Moynihan, with Suzanne Weaver, *A Dangerous Place* (Little, Brown, 1975), pp. 142–46.

61. *The Gallup Opinion Index*, no. 108 (July 1974), pp. 3, 4.

Chapter 7 (pages 130–53)

1. Rowland Evans, Jr., and Robert D. Novak, *Nixon in the White House* (Random House, 1971), p. 11; Richard Nixon, *RN: The Memoirs of Richard Nixon* (Grosset and Dunlap, 1978), p. 825; Charles Colson, *Born Again* (Chosen Books, 1976), p. 42.

2. Interview with Elliot Richardson, January 9, 1978.

3. Interview with Martin Anderson, January 3, 1978.

4. Stephen Hess, *Organizing the Presidency* (Brookings Institution, 1976), p. 121.

5. Interview with Anderson.

6. Interview with Stephen Hess, October 21, 1977.

7. *Nixon on the Issues* (Nixon-Agnew Campaign Committee, 1968), pp. 118, 119.

8. "Report of the Task Force on Public Welfare, to President-Elect Richard M. Nixon," December 28, 1968, p. 9.

9. Gilbert Steiner has pointed out to me that pressure from the industrial states would have been even greater had it not been for enactment of the Kuchel amendment to the Medicaid Act in 1965, requiring the federal government to pay a greater share of the cost of AFDC to states paying high medicaid benefits.

10. Interview with Richard Nathan, August 4, 1977.

11. "Report of the Task Force on Public Welfare," pp. 9–13.

12. Report prepared by Arthur Burns for President-elect Nixon, 1969.

13. Daniel P. Moynihan, *The Politics of a Guaranteed Income* (Random House, 1973), p. 47.

14. Vincent J. Burke and Vee Burke, *Nixon's Good Deed: Welfare Reform* (Columbia University Press, 1974), p. 44. The Burkes provide the most complete overall account of the welfare reform controversy under Nixon. Moynihan, *Politics of a Guaranteed Income*, describes the controversy from the viewpoint of one of the major participants and gives more of the ideological background than is provided by the Burkes. Martin Anderson, *Welfare* (Hoover Institute Press, 1978), describes the controversy from the point of view of those who opposed the family assistance plan. At the time Nixon took office, welfare reform seemed to have found a place on the national social agenda. During 1968 about twelve hundred economists signed a statement calling for income guarantees, and Congress's Joint Economic Committee held hearings on income maintenance. See Gilbert Y. Steiner, *The State of Welfare* (Brookings Institution, 1971), pp. 100–05.

15. Interview with Milton Friedman, March 9, 1978.

16. George H. Gallup, *The Gallup Poll, Public Opinion, 1934–1971* (Random House, 1972), vol. 3, p. 2177.

17. Burke and Burke, *Nixon's Good Deed*, p. 37. The first guaranteed-income bill ever offered in Congress was introduced in May 1968 by Congressman William Ryan, liberal Democrat of New York, who predicted that "some form of the plan" would "undoubtedly" be recommended by the next president, Democratic or Republican. Steiner, *State of Welfare*, pp. 117–18.

18. Burke and Burke, *Nixon's Good Deed*, p. 53.

19. Ibid., pp. 57–60.

20. Interview with Anderson.

21. Ibid.; Moynihan, *Politics of a Guaranteed Income*, p. 144; Anderson, *Welfare*, pp. 81–82.

22. Burke and Burke, *Nixon's Good Deed*, pp. 72–73.

23. Interview with Arthur Burns, September 21, 1977.

24. Interview with Bryce Harlow, November 3, 1977.

25. Interview with Kenneth Cole, December 21, 1977.

26. Interview with Anderson.

27. Interview with Daniel Patrick Moynihan, July 13, 1978.

28. Interview with Burns.

29. Interview with Hess.

30. Burke and Burke, *Nixon's Good Deed*, pp. 83–84.

31. Ibid., p. 87.

32. Interview with Hess.

33. Burke and Burke, *Nixon's Good Deed*, p. 95.

34. Ibid., p. 98.

35. Ibid., pp. 102–07; interviews with Nathan, Moynihan, and Burns; Nixon, *RN*, pp. 426–27; Moynihan, *Politics of a Guaranteed Income*, pp. 213–17; Anderson, *Welfare*, pp. 82–84.

36. *Public Papers of the Presidents: Richard Nixon, 1969* (Government Printing Office, 1971), pp. 637–45.

37. Interview with Moynihan.

38. Ibid.

39. Moynihan, *Politics of a Guaranteed Income*, p. 276.

40. Ibid., pp. 226, 327–45.

41. Byrnes had closely followed the work being done on the negative income tax at the University of Wisconsin's Poverty Institute.

42. Burke and Burke, *Nixon's Good Deed*, p. 152.

43. *Congressional Quarterly Almanac*, vol. 26 (1970), pp. 1032–33.

44. Moynihan, *Politics of a Guaranteed Income*, p. 428.

45. *Congressional Quarterly Almanac*, vol. 26, pp. 16-H, 17-H.

46. *Family Assistance Act of 1970*, Hearings before the Senate Committee on Finance, 91 Cong. 2 sess. (GPO, 1970), pt. 1, p. 3.

47. Ibid., pp. 282–84.

48. Ibid., p. 284.

49. Moynihan, *Politics of a Guaranteed Income*, p. 461.

50. *Family Assistance Act of 1970*, Hearings, pt. 1, pp. 395–96.

51. Interview with John Veneman, September 12, 1977.

52. Interview with Robert Finch, March 8, 1978.

53. Interview with Richardson.

54. *Family Assistance Act of 1970*, Hearings, pt. 2, p. 400.

55. Burke and Burke, *Nixon's Good Deed*, pp. 161–62.

56. *Congressional Quarterly Almanac*, vol. 26, p. 1040.

57. Moynihan, *Politics of a Guaranteed Income*, p. 533.

58. *Public Papers of the Presidents: Richard Nixon, 1971* (GPO, 1972), p. 51.

59. *Congressional Quarterly Almanac*, vol. 27 (1971), pp. 34-H, 35-H.

60. Burke and Burke, *Nixon's Good Deed*, pp. 180–81.

61. Interview with Richardson.

62. *Congressional Quarterly Almanac*, vol. 28 (1972), p. 72-S.

63. Caspar W. Weinberger, "The Reform of Welfare: A National Necessity," *The Journal* (The Institute for Socioeconomic Studies), vol. 1 (Summer 1976), pp. 17–22. In 1981 Weinberger became secretary of defense in the Reagan administration.

64. Interview with Friedman.

65. Interview with Anderson; Anderson, *Welfare*, pp. 10–11. In 1981 Anderson became assistant to the president for domestic policy in the Reagan White House.

66. Moynihan, *Politics of a Guaranteed Income*, p. 215.

67. Nixon, *RN*, p. 428.

Chapter 8 (pages 154–73)

1. The other substantive recommendations made in the initial New Federalism speech on August 8, 1969, were a proposal to remodel the manpower training program, giving more authority over administration to the states, and a plan to reorganize the Office of Economic Opportunity, the continued existence of which was an affront to many conservatives.

2. Paul R. Dommel, *The Politics of Revenue Sharing* (Indiana University Press, 1974), pp. 39–46. Dommel, and Richard E. Thompson, *A New Era in Federalism* (Revenue Sharing Advisory Service, 1973), give overall accounts of the enactment of revenue sharing. Samuel H. Beer, "Adoption of General Revenue Sharing," *Public Policy*, vol. 24 (Spring 1976), pp. 127–95, provides good insights and gives particular attention to the ideological factors involved.

3. Dommel, *Politics of Revenue Sharing*, p. 54.

4. *New York Times*, October 27, 1968; quoted by Dommel, *Politics of Revenue Sharing*, p. 76.

5. "Report to President-elect Richard M. Nixon from the Task Force on Intergovernmental Fiscal Relations," November 29, 1968, pp. 21–25.

6. Dommel, *Politics of Revenue Sharing*, p. 98.

7. *Public Papers of the Presidents: Richard Nixon, 1969* (Government Printing Office, 1971), pp. 665–68.

8. William Safire, *Before the Fall* (Doubleday, 1975), p. 502.

9. Dommel, *Politics of Revenue Sharing*, p. 98.

10. Personal communication from Edwin L. Harper to the author, April 25, 1980.

11. Interview with Edwin Harper, October 26, 1977. In 1981 Harper became deputy director of the Office of Management and Budget in the Reagan administration.

12. *Public Papers: Nixon, 1971*, pp. 54–55.

13. Interview with Richard Nathan, August 4, 1977.

14. George H. Gallup, *The Gallup Poll: Public Opinion, 1934–1971* (Random House, 1972), vol. 3, p. 2285.

15. Interview with John Byrnes, November 2, 1977.

16. *New York Times*, January 26, 1971.

17. Beer, "Adoption of General Revenue Sharing," p. 185.

18. Interview with William Timmons, November 29, 1977.

19. Beer, "Adoption of General Revenue Sharing," p. 191.

20. Interview with Louis Stokes, September 15, 1977.

21. Dommel, *Politics of Revenue Sharing*, p. 138. Governor Jimmy Carter of Georgia also favored giving all revenue-sharing funds to local governments.

22. Ibid., p. 142.

23. Ibid., p. 158.

24. *Congressional Quarterly Almanac*, vol. 28 (1972), pp. 640–41. Gibbons's district was politically little changed by reapportionment and he was easily reelected.

25. Ibid., pp. 641–42.

26. Dommel, *Politics of Revenue Sharing*, pp. 149–50; Thompson, *New Era in Federalism*, p. 103.

27. Interview with Richard Cook, September 16, 1977.

28. Beer, "Adoption of General Revenue Sharing," p. 182.

29. *Congressional Record*, June 21, 1972, p. 21713.

30. Based on *Congressional Quarterly Almanac*, vol. 28, pp. 44-H, 45-H.

31. A few supporters of revenue sharing may have voted no on the O'Neill motion out of general opposition to consideration of bills under closed rules. Members of the Appropriations Committee, too, had particular cause to open the bill to amendments. The vote, however, was viewed by both sides as a critical test of support for revenue sharing itself, and most of those who voted against the closed rule but later supported the bill on final passage may be counted as latent opponents of revenue sharing.

32. Based on *Congressional Quarterly Almanac*, vol. 28, pp. 46-H, 47-H.

33. Ibid., p. 61-S.

34. Staff of the Joint Committee on Internal Revenue Taxation, *General Explanation of the State and Local Fiscal Assistance Act and the Federal-State Tax Collection Act of 1972*, 93 Cong. 1 sess. (GPO, 1973), p. 26.

35. *Public Papers of the Presidents: Richard Nixon, 1972* (GPO, 1974), p. 354.

36. Safire, *Before the Fall*, pp. 219–20.

37. Ibid., p. 220.

38. Publius, "New Federalist Paper No. 1," *Publius*, vol. 2 (Spring 1972), p. 98.

39. Ibid., pp. 99–115.

40. Cato, "Federalism: Old and New," *Publius*, vol. 2 (Spring 1972), pp. 116–24.

41. Ibid., pp. 125–29.

42. Ibid., pp. 129–31.

43. Johannes Althusius, "New Federalist Paper No. 3," *Publius*, vol. 2 (Spring 1972), pp. 132–37. Nathan later elaborated further on his interpretation of the New Federalism, particularly in *The Plot That Failed* (Wiley, 1975), pp. 13–31.

44. *Nixon Speaks Out* (Nixon-Agnew Campaign Committee, 1968), pp. 12–19.

45. Richard Nixon, *RN: The Memoirs of Richard Nixon* (Grosset and Dunlap, 1978), p. 352.

46. See Albert H. Cantril and Charles W. Roll, Jr., *Hopes and Fears of the American People* (Universe Books, 1971), pp. 15–36.

47. Daniel Patrick Moynihan, *Maximum Feasible Misunderstanding* (Free Press, 1969), p. xiii.

48. Cited by Richard M. Scammon and Ben J. Wattenberg, *The Real Majority* (Coward-McCann, 1970), p. 261. Support for desegregation also remained relatively high. *The Gallup Poll*, vol. 3, p. 2122.

49. *The Gallup Poll*, vol. 3, p. 2038. When asked whether they had "a favorable or unfavorable opinion of the Johnson Administration's program,

the Great Society," 32 percent responded favorable, 44 percent unfavorable, and 24 percent gave no opinion.

50. Ibid., p. 2154.
51. Interviews with Nathan and Harper.
52. *The Budget in Brief, Fiscal Year 1970* (GPO, 1969); *The U.S. Budget in Brief, Fiscal Year 1974* (GPO, 1973).
53. Safire, *Before the Fall*, p. 502.
54. Interview with Nathan.

Chapter 9 (pages 174–204)

1. William Safire, *Before the Fall* (Doubleday, 1975), p. 309; Harry S. Dent, *The Prodigal South Returns to Power* (Wiley, 1978), pp. 159–69; interview with Dent, April 3, 1978.
2. *Public Papers of the Presidents: Richard Nixon, 1972* (Government Printing Office, 1974), p. 430.
3. Theodore H. White, *The Making of the President, 1960* (Atheneum, 1961), pp. 321–23.
4. Jules Witcover, *The Resurrection of Richard Nixon* (Putnam, 1970), p. 130.
5. Interview with Dent.
6. Theodore H. White, *The Making of the President, 1968* (Atheneum, 1969), app. B. See also Dent, *Prodigal South Returns to Power*, pp. 94–100.
7. *Brown* v. *Board of Education*, 347 U.S. 495 (1954).
8. *Brown* v. *Board of Education*, 349 U.S. 300–01 (1955).
9. News release issued by U.S. Department of Health, Education, and Welfare, January 4, 1970.
10. *Green* v. *Board of Education of New Kent County*, 391 U.S. 438 (1968).
11. *Brown* v. *Board of Education*, 347 U.S. 493.
12. *Briggs* v. *Elliot*, 132 F. Supp. 777 (D.S.C. 1955).
13. *Taylor* v. *Board of Education*, 191 F. Supp. 193 (D.N.Y. 1961).
14. James Bolner and Robert Shanley, *Busing: The Political and Judicial Process* (Praeger, 1974), provides a narrative account of the busing controversy up to the end of 1973. Gary Orfield, *Must We Bus? Segregated Schools and National Policy* (Brookings Institution, 1978), gives more detail on the social context in which the busing controversy developed and brings the story up to 1977.
15. *Public Papers of the Presidents: Richard Nixon, 1971* (GPO, 1972), p. 849.
16. *Congressional Record*, June 4, 1964, pp. 12715–17.
17. 42 U.S.C. §200(c) (1964).
18. Safire, *Before the Fall*, p. 232.
19. Quoted in Rowland Evans, Jr., and Robert D. Novak, *Nixon in the White House* (Random House, 1971), p. 140.
20. *New York Times*, September 18, 1968.

21. *Nixon on the Issues* (Nixon-Agnew Campaign Committee, 1968), p. 98.

22. Richard M. Scammon and Ben J. Wattenberg, *The Real Majority* (Coward-McCann, 1970), p. 333.

23. *Public Papers of the Presidents: Richard Nixon, 1969* (GPO, 1971), p. 3.

24. Interview with John Mitchell, September 18, 1969.

25. Interview with Robert Finch, March 8, 1978.

26. Interview with John Veneman, September 12, 1977.

27. Leon E. Panetta and Peter Gall, *Bring Us Together: The Nixon Team and the Civil Rights Retreat* (Lippincott, 1971), p. 13.

28. Interview with Leon Panetta, September 19, 1977.

29. Ibid.

30. Ibid.

31. Panetta and Gall, *Bring Us Together*, p. 79.

32. Interview with Dent.

33. Panetta and Gall, *Bring Us Together*, p. 78.

34. Ibid., p. 77.

35. Interview with Mitchell.

36. Orfield, *Must We Bus?* p. 320.

37. Interview with Jerris Leonard, October 31, 1977.

38. Interview with Panetta.

39. Interview with Leonard Garment, October 19, 1977.

40. Panetta and Gall, *Bring Us Together*, pp. 219–21.

41. Ibid., p. 222.

42. Interview with Panetta.

43. Panetta and Gall, *Bring Us Together*, p. 254.

44. Ibid., p. 262.

45. *Alexander v. Holmes County Board of Education*, 396 U.S. 20 (1969).

46. Interview with Panetta.

47. George H. Gallup, *The Gallup Poll: Public Opinion, 1935–1971* (Random House, 1972), vol. 3, p. 2210.

48. Interview with Dent.

49. Interview with Panetta.

50. Ibid.

51. Interview with Garment.

52. Bolner and Shanley, *Busing*, pp. 63–70.

53. *Congressional Quarterly Almanac*, vol. 26 (1970), p. 10-S.

54. Interview with Bryce Harlow, November 3, 1977.

55. *Public Papers of the Presidents, Richard Nixon: 1970* (GPO, 1971), p. 113.

56. Dent, *Prodigal South Returns to Power*, p. 136.

57. Interview with George Shultz, January 4, 1978. The administration proposal to give special financial help to districts undergoing desegregation was turned down by Congress, where it was opposed by liberals on the ground that such funds would be a kind of reward to recalcitrant districts, and by southern conservatives, who regarded it as a means for promoting desegregation.

58. Ibid.; Raymond Price, *With Nixon* (Viking Press, 1977), 206–09.
59. *Public Papers: Nixon, 1970,* pp. 672–73.
60. *Statistical Abstract of the United States, 1978* (GPO, 1978), p. 151.
61. Ibid.
62. Safire, *Before the Fall,* p. 233.
63. Interview with Garment.
64. Safire, *Before the Fall,* p. 280.
65. Ibid., p. 236.
66. Interview with Harlow.
67. *Public Papers: Nixon, 1970,* pp. 304–20.
68. *Swann* v. *Charlotte-Mecklenburg Board of Education,* 402 U.S. 28, 30 (1971).
69. Ibid. at 22–31.
70. 338 F. Supp. 79 (D.Va. 1972).
71. 338 F. Supp. 582 (D.Mich. 1971).
72. Gallup, *The Gallup Poll,* vol. 3, p. 2329. Using a more complicated question—some would say more sophisticated—Opinion Research Corporation in the fall of 1972 found that 21 percent "support busing"; 15 percent "oppose generally, but favor rerouting to increase desegregation"; 7 percent "oppose rerouting, but favor busing as last resort if only way to achieve desegregation"; 36 percent oppose busing; and 21 percent had no opinion. From these figures Bolner and Stanley conclude that 43 percent supported "some form of busing." The Gallup result, based on a direct yes or no question, seems to me a more accurate device for tapping actual public opinion. Whether this opinion was based on popular misconceptions about busing, as Bolner and Stanley, Orfield, and the U.S. Commission on Civil Rights argue, is another question.
73. *Congressional Record,* November 4, 1971, p. 39313.
74. Ibid.
75. Ibid., p. 39302.
76. *Congressional Quarterly Almanac,* vol. 27 (1971), pp. 80-H, 81-H.
77. *Congressional Record,* February 24, 1972, p. S2448.
78. Ibid., p. S2551.
79. *Congressional Quarterly Almanac,* vol. 28 (1972), p. 10-S.
80. Ibid.
81. Safire, *Before the Fall,* p. 480.
82. Bolner and Stanley, *Busing,* p. 154.
83. *Pubic Papers: Nixon, 1972,* p. 428.
84. Ibid., p. 426.
85. Ibid., p. 427.
86. *Public Papers: Nixon, 1970,* p. 232.
87. *Public Papers: Nixon, 1972,* p. 438.
88. Alexander M. Bickel, "What's Wrong With Nixon's Busing Bill?" *New Republic,* April 22, 1971, p. 21.
89. Robert H. Bork, *Constitutionality of the President's Busing Proposals* (American Enterprise Institute, 1972), p. 19.

90. *Congressional Quarterly Almanac,* vol. 28, pp. 72-H, 73-H.

91. Edwin S. Corwin, *The Constitution and What It Means Today,* 13th ed. (Princeton University Press, 1973), p. 240.

92. Ibid., p. xv.

93. Ibid., pp. 245-49; Paul L. Murphy, *The Constitution in Crisis Times: 1918-1969* (Harper and Row, 1972), pp. 311-14.

94. Bolner and Stanley, *Busing,* p. 45.

95. Ibid., pp. 41-42.

96. *Milliken* v. *Bradley,* 418 U.S. 735 (1974).

97. Ibid. at 741-46.

98. Ibid. at 814.

99. Orfield, *Must We Bus?* p. 148.

100. *Public Papers of the Presidents: Gerald R. Ford, 1976* (GPO, 1979), vol. 2, pp. 1908-13.

101. Richard Nixon, *RN: The Memoirs of Richard Nixon* (Grosset and Dunlap, 1978), p. 436.

102. Ibid., p. 444.

103. Ibid.

Chapter 10 (pages 205-31)

1. Arthur F. Burns, "Wages and Prices by Formula," Murray Lecture at the State University of Iowa, November 10, 1964; printed in Burns, *The Business Cycle in a Changing World* (Columbia University Press, 1969), pp. 232-53.

2. Milton Friedman, *Inflation: Causes and Consequences* (Asia Publishing House, 1963), pp. 29-38.

3. *Nixon on the Issues* (Nixon-Agnew Campaign Committee, 1968), pp. 128-29; *New York Times,* December 29, 1968.

4. Data on prices and unemployment are from *Economic Report of the President,* various issues.

5. Interviews with Paul McCracken, October 5, 1978; Arthur Burns, September 21, 1977; and Milton Friedman, March 9, 1978.

6. Interviews with McCracken; and Herbert Stein, November 29, 1977.

7. Rowland Evans, Jr., and Robert D. Novak, *Nixon in the White House* (Random House, 1971), p. 200.

8. Interview with McCracken.

9. *The 1969 Economic Report of the President,* Hearings before the Joint Economic Committee, 91 Cong. 1 sess. (Government Printing Office, 1969), pt. 2, pp. 284-304. An overall account of the steps that led to wage and price controls, beginning with the 1969 game plan, is given by Neil de Marchi, "The First Nixon Administration: Prelude to Controls," in Craufurd D. Goodwin, ed., *Exhortation and Controls: The Search for a Wage-Price Policy, 1945-1971* (Brookings Institution, 1975), pp. 295-352. More detailed accounts of particular

episodes appear in George P. Shultz and Kenneth W. Dam, *Economic Policy Beyond the Headlines* (Stanford Alumni Association, 1977), pp. 65–85; Robert Sobel, *The Worldly Economists* (Free Press, 1980), pp. 175–207; Leonard Silk, *Nixonomics* (Praeger, 1972), pp. 53–61; William Safire, *Before the Fall* (Doubleday, 1975), pp. 509–28; Juan Cameron, "How the U.S. Got on the Road to a Controlled Economy," *Fortune*, January 1972, pp. 74–77; and Herbert Stein, " 'Price-Fixing,' as Seen by a 'Price-Fixer,' " *Across the Board*, vol. 15 (December 1978), pp. 32–43. Nixon's own account is in *RN: The Memoirs of Richard Nixon* (Grosset and Dunlap, 1978), pp. 515–22.

10. Interview with Charls Walker, October 4, 1977.

11. De Marchi, "First Nixon Administration," pp. 310–11.

12. Interview with George Shultz, January 4, 1978.

13. Memorandum in file of Office of Management and Budget, filed under H.R. 13270, December 19, 1969.

14. *Public Papers of the President: Richard Nixon, 1969* (GPO, 1971), pp. 1044–46.

15. Shultz and Dam, *Economic Policy Beyond the Headlines*, p. 44.

16. Interview with Robert Mayo, January 24, 1978.

17. Ibid.

18. Interview with Burns.

19. Interview with Mayo.

20. De Marchi, "First Nixon Administration," pp. 315–16.

21. Arthur Burns, *Reflections of an Economic Policy Maker* (American Enterprise Institute, 1978), pp. 91–102.

22. *Changing National Priorities*, Hearings before the Subcommittee on Economy in Government of the Joint Economic Committee, 91 Cong. 2 sess. (GPO, 1970), pt. 1, pp. 73–75.

23. Interview with Shultz; Evans and Novak, *Nixon in the White House*, p. 205.

24. *Public Papers of the Presidents: Richard Nixon, 1970* (GPO, 1971), pp. 502–09.

25. Herbert Stein, *The Fiscal Revolution in America* (University of Chicago Press, 1969), pp. 127–28, 346–47.

26. *Public Papers: Nixon, 1970*, pp. 600–02.

27. Ibid., pp. 674–76.

28. *Economic Report of the President, February 1971*, p. 60.

29. Arnold R. Weber, *In Pursuit of Price Stability: The Wage Price Freeze of 1971* (Brookings Institution, 1973), pp. 6–7; De Marchi, "First Nixon Administration," p. 326.

30. De Marchi, "First Nixon Administration," p. 326.

31. *Public Papers: Nixon, 1970*, pp. 1088–95.

32. De Marchi, "First Nixon Administration," p. 327.

33. Burns, *Reflections of an Economic Policy Maker*, pp. 103–15.

34. Interview with Peter Peterson, March 23, 1978.

35. Interview with John Connally, August 27, 1979. Connally summarized his political philosophy in a speech before the American Society of Newspaper

454

Editors, April 19, 1972, "Have We Failed So Miserably?" printed in *U.S. News and World Report,* May 1, 1972.

36. Interview with Connally.

37. *The U.S. Budget in Brief, Fiscal Year 1972,* pp. 6–9.

38. Nixon, *RN,* p. 517.

39. Evans and Novak, *Nixon in the White House,* p. 372.

40. *Miami Herald,* February 11, 1971.

41. *Public Papers of the Presidents: Richard Nixon, 1971* (GPO, 1972), pp. 581–87.

42. Burns, *Reflections of an Economic Policy Maker,* p. 118.

43. *New York Times,* February 8, 1971.

44. Interview with Walker.

45. Interview with Burns; Safire, *After the Fall,* pp. 491–96.

46. Interview with Shultz; De Marchi, "First Nixon Administration," p. 341.

47. Interview with Connally.

48. Nixon, *RN,* p. 518.

49. Interview with Shultz.

50. Nixon, *RN,* p. 518.

51. Interview with Shultz.

52. Interview with McCracken.

53. Interview with Shultz.

54. Interview with Friedman.

55. Interview with Paul Volcker, March 24, 1978.

56. Ibid.

57. Interview with Connally.

58. Interview with McCracken.

59. Interview with Shultz.

60. Nixon, *RN,* p. 519.

61. *Public Papers: Nixon, 1971,* pp. 886–91.

62. Interview with Stein; George H. Gallup, *The Gallup Poll: Public Opinion, 1959–1971* (Random House, 1972), vol. 3, p. 2322; Milton Friedman, *There's No Such Thing as a Free Lunch* (LaSalle, Ill.: Open Court, 1975), p. 1.

63. Edward R. Tufte, *Political Control of the Economy* (Princeton University Press, 1978), p. 136.

64. *The U.S. Budget in Brief, Fiscal Year 1973,* pp. 3–10.

65. Interview with Melvin Laird, March 31, 1978.

66. *Statistical Abstract of the United States, 1978* (GPO, 1978), table 884, p. 546.

67. Interview with Shultz.

68. Ibid.

69. *The U.S. Budget in Brief, Fiscal Year 1974,* pp. 17–27.

70. Interview with Shultz.

71. *Public Papers of the Presidents: Richard Nixon, 1973* (GPO, 1975), pp. 61–62.

72. Interview with Stein.

73. Interviews with McCracken, Shultz, Stein, and Volcker.
74. *A Conversation with John Connally of Texas* (American Enterprise Institute, 1978), p. 12. At other times Connally has argued that no one can really say if controls were needed in 1971. In an interview in 1979, he said: "It is really impossible to judge how effective the controls were. It may be that they did have a stabilizing effect, although they dealt with symptoms rather than causes. . . . At any rate, they did not result in the chaos that some eminent economists were predicting."
75. Nixon, *RN*, p. 521.
76. Stein, " 'Price-Fixing' as Seen by a 'Price-Fixer,' " p. 34.
77. Nixon, *RN*, p. 521.

Chapter 11 (pages 232–49)

1. Garnett Horner, "Nixon Looks Ahead," *Washington Star-News*, November 9, 1972; reprinted in Richard P. Nathan, *The Plot That Failed* (Wiley, 1975), p. 164.
2. Richard Nixon, *RN: The Memoirs of Richard Nixon* (Grosset and Dunlap, 1978), p. 717.
3. Interview with Bryce Harlow, November 3, 1977.
4. Interview with Elliot Richardson, January 9, 1978.
5. *Public Papers of the Presidents: Richard Nixon, 1972* (Government Printing Office, 1974), p. 1150.
6. Nathan, *Plot That Failed*, pp. 163, 165.
7. *Public Papers of the Presidents: Richard Nixon, 1973* (GPO, 1975), p. 14. Raymond Price, who drafted the speech, confirmed in conversation a few days after the inauguration that he and Nixon had deliberately aimed to suggest a contrast with the well-known sentence in Kennedy's inaugural address.
8. H. R. Haldeman, with Joseph DiMona, *The Ends of Power* (Times Books, 1978), p. 172.
9. Arthur Schlesinger, Jr., *A Thousand Days: John F. Kennedy in the White House* (Houghton Mifflin, 1965), p. 682.
10. Nathan, *Plot That Failed*, p. 41.
11. Joel D. Aberbach and Bert A. Rockman, "Clashing Beliefs Within the Executive Branch: The Nixon Administration Bureaucracy," *American Political Science Review*, vol. 70 (June 1976), pp. 458–59. Richard L. Cole and David A. Caputo, "Presidential Control of the Senior Civil Service: Addressing the Strategies of the Nixon Years," ibid., vol. 73 (June 1979), pp. 399–413, found that the administration had considerable success moving the senior civil service toward support of its "goals and objectives."
12. Aberbach and Rockman, "Clashing Beliefs," pp. 461–67.
13. Raymond Price, *With Nixon* (Viking Press, 1977), p. 194.
14. Nixon, *RN*, pp. 351–52.
15. Interview with John Whitaker, February 15, 1978.

16. Interview with Frederic Malek, September 13, 1977; see also Frederic V. Malek, *Washington's Hidden Tragedy: The Failure to Make Government Work* (Free Press, 1978), pp. 90–105.

17. Interview with George Shultz, January 4, 1978.

18. Hugh Heclo, *A Government of Strangers: Executive Politics in Washington* (Brookings Institution, 1977), p. 111.

19. Interview with Roy Ash, April 30, 1978.

20. Richard Rose, *Managing Presidential Objectives* (Free Press, 1976), p. 50. The Nixon administration has recently been a kind of happy hunting ground for political scientists studying presidential administrative techniques. Among other books and articles dealing with aspects of the Nixon White House are Nathan, *Plot That Failed*; Malek, *Washington's Hidden Tragedy*; Heclo, *Government of Strangers*; Stephen Hess, *Organizing the Presidency* (Brookings Institution, 1976), pp. 111–39; Harold Seidman, *Politics, Position, and Power*, 3d ed. (Oxford University Press, 1980), pp. 110–24; Raymond J. Waldman, "The Domestic Council: Innovation in Presidential Government," *Public Administration*, May–June 1976, pp. 260–68; John Kessel, *The Domestic Presidency: Decision-Making in the White House* (Hemel Hempstead, Eng.: Duxbury Press, 1975); Thomas E. Cronin, *The State of the Presidency* (Little, Brown, 1975); Richard E. Neustadt, *Presidential Power: The Politics of Leadership with Reflections on Johnson and Nixon* (Wiley, 1976), pp. 1–68; I. M. Destler, "The Nixon System: A Further Look," in Aaron Wildavsky, ed., *Perspectives on the Presidency* (Little, Brown, 1975), pp. 301–16; John Helmer and Louis Maisel, "Analytical Problems in the Study of Presidential Advice: The Domestic Council Staff in Flux," paper delivered at the 1977 annual meeting of the American Political Science Association, Washington, D.C., September 1977; Stephen J. Wayne, *The Legislative Presidency* (Harper and Row, 1978), pp. 45–50, 83–90, 114–18, 184–86; Otis L. Graham, Jr., *Toward a Planned Society: From Roosevelt to Nixon* (Oxford University Press, 1976), pp. 188–263.

21. Interview with Ash.

22. Ibid.

23. Ibid.; Helmer and Maisel, "Domestic Council Staff in Flux."

24. The House Committee on Government Operations voted to disapprove the plan because it denied Congress authority to question the director of the Domestic Council, but disapproval was rejected on the House floor. See H. Rept. 91-1066; and Seidman, *Politics, Position, and Power*, pp. 114–15.

25. Kessel, *Domestic Presidency*, p. 20.

26. Interview with Kenneth Cole, December 21, 1977.

27. Waldman, "Domestic Council," p. 266.

28. Helmer and Maisel, "Domestic Council Staff in Flux," p. 40.

29. Ibid., p. 14; interviews with Cole and Whitaker, and with Louis Engman, February 17, 1978.

30. Helmer and Maisel, "Domestic Council Staff in Flux," p. 15.

31. Interview with Shultz.

32. George P. Shultz and Kenneth W. Dam, *Economic Policy Beyond the Headlines* (Stanford Alumni Association, 1977), p. 161.

33. Interview with Shultz.
34. Interview with Raymond Waldman, January 11, 1978.
35. Nathan, *Plot That Failed*, p. 61.
36. Haldeman, *Ends of Power*, p. 171.
37. Seidman, *Politics, Position, and Power*, pp. 120–21.
38. *Washington Post*, August 24, 1972; quoted in Seidman, *Politics, Position, and Power*, p. 121.
39. Haldeman, *Ends of Power*, pp. 167, 171.
40. Interview with Malek.
41. Nixon, *RN*, p. 682.
42. Interview with Malek; Malek, *Washington's Hidden Tragedy*, pp. 75–80.
43. Interview with Malek.
44. Ibid.
45. *Public Papers: Nixon, 1973*, p. 21.
46. Interview with Ash.
47. Haldeman, *Ends of Power*, pp. 168–69.
48. Nixon, *RN*, p. 850.
49. Helmer and Maisel, "Domestic Council Staff in Flux," p. 15.
50. Hess, *Organizing the Presidency*, p. 137.
51. *New York Times*, June 7, 1974; quoted in Hess, *Organizing the Presidency*, p. 138.
52. *Public Papers: Nixon, 1973*, p. 62.
53. Price, *With Nixon*, p. 121.
54. Interview with Lee Huebner, December 9, 1977.

Chapter 12 (pages 250–61)

1. The most complete account of Watergate, broadly defined, is Theodore H. White, *Breach of Faith: The Fall of Richard Nixon* (Atheneum, 1975). Raymond Price, *With Nixon* (Viking Press, 1977), pp. 215–374, gives a carefully constructed defense of the administration against most of the Watergate-related charges.
2. George H. Gallup, *The Gallup Poll: Public Opinion 1935–1971* (Random House, 1972), vol. 3, pp. 2235–36.
3. A. James Gregor, *The Fascist Persuasion in Radical Politics* (Princeton University Press, 1974), p. 424.
4. Mary McGrory, "A Talk with John Dean," *New York Post*, June 18, 1973; quoted in Arthur M. Schlesinger, Jr., *The Imperial Presidency* (Houghton Mifflin, 1973), p. 380.
5. *The Presidential Transcripts* (Dell, 1974), p. 38.
6. White, *Breach of Faith*, p. 140.
7. For instance, Henry Kissinger in "Dr. Kissinger on World Affairs," *Encounter*, vol. 51 (November 1978), p. 9.
8. Price, *With Nixon*, p. 117.
9. Jefferson wrote in 1807, after spending funds for munitions without

authority from Congress at a time of tension with Britain: "On great occasions, every good officer must be ready to risk himself in going beyond the strict line of the law, when the public preservation requires it; his motives will be a justification." Lincoln argued in defense of his assumption of broad powers during the Civil War, often without authorization from Congress, that "measures otherwise unconstitutional might become lawful by becoming indispensable to the preserving of the Constitution through the preservation of the nation." Quoted in Schlesinger, *The Imperial Presidency*, pp. 24, 61.

10. Richard Nixon, *RN: The Memoirs of Richard Nixon* (Grosset and Dunlap, 1978), p. 496.

11. *Presidential Campaign Activities of 1972*, Hearings before the Senate Select Committee on Presidential Campaign Activities, 93 Cong. 1 sess. (Government Printing Office, 1973), bk. 4, p. 1666; bk. 5, p. 1817.

12. H. R. Haldeman, with Joseph DiMona, *The Ends of Power* (Times Books, 1978), pp. 52–53.

13. Frederic V. Malek, *Washington's Hidden Tragedy: The Failure to Make Government Work* (Free Press, 1978), p. 31.

14. White, *Breach of Faith*, p. 119. Arthur M. Schlesinger, Jr., *A Thousand Days: John F. Kennedy in the White House* (Houghton Mifflin, 1965), pp. 634–40, argues that Kennedy's use of the FBI was "routine."

15. *Public Papers of the Presidents of the United States: Harry S Truman, 1952–53* (GPO, 1966), p. 273.

16. *Public Papers of the Presidents of the United States: Richard Nixon, 1971* (GPO, 1972), p. 53.

17. Interview with Leonard Garment, October 19, 1977.

18. Elliot Richardson, *The Creative Balance* (Holt, Rinehart and Winston, 1976), p. 39.

19. Interview with Charles Colson, January 17, 1973.

20. Taft gave some encouragement to McCarthy early on, but drew a line against him in the debate over the confirmation of Charles Bohlen as ambassador to Russia in 1953. Eisenhower accepted McCarthy's support in the 1952 campaign, but broke with him, as did Vice-President Nixon, in 1954. Eisenhower's farewell address to the nation in 1961 eloquently called attention to the danger of government being dominated by an oligarchic "military-industrial complex."

Chapter 13 (pages 265–87)

1. Gerald R. Ford, *A Time to Heal: The Autobiography of Gerald R. Ford* (Harper and Row, 1979); Jerald F. ter Horst, *Gerald Ford and the Future of the Presidency* (Third Press, 1974). Some of the same material is covered from an unsympathetic point of view by Clark R. Mollenhoff, *The Man Who Pardoned Nixon* (St. Martin's Press, 1976). Briefer accounts are given by Bud Vestal, *Jerry Ford, Up Close: An Investigative Biography* (Coward, McCann, and Geoghegan, 1974); and Dave LeRoy, *Gerald Ford—Untold Story* (Arlington, Va.: Beatty, 1974).

2. Vestal, *Jerry Ford, Up Close*, pp. 50–51.
3. LeRoy, *Gerald Ford—Untold Story*, p. 33.
4. Ford, *Time to Heal*, p. 46. Ford was assisted in writing his memoirs by Trevor Armbrister, a professional writer. According to Armbrister, Ford dictated his reminiscences and ideas onto tapes during long interviews, which Armbrister then reduced to a publishable manuscript.
5. Vestal, *Jerry Ford, Up Close*, p. 58.
6. Ter Horst, *Gerald Ford*, p. 29.
7. Vestal, *Jerry Ford, Up Close*, p. 58; ter Horst, *Gerald Ford*, p. 36.
8. Ter Horst, *Gerald Ford*, p. 36; Ford, *Time to Heal*, p. 53.
9. Ford, *Time to Heal*, p. 50.
10. Ibid., pp. 42–43.
11. Ibid., p. 47.
12. LeRoy, *Gerald Ford—Untold Story*, p. 34.
13. Ford, *Time to Heal*, p. 42.
14. Ibid., pp. 47–48.
15. Ibid., p. 45.
16. Interview with Hugh Morrow, October 18, 1977.
17. Interview with Paul McCracken, October 5, 1978.
18. Ford, *Time to Heal*, p. 56.
19. Ibid., pp. 52–53; Vestal, *Jerry Ford, Up Close*, pp. 60–61.
20. Ter Horst, *Gerald Ford*, p. 9.
21. Ford, *Time to Heal*, p. 63.
22. Ter Horst, *Gerald Ford*, p. 6.
23. Ford, *Time to Heal*, p. 61.
24. Vestal, *Jerry Ford, Up Close*, pp. 79–80.
25. Ford, *Time to Heal*, p. 64.
26. LeRoy, *Gerald Ford—Untold Story*, p. 60.
27. Ford, *Time to Heal*, p. 65; Betty Ford, with Chris Chase, *The Times of My Life* (Harper and Row, 1978), p. 54.
28. Vestal, *Jerry Ford, Up Close*, p. 92.
29. *Congressional Quarterly Almanac*, vol. 6 (1950), pp. 60–61.
30. Ford, *Time to Heal*, p. 70.
31. Ibid., p. 69.
32. Ibid., p. 72.
33. Ter Horst, *Gerald Ford*, p. 77.
34. *Congressional Quarterly Almanac*, vol. 18 (1962), p. 731.
35. Ter Horst, *Gerald Ford*, p. 81. The incumbent chairman whom Ford defeated was Congressman Charles Hoeven of Iowa.
36. Ford, *Time to Heal*, pp. 76–77.
37. Ter Horst, *Gerald Ford*, p. 92.
38. Ford, *Time to Heal*, p. 78.
39. Charles O. Jones, *The Minority Party in Congress* (Little, Brown, 1970), p. 183.
40. *Congressional Record*, January 23, 1967, pp. 1099–1101.
41. Ter Horst, *Gerald Ford*, pp. 107–09.
42. *Congressional Record*, August 8, 1967, pp. 21897–900.

43. Ter Horst, *Gerald Ford*, p. 112.

44. Ford, *Time to Heal*, pp. 85–86.

45. Interview with Charles Goodell, August 30, 1977.

46. Interview with William Timmons, November 29, 1977.

47. Ibid.

48. Ter Horst, *Gerald Ford*, pp. 122–26; Ford, *Time to Heal*, p. 334.

49. Interview with Robert Hartmann, December 8, 1977.

50. *Nomination of Gerald R. Ford to Be Vice President of the U.S.*, Hearings before the House Committee on the Judiciary, 93 Cong. 1 sess. (Government Printing Office, 1973), p. 210.

51. Interview with Hugh Scott, December 6, 1977.

52. Robert N. Winter-Berger, *The Washington Pay-Off* (Lyle Stuart, 1972); ter Horst, *Gerald Ford*, pp. 159–60; Mollenhoff, *Man Who Pardoned Nixon*, p. 159. In the published transcript of the hearings, Winter-Berger's "evidence" was shown to be based on conjectures and dubious recollections. *Nomination of Gerald R. Ford to Be Vice President of the U.S.*, Hearings before the Senate Committee on Rules and Administration, 93 Cong. 1 sess. (GPO, 1973), pp. 204–85.

53. *Nomination of Gerald R. Ford*, Senate Hearings, pp. 128–39.

54. *A Discussion with Gerald R. Ford: The American Presidency* (American Enterprise Institute, 1977), p. 5.

55. John Osborne, *White House Watch: The Ford Years* (New Republic, 1977), p. xviii.

56. Ford, *Time to Heal*, p. 99.

57. Ibid., p. 122.

58. Richard Nixon, *RN: The Memoirs of Richard Nixon* (Grosset and Dunlap, 1978), p. 926.

59. Interview with Joe Waggonner, February 8, 1978.

60. *Public Papers of the Presidents: Gerald R. Ford, 1974* (GPO, 1975), pp. 101–04.

61. Ibid., p. 103.

62. Ford, *Time to Heal*, p. 173.

63. Ibid., p. 160.

64. Mollenhoff, *Man Who Pardoned Nixon*, pp. 93–122.

65. *Public Papers: Ford, 1974*, p. 103.

66. Ford, *Time to Heal*, p. 263.

67. Interview with Robert Goldwin, February 27, 1978.

68. *Seminar in Economic Policy with Gerald R. Ford* (American Enterprise Institute, 1978), p. 3.

69. Interview with Alan Greenspan, January 28, 1978.

70. Ford, *Time to Heal*, pp. 263–64. Ford included a section in his memoirs on his conservative principles at the suggestion of a speechwriter, James Humes.

71. Ibid., p. 10.

72. John J. Casserly, *The Ford White House: The Diary of a Speechwriter* (Colorado Associated University Press, 1977), pp. 72–73.

Chapter 14 (pages 288–316)

1. Interview with Philip Buchen, September 1, 1977.
2. Bob Woodward and Carl Bernstein, *The Final Days* (Simon and Schuster, 1976), p. 215.
3. Gerald R. Ford, *A Time to Heal* (Harper and Row, 1979), p. 25.
4. Woodward and Bernstein, *Final Days*, p. 420.
5. Ford, *Time to Heal*, pp. 129–31.
6. Interview with Gerald Ford, March 8, 1978.
7. Ford, *Time to Heal*, p. 118.
8. Interview with Robert Goldwin, February 27, 1978.
9. Interview with Donald Rumsfeld, January 25, 1978.
10. Ford, *Time to Heal*, p. 126.
11. Interview with Nelson Rockefeller, March 24, 1978.
12. Malcolm Moos, *The Republicans* (Random House, 1956), p. 66.
13. James T. Patterson, *Mr. Republican: A Biography of Robert Taft* (Houghton Mifflin, 1972), p. 141.
14. Interview with Rockefeller.
15. Ibid. A somewhat similar view has been articulated by John Connally (see chapter 10).
16. Interview with Rockefeller.
17. Ibid.
18. Ford, *Time to Heal*, pp. 142–43.
19. *Nomination of Nelson A. Rockefeller to Be Vice President of the United States,* Hearings before the House Committee on the Judiciary, 93 Cong. 2 sess. (Government Printing Office, 1974), pp. 23–57; and *Nomination of Nelson A. Rockefeller . . .,* Hearings before the Senate Committee on Rules and Administration, 93 Cong. 2 sess. (GPO, 1974), pp. 46–60.
20. *Congressional Quarterly Almanac,* vol. 30 (1974), p. 76-S. Voting in the negative besides Goldwater were Republicans Helms of North Carolina and Scott of Virginia; and Democrats Bayh of Indiana, Metzenbaum of Ohio, Abourezk of South Dakota, and Nelson of Wisconsin.
21. Based on ibid., pp. 162-H, 163-H.
22. Interview with Rockefeller.
23. In 1976 Scranton succeeded D. P. Moynihan as ambassador to the United Nations.
24. *A Discussion with Gerald R. Ford: The American Presidency* (American Enterprise Institute, 1977), p. 4.
25. Ibid.
26. Ford, *Time to Heal*, p. 185.
27. Ibid., p. 186.
28. *Congressional Quarterly Almanac,* vol. 21 (1965), pp. 1092–93.
29. Ibid., vol. 23 (1967), pp. 112–13.
30. Ibid., vol. 24 (1968), pp. 824–25.

31. Interview with Rumsfeld.
32. Interview with Goldwin.
33. "Rumsfeld's Rules," 1976, pp. 12, 15, 16.
34. Ibid., p. 8.
35. *Public Papers of the Presidents: Gerald R. Ford, 1974* (GPO, 1975), p. 105.
36. Ford, *Time to Heal*, pp. 232–33; Ron Nessen, *It Sure Looks Different from the Inside* (Playboy, 1978), pp. 78–84.
37. For Hartmann's own lively and candid account of the Ford White House, see Robert T. Hartmann, *Palace Politics: An Inside Account of the Ford Years* (McGraw-Hill, 1980).
38. Ford, *Time to Heal*, p. 145.
39. Interview with Rockefeller.
40. Interview with James Cannon, March 1, 1978.
41. Interview with Ford.
42. Interview with Rockefeller. For further discussion of Ford's use of the Domestic Council, see Kirk Emmert, "The Domestic Council in the Ford Administration," paper prepared for delivery at the Annual Meeting of the Southern Political Science Association, Gatlinburg, Tennessee, November 1979.
43. Interview with Rockefeller.
44. Interview with Rumsfeld.
45. "Rumsfeld's Rules," p. 2.
46. Interview with Rumsfeld.
47. "Rumsfeld's Rules," p. 4.
48. Ibid., p. 7.
49. For a description of the White House organization under Ford, see Stephen J. Wayne, *The Legislative Presidency* (Harper and Row, 1978), pp. 51–58, 89–90, 119–27, 187–88.
50. Ford, *Time to Heal*, pp. 184–85.
51. Interview with Edward Levi, January 24, 1978.
52. Interview with Rockefeller.
53. Interview with Robert Hartmann, December 8, 1977.
54. Interview with Rumsfeld.
55. Interview with Ford. For further discussion on Ford's approach to administration, see Edward D. Feisenbaum, "Transference of Administrative Style: A Case Study of Gerald R. Ford," paper prepared for delivery at the Annual Meeting of the Southern Political Science Association, Gatlinburg, Tennessee, November 1979.
56. Interview with Ford.
57. Interview with Rumsfeld.

Chapter 15 (pages 317–36)

1. Gerald R. Ford, *A Time to Heal* (Harper and Row, 1979), p. 150.
2. Interview with Gerald Ford, March 8, 1978.
3. Interview with Max Friedersdorf, October 27, 1977. For a description

of the White House liaison operation under Ford, see Stephen J. Wayne, *The Legislative Presidency* (Harper and Row, 1978), pp. 158–64. In 1981, under President Reagan, Friedersdorf returned to his old job as director of congressional relations.

4. The exceptions are J. Adams, Jefferson, J. Q. Adams, W. H. Harrison, Taylor, Fillmore, and Garfield.

5. *Presidential Vetoes, 1789–1976*, compiled by the Senate Library (Government Printing Office, 1978), pp. 395–426.

6. Ibid., pp. 437–48.

7. Ibid., pp. 449–65.

8. Ibid., p. 452.

9. Interview with Friedersdorf.

10. Ibid.

11. Ibid.

12. Ibid.

13. Based on *Congressional Quarterly Almanac*, vol. 31 (1975), pp. 60-H, 61-H.

14. Ibid., pp. 116-H, 117-H, 57-S.

15. Interview with Friedersdorf.

16. Ibid.

17. Based on *Congressional Quarterly Almanac*, vol. 32 (1976), pp. 7-S, 55-S.

18. Ibid., p. 56-S.

19. Interview with Friedersdorf.

20. Ford, *Time to Heal*, p. 293.

21. Interview with John Marsh, September 2, 1977.

22. Interviews with John Anderson, September 21, 1977; Richardson Preyer, October 21, 1977; Abner Mikva, November 3, 1977; Barber Conable, September 13, 1977; and Joseph McDade, October 13, 1977.

23. Interviews with Birch Bayh, September 9, 1977; Frank Thompson, October 20, 1977; Charles Mathias, September 22, 1977; and Louis Stokes, September 15, 1977.

24. Interviews with Philip Crane, January 30, 1978; and Jack Kemp, October 4, 1977.

25. Interviews with Preyer; and Bob Dole, September 9, 1977.

26. *Public Papers of the Presidents: Gerald R. Ford, 1974* (GPO, 1975), p. 7.

27. Interview with Marsh.

Chapter 16 (pages 337–57)

1. Gerald R. Ford, *A Time to Heal* (Harper and Row, 1979), p. 30.

2. Interview with Gerald Ford, March 8, 1978.

3. Ford, *Time to Heal*, p. 254.

4. *Public Papers of the Presidents: Gerald R. Ford, 1975* (Government Printing Office, 1977), pp. 463–65.

5. Based on *Congressional Quarterly Almanac*, vol. 31 (1975), pp. 38-H, 39-H.

6. Ibid., pp. 40-H, 41-H.

7. "Kissinger on Oil, Food, and Trade," *Business Week*, January 13, 1975, p. 69.

8. Daniel Patrick Moynihan, with Suzanne Weaver, *A Dangerous Place* (Little, Brown, 1975), pp. 34–35.

9. Ibid., p. 36.

10. Ibid., pp. 36–37.

11. Ibid., p. 61.

12. Ibid., p. 117.

13. Ibid., p. 154.

14. Ibid., pp. 152–61.

15. Ibid., pp. 197–99.

16. Ibid., pp. 212–23.

17. Ibid., p. 216.

18. Ibid., p. 270.

19. Ibid.

20. Quoted in ibid., pp. 274–75.

21. Quoted in ibid., pp. 275–76.

22. Henry Kissinger, *American Foreign Policy* (Norton, 1977), pp. 204–05.

23. Ibid., pp. 370–73.

24. Henry Kissinger, *White House Years* (Little, Brown, 1979), pp. 212–15.

25. *Statistical Abstract of the United States, 1978* (GPO, 1978), p. 258; *U.S. Defense Perspectives, Fiscal Year 1978* (Department of Defense, 1977).

26. *U.S. Defense Perspectives, 1978*.

27. Interview with Ford.

28. *Wall Street Journal*, August 23, 1979.

29. Richard Nixon, *RN: The Memoirs of Richard Nixon* (Grosset and Dunlap, 1978), pp. 924–26; Ford, *Time to Heal*, 227–84; Richard F. Head, Frisco W. Short, Robert C. McFarland, *Crisis Resolution: Presidential Decision Making in the Mayaguez and Korean Confrontations* (Westview, 1978), pp. 110–17.

30. *To Authorize Appropriations during the Fiscal Year 1976 . . .*, Hearings before the Senate Committee on Armed Services, 94 Cong. 1 sess. (GPO, 1975), pt. 1: *Authorizations*, pp. 7–8.

31. John Osborne, *The Last Nixon Watch* (New Republic, 1975), p. 95.

32. Ford, *Time to Heal*, pp. 320–24.

33. Ibid., p. 280; see also Head and others, *Crisis Resolution*.

34. *Congressional Quarterly Almanac*, vol. 31, pp. 362–63.

35. Ford, *Time to Heal*, 324–31; Ron Nessen, *It Sure Looks Different from the Inside* (Playboy, 1978), pp. 155–57.

36. Interview with Donald Rumsfeld, January 25, 1978.

37. Ford, *Time to Heal*, p. 326.

38. *Congress and the Nation, 1973–1976*, vol. 4 (Congressional Quarterly, 1977), p. 878.

39. *Congressional Quarterly Almanac*, vol. 31, pp. 90–95.

40. Interview with Rumsfeld.

41. *Military Posture*, Hearings before the House Committee on Armed Services, 94 Cong. 2 sess. (GPO, 1976), pt. 1, p. 469.

42. *First Concurrent Resolution on the Budget—Fiscal Year 1977*, Hearing before the Senate Committee on the Budget, 94 Cong. 2 sess. (GPO, 1976), vol. 3, p. 124.

43. Interview with Brent Scowcroft, December 1, 1977.

44. Ford, *Time to Heal*, p. 345.

45. Interview with Ford.

46. Ford, *Time to Heal*, pp. 357–58.

47. "The Ford Presidency," White House Office of Communications (August 1976), p. 78.

48. Moynihan, *Dangerous Place*, p. 280.

49. Interview with Scowcroft.

50. Robert W. Tucker, William Watts, Lloyd A. Free, *The United States in the World: New Directions for the Post-Vietnam Era* (Potomac Associates, 1976), pp. 29–33.

Chapter 17 (pages 358–81)

1. Robert Stobaugh and Daniel Yergin, "The End of Easy Oil," in Stobaugh and Yergin, eds., *Energy Future: Report of the Energy Project of the Harvard Business School* (Random House, 1979), p. 18.

2. *Energy Facts II*, prepared for the Subcommittee on Energy, Research, Development, and Demonstration of the House Committee on Science and Technology, 94 Cong. 1 sess., by the Science Policy Research Division, Congressional Research Service, Library of Congress (Government Printing Office, 1975), p. 196.

3. *Energy Policy: The Impact on Budgetary and Economic Goals*, Committee Print, Senate Committee on the Budget, 94 Cong. 1 sess. (GPO, 1975), p. 198.

4. *Statistical Abstract of the United States, 1978* (GPO, 1978), p. 607.

5. *Public Papers of the Presidents: Richard Nixon, 1973* (GPO, 1975), p. 96.

6. George H. Gallup, *The Gallup Poll: Public Opinion 1972–1977* (Scholarly Resources, 1978), vol. 1, p. 230.

7. Robert Enzler, *The Politics of Oil* (University of Chicago Press, 1961), p. 143.

8. David Howard Davis, *Energy Politics* (St. Martin's, 1974), pp. 61–62.

9. *Business Week*, February 28, 1970, pp. 42–44.

10. Richard B. Mancke, *The Failure of U.S. Energy Policy* (Columbia University Press, 1974), p. 27. The original members of OPEC were Iran, Iraq, Kuwait, Saudi Arabia, and Venezuela.

11. Robert Stobaugh, "After the Peak: The Threat of Imported Oil," in Stobaugh and Yergin, eds., *Energy Future*, pp. 23–26.

12. Ibid., p. 26.

13. Interview with Milton Friedman, March 9, 1978.

14. Davis, *Energy Politics*, p. 71.

15. Stobaugh, "After the Peak," pp. 26–27.

16. *Energy Policy*, p. 206.

17. *Public Papers: Nixon, 1973*, pp. 916–21.

18. Carol J. Loomis, "How to Think about Oil-Company Profits," *Fortune*, April 1974, pp. 99–102.

19. *Congress and the Nation, 1973–1976*, vol. 4 (Congressional Quarterly, 1977), pp. 211–12.

20. *Is the Energy Crisis Contrived?* AEI Round Table, July 22, 1974 (American Enterprise Institute, 1974), p. 7.

21. Ibid., p. 8.

22. William E. Simon, *A Time for Truth* (McGraw-Hill, 1978), p. 47.

23. Ibid., p. 50.

24. Ibid., p. 51.

25. Ibid., pp. 47, 55.

26. Frederic V. Malek, *Washington's Hidden Tragedy: The Failure to Make Government Work* (Free Press, 1978), p. 9.

27. Simon, *Time for Truth*, pp. 53–55.

28. *Public Papers of the Presidents: Richard Nixon, 1974* (GPO, 1975), p. 226.

29. *Congress and the Nation, 1973–1976*, p. 224.

30. Ibid. The congressman quoted was James Broyhill, Republican of North Carolina.

31. Stobaugh and Yergin, "End of Easy Oil," p. 18.

32. Stobaugh, "After the Peak," p. 28.

33. Gerald R. Ford, *Time to Heal* (Harper and Row, 1979), p. 228.

34. Ibid., pp. 228–29.

35. Ford first named Andrew Gibson, a former assistant secretary of commerce, to succeed Sawhill, but withdrew the nomination when the *New York Times* disclosed that Gibson was to receive an $880,000 settlement over a ten-year period from his former employer, an oil-shipping firm. Zarb, like Sawhill, had formerly served as associate director of OMB in charge of energy matters.

36. Interview with Gerald Ford, March 8, 1978.

37. *Public Papers of the Presidents: Gerald R. Ford, 1975* (GPO, 1977), vol. 1, pp. 39–43.

38. On May 28 Ford, observing that Congress had still failed to produce an energy program, went ahead with the second $1 import fee increase. In August a federal court of appeals held that the president had exceeded his authority in raising the fees. The fee increases remained in effect, however, while the administration appealed to the Supreme Court, until they were lifted by Ford when he approved the compromise energy bill in December 1975. In 1976 the Supreme Court ruled that the president had indeed possessed authority to raise the fees.

39. *Congressional Quarterly Almanac*, vol. 31 (1975), pp. 194–95.

40. Ibid., pp. 208–09.

41. Ibid., pp. 211–14.
42. Ibid., pp. 214–19.
43. Ibid., p. 221.
44. Ibid., based on roll call on pp. 106-H and 107-H.
45. Ibid., based on roll call on p. 57-S.
46. Ford, *Time to Heal*, pp. 340–41.
47. Simon, *Time for Truth*, p. 79.
48. *Congress and the Nation, 1973–1976*, p. 259.
49. *Energy Facts II*, p. 47.
50. I. C. Bupp and Frank Schuller, "Natural Gas: How to Slice a Shrinking Pie," in Stobaugh and Yergin, eds., *Energy Future*, p. 61.
51. Ibid., p. 64.
52. *Energy Facts II*, p. 196.
53. *Congressional Quarterly Almanac*, vol. 31, pp. 252–59.
54. Ibid., based on roll call on p. 64-S.
55. Ibid., p. 259. For a full discussion of the natural gas price control controversy, see Pietro S. Nivola, "The Natural Gas Policy Act of 1978: The Politics of Enactment," paper prepared for delivery at the 1979 Annual Meeting of the American Political Science Association, August 31–September 3, 1979.
56. *Energy Independence Authority Act of 1975*, Hearings before the Senate Committee on Banking, Housing, and Urban Affairs, 94 Cong. 2 sess. (GPO, 1976), p. 6.
57. Simon, *Time for Truth*, pp. 76–77.
58. *Energy Independence Authority Act of 1975*, Hearings, p. 383.
59. Dennis Farney, "Mr. Ford's $100 Billion Elephant," *Wall Street Journal*, September 20, 1976.
60. Interview with Donald Rumsfeld, January 25, 1978.
61. *Public Papers of the Presidents: Gerald R. Ford, 1975* (GPO, 1977), vol. 2, pp. 1494–98.
62. Interview with Ford.
63. Farney, "Mr. Ford's $100 Billion Elephant."
64. Interview with James Lynn, September 8, 1977.
65. Interview with Nelson Rockefeller, March 24, 1978.
66. Interview with Rumsfeld.
67. *Energy Independence Authority Act of 1975*, Hearings, p. 354.
68. *Congressional Quarterly Almanac*, vol. 31, p. 268.
69. *Energy Interdependence Authority Act of 1975*, Hearings, pp. 430–31.
70. Interview with Rockefeller.
71. This analysis of what conservatives believe is based mainly on statements by conservative politicians and officeholders, including those set forth in earlier sections of this chapter. For more systematic presentations of contemporary conservative economic philosophy, see Milton Friedman, *Capitalism and Freedom* (University of Chicago Press, 1962); Friedrich A. Hayek, *A Constitution of Liberty* (University of Chicago Press, 1960); and Alan Greenspan, "Economic Policy," in Peter Duignan and Alvin Rabushka, eds., *The*

United States in the 1980's (Hoover Institute Press, 1980), pp. 31–48. Friedman and Hayek are reluctant to be identified with a more general conservative social philosophy. For a discussion of the effects of ideology on the formation of energy policy, see David Howard Davis, "Energy Policy and the Ford Administration: The First Year," in David A. Caputo, ed., *The Politics of Policy Making in America* (San Francisco, Calif.: Freeman, 1977), pp. 39–70.

72. For representative statements of contemporary liberal economic philosophy, see John K. Galbraith, *The New Industrial State*, 3d rev. ed. (Houghton Mifflin, 1978); and Arthur Okun, *Equality and Efficiency: The Big Tradeoff* (Brookings Institution, 1975). Lester C. Thurow, *The Zero-Sum Society* (Basic Books, 1980), offers a modified liberalism, tempered by the experience of the 1970s. John Rawls, *A Theory of Justice* (Harvard University Press, 1971), presents a carefully worked out rationale for the underlying values of contemporary liberalism. For an analysis of the relationship between liberal intellectuals and liberal public officials, though in an earlier period, see Henry J. Aaron, *Politics and the Professors: The Great Society in Perspective* (Brookings Institution, 1978).

Chapter 18 (pages 382–406)

1. News release from the Department of the Treasury, June 18, 1976.

2. Interview with Gerald Ford, March 8, 1978.

3. *Public Papers of the Presidents: Gerald R. Ford, 1976–77* (Government Printing Office, 1979), vol. 1, pp. 18–19.

4. The secretary of labor was formally named to the Economic Policy Board executive committee in the same executive order in June that added the secretaries of state and commerce. In reality, however, Dunlop had been functioning as a member of the executive committee since February. I am indebted to Roger Porter for his description of the internal operations of the board. Letter to the author, May 1, 1980. See also Roger B. Porter, *Presidential Decision Making: The Economic Policy Board* (Cambridge University Press, 1980), pp. 30–56.

5. Interview with William Seidman, November 16, 1977.

6. Interview with Carla Hills, May 19, 1978.

7. Interview with William Coleman, December 19, 1977.

8. Interview with Alan Greenspan, January 28, 1978.

9. Interview with Seidman.

10. Ibid.

11. Interview with Coleman.

12. Interview with Rudolph Penner, January 11, 1978.

13. Interview with Greenspan.

14. Ibid.

15. Porter stresses the "collegial" nature of the board's operations. It was his finding, on the basis of a tabulation he made of executive committee

votes, that "no one individual or group of individuals consistently dominated the process." Letter, May 1, 1980.

16. Interview with William Simon, October 18, 1977.

17. Rand's best known work, which sets forth her social philosophy through long speeches by her central character, is *Atlas Shrugged* (Random House, 1957), especially pp. 1010–59.

18. *Inflation and Unemployment* (Congressional Quarterly, 1975), pp. 83–84.

19. *Statistical Abstract of the United States, 1977* (GPO, 1977), p. 247.

20. Ibid., p. 278.

21. *Statistical Abstract of the United States, 1978* (GPO, 1978), p. 908.

22. Ibid., p. 257.

23. Press release on a speech delivered to the Missouri Industrial Development Conference on March 23, 1976.

24. Personal communication to the author, January 24, 1978; published in "How Government Makes Its Living," *Commonsense*, vol. 1 (Fall 1978), p. 27.

25. *Economic Report of the President, 1976* (GPO, 1976), p. 173.

26. Ibid., p. 199. Roger Porter has pointed out to me that the tentative figure reported at the time was 5.4 percent. Letter, May 1, 1980.

27. Interview with Greenspan.

28. *Economic Report of the President, 1976*, p. 172.

29. *The Economists Conference on Inflation: Report*, vol. 1 (GPO, 1974).

30. *Public Papers of the Presidents: Gerald R. Ford, 1974* (GPO, 1975), pp. 235–36.

31. *Economic Report of the President, 1976*, pp. 173, 199.

32. Interview with Greenspan.

33. *Public Papers of the Presidents: Gerald R. Ford, 1975* (GPO, 1977), vol. 1, pp. 37–39.

34. *Congress and the Nation, 1973–1976*, vol. 4 (Congressional Quarterly, 1977), pp. 67–69.

35. Interview with James Lynn, September 8, 1977.

36. *Public Papers: Ford, 1975* (GPO, 1977), vol. 2, p. 1973.

37. Based on *Congressional Quarterly Almanac*, vol. 31 (1975), pp. 180-H, 181-H.

38. *Congressional Quarterly Weekly Report*, December 27, 1975, p. 2871.

39. *Congressional Quarterly Weekly Report*, December 20, 1975, p. 2763.

40. *The U.S. Budget in Brief, Fiscal Year, 1980*, p. 71; *Congress and the Nation*, vol. 4, p. 67.

41. Interview with Greenspan.

42. Interview with Ford.

43. Ibid.

44. Gerald R. Ford, *A Time to Heal* (Harper and Row, 1979), p. 342.

45. Ibid.

46. Interview with John Marsh, September 2, 1977.

47. George H. Gallup, *The Gallup Poll: Public Opinion, 1972–1977* (Scholarly Resources, 1978), p. 601.

48. *Pubic Papers: Ford, 1975,* vol. 2, p. 1995.

49. Interview with Ford.

50. Interview with Greenspan.

51. Interview with Simon.

52. Interview with David Gergen, February 2, 1978. In 1981 Gergen returned once more to the White House, as an assistant to President Reagan.

53. Interview with Lynn.

54. *Economic Report of the President, 1977,* p. 221.

55. Press release, March 12, 1976.

56. Press release on testimony by Alan Greenspan before the Subcommittee on Manpower, Compensation and Health and Safety of the House Committee on Education and Labor, April 14, 1976.

57. "The Economic Impact of a Federal Program to Achieve 3 Percent Unemployment by the End of 1976," report issued by the Congressional Research Service, Library of Congress, by Warren E. Farb and Peter Henle, May 29, 1975.

58. Press release on statement of Charles L. Schultze before the Subcommittee on Unemployment, Poverty and Migratory Labor of the Senate Committee on Public Welfare, May 14, 1976.

59. Humphrey-Hawkins, in substantially watered-down form, was finally passed by Congress and signed by President Carter in 1978.

60. Hills managed the reelection campaign of Senator Thomas Kuchel in 1968, and the gubernatorial campaign of Huston Flournoy in 1974. Both were progressive Republicans, and both lost—Kuchel in the primary, and Flournoy in the general election.

61. Interview with Roderick Hills, November 17, 1978.

62. Interview with Philip Buchen, September 1, 1977.

63. Interview with Edward Schmults, November 16, 1977.

64. Interview with Nelson Rockefeller, March 24, 1978.

65. *The Challenge of Regulatory Reform,* a report to the President from the Domestic Council Review Group on Regulatory Reform (GPO, 1977), p. 42.

66. Interview with Ford.

67. Interview with Greenspan.

68. Interview with Seidman.

69. Interview with Robert Hartmann, December 8, 1977.

70. Interview with Greenspan.

71. Ibid.; interview with Ford.

72. Interview with Rockefeller.

73. Interview with Greenspan.

74. Memorandum, Sidney L. Jones, "Economic Policies and Prospects," January 21, 1977, p. 15.

75. Interview with Greenspan.

76. Interview with Ford.

77. Interview with Hartmann.

78. Interview with Marsh. In 1981 Marsh became secretary of the army in the Reagan administration.

79. Interview with Ford.

80. Fred Hirsch, "The Ideological Underlay of Inflation," in Fred Hirsch and John C. Goldthorpe, eds., *The Political Economy of Inflation* (Harvard University Press, 1978), p. 270.

81. Arthur F. Burns, *Reflections of an Economic Policy Maker* (American Enterprise Institute, 1978), p. 221.

82. Interview with Ford; Ford, *Time to Heal*, pp. 349-53.

83. Interview with Ford.

84. Interviews with Ford, Coleman, and Hills. Coleman recalled one occasion on which the president decided in his favor on eight of nine disputed items. Hills's reputation for winning the president to her point of view was so strong that OMB eventually tried to avoid taking disputes with her to the Oval Office.

85. *President, 1976* (Congressional Quarterly, 1977), pp. 96-97; *The Presidential Campaign, 1976*, vol. 2, pt. 2: *President Gerald R. Ford* (GPO, 1979), pp. 709-10.

86. *The Gallup Opinion Index*, no. 137 (December 1976), p. 29.

87. Carter received 50.1 percent of the popular vote and Ford 48 percent. In the electoral college Carter won by 297 to 240. A shift of 10,000 votes in Ohio and Hawaii would have given Ford the election.

Chapter 19 (pages 407–19)

1. *Nixon on the Issues* (Nixon-Agnew Committee, 1968), p. 125.

2. Television interview with David Frost, May 19, 1977; transcript in the *Washington Post*, May 20, 1977.

3. Louis Hartz, *The Liberal Tradition in America* (Harcourt, Brace, 1955), especially pp. 3-20, 71-78, 145-158; Samuel H. Beer, "In Search of a New Public Philosophy," in Anthony King, ed., *The New American Political System* (American Enterprise Institute, 1978), pp. 15, 37-41.

4. Very recently, some liberals have developed doubts about the effectiveness of some kinds of government regulation, and have even joined efforts to achieve deregulation in limited areas. But broad forms of regulation, like wage and price controls and rent control, remain much more popular among liberals than among conservatives.

5. Theodore H. White, *Breach of Faith: The Fall of Richard Nixon* (Atheneum, 1975), p. 224.

Index